# The Three Times of the Law

*Alain Didier-Weill*

*Translated by Andrew Weller*

**THE SEA HORSE IMPRINT**

Paola Mieli, *Publisher & Director*
Mark Stafford, *Editor*
Marie-Claude Hays, Jean-Michel Vives, Martin Winn, *Editorial Support*

*This book is published under the aegis and with the financial assistance of Après-Coup Psychoanalytic Association, New York*

Alain Didier-Weill

# The Three Times of the Law

*The Stunning Commandment,
the Injunction of the Superego,
and Musical Invocation*

*Translated by Andrew Weller*

Agincourt Press
New York, 2017

Originally published as:
*Les Trois Temps de la loi*
Éditions du Seuil, 27 Rue Jacob, Paris, France 1995, Second Edition 2008
All rights reserved
English language rights the author

Copyright © 2017

ISBN: 978-1-946328-08-3

*Copyedited*
Zachary Slanger

*Design and typesetting*
Danilo Montanari

Agincourt Press
P.O. Box 1039
Cooper Station
New York, NY 10003
www.agincourtpress.org

Cover image: René Magritte, *The Mysteries of the Horizon*, 1955

The publisher welcomes inquiries from copyright-holders he has been unable to contact.

For Jacques Lacan, for the "blue note,"

*and of course for:*

Billie H., Lester Y., Django R., Nina S., Chris M., and Ernie C.;
Eric, Michel, and J. D. Salinger;
Jean Kestemberg;
Marie-Emmanuelle;
M. Assabgui, C. Azouri, P. Krejbich, M. Malandrin, J.-P. Winter;
Léon Poliakov;
François Wahl;
J. Clavreul, M. Guibal, P. Landman, B. Milan, J.-J. Moscowitz;
J. Spirko;
Michel Silvestre;
Claude Lanzmann;
Raphy Marciano;
J. Dujardin;
B. Dupuy;
G. Petitdemange;
and B. Vergely.

Editorial Note

In the interest of the readability of an already complex text, the editors decided to maintain the use of the masculine pronoun, which refers to both sexes in the original French. Notes in brackets indicate additions to the text for the purpose of further clarification of terms or references that may be unfamiliar to English language speakers.

## TABLE OF CONTENTS

| | |
|---|---|
| PROLOGUE | 11 |
| CHAPTER ONE – ASTONISHMENT IN EVERYDAY LIFE | 13 |
|    A) First Astonishment: The Adult and Play | 16 |
|    B) Second Astonishment: Art | 21 |
|    C) Third Astonishment: The Child | 24 |
| CHAPTER TWO – THE THREE SUPEREGOS | 29 |
| Introduction | 31 |
|    A) The Archaic Superego: "Not a Word!" | 33 |
|    B) Second Superego: Censorship | 35 |
|    C) The Third Superego | 39 |
| I. The First Superego: "Not a Word!" | 39 |
|    A) The Madman, the Chicken, and the Silence of the Cursed Part | 39 |
|    B) Three Silences: Night, Darkness, and the Abyss | 44 |
|    C) The Silence of the Monster | 55 |
|    D) The Dream of the Black Point: The Silent Malediction | 62 |
| II. The Second Superego: "Don't Insist!" | 67 |
|    A) The Gaze of the Evil Eye | 69 |
|       a) To Guard—To Regard | 69 |
|       b) The Stolen Secret | 70 |
|       c) The Confession of the First Fault | 72 |
|       d) The Evil Eye against the Painter's Eye | 73 |
|       e) True Secret or False Secret | 74 |
|       f) The Problem of Fixedness | 78 |
|    B) Freud and the Superego | 82 |
|    C) Abuse, Insult, Malediction | 86 |
|       a) Abuse and Insult | 87 |
|       b) The Malediction: Oedipus and Polyneices | 90 |
| III. The Third Superego: "Are You Going to Persevere?" | 101 |

*Table of Contents*

## CHAPTER THREE – THE QUESTION OF THE STUNNING COMMANDMENT — 111

I. Freud and the Commandment of *Verblüffung* — 113
  A) Bewilderment and Illumination: Freud and Witticism — 113
  B) Sideration without Light — 121
    a) Freud and the 11$^{th}$ Commandment of Censorship: "Don't Let Yourself Be *Verblüfft!*" — 121
      1. The Repression of the Signifier — 121
        α) The Two Provincial Travellers — 121
        β) The Determination Not to Change and False Thinking — 125
        γ) Falsified Thought and the Ethics of Psychoanalysis — 128
      2. The Murder of the Stunning Face and the Foreclosure of the Signifier — 134
    b) The Subject Remains Stunned: Stupor and Stupidity — 138
    c) Anticipatory Expulsion of the Stunning Signifier: Drugs — 139
  C) The Foreclosure of the Stunning Signifier — 139
    a) The Witticism and the Call — 141
    b) Lacan's A-Father [*l'Un-père*] and the Question of Procreation — 143
      1. The Foreclosure of the Mother's Call — 143
      2. Assumption or Foreclosure of the Call: The Question of Fear — 147
  D) The *Après Coup* Light: The Freudian Time of Interpretation — 151
    a) First Logical Time: The Subject Is Overwhelmed — 154
    b) Second Logical Time: The Subject at an Impasse — 155
    c) Third Logical Time: The Sleight of Hand — 157
    d) Fourth Logical Time: Freud's "Pass" — 160

II. Sideration beyond the Pleasure Principle: The Question of Unconscious Choice — 163
  A) Freud and the Question of the Unconscious Choice — 163
  B) Beyond the Freudian Conception of Beyond the Pleasure Principle — 171
  C) The Fall of the Signifier of the Name-of-the-Father into the Real: *Ausstoßung, Verwerfung, Werfen,* and *Verblüffung* — 179

III. An Attempted Translation of the Stunning Commandment — 180
  A) What Is Your Debt? — 181
    a) The Justness of the Question — 181
    b) The Forgetting of the Question: Saying No to Injustice Rather than Yes to Justness; Paul of Tarsus — 183
    c) The Quarrel with the Law — 187

| | |
|---|---|
| B) "Where Are You?" | 192 |
|   a) The Revelation of the "Where" | 192 |
|     1. Adam | 192 |
|     2. Music | 196 |
|   b) The Forgetting of the "Where Are You?" | 198 |
|     1. Witticism or Slip of the Tongue?: The Question of Shame | 198 |
|     2. The Conformist | 203 |
| C) "That's Not All You Are!" | 207 |
|   a) Being and Existence | 207 |
|   b) Forgetting the Question: The Tramp | 208 |
| IV. Question to Lacan and Question of Lacan "He Knows (that I Know (that He Knows (that I Know)))" | 209 |
|   A) Three Observations Involving the Statement "He Knows (that I Know (that He Knows (that I Know)))" | 210 |
|     a) First Observation: A Rejection of Sideration | 210 |
|     b) Second Observation: A State of Sideration without De-sideration | 212 |
|     c) Third Observation: A Case of Sideration Followed by De-sideration | 218 |
|   B) The Seminar of February 15, 1977 | 225 |
|   C) The End of an Analysis: Unknotting and Re-knotting | 229 |
| **CHAPTER FOUR – THE TIME OF THE OTHER: MUSIC** | **233** |
| I. Untranslatability | 235 |
| II. The "Blue Note" | 247 |
| III. Rhythm, the Invocatory Drive, and Dance | 249 |
|   A) Dance and the Generation of Time | 249 |
|   B) Foreclosure of Time | 254 |
| IV. The Trauma, Speech, and Music | 257 |
| **CHAPTER FIVE – THE TIME OF THE SUBJECT OF THE UNCONSCIOUS: SPEECH (Theory of Primal Repression and Originary Bewilderment)** | **263** |
| I. Originary Bewilderment and the Way out of Trauma | 265 |
|   A) Entering the Trauma | 265 |
|     a) Betrayal | 267 |
|     b) The Loss of the Call | 268 |
|     c) The Medusa's Gaze and the Loss of Being Incognito | 270 |

| | |
|---|---|
| B) The Way out of the Trauma | 275 |
| a) The First Time of Exit from the Trauma: Originary Bewilderment | 277 |
|     1. The "You" that Precedes the "There" | 277 |
|     2. The Traumatic Dilemma | 278 |
|         α) Existence of the Dilemma | 278 |
|         β) The Four Possible Responses | 279 |
| b) The Second Time of Exit from the Trauma: Paternal Metaphor and Primal Repression | 281 |
|     1. Passivity or Sensibility of the Subject | 285 |
|     2. Primal Repression as an Originary Metaphorical Pact | 288 |
|         α) The Originary Pact | 290 |
|         β) The Institution of the Triple Veil | 291 |
| II. Overcoming Bewilderment and Emerging from Primal Repression | 306 |
| A. The Game of Tennis and the Analytic Game | 306 |
| B) The Unforgettable Forgetting | 314 |
|     a) The Urgent Necessity to Forget: Of the Psychotic, the Mystic, and the Psychoanalyst | 314 |
|     b) What Unforgettable Forgetting Is | 317 |
|     c) The Contribution of Derrida | 320 |
| TO CONCLUDE: THE CONQUEST OF TIME | 325 |
| Dialectic of the Interruptions and Resumptions of Time | 326 |

# PROLOGUE

What is so fearsome about speech that we so often choose to accept to produce only small talk rather than having to speak? It is in the nature of a challenge that we may wish to avoid.

What, indeed, do we discover the moment we take up this speech that we seem to have been given with no strings attached? We discover that this speech with which we thought we could innocently speak begins to speak to us by asking a stunning question that tears us away from any possible innocence: "What gives you the right to speak?"

It is a fearsome question because, as soon as I heard it, I began to discover what I had always known without having learned in school: its accuracy.

It is so accurate, so right, that I find myself unable to deny, at least in the moment it confronts me, its absolute veracity. So then, this thing, which I counted on as the only thing given to me for free, asks me to pay up by informing me of the price of my gift as follows: "You who speak because you have the power of speech, have you forgotten that I am yours only because you were mine first? Have you forgotten that you are my subject?"

This line of questioning reminds me that I am on trial: a trial in which I am facing a grand jury questioning not *what* I am saying, but questioning rather the very fact *that* I am saying.

Why does this trial prove so harrowing? Because, responding to the question addressing the fact *that* I speak, it isn't possible for me to justify myself the way I would if I were asked to account for *what* I say. When I am questioned as to *what* I say, I know how to plead my case and explain myself; but I am stunned, reduced to silence, if I am asked to justify the fact *that* I am a speaker. Why am I struck dumb by this questioning that is not a calling into question? Why am I unable to challenge it?

If I do not argue against this challenge, it is because it does not present itself as an authority that I have to obey simply because I am

*Prologue*

unable to say "no"; on the contrary, it presents itself as a questioning to which I would assent without being able to say why.

The subjective experience I encounter at this point is one of amazement: speech that amazes is the opposite of speech that intimidates, which only obtains a "yes" because the "no" is made impossible for the subject.

The internal act through which I allow myself to be amazed is an act through which a movement of recognition makes me utter a "yes" that is not the effect of an irresistible constraint. It is instead the effect of the internal acquiescence to a presence that is other or foreign, a presence that, stupefied, I discover is not foreign to me.

As a result of this "yes," this form of *Bejahung* through which I consented to being dumbfounded, the difficulties begin.[1] If I know, without having needed to learn it in school, that this question is just and that it requires from me a well-said answer, it is because I come to acknowledge my debt to speech, even though I did not know we (speech and I) were bound by a contract.[2]

Thus, the question of amazement reminds me that speech is not an *élan vital*, bursting forth immediately in the innocence of a movement that would free it from the rule of law. Rather, speech is the manifestation of a law that asks the subject this question: "What have you done with the speech that you were given?"

---

[1] *Bejahung* translates as "affirmation" and is used by Freud in his paper on "Negation." It refers to a particular form of affirmation that will be thoroughly discussed in this book.

[2] [Psychoanalysis is defined by Jacques Lacan as an ethic of "well saying": a bene-diction (*béne-diction*). To the well saying is opposed a "badly spoken word" (*malédiction*) that assigns the subject who suffers it to the position of a cursed object.]

# CHAPTER ONE

# ASTONISHMENT IN EVERYDAY LIFE

The French language privileges the "clap of thunder" when speaking about the subjective experience of astonishment that reveals that the ordeal of a sudden event has the power to introduce, into the continuity of knowing, the gaping hole of discontinuity. This gaping hole that opens up—in the form of leaving me "open-mouthed" or flabbergasted—informs me of the fact that, at the moment when the thunder rumbles, I am brutally dispossessed of everything I knew about its electromagnetic causes and I am momentarily seized by this astonishing encounter with Zeus thundering from Olympus. Though the clap of thunder is not as frightening for me as it might be for an animal, it astonishes me because it commemorates the originary moment when, without any softness, without any harmony, I was "one day" uprooted or torn from the *nihil* by the thunderbolt of the Word (*verbe*). We will thus be led to interpret astonishment as the effect of a subjective destitution produced by a special signifier to which I will subsequently give the theoretical signification of the signifier *Verblüffung*, which Freud isolates in *Der Witz und seine Beziehung zum Unbewußten* (1905), and which Marie Bonaparte translated into French as *signifiant sidérant*.[3] Before giving its psychoanalytic status to the question of *sideration*, it is first necessary to situate it within a framework that goes beyond that of clinical psychoanalysis, one in which

---

[3] [The German word *Verblüffung* (Fr: *sidération*) is translated as "bewilderment" in the Standard Edition—in *Jokes and their Relation to the Unconscious* (1905) and in *Leonardo da Vinci: A Memory of His Childhood* (1910). The term is used in conjunction with "illumination" to stress the aspect of being "stunned" with surprise or astonishment, so that one is temporarily unable to think or react. Throughout this book, the words *sidérante*, *sidération*, and *sidéré* will be translated using different English terms according to the context (stunning, astonishment, surprise, etc.) The verb *sidérer* means to stun, stagger, or shock. *De-sidération*, *un-stunning*, refers to the process of overcoming this state. Desire etymologically refers to an act of *de-sideration*. Desire is what makes it possible to escape from the stunning effect, from the sideration, provoked by any object.]

the human world socializes the reception given to different forms of astonishment that a subject is capable of experiencing. In this respect, we will have to ask ourselves in what way society restores to the adult, through sport and art, the possibility of rediscovering the astonishment that has deserted him since that time when he was a child who was astonished by everything.

## A) FIRST ASTONISHMENT: THE ADULT AND PLAY

At this juncture, when we are asking ourselves what the aptitude to be astonished consists of, there is one question that cannot be avoided: Why does this aptitude, which is characteristic of the child, apparently tend to decline at the age of reason? If we want to pose the question correctly, we need to qualify this affirmation by observing that it is not a question of a pure and simple decline, but rather of the institution, in adulthood, of a split with respect to astonishment: it is as if astonishment had deserted the domain of daily existence in order to be recuperated, institutionally, in theaters or gyms, that is to say, in places that restore it at fixed times.

Take the example of those games governed by that strange object, the ball: How are we to explain the power that this small ball has over thousands of humans who, in stadiums or on television, watch it going back and forth for hours on end? What is the nature of the astonishment that is provoked each time the ball disorients one of the partners sufficiently for him or her to let it go by? And what does the spectator's desire to be astonished by this ephemeral instant relate to? Is it because human beings are unable to experience these fleeting instants of astonishment in their own lives that they attend by the thousands these football or tennis matches, which are all stages on which the astonishing disappearance of a ball behind the scenes can be enacted?

Before the moment of rupture introduced by the winning shot, a sort of alliance, which functions for a certain time, is formed between me and my opponent: the ball that is being exchanged between us establishes a link in which each of us is alternately the one who receives the ball before being the one who returns it. In this type of exchange, the movements of the ball back and forth are governed by a specular control that only gives rise to symmetrical shots: each partner only returns the ball to the point where the other is expecting it. In this kind of dialogue, what is involved is a certain complicity between two players ensuring that they share the same specular space in three dimensions: each one knows that at the very moment when the fourth dimension, that of time, intervenes, space, ceasing to be sharable, will no longer allow the two players to share the ball; as a result, one of them will necessarily miss it. What makes a great champion in this respect, apart from muscular aptitude, is a poetic aptitude giving him or her the capacity to know, like Alice, how to get to the other side of the mirror and into a fourth dimension by means of the ball. What happened in the fleeting moment when my partner, having placed the ball where I saw nothing at all, transformed it into an invisible object? Well, he effected an authentic transformation whereby an object of exchange, moved by symmetry, acquired the astonishing privilege of being withdrawn from the regime of the specular exchange and transformed into a lost, non-specular object to which we can give the original name that Lacan gave to it, namely, "*objet (petit) a*."[4] I missed the ball because my partner placed it in an area where it is my knowledge that is missing, in such a way that at the moment when, having been visible, it becomes invisible, it is not only the ball that is lost: I am too. I am lost because I am stunned, in the same way as I would have been by a witticism; this ball that has become invisible leads me, does it not, to the threshold at which the enigmatic becomes stunning or bewildering?

Just as a witticism succeeds in transforming, generally by means of ambiguity, an unsurprising word into a surprising one, the spirit of a winning shot consists in a comparable success: the ball that has suddenly acquired a status of invisibility by separating itself from the reign of specularity plunges me into a state of stunned astonishment. For as the reference points that I had hitherto had (high and low, left and right, in front and behind) are of no further use to me for identifying the strange place where the ball has been placed, they allow a situation

---

[4] [The object *a* is not specularizable, nor is it symbolizable; it cannot be transmitted or exchanged. Following the relation of the subject to the caretaker, it emerges in the gap existing between the demand address to the other and the satisfaction of the need, and takes the form of "four episodic substances." The oral object refers to the demand to the Other, the anal object to the Other's demand, the scopic object to the desire towards the Other, and the vocal object to the desire of the Other. As that which can never be attained, object *a* becomes the object cause of desire, orienting its course.]

## Chapter One – Astonishment in Everyday Life

of "not knowing" to emerge, to which I have been subjected as a result of being astonished.

To understand the transformation whereby a subject manages, like Alice, to escape from the specular world by means of a little ball and to get through to the other side of the mirror, it is necessary to understand the nature of the message that a player receives from a ball each time it comes back to him or her. This message could be expressed as follows: "I know where you are, and I know where to find you so that I can come back to you." In a certain way, it conveys to the player the following message originating in the superego: "I am watching you; nothing about you is unfamiliar to me."

Will the player receiving this ball respond to this command obediently? If he does, he will be there where he is expected to be. He will only become surprising if he responds to the command "You are there" by contesting it, by creating *ex nihilo* a ball that has acquired another signification: "I am not there, I am elsewhere." It is through the emergence of this "elsewhere," of which my spatial orientation is totally unaware, that I am disoriented and so lose the point. This temporo-spatial disorientation is not only the effect of a loss of knowledge; at the same time, it is the effect of the appearance of a hole in knowledge, a sort of navel by means of which the not-knowing communicates with the scene through a non-specular hole. It is into this hole, which opens out onto the "elsewhere," that the ball that stuns me falls. How is it that my opponent is able to gain access to this "elsewhere" before me? I only have access to it, in fact, by means of the ball that he has *already* hit, and that presents itself to me as an interpretation.

Rather than pertaining to my unconscious knowledge—that of secondary repression—this interpretation relates to an impossibility of knowing that depends on primal repression. This interpretation coming from my opponent derives its power from the very particular desire that informs it. If he was able to astonish me in this way, it was because, with this precise shot, his relation to desire was structured differently from mine: at the moment he hit the ball, it was not *that ball*—the ball that was indeed present—that sustained his desire, but rather it was the ball as *already* what it was going to become inasmuch as it was destined to make itself absent, to be transformed into a lost object. His desire is not caused by the presence of the ball, but rather by its absence to come insofar as it is already a vehicle of this fourth dimension that space acquires when it is generated by time.

To enter this new dimension, let us ask ourselves the following question: What is it that drives thousands of spectators each week to watch two players hitting a ball back and forth to each other? I assume that, apart from interest in the rally itself, there is yet a deeper interest in the interruption of the rally. This interest only exists if the player plays well, that is, if the interruption is not caused by the error of the player playing badly, but rather by the success of a winning shot. It is my contention that it is in the astonishment that such a success arouses in the spectators, when it is fully realized, that they encounter what they have come for: the desire to be astonished. What can the meaning of such a desire be?

The first major observation is that the affect induced in me by astonishment is the only affect that I am capable of experiencing as if it were presenting itself for the first time; even when repeated, I do not experience it as a repetition. What is boring and monotonous in a repetition resides in the fact that each repetitive cycle takes me back to the reminiscence of a *"déja-vu"*: the oppressive feeling that the repetition-compulsion confers on the reproduction of the same consists in the fact that the subject cannot forget the similarity between what has just happened and what has already happened.

What is distinctive about astonishment is that it is forgotten each time it occurs and, when it occurs, it does not evoke the memory of the precedent state of astonishment. That is why I am able to watch a game of tennis without growing weary of it: it is not so much that this or that particular shot by Borg is astonishing, but that it is *always so* astonishing.[5] Why, in short—since, from an objective point of view, it is perhaps always the same shot—is it not possible for me to get used to it and apprehend it by locating it within the cycle of the repetitive? The reason is that it is not a shot that is *repeated*, but rather a shot that *recommences* a commencement that is impossible to get used to, for this commencement is constitutive of the first human undertaking.[6]

---

[5] Björn Borg (born June 6, 1956) is a Swedish former world-number-one tennis player, widely considered to be one of the greatest in tennis history. Between 1974 and 1981, he became the first male professional to win eleven Grand Slam open era singles titles.

[6] In *La Beauté du geste* (Paris: Calmann-Lévy, 1994), 49, Catherine David aptly points out that an act that is performed for "the first time" has the power of transgressing habit: "Habit weaves a protective network, a sort of manual of the body. . . . Among the thousands of acts accomplished in the course of a day, only a few are recalled: they are the ones that escape habit—the sidesteps, impulsions, failures, the first times."

## Chapter One – Astonishment in Everyday Life

It is impossible to recall this commencement with which memory once began. Astonishment is not an act of remembering this commencement, but of commemorating a psychic act (primal repression) of which the subject's memory has no representation. In our example of the game of tennis, the subject who transforms the specular ball into a stunning ball converts the attributes of this ball that are linked to representations (it has such and such a color, weight, and sound) into attributes stripped of all representation (it is invisible, immaterial, and incredible). During the ephemeral instant when it becomes invisible like a painting, immaterial like a dancer, and incredible like a note of music, the ball is the work of an artist. If this astonishing instant presents itself as the recommencement of a commencement that is both forgotten and unforgettable, it is because it is a break in temporal continuity by means of which I am authorized to explore that secret, discontinuous dimension that is ahistorical time.

The fact that I can travel in time by evading historical determinism—receiving, like a poet, the favor of a scrap of eternity fleetingly liberated by the encounter with a commencement that recommences—corresponds, does it not, to what Freud identified in discovering that the unconscious is ignorant of time?[7] That the unconscious is ignorant of time does not mean that it denies it, but that there exists a subject of the unconscious that, unlike the ego, is not exclusively determined by history and is therefore in a position, when it is stunned, to return to that point of time before historical time, comparable to the "starting-point." From this point, from which a new departure is possible, the subject can stop repeating and start again differently.

Beginning again in a different way is what can happen to a tennis ball when, having been hit to the other player, it comes back to the sender with a reply that raises it to a level of alterity that it did not have before: it becomes Other, travelling in "another" time and "another" space, no longer topographical but rather topological. This intertwin-

---

[7] In *L'Ange de l'Histoire* (Paris: Éditions du Seuil, 1992), Stéphane Mosès studies the conceptions of time of Franz Rosenzweig, Walter Benjamin, and Gershom Scholem, offering a radical critique of historical reason and its axioms, namely, the idea of continuity, the idea of causality, and the idea of progress. Against the Hegelian conception, all three set the idea of a discontinuous history, the effect of an irruption, at the heart of time, of an absolute alterity emerging from the unpredictability of the radically new. We may well ask ourselves why Bergson, who inaugurated this critique, *did not see that it had its place in a Jewish conception of time*.

ing of time and topology (to which Lacan devoted his last seminar) is knit together by a very particular desire that I have called "desire X," while noting that such a desire is not structured around the visible actuality of the ball, but rather around an anticipation concerning its future invisibility—anticipation, that is, concerning the creation of a new object of poetic structure.[8]

Can this desire X, which is both sustained by and the bearer of a metaphorization, be psychoanalyzed? Is it reducible to certain underground events that the subject's biography might shed light on? No, analysis would exhaust itself trying to give an account of it.

B) SECOND ASTONISHMENT: ART

There exists a second sort of astonishment, which is produced by the magician that is the artist. In the aesthetic enjoyment I derive from looking at a painting or from listening to music, there is, is there not, the experience of a paralysis of intelligence that we have discovered at the origin of astonishment? This crippling of intelligence is, is it not, at the source of aesthetic enjoyment? Is it not the case that I find that, if I remain lost in my thoughts, I will not be affected by music?

This frigidity towards music is not fundamentally different from sexual frigidity, the analysis of which teaches us that it is so often linked to the impossibility of ceasing to think. Music, and art in general, has its effect at the point where man is divided between what touches him and what he thinks. The fact that "touching" is not "thinking" relates to that dissociation between intellect and affectivity wherein the subject feels separated from what he feels *life* is when he thinks about it, whereas it takes possession of him when he ceases to think about it in order to feel it.[9] In this respect, if a piece of music or a painting astonishes us, it is because it has the power to "touch" us and so gives us the feeling that we can touch what we call "life"; consequently, we cease, momentarily, to be separated from its "presence" that was concealed by this re-presence that is psychic representation.

---

[8] Jacques Lacan, *La topologie et le temps*, unpublished seminar.
[9] Eugène Delacroix, 1798–1863.

However, it is not because we touch this life when we don't think about it that it is a pure, inaccessible real.[10] The stunning signifier is, for me, the possible *passeur*[11] of the real.[12] The astonishment caused by art is not the same as that produced by the domain of play, and this raises the following question: What difference is there between the artistic object and the tennis ball? While the ball acquires its specificity by *disappearing* suddenly from the scene where it was present, the artistic object is characterized, for its part, by the specific surging forth of something that had hitherto been latent and absent, but that is now suddenly *brought to the state of appearing (apparition)*, like the actor emerging from the wings to make his appearance on the stage. In both cases what is involved is the process that reveals an existence, with the difference that, in the case of play, it is an existence revealed by its "presentification," that is, by the very fact of being presented.

What does a painting show us? It shows us that the presence of the invisible—banned from the everyday world—ceases to be banned by finding a path to our eye, which, in this astonishing encounter, "lays down its weapons."[13] What does music make us hear if not the presence of something incredible that was hitherto banned from the humdrum of daily chatter? There is, however, one fundamental point

---

[10] [Used by Lacan as a noun, the term "the real" articulates itself with the imaginary and the symbolic. The real is not reality, and is defined as "the other face of the symbolic" (*Television*). It is outside the field of significations.]

[11] [The *passe* is the term employed by Lacan in 1967 to name the procedure, radically new in the history of psychoanalysis, aimed at accounting for the desire to become an analyst. This procedure permitted an analysand—passant (*passant*)—desiring to accede to the title of Analyst of the School to transmit to two analysts—passers (*passeurs*)—the elements of his cure that lead him to wish to pass from the status of analysand to that of analyst. These passers of the speech of the passant had, in a second time, the charge of transmitting to the Jury of Approval (*jury d'agrément*) what had passed from the passant to the passers in regard to his desire to become an analyst. The passers are thus in the position of mediators between the desire of the passant and the jury.]

[12] By paralyzing intelligence, this experience of being "stunned" by surprise [*sidération*] opens out onto a dimension beyond meaning, towards a multidimensionality of the subject.

For Heitor O'Dwyer de Macedo in *De l'amour à la pensée* (Paris: L'Harmattan, 1994), 182: "It is with Brecht that this multidimensionality of the subject emerges on the theatrical stage: for him, theatre is the place where it must be shown that a subject is inextricably bound up with the unexpected, the now never providing any certainty as to what will come later."

[13] Jacques Lacan, *The Seminar of Jacques Lacan, Book XI: The Four Fundamental Concepts of Psycho-Analysis*, trans. Alan Sheridan (London: Hogarth Press and The Institute of Psycho-Analysis, 1977), 101.

in common between play and art: both strive to extract man from that strange thing—silently distilled by daily life—that is called boredom. A boring person is someone, is he not, who is unable to astonish me, someone whose utterances seem so predictable that I perceive them as devoid of unpredictability, of alterity? How are we to understand the fact that the alterity of my *alter ego* can be so altered that it is no longer perceptible to me? Is this repression of the dimension of the Other his own doing or mine?

There is no doubt that certain types of identification—hysterical identification, collective identification with the leader—are available to help me avoid opening myself to symbolic alterity, and that consequently I can choose to alienate myself by alienating the Other in the unsurprising form of the "same." The more this identification with the "*right form*" is successful, the more conformity will tend towards conformism and uniformity, and the more the repression of this stranger, in the form of living speech, will intensify its vigilance so as to not let this unwelcome dimension the slightest chance of manifesting itself and being a cause of stunning surprise. So, behind the repression leading the ego to replace the astonishing alterity of speech with the alienating identity of the conforming form is an act of obedience towards the 11th commandment, "Don't let yourself be astonished!," which we shall study later.[14] In this respect, the question of the so-called "boring" person can now be reframed: Is he the one who, by obeying the 11th commandment, has repressed in himself the alterity of speech or, rather, is it I who, by obeying this 11th commandment, am in fact incapable of being astonished? That the negation of the Other can have a bearing on my own speech or on that of my fellow creature is thus, in both cases, a psychic act with which I obey this 11th commandment. It is indeed a strange obedience, given that it establishes a psychic field from which astonishment is banished while leaving another psychic field—that of play and of art—the possibility to play with and delight in astonishment.

The existence of man is thus split into two separate domains by a relatively impermeable barrier: the first domain, that of grave and serious reality, stands opposed to the second, that of artifice. From this

---

[14] See further on, in Chapter Three, "Freud and the 11th Commandment of Censorship," 121-139.

dualistic perspective, the seriousness of reality is defined negatively, as that which does not proceed from this artificial world that man has invented for his amusement in order to escape the monotony of a "reality" whose seriousness is guaranteed by the fact that it does not lend itself to astonishment. The existence of this dualism generates two questions: 1) Why is "reality" less desirable than the realm of fiction? What is it that prevents man from finding in his daily life the same enthusiasm that he has for watching a little ball going back and forth over a net for several hours? 2) Conversely, why does the realm of fiction only arouse desire of no consequence? Why is this desire, which has the possibility of expressing itself in the realm of fiction, nothing but a form of entertainment or recreation that is devoid of seriousness and that is to be enjoyed in the present instant because it is without any ethical consequences?

C) THIRD ASTONISHMENT: THE CHILD

Both these questions are legitimately raised by the child, for his or her world is not split, like the adult's, between an entertaining world that allows room for astonishment and a world of serious reality obeying the 11th commandment, "Don't let yourself be astonished!"

If a child's play is not the pure distraction of a desire without repercussions, cut off from the real, it is because, on the contrary, it brings into play a desire engendering the real. Furthermore, the aim of this play is not to escape from the boredom created by the monotony of daily life, for everyday life is not for the child, as it is for the adult, a source of monotony: rather, it is a permanent source of astonishment, and even of wonder, that is incomprehensible to anyone who does not experience it. How can an adult who knows, or thinks he knows, what a little stone or a blade of grass is understand the child's astonishment upon seeing this small stone?

This adult supposes that the child is astonished because, unlike him, he does not know that a stone is a mineral object that consists of calcium and is used for this and that, and that it can be found here and there, on a riverbank or on a beach. This adult does not suspect that the child's look of astonishment shows that he sees something that the adult can no longer see. What does the child see, then? He sees what the painter strives to see, or, more exactly, what the painter strives to see again: Did not Picasso once say, in an interview, that the compass that guided his research was the attempt to recapture the vision he had had at the age of two? Did he mean by that that the painter's vision involves rediscovering an innocence that authorizes, thanks to the absence of mediation through knowledge, access to an immediate vision of the real? No doubt, the idea of the inaugural freshness of a mind devoid of all prejudice instilled by knowledge is not foreign to what Picasso wanted to say, but it is not the real meaning. In this instance, he is surely not asserting, as some are tempted to do, that the child's astonishment is the consequence of knowledge that has not yet been acquired. This interpretation of innocence eludes the very question of astonishment. In fact, independently of his innocence with regard to knowledge, the child is less innocent than the adult in relation to the real; if he is astonished by a small stone, it is because he does not share the adult's static conception of the real. For him, his stone is not something immobile and frozen in a fixed space, but rather it is something in movement, something mobile that suddenly emerges, whose incommensurable momentum continues to perpetuate itself in spite of the apparent stability of its commensurable form.

The perception of this movement is the perception of a commencement of time, from which point that which did *not yet* exist is brought to a commencing existence that continues to commence. In short, what the child is faced with, in his astonishment at the existence of the little stone, is the metaphysical question *par excellence*: "Why is there being rather than nothing?" He does not need to be a professional metaphysician to ask this question. But if a metaphysician, or a Picasso, needs to rediscover his childlike capacity for astonishment in order to take in the full force of this question, it is because they have to struggle against the impulse to obey the commandment prescribing the repression of astonishment. By perceiving the movement whereby the stone is rescued from non-being, the child apprehends the fourth dimension from which movement is deployed as a knot between time and topology: a knot between, on the one hand, time that is beginning to ensure that the created emerges and, on the other hand, the place from which this created emerges *ex nihilo*.

Somewhat in the same way as he discovers on his body, at the level of the navel, the mysterious trace left on him by this place from which he emerged when, at a certain moment, time sovereignly decided to extricate him from the uterine wings or backstage (*coulisses*) where he was in waiting, the child discovers on his little stone a sort of navel through which the backstage from which he was extricated has left a mysterious trace. This trace, the signature of his creation, is the means by which the child's vision, his painter's eye, is reminded that the void from which the stone emerged continues to exercise rights over him. It is as if, from the nothingness where it did not exist before it emerged, the stone had retained an imprint reminding it of its debt towards this originary backstage. The adult needs the artifice of art to see this backstage: in this respect, the stage reminds him that it only gives the actor his strange presence because it is in communication with a backstage whose absence remains stuck to the actor's feet. The actor is thus the one who, passing from the invisible to the specular, has become the *passer*, for the astonished spectator, of the obscurity that reigns backstage. But the child has no need of such an artifice to see that such a backstage exists in the visible world. It is because he has access to this secret backstage from which the specular world derives its substance that this world astonishes him.

How is the secret of its creation that the stone contains within it to be characterized? It is not dissipated—as other secrets are—by light; on the contrary, it is illuminated by it. This illumination, which reveals the existence of a subtraction in what is illuminated, shows that it is not a question of a secret like others: in general, a secret is something that acquires its substance by being concealed from the clarity of daylight and by maintaining an affinity with darkness. The characteristic of such a secret, concealed by obscurity, is its fragility: indeed, obscurity deeply fears the light that makes it disappear. The fragility of a secret shrouded in obscurity—no aspect of which can survive the vengeance of clarity—stands in stark contrast to the secret of a child: the latter is astonishing precisely because it does not need obscurity to survive but, on the contrary, it needs light in order to *appear* with complete clarity. It needs light to reveal itself, for what light reveals is the power inherent to the secret of the stone that consists in *re-vealing* itself, that is to say, in *veiling itself again* by deploying through its own means a sort of veil, of strange obscurity, that is not *absence of light*, but rather *absence in light*.

We have seen that the astonishment created in the adult by play and the astonishment engendered by art do not have the same structure. While play tends to conceal the ball that was visible, the painter reveals the invisible, the musician reveals that which is unprecedented, unheard-of, (*l'inouï*), the dancer reveals that the dancing body accedes to immateriality. The child does not recognize this distinction between what disappears and what appears because, for him, there is no fundamental difference between the stone, which, like a sculpture, shows him its dimension of invisibility, and the invisibility that he acquires by playing hide-and-seek: in both cases, it is a matter of the same movement whereby that aspect of the stone that is revealed is the existence of a secret that *remains hidden*, and whereby what is concealed, when he plays hide-and-seek, is a secret that does not merely constitute a momentary distraction. Indeed, he sees the discovery of this secret as being linked to the discovery of a command enjoining him to realize that there is such a secret within him and that it is for him to realize himself in this transcendent place of incognito.

This movement towards the *"pas de sens"* is one that accompanies the child when, in dancing and jumping, he brings immateriality into existence; or when, in singing, he discovers as a musician that he becomes extraordinary; or when, by hiding, he acquires that invisibility that solicits the painter's eye.[15] So, for the child, the path towards fulfilling the command to realize himself is something serious and grave because it is foundational for reality. The mystery that he discovers in his little stone, and that must become his own, implies that he will have to find a way to constitute himself as a secret that can tolerate being revealed without fear.

One of the means of grasping the division of the subject involves taking into account the two antinomical ways in which he is led to apprehend the reality of the world: either through astonishment, as a "real" that he has never seen before, or through the repetitive dimension of *déjà-vu*. To the extent that the superego is precisely that agency [*instance*] which, tending to strip man of his aptitude for astonishment, lets him fall into the *already-known*, we cannot avoid analyzing the fall that it induces.[16]

---

[15] [In *pas de sens*, there is a pun on *"pas,"* which means both "no" and "step"; thus, something that may apparently have no meaning at one point may subsequently be seen as a step of/towards meaning at another.]

[16] [The French word *instance* can be translated either as "authority," in the sense of legal authority, or as "agency," as in Freud's work.]

# CHAPTER TWO

## THE THREE SUPEREGOS

## Introduction

The three knocks, which, from the wings, announce the imminent entrance on stage of speech, alert us to the fact that the speech that is on the verge of being uttered is announced by a knocking spirit that knocks three times. This precedence of the announcement over the saying is the effect of an enigmatic precedence of the Other in relation to the subject: why, indeed, is it necessary for this voice of the Other, whose vocation is to suppose the existence of a speaking subject, to insist three times before the subject whom it is calling is able to come into being? Why can't this graft of speech (which is the speaking subject) grow at once? Could there be, in this sort of promise whereby the Other predicts that a subject is soon going to speak, a structural fact that, by acting as a rupture of the promise, puts the signifier in the position of insisting sufficiently—three times—so that the prediction is accomplished? It is because such a structural fact exists—the superego—that, when speech knocks at the door, the subject is not in a position to answer immediately: "Yes, do come in, make yourself at home!"

Since Freud, we know that the subject, although brought into being by the fact of having "one day" said "yes" to speech, will henceforth devote his time to saying to it: "No, you cannot come in because you are not welcome." By showing, in a brilliant way, that the structure of this "no"—which he calls repression—is governed by the process of the pleasure principle, Freud raises an implicit question that he does not go into more deeply: if repression has the effect of excluding a signifier causing unpleasure, what becomes of this "unpleasure" encountered by the subject if he chooses not to repress it by obeying the superego, but rather to assume responsibility for it? How is the unpleasure to which the "ego" says "no" to be distinguished from that which affects the subject when, unlike the "ego," he says "yes" to the signifier that is the cause of unpleasure. To do this, it will be necessary to detach the Freudian term of "unpleasure" from its economic connotation and to link it up with the metaphorical dimension that is proper to it, insofar as speech is a "cause of unpleasure" because it constantly puts the following formidable question to the subject: "What have you done with the speech that has made you a speaking subject?"

To this absolute question, one that I will qualify as stunning, the stunned subject has the possibility of answering "yes" or "no": if he answers "yes," he will embark on the path of *dé-sidération*, un-stunning, which is the path of the *desiderium*; if he answers "no," he will embark on the path of repressing the question of the symbolic debt. The possibility of answering "yes" or "no" to the stunning *Che vuoi?* stands in contrast to his incapacity to answer "yes" or "no" when called upon to do so, called upon not by the questioning aspect of the superego but by that side of it that is a stupefying injunction. In this respect, we will be led to define the archaic superego as the injunctive gaze of an evil eye that the subject only attests because it is impossible for him to contest it.[17] While the subject may agree to say "yes" to the *Che vuoi?* because he has chosen not to answer "no" to it, his obedience to the injunction of the superego is not a willing acquiescence, for it is the very effect of an impossibility of saying "no"—an impossibility that explains the fact that obeying the archaic superego is not the result of a symbolic assumption. Between the fascination of the subject who is incapable of saying "no" to the archaic superego and the astonishment of the subject who is capable of saying "yes" to the questioning superego, there exists an intermediate position. This is the position of the superego of censorship, in relation to which the subject will be put in the position of replying "yes-no." If speech has to be announced three times, it is because each of the three announcements made by the Other is followed by a specific response in which the superego contests the subject's right to speak.

We will thus be led to distinguish three superegos. The injunction of the first superego—namely, the archaic superego—which tends to introduce an absolute silence, may be translated by: "Not a word!"

---

[17] [*Che Vuoi?*, "What do you want?," is the question that the subject addresses to the Other. Lacan articulates this in *Seminar XI* (drawing from *The Devil in Love* by Jacques Cazotte) in his development of the concepts of alienation and separation of the subject in relation to the Other.]

Through its second prohibiting command, the superego, which has to take account of the fact that a first word has been uttered by the subject, will tend, in its role as censor, to convey the following message to the subject: "Don't insist, you have already uttered one word; you will not utter two!" As for the third superego, confronted with the fact that the subject has transgressed the censorship with a view to embarking on the path of insistence, it will cease to be injunctive in order to provide support for the question: "Will you find the third word that will transmute your insistence into perseverance?" Lacan asked me to give an account of this triple conception of the superego in his seminar of May 5, 1979.[18]

The study that follows is an amplification of that lecture.

A) THE ARCHAIC SUPEREGO: "NOT A WORD!"

To what subjective position is the subject sent back, the subject who is unable to answer "yes" to the symbolic command that says to him, "Where it was, there speech becomes," for he is unable to say "no" to the command of the superego that says, "Do not become"? The story of the madman and the chicken may help us to answer this question. It makes us laugh because it shows in an exemplary way the radical way in which the first superego presents itself as the agency transmitting to the subject the injunction, "Not a word!," whose enigmatic character resides in the fact that the subject is absolutely unable to contest it. Every time the subject radically loses his capacity to speak because he is unable to say "no" to this absolute imperative—even though he does not choose to say "yes" to it—he is dealing with this first superego, which, as we shall see, cannot be identified with censorship. Here, then, is the story: a madman who thinks he is a grain of wheat is cured and leaves the hospital unit to which he has been confined. Upon leaving the hospital, he meets a chicken and he is terrified; so he makes an about-turn and promptly asks his psychiatrist to confine him again. Astonished, the psychiatrist says to him: "I don't understand; five minutes ago, you were cured; you knew that you are

---

[18] Jacques Lacan, *La topologie et le temps*, unpublished seminar.

not a grain of wheat." The madman replies: "Yes, I know that, but does the chicken know it?"

Before analyzing at greater length this question of the madman and the chicken, let us just note succinctly for the moment that the nub of this story lies in a common fact of experience that is illustrated by our daily clinical practice—namely, that the destiny of a subject can be guided by a radical impossibility of saying, "No, I am not only that; I'm not only a grain of wheat," to an Other who incarnates for him the archaic superego and who is constantly *speaking badly* of him, cursing him with a silent malediction that condemns him to this state of degradation: "That's all you are; just a grain of wheat." As an incarnation of the dregs of symbolization, this "grain of wheat" is the term employed in this witticism to name the refuse that the madman is in not gaining access to the status of a lost object. He thus personifies the possible destiny of the subject who does not fail to obey the symbolic command and so falls into a state of degradation created by the imperative of the superego. Is not the analyst constantly obliged to recognize, in the light of his clinical experience, the extremes to which a subject can be driven if he does not have the possibility of contradicting the voice of the superego? This voice is expressed through a series of utterances that, in their infinite variety, have the common feature of presenting themselves as absolute knowledge about the subject's "being." Whether he says, "You are nothing but a grain of wheat, an idiot, a jerk, a loser, deficient, or a good for nothing...," what he is really saying is, "You are only that," which is to say, "nothing but that."

Insofar as the subject can devote his life to the deadly *jouissance* of embodying the "being" of such a state of degradation, I would say that this voice of the superego is the "bad saying" [*maldire*] of the malediction.[19] The reason why I will spend some time elucidating the issues involved in the story of the madman and the chicken is that it depicts in a spectacular way the primordial alienation as a result of which each human being is this potential madman, inasmuch as he is under the yoke of a silent malediction to which he devotes himself all the more fervently in that he is unaware of it.

---

[19] [In Latin, *maledicere* means "speaking evil."]

## B) SECOND SUPEREGO: CENSORSHIP

We will study this second form of the superego—that is, censorship—with the help of a fragment of analysis that contains a slip of the tongue in which a witticism could have been produced. "It happened at the Gare de Lyon in Paris. I saw her getting off of the train, encumbered (*embarrassée*) by a suitcase that was clearly too heavy for her. She was very attractive. I rushed forward to offer her a helping hand, as any courteous man would have done on seeing a woman so encumbered. I can still hear myself saying to her: 'Allow me to help you because you seem to be very *kissed* (*embrassée*). So, *embrassée* instead of *embarrassée*.'" The man speaking—I will call him Robert—was lying on the couch. He paused, and then remarked: "If she hadn't been so attractive, I don't think I would've made this slip of the tongue, and I wouldn't have blushed with shame." There was a long silence, much longer than the previous one, before the analysand asked this crucial question: "It was a slip of the tongue, but, after all, why could it not have been a witticism?" The pertinence of this question that is related to the dividing line—in reality, a very complex one—between a witticism and a slip of the tongue resides in the fact that Robert knows that he has made a slip of the tongue, but also claims to know that the word "*embrassée*" *could have* been a witticism. What does this *could have* mean, if not that the same enunciation can convey two heterogeneous meanings between which the subject must choose, in such a way that the words "you are very *embrassée* (kissed)" *could have* been a witticism if the desire of the subject of the unconscious had chosen not *to be* revealed by a slip of the tongue, but rather to reveal *himself* by being witty?

If the lady had heard in the words, "you are very kissed," the presence of a subject who was revealing "himself," we may suppose, as Robert does, that she could have responded by laughing, thereby authenticating the existence of a witticism, rather than by looking at the subject with contempt, causing him to blush shamefully. If one does not take into account this subjective dimension of shame, one cannot distinguish, in certain cases, between a slip of the tongue and a witticism. In this connection, here is an example taken from Freud's *The Psychopathology of Everyday Life*.[20] It is a story that took place in

---

[20] Sigmund Freud, *The Psychopathology of Everyday Life* (1901), *The Standard Edi-*

Chapter Two – The Three Superegos

a camp of interned prisoners after the war of 1870. A professor had to give a lecture before a crowd of French prisoners-of-war and German officers. This event probably took place shortly before the armistice was signed. The lecturer, of Swiss origin (we do not know if his sympathies lay with the French or the Germans), had repeatedly told himself: "I mustn't say the word '*boche*' in my lecture." At a certain point in his lecture, he told a story concerning a German schoolmaster who, whenever he put his students to work in the garden, was in the habit of saying: "When you hit the clods of earth with your rake or spade, tell yourselves, in order to take courage, that each clod of earth that you break up represents a French skull." But this is what he said when citing the schoolmaster's words: "*Imaginez-vous qu'en chaque moche vous écrasez le crane d'un Français.*" That is to say, he said *moche* (ugly) instead of *motte* (clod). Now, was it a slip of the tongue or was it a witticism? We may suppose that the French audience laughed, taking it as a witticism. And we may equally suppose that the German officers forced themselves to laugh. If we do not know what the subjective position of the speaker is, do we have any elements at our disposal to help us decide? In the case above, did he "acquiesce" to the forced laughing of the Germans or did he acquiesce to the hearty laughing of the French? In which form of laughing did he recognize himself? The story does not say. If we do not know how he responded subjectively to the different types of *jouissance*, we cannot know if he regarded this word as a slip of the tongue or as a witticism. The matter cannot be settled, then, on the basis of the word alone.

Here is another story to show how this dividing line between the slip of the tongue and the witticism is far from evident.[21] Freud includes in the category of slips of the tongue the following witticism: "A recently married man, whose wife was concerned about preserving her girlish appearance and only with reluctance allowed him to have frequent sexual intercourse, told me the following story that in retrospect both he and his wife had found extremely funny. After a night in which he had once again disobeyed his wife's rule of abstinence, he was shaving in the morning in the bedroom that they shared, while

---

tion *of the Complete Psychological Works of Sigmund Freud VI* (London: Hogarth, 1961), 73–74.

[21] This paragraph is an extract from Alain Didier-Weill, "Lapsus ou mot d'esprit," *Apertura* 4 (1990).

his wife was still in bed; and, as he had often done to save trouble, he made use of his wife's powder-puff that was lying on the bedside table. His wife, who was extremely concerned about her complexion, had several times told him not to, and therefore called out angrily: 'There you go again, powdering *me* [*mich*] with *your* [*deiner*] puff!'" (She had meant to say: "You are powdering *yourself* [*dich*] again with my [*meiner*] puff").[22] Freud adds that when she saw her husband burst into laughter, she herself burst out laughing.

I would say that this was more a witticism than a slip of the tongue, as Freud supposes: the wife laughs, it seems to me, in a way that is less associated with the shame of a slip of the tongue than with the *bien-dire*, the *well-saying*, of a witticism.[23] This was how Robert knew—without any manner of doubt, owing to the shame he felt when the woman looked at him contemptuously—that what he said was not the *well-saying* of a witticism but the *mal-dire, the saying* it *badly*, of a slip of the tongue.[24] Further analysis led us to understand that the woman's contemptuous look took him back, in fact, to a look that he was expecting, for he "already" knew it. He thus discovered, without knowing it, that just as he was about to speak, he was "already" under the sway of this *deja-vu* look that had forever been telling him: "Be quiet; if you speak about your desire, you will stammer." So he was not in fact astonished by the woman's contemptuous look, which, by showing her contempt, simply confirmed the message of the look under whose sway he had always been.

This dimension of shame, which Freud identifies as one of the parameters in slips of the tongue, introduces us to the essence of what differentiates the *bien-dire, the well-saying*, of the witticism from the *mal-dire, the saying* it *badly*, of the slip of the tongue: whereas, when a witticism is being told, I learn that the witticism has been successful because the listener reacts with surprised laughter, the person who has made a slip of the tongue is not informed of his *saying* it *badly* by the listener's joyful laughter, but rather by the silence of a look that causes his shame and that for him has the characteristic of the

---

[22] Sigmund Freud, *The Psychopathology of Everyday Life*, op. cit., 77.
[23] See footnote 2.
[24] Throughout this chapter, Robert's question will be introduced in relation to the different aspects of the theoretical discussion.

"*déjà-vu.*"[25] By virtue of this fundamental difference in the Other's response, whereby he shows that he is either hearing or looking, the subject learns that there are two radically different ways of revealing himself: either he blushes shamefully before the gaze of the Other or he demonstrates that he is saying something extraordinary over which the gaze has no control because what is involved is invisible and does not lend itself to being heard.[26] This dissymmetry between the fact that the subject can show himself or demonstrate himself returns him to his most intimate relation with speech: As a potential author of his speech, does he or does he not *authorize* himself to speak? Let us say, in this respect, that Robert, inasmuch as he had already consented, at the very moment of speaking, to place himself under the sway of a contemptuous gaze, had not in fact authorized himself to transgress this gaze that was saying to him, "You are going to stammer." We will see that the destiny of speech thus resides in the way that the subject reveals the choice he is faced with between that which pushes him to speak and the power of the gaze that obliges him to keep quiet by saying to him, "Be quiet; if you speak, you are going to utter insanities."

So, the question Robert asks himself, "What would have been required to turn my slip of the tongue into a witticism?," is a pertinent one. By asking this question, he understands that it is not the word "*embrasser*" (kiss) itself that makes it possible to decide whether it is a good or bad word: it *could have* been a good word, if the woman had heard, through its enunciation, that Robert had unconsciously assumed responsibility for revealing himself. Why, in this case, would the lady not have responded by looking at him with contempt? Because someone who is told a joke receives the following unconscious homage: "You are the one thanks to whom my unconscious desire was able to speak with wit; for you do not recognize the definitive right of that demanding master, the eye of my conscience, to keep watch over desire." In short, this contempt in the woman's gaze was not directed *at* Robert's desire, but rather at his unacknowledged desire that was disavowed by a slip of the tongue just as it was promising to assert itself with wit. If man has the power to propose, it is up to the woman

---

[25] Sigmund Freud, *The Psychopathology of Everyday Life*, op. cit., 83.
[26] We will see later that the look or gaze to which I am referring has the greatest affinity with the gaze of a blind man; that is why it cannot be identified with the gaze analyzed by Sartre.

to dispose of this proposal by judging, sovereignly, whether his words are equal to what he seems to promise or whether it is not simply a false promise by means of which the subject denounces, in his slip of the tongue, what he has announced. In connection with this duplicity whereby, in the slip of the tongue, the subject yields to desire that he is unable to accept, Freud refers to the enigmatic "inner insincerity" that the slip of the tongue exposes.[27] It is this "inner insincerity" that we will have to interpret as the effect of censorship undermining not the existence, but rather the insistence of desire.

In order to highlight the specificity of the first and the second superego, I will be led, in light of the requirements of my theoretical development, to introduce the structural difference inherent to the question as it is posed by Robert, on the one hand, and by the "grain of wheat," on the other.

C) THE THIRD SUPEREGO

Insofar as we have interpreted the slip of the tongue as the effect of an insistence interrupted by the act of censorship, the following question is raised: If, as in the case of a witticism, the censorship is transgressed and, as a result, the insistence of desire has gotten through, what are the conditions required to ensure that this insistence is not retracted, but rather is transmuted into perseverance that is fully assumed? At this point, the question of the *Che vuoi?* emerges, which may be identified as the agency of a third superego.

### I. The First Superego: "Not a Word!"

A) THE MADMAN, THE CHICKEN, AND THE SILENCE OF THE CURSED PART

Each stage of this story of the madman is significant: the first phase shows us that he is cured, for he tells the psychiatrist that he knows that he is not a grain of wheat. During the second phase, the

---

[27] Sigmund Freud, *The Psychopathology of Everyday Life, op. cit.*, 86.

## Chapter Two – The Three Superegos

confrontation with the chicken reveals his alienation: the fundamental problem lies in the fact that there is no exchange of words between them, so that they are face to face, silently, in a relationship whose sole support is the chicken's gaze, which conveys the message to the madman, "You are a grain of wheat." In the third phase, the madman turns and flees. In so doing, he shows that if it was impossible for him to contradict the chicken with words by saying to it, "No, I am not a grain of wheat," then he only has one possibility left, that is, fleeing in silence, thereby removing himself from the chicken's gaze. It is worth noting already that if the chicken's gaze had been what the Greek myth identifies as Medusa's gaze, he would not have been able to remove himself from it, but would have remained in its grip, in a state of melancholic petrification that would not have allowed him to flee. This flight carries him, in the fourth phase, towards the only place where he can say to a third party—the psychiatrist—what he was unable to say to the chicken: "It's mad; it takes me for a grain of wheat."

The difficulty of the question posed is this: If it is true that "it" is crazy, why does the story say that *he* is the one who is mad? Is it because he is the one who is faced with the mad *jouissance* of the superego embodied by the chicken, by the mother hen? Is he really mad because he asks to be interned? No, the very fact that he asks to be confined offers a glimmer of hope of rediscovering a lost freedom. How does this hope manifest itself? Well, by saying to the psychiatrist, "It does not know that I am not a grain of wheat," he shows that he still has a degree of freedom because he is not identical to what the superego, embodied by the chicken, thinks. This thought of the superego, which he receives as the injunction, "You are a grain of wheat," in fact signifies: "You are nothing other than a grain of wheat." What does this "nothing other" mean, if not: "There is nothing in you other than what is visible; there is no alterity that can escape my gaze"?

The fact that a foreclusive judgment concerning the very existence of the dimension of this Other, namely, the subject of speech, is affirmed by this silent imprecation raises the following question: Why can the subject not contest this judgment? Why can he only take flight without saying a word, without saying, in this case, to the chicken (thereby manifesting that he is a speaking subject): "What you say is false; that is not all I am"? This brings us to the heart of the dialectical contradiction inherent to the statement of the superego: the subject is perfectly capable, insofar as he is accessible to truth, of seeing that this statement is discordant with the truth, for he knows "that it [the chicken] does not know that he is not just a grain of wheat." However, this truth to which he has access is without consequence, without hope, since he is unable to *say* it in the superego's presence—a superego, precisely, that is incapable of recognizing the truth of the subject. The fact that the possibility of attesting the truth is not enough to be able to contest the superego's judgment means that the subject knows perfectly well that what confers this judgment is that it does not derive its efficacy from any form of relationship to the truth, but rather from a relationship to the real. If, indeed, the superego's statement were nothing but a false judgment, the subject would not be annihilated in his speech. Are we annihilated when we are faced with someone who denies the truth? No, common experience teaches us that, when the truth is denied in the form of negation (*Verneinung*) by an interlocutor, we are not reduced to silence. The mere fact that we can be witnesses to a negation of the truth tends to result in our being called immediately to the bar of witnesses, from which we make an appeal in order to reject the false testimony.

If, on the contrary, we do not have the possibility of appealing against the superego, it is because it is supported by something that, as Lacan points out, is the "contrary of the truth," and that he calls "the real." Indeed, the great paradox of the real lies in the fact that, while it is the "contrary" of the truth, it is not, however, falseness: falseness is not the contrary of truth since, through the operation of negation, it is the privileged path by means of which the question of truth can be posed insofar as the latter is denied. What establishes the mother hen as the power of the superego is not so much the fact that it flouts the truth as the fact that it embodies absolute knowledge over those aspects of the subject that are real, that is to say, over those aspects of him that elude the reign of the signifier insofar as it allows the question of truth to be posed.

How can the subject assume or acknowledge this truth? How can he say "yes" to it? This "yes" that can occur during an analysis is a "yes" whose complexity resides in the antinomical articulation that it has to produce: the subject must say "yes" both to that part of himself that is most real ("I am only that") and to that part of himself that contradicts the real ("I am not only that"). This "affirmation of affirmation," whereby the subject accepts being both "that" and "not only that," is the act whereby he will accept his division as a speaking subject whose saying will never be more than a half-saying of "the" truth.[28] It is insofar as he will not say "the whole" truth that his saying will transmit, through the very intermediary of this "not-all," the human real as the contrary of truth. Whereas truth, in order to be human and non-dogmatic, must be disturbed by this real of the grain of wheat that we carry within us, the real to which the superego tends to reduce us univocally must be contested so that the truth can be attested as "not all."

This raises the following question: Why does the "yes" by means of which the madman attests in the psychiatrist's presence that he is a speaking subject not have the effect of making him capable of contesting the chicken face-to-face, that is, without having to flee from it? Because his "yes" to the truth and his "yes" to the real are not, insofar as they are dissociated, real "yeses." If this "Yes" given to truth is not authentic, it is because it has the structure of a negation of negation: "I am *not just* a grain of wheat." Now the signification of the "yes" produced by a double negation proceeds, as Freud points out in his article on the *Verneinung* from an "intellectual" signification.[29] It does not result, however, in the absolute affirmation, the unconscious "yes" that Freud recognizes in the act of *Bejahung*.

While the "yes" given to truth through the intermediary of the psychiatrist is not a real assumption, the "yes" given to the chicken—given the impossibility of contesting the chicken—is no more a real "yes" given to the real. Uttering a "yes" that is an authentic "yes" implies, does it not, that the subject, even if he did not say "no" to the chicken, could, at least, have done so? "No" to the notion that he is *only* a grain of wheat. But what is the difference between "being" a grain of wheat and "existing" as a grain of wheat? That the body incarnates speech signifies that it can be inhabited by an alterity. Uprooted, therefore, from the fact of only "being" what it is subjects the body to an elsewhere, which elevates it to being other than what it is. Is it by playing with this dimension of the "elsewhere" that the body can dance and transmit that dimension beyond gravity and the visible through which the immaterial and invisible aspects of it are bestowed on us?

---

[28] [Ce «oui-de-oui», par lequel le sujet assume d'être et «ça» et «pas que ça», est l'acte par laquel il assumera sa division d'etre parlant dont le dire ne pourra jamais être plus qu'un mi dire de «la» vérité.]

[29] Sigmund Freud, "Negation" (1925), *The Standard Edition of the Complete Psychological Works of Sigmund Freud XIX* (London: Hogarth, 1961), 235–239.

Would this conquest of the immateriality of the body, through the transgression of its materiality, be possible if the assumption of this material part—that is, our body, inasmuch as it belongs to the real—had not already occurred? If the assumption of this "grain of wheat," the body, is not realized, then the body, rather than being brought into existence, is left on the side of "being": it becomes this purely material thing, identical to itself, destined, as a pure object stripped of alterity, to be subject to the sole law of the real—the law of gravity. It then becomes this heavy body, which, subject to the pressure of falling bodies, has the experience, in depression, of being "only that," only a grain of wheat. So it was because he did not accept the fact of "existing" as a grain of wheat, in order to "be" this grain of wheat, an object of *jouissance* of the superego, that the madman in our story was unable either to say a real "yes" or a real "no" to his persecutor. This "neither yes nor no" is evidence of a silence whose profoundly enigmatic character lies in the fact that it does not succeed as an act of speech, but rather precedes all speech: unlike Robert, who speaks to the psychoanalyst about the silence following his slip of the tongue, the madman speaks to the psychiatrist about a silence that precedes his speech. The fact that he did not speak to the chicken created a resounding silence from which he has, in reality, still not emerged: his terror shows that, in spite of fleeing, he did not in fact separate from the chicken. To do so, it would have been necessary to take leave of the chicken through an act. But his flight does not deserve to be considered as such: if there had been an act of separation, the madman would have ceased to be mesmerized by the chicken's fascinating gaze. By fleeing, he thought he was getting away from the chicken, but he was overlooking the fact that it was not the dimension of space that had the power to shield him from the command of the fascinating gaze. The mere fact that he thought that he could escape from the chicken by putting between them the spatial barrier of a wall indicates that he still did not know that what he was fleeing was the very non-existence of that human limit that is symbolic prohibition. Admittedly, if he flees, it is because it is possible for him to suppose that there exists, somewhere, a world structured by the protective symbolic prohibition. Insofar as it is purely silent, his flight shows that this supposed place is not yet part of this world. The impossibility of supposing that a symbolic world exists stems from the fact that the power of the fascinating gaze consists precisely in showing him the other side of the symbolic:

the world of abjection (*immonde*), which is not governed by the law of speech.

In this waste matter of the world, there reigns an absolute silence that we now need to try to speak about, while bearing in mind that no words can express it; for, precisely, it is not the human silence that the act of speaking can lead us to hear, but rather the inhuman silence that can be found in this "depth of depths" where speech is unable to reach us.[30]

B) THREE SILENCES: NIGHT, DARKNESS, AND THE ABYSS

Why are we under the spell of the world if we abhor abjection? The world and nature present themselves as a real that speaks to us and makes poets of us, whereas the real of the formless void (*tohu-bohu*) is only transmitted to us through an absolute silence. To understand this primal split between nature and chaos, we need to grasp how part of the real is informed by the symbolic, while another part receives no information from it.[31] Commenting on the first verses of Genesis, Lacan is led, in the wake of Jewish and Christian commentaries, to note that this symbolic information is not single but double, since the symbolic acts in two successive phases:[32] in the first, there is the act of creation *ex nihilo* by means of which, on the basis of a signifying enunciation, *Fiat lux*, the real comes into "being"; and in the second, there is the act of nomination whereby the created real—"light"[33]—is called "day."[34] It was the necessity of distinguishing these two phases

---

[30] See further on, 97.

[31] Different cosmogonic systems (that of the Greeks, that of the Dogons, etc.) were used to distinguish the three types of silence that I want to analyze. If I have chosen to draw on the first verses of Genesis to support my argument, it is because I think it is possible to import the signifiers "night," "darkness," and "abyss" that appear there into the field of the genesis of the psyche insofar as they qualify three types of the real that are constitutive of the human order.

[32] In the seminar of May 13, 1975, from *RSI* (unpublished seminar), Lacan says: "But one does not notice that the creationist idea of the inaugural 'Fiat lux' *is not a naming* [author's emphasis]. The fact that the symbolic emerges from the real—that's what the idea of creation is—has nothing to do with the fact that, *in a subsequent phase*, a name is given...."

[33] Genesis 1: 3.

[34] Genesis 1: 5.

that led Lacan to make a division in the symbolic function, on the basis of which he introduced a shift from the Borromean knot with three rings to the Borromean knot with four rings.

This question of a creation *ex nihilo* concerns psychoanalysts, for "each time we utter a word, we make something emerge from nothingness, *ex nihilo*, which is our fate as being humans."[35] However, this conception of creation is fundamentally different in religion and in psychoanalysis. Whereas, from the Biblical point of view, the created real is "light," that is, the unary trait (*trait unaire*), from a psychoanalytic point of view, the created real is the effect of the *Urverdrängt* (the original, primal repression) created by the unary trait.[36] It is at this level that the distinction occurs between the *creation* of the hole of the *Urverdrängt* (not *Fiat lux* but *Fiat hole*) and the *nomination* of this hole.[37]

The positions of Freud and Lacan in relation to this hole are dialectical: while Freud called this hole, which has since existed as the unconscious, the "Freudian thing," Lacan tries to "reduce this nameable thing" by identifying it with the topology of the Borromean knot:

"I am trying to reduce this nameable thing because like that one can allow oneself to cover all sorts of things with names; this has always been done and it has even been done indiscriminately.... I identify this hole with topology.... Topology cannot be conceived of without this Knot.... This is the first time that we have seen something that combines the mental and the real to this extent: the mental also forms a knot...."[38]

The question that remains open concerns the difference between what Lacan calls "symbolic nomination," with which he identifies the activity of nomination whereby a name is given by Adam to each animal, and the nomination of the real that he imputes to the naming father.[39] This nomination can be identified in the naming act

---

[35] Jacques Lacan, "Clôture des journées d'avril 1975," *Lettre de l'EFP* 18 (1975), 270.

[36] Jacques Lacan, *The Seminar of Jacques Lacan, Book X: Anxiety*, trans. Barbara P. Fulks (Boston: Polity, 2014), 21: "In the beginning was the Word; that means, in the beginning was the unary trait [*trait unaire*]." [Lacan appropriates Freud's expression *Ein Einziger Zug* (in Chapter VIII on Identification from *Group Psychology and the Analysis of the Ego*), and translates it as *trait unaire* (unary trait), further developing the concept. The unary trait is the trait of identification as trait of difference.]

[37] Jacques Lacan, "Clôture des journées d'avril 1975," *op. cit.*, 267.

[38] *Ibid.*

[39] Jacques Lacan, seminar of May 13, 1975, *RSI*, unpublished seminar.

that transmutes "light" into "day." Is the absolute silence in which the *Fiat hole* resounds hospitable or inhospitable to this speech? Does it appear as a blank page on which speech has been written or does it not support speech in this way?

The Christian and Jewish traditions are radically opposed on this question. While the Christian conception envisages an absolute beginning—"In the beginning was the Word,"[40] from which the world emerges, from head to toe, as an absolute and complete success, where Logos, having got the better of silence, reigns as master—the Jewish conception has always taken into consideration the primal silence evoked by the enigmatic second verse of Genesis:[41] "Now the earth was formless and void (*tohu-bohu*),[42] darkness was over the surface of the deep, and the Spirit of God (breath of *Elohim*) was hovering over the waters."[43]

The three terms used to name the real—"formless void" (*tohu-bohu*), "darkness," and "the abyss"—signify, in Jewish thought, the persistence of a realm of silence, of abjection, at the heart of the human world of speech, which implies not only that creation is not complete, but also that, at any moment, the real of the "formless void" (*tohu-bohu*) may, if man is not careful, be unleashed and annihilate the dimension of the symbolic law established by the *Fiat hole*. A new question arises then: In what way does the silence of the lawless world, of the formless void, exist side-by-side with the silence present in a world governed by the law of speech? Does the passage from the second to the third verse signify two types of creation that follow each other chronologically, in such a way that, before the creation of speech by the speech of the third verse (*Fiat lux*), there is an enigmatic creation in the first verse—concerning which it is not stated that it involves speech ("In the beginning God [*Elohim*] created the heavens and the earth")—that engenders, in the second verse, the formless void and darkness? Are we to understand, then, that, between the first

---

[40] John 1:1.

[41] See André Neher, *l'Exil de la parole* (Paris: Éditions du Seuil, 1970), Chapter 1, "L'inerte" and Vladimir Jankélévitch, *Le Nocturne* (Paris: Albin Michel, 1957).

[42] [The Hebrew term for the condition of the earth before God said, "Let there be light."]

[43] [Rendered in English translations of the Bible as the "Spirit of God." However, the Hebrew word behind spirit or breath (Fr. *souffle*) is *ruach*, meaning "air in motion."]

two verses and the third, there is a progression in the work of the Creator that initially manifests itself silently ("the breath of *Elohim* was hovering over the waters") and then subsequently through his enunciating Word: *Fiat lux?*

For my part, I will follow Rachi's conception because it is astonishingly evocative for a psychoanalyst.[44] Rachi considers that the verses do not give "the order of creation in order to tell us that the elements—heavens and earth—were created first"; for, he points out, "if that were the case, it would not have been said, 'In the beginning God created the heavens and the earth,' but rather, 'In the first place, God created the heavens and the earth.'" So he proposes the following reading of these three verses: "At the beginning of the creation of the heavens and the earth, when the earth was formless and void, and full of darkness, *Elohim* said: 'Let there be light.'" In a certain way, insofar as it places the divine Word at the very origin of creation, this interpretation seems to simplify things in the extreme; but, in fact, it implicitly raises the following formidable question: If it is indeed the *saying* of God that is at the origin of the created, then it has to be recognized that this *saying* is not only a *well-saying* organizing the human world, but also *an ill-saying* whose effect is to reveal, monstrously, an inhuman world.

The fact that, through the *saying* of the father, well-saying and *ill-saying*, benediction and malediction, can thus be inextricably associated, takes us back to Lacan's late conception according to which the symbolic only takes possession of man—by transmitting meaning to him—insofar as he is structurally foreclosed from the real:[45] the foreclosure in question here is quite different from the pathogenic foreclosure of the signifier of the Name-of-the-Father, since it is structurally linked to the transmission peculiar to the symbolic.[46] For the moment, it is important to note that, in this transmission, something is perverted, as if the father could not structurally transmit "all" the

---

[44] Genesis 1 in *Le Pentateuch en cinq volumes (The Pentateuch in five volumes)*, commentary by J. Rachi, translated into French by J. Bloch, E. Munk, I. Salzer, E. Guggenheim (Paris: Fondation Samuel et Odette Lévy, 1976).

[45] Jacques Lacan, *The Seminar of Jacques Lacan, Book XXIII: The Sinthome*, trans. A.R. Price (Boston: Polity, 2016), Chapter 6.

[46] See the study by H. Yankelevitch, "Un Joyce pour les analystes," *Esquisses psychanalytiques* 19 (1993), 80–81.

## Chapter Two – The Three Superegos

symbolic. This is due to the price of the nonsense of the real exacted from the transmission of sense. We shall see later how the perversion of the symbolic will have to be articulated with the structural function of *"père-version"* (per-version), which Lacan attributes to the father.[47]

Our question is this: How are we to conceive of the articulation between the real of the hole created by the *Fiat hole* and the real of the formless void insofar as it is not included within the domain of speech, since *Elohim is not present in it through his Word* but rather *through his breath* hovering silently over the surface of the waters?

The difference between the second and the third verse lies in a tension between abjection and the world: the created elements, dispersed in the formless void (the spirit of God, the deep, the surface of the waters), will be uprooted from their chaotic confusion and organized in a world that will be governed by the order of speech affirming that *"y a de l'Un"*; the light appearing with the *Fiat lux* is not in fact the light of the lights (which only appears in verse 14), but that of the founding Word, to which Lacan attributes the creation *ex nihilo* of the *Fiat hole*.[48]

In order to understand the mutation that occurs between the hole of "the abyss" of the second verse and the Borromean hole of the third verse, it is necessary to understand the difference established by Lacan between the *Names*-of-the-Father and the *Name*-of-the-Father. Referring to the interrupted seminar on the *Names*-of-the-Father, Lacan says: "It was not without good reason that I did not speak of

---

[47] [*Père-version*: the "father-version" or turning to the father. This turning towards the one who occupies the position of the father corresponds to the third logical time of the Oedipus as Lacan describes it, that in which the father is preferred to the mother, as the one who has the phallus, the signifier of the mother's desire. At this point of crossing the Oedipus, the child, whatever his sex, passes through the desire to be loved by the father as a woman and to receive a child. It is the anguish of castration that will cause him to renounce such a desire. For this turning towards the father to occur, it is necessary that the first two logical steps of the Oedipus have been crossed: that the mother has been dispossessed of the imaginary phallus and that the child has given up his attempt to fill this lack in the mother, to be her phallic object. What makes this renunciation possible is the way in which the mother refers to the father's speech.]

[48] [The formulation *"y a de l'Un"* could be translated as "There's some One," but this translation *does not reflect* its complexity. *Un* in French designates both the indefinite article "a" and the number one. In addition, Lacan accentuates the double nature of the signifier with a pun: *"de"* (which Lacan sometimes writes *d'*) can be heard as both the partitive article "some" and the number two (*deux*). Finally, *Un* in French evokes Lacan's use of the German term *Unbewusste*—unconscious—since it underlines the *Un* of Un*bewusste*.]

the *Name*-of-the-Father: when I began, I spoke of the *Names*-of-the-Father. The *Names*-of-the-father are the symbolic, the imaginary, and the real. These are the first names insofar as they name something."[49]

Are not these *Names*-of-the-Father what we can read in the second verse where a formless void is depicted in which three elements are juxtaposed in a confused manner:

— the "breath of God," hovering without speaking, seems to me to be this first Name by which the symbolic is named;
— the deep, which seems to me to be the first Name of the real;
— and the "surface of the waters," or the first Name of the imaginary.

How are we to understand the fact that these first Names, inasmuch as they are dissociated from each other, can sustain a chaotic real governed by dissociation and confusion? Indeed, one question that each neurotic and each psychotic is faced with is that of the problem of his proximity to the lack of consistency of filth, of abjection.

The other side of the question is just as enigmatic: How is it that these first Names—the symbolic, the real, and the imaginary—can be bound together in such a way that, for three distinct Names, one can substitute just one Name—the Name-of-Name-of-Name—which is what Lacan identifies as the Name-of-the-Father insofar as it is "nothing other than this 'knot' that holds the R.S.I. together"?[50]

The enigma we are faced with lies in the fact that the symbolic can manifest itself in two different ways. Either it is transmitted as the breath of *Elohim*, which, given that it hovers silently over the real of the formless void, is not part of this real, or it ceases to hover over the real and becomes part of it, thereby acquiring, as light, the function whereby the unary trait is at once indissociably real and symbolic. "Light," as Lacan points out, is not a nomination but a creation *ex nihilo* in which "the real emerges from the symbolic."[51] This primordial knot between the real and the symbolic also implies the first Name, the imaginary, inasmuch as, in the following verse—"*Elohim* saw that the light was good"—the dimension of vision is put into perspective. Thus, in the verse where, at the level of "light," the three first Names are knotted

---

[49] Jacques Lacan, seminar of March 11, 1975, *RSI*, unpublished seminar.
[50] *Ibid.*, and Preface to F. Wedekind, *L'Éveil du printemps* (Paris: Gallimard, 2005).
[51] Jacques Lacan, seminar of May 13, 1975, *RSI*, unpublished seminar.

together, I want to suggest that "light," as Name-of-Name-of-Name, is one of the possible ways of defining the Name-of-the-Father.

For the time being, the tension between the *Names*-of-the-Father and the *Name*-of-the-Father may be summarized as follows: on one side, the introduction of the *Name*-of-the-Father is expressed by a transmissible enunciation—"light"—which, by binding together the first *Names* (breath of *Elohim*, the deep, surface of the waters), subjects them to the symbolic law by means of which the *Name*-of-the-Father proffers that *"y a de l'Un."*

This One—founded by the continuity of the three dimensions of the real, the symbolic, and the imaginary (R.S.I.)—is thus the effect of a binding *saying*. But as this *saying* that holds together the human world is only a *half-saying*, it does not have the power to hold together "everything" that is named by the first Names. At the same time something falls as the human world, something falls away: the realm of what is abject is nothing other than the persistence of a formless void that, refractory to the chaining power of speech, subsists as an unchained, unbridled world.

If we retain the interpretation of Rachi as being the closest to the interpretation that psychoanalysis can give of the origin of the human psyche, we are led to suggest that psychic reality is put into perspective inasmuch as the *infans*, as the subject supposed by the Name-of-the-Father to gain access to speech, finds himself in the position of responding to the enunciation *Fiat lux* by giving it two antinomical, and no doubt simultaneous, responses. With the first response, the pre-subject attests to the Name-of-the-Father by responding to it with this "yes" in which Freud identifies the enigmatic, originary *Bejahung*. With his second response, the primordial ego contests the enunciation of the Name-of-the-Father by opposing to it a "no" whose radical nature is not that of negation, but rather that of a foreclosure, translated by Freud, in his text on negation, by the term *werfen* (expelled).[52] Through the association of this originary foreclosure and *Bejahung*, there is a simultaneous emergence of a human world in which the reign of speech acts by unifying, by binding together, its three components (real, symbolic, imaginary), and a world uninhabitable by hu-

---

[52] [Alain Didier-Weill isolates, in Freud's essay "Negation," the German term *Werfung*, which he differentiates from *Verwerfung*. *Werfung* would be a non-irreversible rejection, whereas *Verwerfung* would be an irreversible rejection, translated by Lacan as foreclosure.]

mans, insofar as it is a formless void in which the symbolic, hovering as breath over the surface of the waters and the abyss, is not tied or knotted to the real and the imaginary. We thus arrive at a conception where, from the beginning, the *saying*—split between *well-saying* and *saying badly*—engenders both a world of speech, in which things are bound, and a world of absolute silence, in which they are unbound.

Are these two worlds in communication or are they parallel? Is the frontier between them porous or impassable? To this topological question, psychoanalysis can only respond by noting that the complexity of this frontier lies in the fact that, if there is a possibility of crossing it, there is, at the same time, an irreducible impossibility of crossing it. Maintaining that there is both continuity and discontinuity between the reign of speech and that of absolute silence leads us to oppose two types of silent real:[53] a silence that is capable of being visited by speech, and another that is irremediably inhospitable to speech.[54] For the moment, these two types of silence—which I shall be exploring later with reference to a clinical observation—can be accounted for by noting that the silence of the formless void does not have the same structure depending on whether it is that of the darkness or that of the abyss; indeed, we learn from later verses that though the "darkness" is divided from silence (verse 4)—inasmuch as after the *Fiat lux*, it is called "night" by the Creator—the abyss, on the contrary, designates a point of the real that no nomination will succeed subsequently in raising to the level of existence.

The word "abyss" thus designates a real that, as it is inaccessible to the naming power of the Creator, incarnates the very point, at the heart of his *saying*, of an unnamable abyss that has been created by this primal repression: the abyss incarnates a type of silence that attests to the limit that the symbolic power of the *Bejahung* receives from the *Ausstoßung*.[55] Insofar as the abyss designates the place of the real that will not be named in any way, the silence that it makes us hear

---

[53] Alain Didier-Weill, "Les trois silences," in Mouvement du coût freudien, *Fin d'une analyse, finalité de la psychanalyse* (Malakoff: Solin, 1989).

[54] Each of these silences is the effect of a specific structural foreclosure: the first is, in my opinion, induced by the act of *Ausstoßung*, generative of primal repression; the second is induced by the process of *werfen*. See 290–306 for a development of this theoretical question.

[55] See 291ff.

is radically different from the silence that the darkness makes us hear, to the extent that the latter, waiting to be named, resounds with a desperate silence—that is to say, a silence that nonetheless contains the hope of a possible speech. It is the perception of the absence of this possible speech that confers the silence of darkness with its frightening character, something experienced by any child when he or she is in the grip of night terrors. If the extraordinary silence of the abyss is not desperate, it is because it does not incarnate a real that has been cast off from the symbolic, but, on the contrary, a real that never ceases to expect to come within its scope.

The complexity of the frontier between the real and the symbolic consists in the fact that it stands in a twin relationship of discontinuity and continuity, where the real and the symbolic both act on each other, but dissymmetrically, through discontinuity and continuity. While introducing, through foreclosure—*werfen*—a discontinuity with the symbolic, the real tends, at the same time, to corrupt the symbolic limits when contact with the symbolic, ceasing to be prohibited by the taboo, creates the conditions of a monstrous continuity between the real and the symbolic.[56] This continuity, whereby the symbolic form is invaded by formlessness, is, as we shall see, the condition of the appearance of what we call a monster.[57]

Conversely, the symbolic tends, through the symbolization—*Bejahung*—of the silent real, to re-establish continuity with it; but this continuity is achieved by means of introducing the symbolic law, which creates a discontinuous relation with the real brought into existence by nomination.[58]

How, then, are we to understand the mode of proximity of the nameable real (darkness that has become night) with that of the unnamable real (abyss)? And how does the unnamable real, as an effect of structural foreclosure—*Ausstoßung*—differ from the real that, in a delusional hallucination, is the consequence of a pathogenic foreclosure?

---

[56] See 291.

[57] See 55–62.

[58] This separation between the real and the symbolic, made possible in the analytic *cure* by the transference-love, leads Shmuel Trigano to say ("Une voie hors du temps qui passé et se perd," *Pardès* 17, (1993)): "How paradoxical is this love whose first act produces separation! It is contrary to what one might think of love, of the immediateness of the rapprochement."

To answer these questions, I would like to comment on the rapprochement established by Lacan between the originary *Fiat lux* and the *Borromean Fiat hole*, and to suggest that, for the Name-of-Name-of-Name that is *lux*, insofar as it holds together three first Names, to be transmissible to the pre-subject, the latter must be able to say "yes" to it, must be able to turn it into the *Bejahung*. Without this assumption, the Name-of-the-Father would not be transmuted into the signifier of the Name-of-the-Father. The assumption of this signifier is the means whereby the "light" of this signifier is transmitted, for the subject, as a graft of the light that is the symbolic law inasmuch as it informs us about the real. The effect of this law is not to make the real disappear from the abyss that inhabits the subject, but rather to bind the bottomless and limitless hole that is the abyss by transmuting it into the well-circumscribed hole in the form of the Borromean *Fiat hole*.

The problem posed by this binding of the real is that, although it is fragile, it is efficient for an indefinite period of time. If this real becomes unbound, the subject is not completely helpless, because he can rely on the help of the signifier of the Name-of-the-Father to bind the realm of abjection to the symbolic chain that holds the world together. For example, when a child discovers that nocturnal darkness has the power of unleashing monsters, he has the possibility of switching on the light of a lamp whose capacity to dissipate horror resides in the fact that the light dispensed is none other than the clarity by which the symbolic law substitutes the distinct for the diffuse and discrimination for confusion. If the delusional subject does not have this recourse, it is because the foreclosure of which he is the victim is another type of foreclosure whose effect is to prevent the assumption of that Name-of-the-Father that is "light": if he is assailed by monsters, for instance, in the form of hallucinations, he does not have a lamp to switch on; his lamp does not work anymore. If this "darkness" into which he is plunged is so desperate, it is because it has lost all hope of becoming "night": if it had become night, the arrival of time would have carried it away and, by removing it from its timelessness, would have bound it to the rhythm of the alternation between day and night.

The despair, the angst, that exists in the silence of darkness comes from its link with obscurity that, induced by a foreclosure of light, retains—to use Freud's terms—an "inner perception" of this mechanism of foreclosure whereby the signifier "light," inasmuch as it has been rejected from the symbolic, returns, in the real, in the form of darkness. In this respect, the great difference between the silence of darkness and the silence of the abyss resides in the fact that the silence of darkness is the consequence of the absence of the signifier "light" inasmuch as it is foreclosed, whereas the silence of the abyss occurs paradoxically in the presence of the signifier "light," *at the very heart of this signifier*: it is not the absence of presence, but, rather, that absence in presence that is introduced by primal repression. That this absence in presence is signifiable, while remaining irreducible, is what Lacan introduces through the signifier of absence in presence that he writes S (A̸).

The fraternity that exists between the neurotic and the psychotic consists in the fact that the absolute silence with which every subject is confronted, owing to the structural foreclosure that faces him with what I have called the abyss, is not identical to, but rather is comparable with, the absolute silence that reigns in that darkness where the light is foreclosed and that is frequented by the psychotic; it is not the cause of the silence that is comparable but rather the phenomenological, clinical character of this silence insofar as it is silence of silence.

This silence of silence is literally the sense of terror to which Psalm 22 refers, when the psalmist cries (verse 2): "...and the night season, and am not silent."[59]

Through the expression "*lô dûmya*," the psalmist evokes the experience of a non-silence of God; the strangeness of this experience consists in the fact that there can be a "non-silence" that is not speech. As André Neher points out, "If the negation of speech—non-speech—is silence, non-silence is not automatically, or necessarily, speech. This non-silence is a silence more silent than silence."[60] Thus the silence of silence revealed by night silences what can be transmitted by the silence of daytime: "a silence that speaks."

To get an idea of the silence that speaks, think of the silence that music makes you hear: the moment it stops speaks of something so essential that a music lover was able to say elegantly that, when a concerto of Mozart ended, one could then hear the whole of Mo-

---

[59] [The complete verse (verse 3 in the Hebrew Bible, but verse 2 in English translations) reads: "Oh my God, I cry in the daytime, but you hear not; and the night season, and am not silent" (King James 2000 Bible). The French text reads: "*La nuit, pour moi, point de silence.*"]

[60] André Neher, *L'exil de la parole, op. cit.*, 75.

zart. In fact, this silence that speaks does much more than perpetuate the speech that preceded it: not only does it cause the memory of the speech that has died out to resonate but, above all, it also makes one hear the silent support—a veritable blank page—on which speech has been inscribed; and, in so doing, it teaches us that silence can be buzzing with speech already uttered. Is not the silence of nature this buzzing silence that is unable to forget the enunciation of the originary words, *Fiat hole*, insofar as they continue to reverberate? Are not the poems that are dictated to the poet by silent nature evidence of this? If the *Fiat hole* continues to resonate in the silence of nature, it is because this silence is not the silence that preceded it, but the one that succeeded it: whereas the silence that precedes the *Fiat hole* harks back to the *ex nihilo* of the uncreated, the silence following it is the effect of a creation whereby the silence is not defined negatively as non-speech, but rather positively as a locus of habitation for speech.[61]

It is because it is inhabited that silence can be heard; and it is because it speaks to us silently that nature conveys to us a peaceful interpretation of the meaning of its silence. This silence that can be heard may be contrasted with the silence that, as it is not induced by an act of creation but rather by structural foreclosure, is a silence that cannot be heard, a silence of silence.

It is impossible for me, by using my imagination, to picture what this silence that cannot be heard is, if only because I can only encounter the horror of such a silence if I have already lost the possibility of resorting to imagination.

## C) THE SILENCE OF THE MONSTER

We can get an idea of the absolute silence that I have just been discussing by asking ourselves what, for us, the signification is of that which the mythological and folkloric tradition calls a monster. Even if we have never encountered such a creature, we are capable of imagining—even without going to see horror films—the horror caused by encountering a monster. For each one of us, as a subject created *ex*

---

[61] See 24–27: while Robert speaks to the psychoanalyst about the silence that followed what he said, the madman speaks to the psychiatrist about a silence preceding what he said.

*nihilo*, maintains an intimate relationship with that part of the real that, because it has not acceded to the nomination that makes the world exist, persists as *abjection*—as that absolute silence, namely, the silence of silence.

Why is the horror that grips us if we meet a monster comparable to that of the madman meeting the chicken? Because, like the madman, confronted with the encounter of a real that "is" silent, even though it does not exist, we are suddenly reminded of that real that does not exist in us because it has been withdrawn from the power of speech. What outcome will our companionship with this monstrous twin, the real, have? The monster thus possesses the power to send us back to that place in our being where absolute silence reigns, which shows that, in the creative *saying* by means of which an originary *Fiat hole* appeared, both a symbolic success and a failure of the symbolic occurred at the beginning. This partial-success is thus the result of the fact that the original *saying* can only be a *half-saying*. Through it is announced both a *well-saying*, attesting to the meaning of the world, and a *saying badly*, the cause of this abjection that will forever continue to contest this meaning.

The fact that the analyst knows that there is a share of *saying badly*, of malediction of a structural order, in the original *saying* that the *infans* receives from his or her ancestors has consequences for his practice: he will not conduct himself like Don Quixote, attacking windmills blindly. He knows that—beyond the real possibility of a perversion of the ancestors, who, like Oedipus with his son, can really curse their descendants, that beyond this historical reality—there is, in speech itself, a fact of a-historical structure that acts on him in such a way that he can only produce a *well-saying* in association with a *saying badly*. Generally speaking, it is only when the analysand has exhausted all the reproaches they can address to their parents that they encounter the question of the sway that the *saying* and the *curse* have over them.

How is the sway that the absolute silence has over the subject—a silence to which he is sent back by the monster—expressed phenomenologically? It is expressed by the fact that, when he comes face-to-face with the monster, the subject does not conduct himself—or at least not yet—as Beauty does with the Beast: if, indeed, he could speak to this Beast, it would cease, as the fairytale tells us, to be a Beast and recover its human form immediately. This is, perhaps, what expresses most eloquently the fact that, faced with the absolute silence of the monster, the subject can no longer speak and manifests himself through the sole vocal act that remains available to him, that is, by screaming.

Screaming, indeed, is the simplest sound vibration. It attempts, not to break the silence, but rather to make it heard; it is the means whereby one hears that it is this silence that is screaming with pain. Is not this pain of not being able to get out of oneself the effect of the part of the signifier that, remaining inexorably in abeyance, dooms the cursed part of the subject to remain in exile in a place that is absolutely inhospitable to speech? The silence is so absolute that, from this place, the subject does not even have the possibility of calling for help. Being able to call on the recourse that is the symbolic would imply the manifestation of a presence that can only call because it has itself already been called into being. We may suppose that, in the inaugural call addressed to the subject, something functions as an evil call, as a malefic call comparable to the evil spell cast by the wicked fairy on the infant in the cradle. This produces a foreclosure of the symbolic, cause of an uncreated part in the subject. Owing to this primordial spell, the subject is reminded of the fact that there is a point of foreclosure in him where there was no creation of unconscious representation. It is from this place where there can be no unconscious thought that he learns, through the very presence of the monster, that this presence presents itself to him devoid of representation. Because the monster is unrepresented and unrepresentable, it is characterized, as real, by the fact that it transmits its presence not through the intervention of unconscious thought but through the intervention of what Freud calls "internal perception."[62] Through this "internal perception," the subject, gaining access to the real without signifying mediation, undergoes the deadly experience of the world of iniquity, which is a lawless world: indeed, the law introduces a signifier of alterity that, interposing itself between the subject and the real, has the effect of prohibiting the real from offering itself to the subject's internal perception, only permitting him to be symbolized in a *saying*.

There is an enigma in the symbolic prohibition: If it is sufficiently effective to allow the subject to live in a world that is not perpet-

---

[62] For example, Sigmund Freud, *Totem and Taboo* (1913–1914), *The Standard Edition of the Complete Psychological Works of Sigmund Freud XIII* (London: Hogarth, 1961), 68.

ually invaded by abjection, how are we to understand the fact that the power of this prohibition is so limited? A return of obscurity, for instance, is all that is required for these nocturnal anxieties to appear through which the child "senses" the proximity of the monster that might "touch" him. This horror of being touched (return to the real of the "internal perception") takes us back to the appearance of the taboo prohibiting contact and raises the following question: What fundamental difference is there between the prohibition induced by the interdiction and that induced by the taboo?

For the time being, I understand this difference as being linked to the structural fact that, as a *saying*, the interdiction is only a *half-interdiction* and that, as such, it cannot assume responsibility for the symbolization of "all" the real. In my view, it is for this reason that what has been withdrawn from the symbolizing power of the interdiction returns to the real as an untouchable cursed part. This prohibition of contact with the impure is from that moment on, at the point where the interdiction is lacking, the ultimate barrier that the taboo sets up against the real.

But this prohibition is eminently fragile, for the taboo—contrary to the interdiction that is said to "introduce distinctions"—is fundamentally silent, in such a way that, although the symbolic law clearly *precedes* the infraction, the taboo only manifests itself silently *after* the infraction: the fact that it then takes vengeance—generally by passing the death sentence, without a judicial procedure, without symbolic instruction—introduces us to the very heart of the possibility of understanding what the baleful power of the real is.

Why does the taboo on touching expose one to death if it is violated? Because, in the absence of interdiction, if there is contact between the subject and the real, a complex operation occurs whereby it turns out that the real, insofar as it is foreclosed from the symbolic, is characterized by the very fact of not knowing the signification of the human limit bestowed by the law, of not being limited by this law. The confusion of limits is shown by the monster, to the extent that its monstrosity is the monstration of the mingling of shapelessness with the human shape. If this confusion is so threatening to the subject, it is because it reminds him that within the human limit there is a fundamental porosity, a deficiency, through which a continuity can be substituted for the discontinuity established in him by the symbolic law, and, by this means, the inhuman can take possession of what, in him, is human.

In this respect, why do we find it so particularly horrifying if the human is transformed into the inhuman, if man is transformed into a werewolf? Through the spectacle of this process, we witness an internal struggle in which, for a certain time, the human frontier resists the internal assault of an anonymous force pushing it to renounce what it is, gradually making way for the new frontier of bestiality.[63] What is frightening is not the final substitution of the stable form of a wolf for the human form, but rather the work of metamorphosis that has taken place before our eyes and that has made us witnesses of a sort of hesitation between the human decision to persevere in the direction of the human and the anonymous decision to go towards the inhuman.

I suppose that if the spectacle of this indecision between speech and absolute silence has the power of fascinating us to the point of making us cultivate this fascination, it is because it tells us this: our horror of monstrosity is nothing other than a commemoration of the profoundly enigmatic originary act, which, as it has not created a humanity in us that is fully accomplished and defined by the symbolic law, has allowed a residual part to come into being as a result of this very incompletion linked to the *half-interdicting*. As this residual part escapes the human law, it is has not been visited by speech and thus remains the place of a monstrous silence, juxtaposed in a radical dissymmetry with the place where speech reigns.

This dissymmetry between speech and silence resides in the fact that, if the speaking part of the subject knows about monstrosity (owing to the mere fact that it is capable of being horrified), *this monstrous part does not, however, have the symmetrical knowledge of speech*. The monster is in a silence of silence, the fundamental meaning of which is precisely that of not knowing about the existence of speech: just as the chicken does not know that the madman is a speaking subject, whereas he knows in what silence the chicken remains, the man transformed into the werewolf no longer knows that he was a man, whereas, once he has become a man again, he knows, or can know, that he was a wolf, that he was inhabited by the non-human silence of the cursed part.

---

[63] A force that may be identified with the 'there is [*il y a*]' of Levinas.

Although this monstrous silence is generally forgotten, as was the case at the Nuremburg trials, such forgetting is not, in essence, inexorable.

This dissymmetry between the power of the real and that of the symbolic lies in the antagonistic modalities according to which the symbolic and the real are transmitted: whereas the symbolic, being transmitted via the law of speech, tends, by naming a part of the real, to make it exist at the level of symbolic, in such a way that there can be no contact between the subject and the real, the real is transmitted via a topological point that, having escaped the power of the real, is put in the position of transmitting itself through the "internal perception" of a contact between itself and the subject. As a result of this contact—which is made possible structurally by the fact that the wall of the symbolic interdiction, as *half-interdicting*, is porous—there only exists, as the last prohibition of the real, the taboo that prohibits contact. So when circumstances are such that the subject is plunged into a lawless world where he can draw support neither from the symbolic interdiction nor from the taboo, he has the experience of deadly contact with the real. This contact creates a traumatic rupture in the psychic envelope that Freud calls the "stimulus barrier" through the intervention of a bite made by the monster (for example, the vampire) or of the evil eye of the monster (the Medusa).[64] In any case, the enigmatic effect of the contact is that which tradition identifies as being linked to the production of soiling.[65] The enigmatic notion of soiling implies the register of a transmission whereby the soiled body is silently invaded by a process of continuous progression that is ignorant of the body's limits. Step by step, the soiling abolishes the discontinuity of these limits, replacing it with the deadly reign of chaotic continuity. It is because this transmission by contamination—which is reminiscent of the mode of transmission of the cancerous cell—is ignorant of the discontinuous character of the law that nothing can stop it and that it can spread by ceasing to obey the ascendancy of speech, by virtue of which the symbolic order prevailed as a discontinuous process. It is in this way that

---

[64] Sigmund Freud, *Beyond the Pleasure Principle* (1920), *The Standard Edition of the Complete Psychological Works of Sigmund Freud XVIII* (London: Hogarth, 1961).

[65] Cf. Jean-Pierre Vernant and Pierre Vidal-Naquet, *Mythe et Tragédie en Grèce ancienne* (Paris: Maspero, 1972), chapter 5; Mary Douglas, *De la souillure* (Paris: Maspero, 1981).

it can invade the subject: by reducing him to that pure real, the pure "grain of wheat" stripped of all significant alterity.

Whether man is transformed into a werewolf through the contact of a bite or into a stone statue through the petrifying contact of the Medusa's gaze, in both cases he acquires the specific character of the monstrous real, which is that of absolute silence.

If the silence of the monster can enter the subject in this way, it means that between them there is the affinity of a discontinuity whose enigmatic character never ceases to pose the following question: How is it that, in the case of the dumbfounded being, the monstrous real of the stupefying gaze is able to take possession totally of the subject by establishing an absolute and definitive continuity with him, whereas, in the case of the subject fascinated by the chicken, it turns out that the fixedness of the chicken's gaze does not possess the power of the Medusa's gaze to impose an immobility of stone,[66] for ever, on the subject?[67]

How is it, in short, that the cursed part of the madman, fascinated by the chicken, is able to detach itself, at a given moment, from the evil eye that has cursed it? How can this cursed part escape its state of degradation and be put back into a transferential relationship with the symbolic from which it has been foreclosed?

This question leads us to a radical distinction between the most archaic superego of the neurotic and the psychotic superego. The psychotic superego is the effect of a pathogenic foreclosure linked to the specific history of a subject to whom the signifier of the Name-of-the-Father has not been transmitted, owing to a certain perversion of the function of transmissibility vested in ascendants. The archaic superego of the neurotic—as it is portrayed in the scenario of the madman and the chicken—seems to me to be the effect of a foreclosure that is not pathogenic but structural, introducing into saying the dimension of cursing.

The clinical distinction introduced by these two types of foreclosure is manifested through two kinds of gaze emanating from the superego: on the one hand, the gaze directed by the Medusa towards

---

[66] See Danièle Epstein, "Autour de la Méduse," *Correspondences freudiennes* 40–41 (December 1993); see "The Medusa's Gaze and the Loss of Being Incognito," 284.

[67] On the difference between a stupefying gaze and a fascinating gaze, see "The Dream of the Black Point: The Silent Malediction," 62–66.

her victim; and, on the other, the gaze directed by the chicken towards the madman. While the dumbfounded subject finds himself forever petrified into a statue that has the eternity of stone, the madman of our story is not totally invaded by the monstrous gaze because he can avoid it. This possibility of rupture shows that the monstrous continuity established between the silence of the grain of wheat and that of the fascinating gaze remains in fact under the sway of a signifier that establishes a possible discontinuity between the cursed side of the subject and the cursing side of the Other that is the evil eye.

## D) THE DREAM OF THE BLACK POINT: THE SILENT MALEDICTION

The analysis of the following dream allows us to closely identify the process whereby the separation of the subject from the fascinating gaze involves the intervention of a signifier that has the power of metaphorizing the cursed part of the subject and of constituting the fascinating object as a lost object.

Here is the text of the dream: "A man was looking at me and I noticed a little black point, a sort of spot, at the corner of his mouth. I was so fascinated by this black point that I couldn't help looking at it, and I remained like that, silently, for a period of time that went on forever. Then a woman approached the man and asked him if he had a light. The man got out his Dupont and lit the woman's cigarette. I told myself that I was going to count to three and then leave, and I left."

The first sequence of the dream depicts what becomes of a subject who encounters the existence of what can only show itself in the real, since it cannot be demonstrated by means of speech: what the "black point" monstrously designates is thus the real insofar as it manifests that which has neither been created nor symbolically named. By virtue of its fixedness, the black point silently imposes itself on the subject of the dream in such a way that this subject—who is unable to move, like the madman under the chicken's gaze—tends to remain stupidly in a state of absolute immobility for an indefinite period of time. Why is he no longer able to move, no longer able to think? Because the body's capacity to move, like that of the mind, is only rendered possible by living speech; and it is precisely this speech that has been put to death by the silent message conveyed by the gaze of the black point: "That is all you are, this fixed real, devoid of all speech, which can no longer move around; for there is only one place left for you, the one that is fixed by my gaze."

The first part of the dream thus represents the indefinite period of time during which the immobilized and silent part of the subject is under the absolute sway of this blackness of the Other, in the form of this black point incarnating what we are. With the expression "blackness of the Other," I am evoking that obscure part that signifies that there is a point in the Other where there remains a structural foreclosure of the signifying light. The black point, in my opinion, is that point of the real—inasmuch as it has not yet been lost—which is encountered by the *infans* at the dawn of his days when he discovers, in the signifying chain transmitted by his ascendants, a real hole at the level of which he does not find the support of any significant light to welcome him. It is because the subject can fall into such a hole, without there being anything to restrain him, that the human terror of nocturnal darkness appears.

But this terror can be dialectized: If this bottomless and borderless hole acquires, through the signifying metaphor of the paternal metaphor, a limit imposed by the symbolic law of the *Fiat hole*, then it is possible for the subject not to fall into or yield to the dizziness of deadly fascination by the black point and, like at the end of the dream, he can then separate from the black point, turning away from it in order to resume his own movement at the point at which he had broken it off.

What does the dream teach us about this moment of overcoming in which the subject rediscovers speech and movement? It teaches us that the subject is freed from the deadly sway of the superego's gaze at the very moment when the man with the black point is snatched from the silence in which he found himself, because he has been put in touch with the speech of a woman who asks him the question: "Have you got a light?" The meaning of this question (to which I will devote an analysis later on, 141ff) is the same as that of the question that the unconscious of a mother puts to the unconscious of her child's father: "Will you be able to transmit to this newborn baby the flame of the signifier under which you yourself were already born, having received it from something higher than yourself?" This is a formidable question that reminds the father that, if he is a father, it is because—having, in an initial metaphorical phase, received the flame of this symbolic command: "You will be the one who will be father"—he must, subsequent-

*Chapter Two – The Three Superegos*

ly, bring into existence the "I" presupposed by the "who will be." This "who will be" presupposes the procreation of such an unconscious "I" inasmuch as it is written in the second person singular and not in the third person singular, which, in this case, would tend to foreclose the presupposition of the "I."[68]

The dream thus depicts the transition whereby the figure of the man with the black point, interpellated as the receiver of the question, "Have you got a light?," is transformed into an emitter producing the signifier "Dupont" ("The man got out his Dupont"). By means of this signifier, the man with the black point tears himself away from the blackness of a pure fascinating gaze (first superego), for the signifier "Dupont" introduces, in a divided way, both the *metaphorical* function and the function of *nomination*: the analysis will reveal, in fact, that the metaphorical function refers to the maternal grandfather and the function of nomination to the real father.[69] By virtue of the ambiguity with the lighter, the signifier "Dupont" transmits the metaphor of fire bestowed by the "late maternal grandfather."[70] But "Dupont" also transmits the patronym of the real father, for it is consonant with "Dupont."

Thus, through this brief sequence that articulates two productions of the unconscious—"Have you got a light?" and "Dupont"—the subject of the dream showed that the gaze of the archaic superego embodied by the black point was not the pitiless gaze of the Medusa, but rather a gaze bearing witness to the existence of a real that is not unnamable. The "bridge" that "Dupont" establishes between the real and the symbolic outlines this narrow passage by means of which the subject depicted in the dream will be able to pass, finding at the end of the dream his freedom of thought ("I told myself that I was going to count to three") and of movement ("and I left").

---

[68] In relation to Lacan's commentary on this question (*Le Séminaire livre III: Les Psychoses*, ed. Jacques-Alain Miller (Paris: Éditions du Seuil, 1981), 316), the transcription of the seminar contains an error on page 344. It is written: "Tu es celui qui *sera* père," whereas it should read, "Tu es celui qui *seras* père." [Jacques Lacan, *The Seminar of Jacques Lacan, Book III: The Psychoses*, trans. Russell Grigg (London: Routledge, 1993).]

[69] On the question of the division of the symbolic, see 44ff and Chapter Three: "The Question of the Stunning Commandment."

[70] [*Dupont* was a very common brand of lighter, such that it was a proprietary eponym for a period in France.]

This dream appeared, in this analysis, like a sort of *coup de théatre*, introducing the subject to a new relationship with both his mother and his paternal filiation. While, for him, his mother was nothing but this mother hen, fixing him with a gaze whose omnipotence was only equaled by its profound stupidity, expressing its ignorance of the symbolic, here she reappeared in a dream in the guise of a woman questioning the "fire" of the signifier of the Name-of-the-Father. The dreamer, astonished by her new appearance, asked himself the following question: "Is this the mother of my fantasies or is it a side of my mother that was turned, without my noticing it, towards the signifying fire?" It was by virtue of this question that the subject would gradually be led to return to the image of his mother and to recognize that her stupid gaze was, in fact, the gaze that she had directed at her husband insofar as, in her relationship with him—he was a brilliant lawyer—she felt she was as much despising as she was despised: despising in relation to the speech of this man, which she regarded as futile, and despised because she considered herself, in comparison with him, an uneducated half-wit.

The analysand thus recognized, for the first time, that the silent and stupid gaze with which his mother seemed to have categorically rejected the order of speech had been, in fact, the last veil by means of which the latter had kept inside herself, in a silent suffering, the burning question that she was constantly addressing, in fact, to the signifier of the Name-of-the-Father: "Have you got a light?"

The progress of the analysis consisted in the fact that the subject was one day able to recognize that, beyond her mother hen's superego gaze, there was, in fact, in his mother's unconscious, a silent quest calling on the signifier of the Name-of-the-Father to transmit itself as "fire" to her son.

Does the fact that the man with the black point was recognized as the grandfather of the dreamer mean that, in the mother's unconscious, the signifier of the Name-of-the-Father could only be transmitted to her son through the intercession of the grandfather? In fact, the breakthrough established by the dream stems from the fact that, if the man with the black point refers, on the one hand, to the maternal grandfather as intercessor of the signifier of the Name-of-the-Father, he also refers to the dreamer's real father in his function of naming father, for the name of the lighter dispensing flame—"Dupont"—rhymed with the patronym of his father.

## Chapter Two – The Three Superegos

It should be emphasized, in conclusion, that two generations are necessary for structuring the archaic superego: The superego gaze of the mother hen is, in fact, the response, is it not, that was induced in her by the man with the black point, that is to say, by this absolute point of silence that she encountered in her own father, whose "fire" she had constantly tried to reach in vain throughout her life? The fact that it was in the dream of his grandson that the man with the black point, responding to this appeal, gave the green light by giving his "Dupont" teaches us that the analysand can succeed in his analytic task where his ascendants failed: by intervening verbally in the dream of his grandson, the grandfather ceases to embody for him the black point that he was for his daughter. The black point embodies the persistence of a real that, like the hallucinatory real, does not yet exist in the symbolic order. This is the source of the fascinating archaic superego. Insofar as it is not the real that exists in the symbolic—which Lacan writes as bar on the big Other ($\cancel{A}$)—we have the greatest difficulty in understanding its generation.

Because we interpret its genesis as a non-genesis—as the effect of a waste residue of the signifying operation of the *Fiat hole*—we must accept the following paradox: while being something base—unnamable—the abject real, by virtue of the mere fact that we can speak about it, is not a pure real; it is already a mixture, revealing that, as a signifying waste product, it retains, as it were, the scar of the passage of this foreclosed signifier. I understand this scar to be the unnamable—since it is untranslatable—trace left by this Name-of-the-Father that is the first Name of the real.[71]

That this first Name of the real can be tied to the symbolic by the question of the *Fiat lux* ("Do you have a light?") is a possibility represented by the dream of the fascinating black point. If the structure of this black point had been the cause of a stupefying gaze—from which the subject would not have been able, under any circumstances, to detach himself—he would have incarnated not what I have identified as the archaic superego, but rather a psychoticizing superego.

---

[71] Jacques Lacan, seminar of March 11, 1975, *RSI*, unpublished seminar.

## II. The Second Superego: "Don't Insist!"

Insofar as we are led to consider the infinitesimal instant when Robert had the unconscious choice between the possibility of making a slip of the tongue or a witticism, we will try to reconstitute the moment when Robert, initially driven to express his desire, was led subsequently to retract what he had said.

Within this infinitesimal interval of the choice is posed the enigmatic question of the choice of the neurosis.[72] The subject is confronted with the fact that the law, depending on whether it is understood in symbolic terms or in terms of the superego, presents him with two antinomical possibilities. The symbolic law presents him with the command that says he has a duty to become, a "*soll ich warden*," which expects from him the advent of a new signifier that will divide him; on the contrary, the law of the superego, embodied in our clinical example by the lady's contemptuous look, issues him with the command: "Disavow in yourself the future of speech."[73]

Robert agreed to this disavowal by choosing to obey the gaze of the superego that asked him to give up his attempts to show that he could be a speaking being and to show, monstrously, that silently he was only a blushing thing. What, indeed, is the subjective pain involved in blushing if not the experience in which the subject is led to realize that he has in fact agreed to disown himself as a speaking being. The patent character of this renunciation is revealed by the fact that the act of blushing is essentially a silent act whereby the subject conveys the message to the gaze that fixes him: "Look at what remains of me when I obey you, and when, having given up the possibility of speaking, I once again become this silent being whom you have the absolute right to observe...." This obedience to the silent message conveyed by the gaze is an enigma for me: how can one explain what is at the basis of the power of the gaze?

The following dream, which Robert had at the beginning of his analysis, enables us to tackle this question:

"I am at home and I suddenly have to go out because, outside, someone is calling for help. But my cat is staring at me and the way it

---

[72] See "Freud and the Question of the Unconscious Choice," 163ff.
[73] See 35ff.

is looking at me is telling me, 'Stay there!' Even though I know that I should go out, I cannot leave the room because of this gaze."

From the associations to the dream we learn that it was not the *signification* of the message that he received from the cat ("Stay there!") that made the dreamer obey, but rather the fact that the cat was silent. Indeed, if the cat had *said* to him: "Stay there!," he *could* have disobeyed it, for he would have contradicted it immediately in the following way: "I will not stay there because someone is calling me to go outside!"

In the same way, Robert is led to realize that, if the woman had *said* to him, "You're a very uncouth person," he would not have been paralyzed in the same way that he was by the woman's scornful look; he could have replied, for instance, that it was a slip of the tongue and apologized for it. But the problem lies in the fact that this simple possibility was absolutely excluded from the moment he agreed that the woman's gaze could incarnate itself—the deepest meaning of this consent being that of not replying, of not contradicting it. This impossibility of replying raises, among others, the following question: If Freud's "Case Histories" confront us with a bestiary in which the wolf man, the rat man, and the horse child cohabit, is it not because an animal embodies for human consciousness a fundamentally gazing presence?

The force of this gaze is greatly increased, is it not, by the fact that an animal cannot speak and is thus apprehended by the unconscious as the repository of an absolute knowledge that silently says: "I have the advantage over you of a form of knowledge to which speech, which can only offer you a half-saying, cannot accede: *what, in you, remains inaccessible to speech is not inaccessible for me*"?

It is the fact that the possibility of gaining access to the inaccessible is the privilege of the gaze that leads man to assign the gaze with the possibility of passing absolute judgment on him, a last judgment, which makes of him a man on trial, especially if he does not know the nature of the charge. That the gaze lends itself particularly to the superego's faculty for condemnation is the point that we are going to examine.

*Chapter Two – The Three Superegos*

A) THE GAZE OF THE EVIL EYE[74]

*a) To Guard—To Regard*

Our clinical experience teaches us that the major effect of the gaze is to strip the subject of what he was unaware of possessing before suddenly being deprived of it: indeed, he has to be reduced to silence, to immobility and transparency, in order to learn retrospectively that the human "Thing"—*das Ding*—that was in him, before being undermined by the gaze, was the means by which he had been bestowed with a radical incognito, the source of that life that is speech.[75]

Why does this human Thing not have the capacity to "guard" or protect itself when it is "re-garded"?[76] The semantic dissymmetry

---

[74] This research on the evil eye, which draws exclusively on psychoanalytic practice, needs to be amplified by certain contemporary ethnographic research studies on Mediterranean societies.

See, on this subject, the work of Muriel Djeribi: "Le mauvais œil et le lait," *L'Homme* 105; "La fabrication mythique des enfants" (Paris: Navarin, 1988), 35–40; "Œil d'amour, œil d'envie," *Nouvelle Revue de Psychanalyse* 38; "Le Mal" (Paris: Gallimard, 1988); "L'incantation mythique: noms et écriture," *Ethnologie française*; "Textures mythiques" (Paris: Armand Colin, 1993), 1; "La goule dans les rêts de l'écrit," paper read May 6, 1994 at the seminar of N. Belmont at *L'Ecole pour hautes études en sciences sociales* (EHESS), sessions devoted to the writing of orality.

Among other psychoanalysts who have spoken of the malefic function of the gaze, let me cite: Pascale Hassoun, "L'envie," *Filigrane* 2 (1994) and "Un reste d'envie," *Che vuoi?* 1 (1994); Imre Hermann, *L'Instinct filiale*, trad. Française G. Kassai (Paris: Denoël, 1972), 165–171 and 343–345.

I have discovered, unfortunately at a late stage, Jean Clair's remarkable book *Méduse* (Paris: Gallimard, 1979).

[75] [On *das Ding*, see Jacques Lacan, *The Seminar of Jacques Lacan, Book VII: The Ethics of Psychoanalysis*, trans. Dennis Porter (New York: W. W. Norton, 1997), Chapters IV and V. In his reading of Freud's "The Project for a Scientific Psychology" (1895), *The Standard Edition of the Complete Psychological Works of Sigmund Freud I* (London: Hogarth Press, 1961) Lacan isolates the notion of *das Ding*, "the Thing," as the element that remains foreign to the subject in his encounter with the fellow human being, the *Nebenmensch*. The Thing is that part of the primary object that cannot enter into language, that is expelled, that is a true empty space at the heart of subjectivity. Reality, therefore, does not cover the term real, not even that of exteriority. Reality is what screens the void of the Thing. Reality is thus what will come to mask the absence of the Thing, creating a signifying organization of representations around the void. Lacan evokes the Thing as the impossible to attain—forever lost to the quest and to desire—as the dimension that is lacking in the invested objects, making them dissatisfactory.]

[76] On the "Thing" (*la Chose*), see the work of Erik Porge in *Lettres de l'école freudienne* 18 (April 1975), 158–165.

that one finds between the act of "guarding" (*garder*) and that of "regarding" teaches us two things: the subject "on his guard" is in a state of anticipation in which he tends to guard against the gaze. He knows that, if he happens to be regarded, he will then be fixed in a place that is much more dangerous than that of merely "under guard." The prisoner kept under arrest by a guard, the patient watched over by a hospital orderly, the child placed in the care of a nanny, they always have the possibility of escaping: the power of the guardian—for example, that of a goalkeeper—can always be found wanting, unlike the power of the gaze.

Two dissymmetrical vicissitudes are reserved for that which is not well-guarded: either the prisoner who is not well-guarded by his guard recovers his freedom; or, that which is not preserved properly—such as wine that decomposes because it has not been kept in the cellar or an apple that goes bad because it has not been kept in the storeroom—degenerates because it is no longer supported by what generated it.

Why is the human Thing poorly guarded? Why, if it is "regarded," does it degenerate by losing its freedom to generate speech? That is the question that introduces us to the root from which the superego's gaze derives its formidable efficacy.[77]

The psychic pain of the subject who has the experience of the evil eye, like that of the woman's gaze in the case of Robert, goes through an ordeal of dispossession: dispossessed of speech, he is reduced to a feeling of shameful transparency, that is to say, of being dispossessed of his specular image.[78]

## b) *The Stolen Secret*

The conjunction of this double dispossession is expressed by a sense that one's thoughts have been seen through, the subjective

---

[77] Jean Clair (*Méduse, op. cit.*, 28) offers a striking point of view on the malefic origin of the gaze by reminding us that the function of the first works of art was born of the necessity to ward off the power of the dead and to prevent their return. From this perspective, this first statue was not intended to be seen by humans, for it was buried in the tumulus with the dead person: "Its gaze turned towards the invisible... must not meet the gaze of humans ... it is inflicted with invisibility because no living being could bear seeing it."

[78] See 69–86.

translation of which is: "I felt I had been seen through, despoiled of an intimate incognito; and I did not know, before it was undermined by the gaze, that it was precisely what had guaranteed the sense of permanence of my existence." It will have been necessary, therefore, for the subject to go through this enigmatic experience of thought-divination—in which he discovers, traumatically, that he holds no further secrets for the Other—for him to learn that there was in him the secret of an absolute incognito whose existence he only discovered at the moment when he disappeared under this gaze.

It is thus the disappearance of this incognito that exposes the subject to the feeling, bordering on psychotic experience, of being seen through by the gaze, of suddenly being absolutely transparent: no aspect of him, in fact, can be hidden any longer from the Other.

The subject feels persecuted by this experience of transparency that gives him the feeling either of being profoundly stupid or of being absolutely ugly.

If the fear of being "stupid" or "foolish" gives him the impression that he has "nothing to say," the fear of being ugly gives him the feeling that, once he has been seen through, he is deprived of the mystery that underlies beauty. In this respect, we are led to understand what prevented Freud from recognizing the force of the feminine superego as well as the fact that the expression of this superego was conveyed through the prescription, "Be beautiful and keep quiet."

This "Be beautiful and keep quiet" interests us because, by connecting the dimension of the specular image ("be beautiful") and that of speech ("be quiet"), it teaches us that the substance of the image does not come first; it is dependent on its relation to speech.[79]

The traumatic experience of transparency can now be understood as an experience in which the subject loses his appearance solely because he has already lost the use of speech.

The way he accounts in analysis for this loss of speech puts us on the tracks of what is really at stake for the subject who has been reduced to silence by the gaze. What does he say in fact to justify this

---

[79] If, when the time comes for her to speak—especially in public—a woman, more than a man, may have the persecutory sense that at any moment she is going to be transparent, it is because of her relationship with the evil eye that condemns her to being beautiful so as not to be transparent. Beauty, in fact, is not definable as narcissistic, as Freud thought, but rather as a specific response that the feminine has at its disposal to disarm the evil eye.

silence? He says: "I keep quiet because I don't know what to say." The error committed by the subject in making such a statement resides in the unjustified assumption that the subject speaks because he "knows" what to say; indeed, if the subject can speak, it is precisely to the extent that, at the very moment he speaks, he "does not know" what he is saying. He does not know because if he is speaking as a subject this means he is speaking while forgetting himself. But can the subject forget himself if he cannot forget the gaze with which the Other fixes him. Is it not the case that it was because Robert was unable to forget this gaze that he was equally unable to forget himself and to make a successful witticism?

The paradox in which the subject who does not speak because he "does not know what to say" finds himself lies in the fact that the very fact of asking himself this question means that he knows unconsciously what he is afraid of saying: he knows this because, living under the gaze of the Other, which he does not forget, he speaks while observing himself, while watching himself closely, so as to avoid making the slip of the tongue that the gaze is *already* expecting from him. What the subject who "does not know what to say" is suffering from is not a lack of knowledge but, quite to the contrary, a lack of rapport to not knowing: Robert could have made a witticism if he had not been held by the knowing gaze of the Other, but sustained by the lack of knowledge specific to his incognito.

In short, to speak while forgetting oneself is to speak while forgetting the eye of conscience: it is to speak while not being duped by the uncanny stranger in the form of the gaze, but rather by the Other stranger, namely, the unconscious, which, for its part, is not transmitted as "already seen" but as this "never heard" that a witticism can make us hear.

### c) The Confession of the First Fault

We are justified in asking ourselves if the shame that took hold of Robert when he made a slip of the tongue does not raise the question of the "first fault" that Lacan examines in his seminar on Joyce;[80]

---

[80] Jacques Lacan, *The Sinthome, op. cit.*, 5.

there, he interprets the sinthome as coming "at the site where the knot fails, where there is a kind of slip of the knot."[81]

Let us follow the hypothesis that Lacan formulates a few lines further on—"Is the first fault, which conscience regards as a sin, of the order of a slip?"—by bringing some elements that may give it substance. In what governs Robert's shame there is in fact a very instructive paradox that allows us to provide a new definition of the first fault.

The paradox brought to light by the interpretation of his shame resides in the fact that although he experienced the gaze as a presence that robbed him of his most personal incognito, he discovers subsequently, from a subjective point of view, that it is he—the one who has been robbed and usurped—who is in fact led to admit that he is a robber and a usurper.

What was Robert doing when he blushed if not admitting that he was a liar who was finally acknowledging that he had been lying constantly up until then? The confession of this lie, of which he had hitherto been completely unaware, resulted from the fact that, by revealing the most intimate aspects of himself, his blushing revealed that he was not covering up with impunity the existence of a certain hiding place whose trail we are on.[82]

### d) The Evil Eye against the Painter's Eye

How is it that the human Thing—*das Ding*—which refers to that, in us, which is the most veiled real, can be revealed either through shame, as a blushing thing that has lost its secret, or through an aesthetic production? Through the mediation of beauty, a secret is presented whose absolute character lies in the fact that it disarms not only knowledge but also the malefic power of the gaze.

In the penetrating interpretation that he gives of the pacifying power of a painting, Lacan shows that the painter "invites the person to whom the picture is presented to lay down his gaze there as one lays down one's weapons. This is the pacifying, Apollonian effect of

---

[81] *Ibid.*, 80. Lacan notes a slip [*lapsus*] of the knot, *lapsus* referring to a "slip of the tongue."

[82] See 76 and 208ff on the "he knows (that I know (that he knows (that I know)))."

painting."[83] Why is this laying down of the gaze so pacifying? Because, for Lacan, as for Robert, "the true function of the organ of the eye, the eye filled with voracity... is the evil eye.... It is striking, when one thinks of the universality of the function of the evil eye, that there is no trace anywhere of a good eye, of an eye that blesses."[84]

This possibility given by the painting to man to avoid not only the gaze of the Other—"a gaze that surprises me and reduces me to shame"—but also his own malefic gaze, which he leaves on one side, raises the following question: as a being who is looked at, does man have the choice between being under the gaze of the evil eye or under that of the painter.[85]

If such an unconscious choice exists, it allows us to reformulate Robert's incessant question—"Did I have the choice between a slip of the tongue and a witticism?"—in the following way: Could he have welcomed the woman's gaze as a painter's gaze, seeing it not as something "*déjà-vu*," stripped of all incognito, but as something "never seen," transmitting his incognito? In short, at the moment when Robert was on the point of unveiling, through what he said, what was most intimate in him, what was most veiled, did he have the possibility of choosing a mode of unveiling in which his incognito would have kept its secret, or could he only be unveiled shamefully by an evil eye that has the right to watch him?

My answer to this question is that the mode of unveiling of the Thing is subjected to the way in which its veiling is structured. In this respect, we must recognize the existence of two types of heterogeneous veils and the fact that they induce two types of unveiling.

## e) *True Secret or False Secret*

The two heterogeneous veils that I am speaking about refer respectively to what I call "true secret" and "false secret." Every secret that is determined by the act of being hidden in an underground recess of obscurity, thereby deriving its substance from being sheltered from the gaze or the thought of the Other, is "false": the false secret

---

[83] Jacques Lacan, *The Four Fundamental Concepts, op. cit.*, 101.
[84] *Ibid.*, 105.
[85] *Ibid.*

necessarily fears the ray of light by means of which it will be dissipated. Conversely, the secret that not only does not fear the light but also, like the painting we have been speaking about, needs light to be revealed, is "true": the true secret is not a secret for me because I cannot see where it is concealed, but rather because I can see clearly that in it which eludes the clarity of my knowledge.

Thus the fundamental difference between the unveiling of these two types of secret lies in the fact that light falling on the object hidden in the darkness has the power of destroying this hiding place, by showing that it is without substance, whereas the light elucidating the secret of the painting serves, on the contrary, to give it life by revealing that it does not derive its substance from a gaze that does not see, but rather from a gaze that sees clearly. Man thus has at least two ways of living this "human thing" that institutes in him what is radically secret: if, like a painting, he does not need to *hide himself* in order to *be hidden*, he will not veil or conceal himself from the Other: why would he develop secrets if he is secret?

It is when this secret is without substance that he is led to "develop" secrets, to conceal, by means of secondary repression, the true secret of primal repression. The effect of this concealing, through which the incognito of the subject is dissimulated from the gaze of consciousness, is exactly the contrary of the effect produced by the secret revealed by the painting. When there is a true secret, the gaze "is laid down as one lays down weapons," while when there is repression, the gaze is not laid down but rather imposes itself. The peculiarity of the act of concealment from the gaze is to incite, to provoke the gaze into being excessively vigilant, putting it in the position of eventually discovering what has been covered over: When he hides "the purloined letter," does not the minister *already* make a transference onto the gaze that might see this hiding place, such that this gaze will come back through the intermediary of Dupin, who will be able to reveal what was so well concealed?[86]

This brings us closer, then, to the signification of Robert's slip of the tongue. If this slip elicits a gaze under which he discovers, in shame, that he can no longer hide anything, it is because the veil that

---

[86] Edgar Allan Poe, "The Purloined Letter," in *Tales of Mystery and Imagination* (London: Everyman's Library, 1993).

maintained his incognito instituted what I call a false secret, namely, a secret whose falseness showed through in the fact that it could only have consistency in obscurity but could not persist, like the painting, in the light.

The fragility of the secret "placed in obscurity" resides in the fact that the eye of consciousness must not know, beyond *what is hidden*, *what is hiding it*.

The expression given by Robert to his shame translates eloquently what the act of hiding consisted in; unveiled, Robert recognizes after the event:

— that, on the one hand, "he (2) was hiding the fact that there (1) was something hidden in himself,"

— that, on the other hand, "he (3) did not know that he (2) was hiding that there (1) was something hidden."

Three "*ils*" of different structures are thus compared: the first ("*there* was something hidden") refers to the incognito of the subject of the unconscious, whereas the second ("*he* was hiding") refers to the act whereby the ego, by hiding the fact that a part of the real is rooted in the symbolic, wanted to signify, through this act of mastery, that if "*there* was something hidden," it was not because the real *was hidden from it*, but because it *had wanted to hide this real*.[87]

As for the third ("*he* did not know"), it is the means by which the denial intensifies and extends secondary repression.

We will progressively discover the complexity of the affection of shame. While we had interpreted the psychic pain of shame as being linked, for the subject, to the fact of being unveiled or revealed, we can now understand that, beyond this unveiling, Robert is in fact reminded of a deeper fault, namely, the first fault whereby he did not accept or own the fact that the absolute secret that he had within him could have, like that of a painting, been revealed through a witticism without losing anything of its extraordinary character. It was a fault that consisted, in short, in substituting for the true secret that it could have *been* the false secret that he wanted to *have* by hiding what did not need to be *hidden* in order *to be* secret. No one can master with impunity what is unmasterable without exposing himself immediately to an

---

[87] [The French pronoun *il* may mean *he*, *it*, or *there*, according to the context.
—*que, d'une part:* "*il (2) cachet qu'il (1) y avait du caché en lui*"
—*et que, d'autre part:* "*il (3) ne savant pas qu'il (2) cachet qu'il (1) y avait du caché*"]

act of vengeance. The gaze of the superego is the expression of such vengeance whereby the ego, like the ostrich believing that it is not seen because it cannot see, succumbs to a gaze. This gaze says silently: "Didn't you know that by hiding yourself from me you would make me come back in the form of a gaze that would torment you constantly by asking you: 'Where are you when you think you are hidden and learn that I can see you? When this lie with which you are simulating that you are not dissimulating collapses?'"

To the extent that, by blushing, Robert discovers that he confesses to being such a liar, he is faced with the paradox of the following obscure satisfaction: "Before blushing, I didn't know that I was a liar and no doubt I suffered from not knowing it. By blushing, I am, as it were, relieved, because now I know what I was suffering from."

If we want to set out the steps by which Robert would progress from thereon towards a subjectivization of speech, we can say that the first step consisted in this lifting of the denial: "I (3) am not unaware that I (2) hide the fact that there is something hidden (1)."

But for his symptom to be authentically lifted, the lifting of the denial was not sufficient: for the symptom to yield, it was necessary to arrive at a situation in which the lifting of the repression was introduced by the *new* subjective *position*: "I am not hiding from myself the fact that there is something hidden." It is only in this new position where he gained access to a *Bejahung* towards the irreducible "there is something hidden" that Robert ceased to live under an omnipresent and omnipotent gaze of the superego.

Let us say that, through this *Bejahung*, Robert rediscovered the signifying support that allowed him to extricate himself from the persecutory feeling of being transparent; he had rediscovered the possibility of trusting in the signifier by renewing with the engagement of the originary pact of primal repression[88] in which he had lost confidence.[89]

---

[88] See "Primal Repression as the Originary Metaphorical Pact," 288ff.

[89] On the subject of this question of the fragility and confidence restored by the painting, see Jacques Derrida, *La Vérité en peinture* (Paris: Flammarion, 1990), in particular 398ff.

## f) The Problem of Fixedness

We have been led to subject the shame of the subject who feels he is being watched to the fact that the secret induced by secondary repression loses all substance when it is tested by the penetration of the gaze. This character of the gaze leads us to ask ourselves what is it based on. It is important to know this because the process by which a subject learns, in analysis, that he can appeal to speech is condemned to failure if the subject encounters the irrevocable judgment of the superego's gaze.

Why is the subject no longer able to appeal to speech when he is prey to the penetration of the gaze? If the movement of speech can disappear, leaving only a fixed place for the subject fixed by the gaze, how are we to explain the ascendancy of fixedness over movement?

It was by reflecting on the dream of the cat that Robert was able to get to the heart of this question: Why had he been unable to contest the silent order by which the cat's gaze was telling him, "Stay there"?[90] While he could have disobeyed a verbal command to "stay there," Robert understood that if he was unable to disobey the cat's gaze, it was because of the structure of what is silently conveyed by the gaze. If the message—"Stay there!"—had been transmitted in words, deployed in time, he could have found in the dimension of these words the signifying element that, by representing him as a subject for another signifier, would have given him the possibility of replying as a speaking subject. But as this signified was transmitted to him via the gaze—that is to say, via this presence whose fixedness is characterized by not being subject to temporality—he was sent back to the cursed part that, withdrawn from the capacity in him for becoming, is entirely given over to the power of that which is fixed, namely, the power of the real that incarnates that which always returns to the same place. We have already said that nothing incarnates this fixedness better than the purity of an animal's gaze, for there is no risk of it being contaminated by the impurity of speech. It is impossible to speak directly of fixedness for, by essence, it contests the specific movement of speech; it is only approachable negatively, by speaking of the interruption of movement. There is thus a correlation between the appearance of the fixedness

---

[90] See 67.

of the *gaze* and the disappearance of the movement characteristic of sight.[91] Sight, which proceeds from a form of activity requiring rapidity and vivacity, leaves the gaze with the possibility of appearing when it slows down or is interrupted. It is true, is it not, that the eye of my fellow man only has to cease to glance at me, to stop, if only for a moment, and fix me, for the gaze to appear? The word "appearance" is to be taken in its literal sense here, for, with the gaze, it is the dimension of "appear to," that is to say, of specular symmetry, that disappears to make way for "to appear."

That the fixedness of the gaze has the eminently dangerous power or capacity to requisition that in us which is of the order of fixedness is what is shown by the human aptitude for being petrified by the gaze, for allowing that mineral fixedness to appear, which, by reminding us of it, reminds us of the fixedness of the corpse.

Why do the eyes of a dead person have to be closed? Because, since he stopped seeing, the dead person is able to gaze at the secret in me that the guardian that I am is no longer able to protect if he is being gazed at by a dead person. Nothing metaphorizes the gaze better than the appearance of this gift of double sight that death confers on someone who has lost the capacity to see earthly things. Owing to a transfer of power, the blind man thus finds he is invested with the capacity of someone who is dead to gaze at me while ceasing to see me. It was undoubtedly Fritz Lang, among other film directors, who was best able to exploit the power of those two white eyes that a blind man can fix on us. We know quite spontaneously how to use this power: The fact that we know how to glower at a child to intimidate him shows, does it not, that we know how to use our gaze? We know that to do this we have to replace the mobility of our eyes with their terrible immobility. Even if we do not perceive consciously that it is from the springs of death that we draw this enhanced power of the gaze, we know that it is in fixedness that it finds its force. By interrupting the movement and by bringing to light a point of real that was veiled by movement, fixedness can be revealed, something akin to an interpretation. A woman thus once came to see me because she had been stupefied by the terrible expression that she had seen of herself in a photograph: her stupor was all the greater in that she was used to

---

[91] See "The Medusa's Gaze and the Loss of Being Incognito," 270ff.

being filmed very often and had never seen this expression appear in the context of a film—an expression that the photo had fixed by virtue of its power to interrupt the succession of images. The expression of this dimension of the fixed is as much a cause of angst as of laughter. If the man who has fallen to the ground breaks out into particularly ferocious laughter, is it not because he has left the symmetrical field of reality to fall into the monstrous field of the real? Into that place of fixedness where the law of the real, namely, the law of falling bodies, reigns supremely? This law, whereby each object tends, owing to its inertia, to fall towards the center of earthly gravity, liberates itself at the moment when a body falls insofar as, when it falls, the body loses the lightness that had been bestowed on it by the signifier and is reduced to that aspect of it that is fixed, namely, its weight.

We are generally surprised by the weight that the body acquires in death, whereas we ought really to be surprised by the counterweight that the living body receives from the signifier: the signifier frees, in effect, the body from gravity by making it stand up again and fly away to dance. This dialectic whereby the body is a point of articulation between gravity and weightlessness, between fixedness and movement, is one of the major coordinates of the articulation of unconscious desire. Desire sags and this body begins to sag under its weight, as if each pound reminded the subject of the painful effort required to resist the fixedness of the earth's attraction. The perception of this resistance, which is nothing other than the perception of the heaviness of the body, of this double that is the fixedness of the corpse, is generally the first symptom of what is called depression. In depression, the pressure that the body receives from the earth's attraction becomes oppression, for there is a suppression of the unconsciousness of what, in the body, is fixed, namely, its weight.

The joy that the dancer communicates to us comes, does it not, in this respect, from the fact that the dancer has the power to help us to forget the fixedness of our weight? A question arises: what is the relation between this joy aroused by the ascension of a body that, by flying away, defies the fixedness of the earth's gravity, and the child's joy in seeing the contrary situation of a clown falling on the ground? The dancer only needs to make the slightest false step, to show the slightest hesitation, to catch my gaze, a cruel gaze whose malignity resides in establishing a mortal identity between its fixedness and what it fixes: as long as the dancer's body contests, through its movement, any identification with the order of fixedness, I am preserved, as a spectator, from the emergence of my gaze, of my evil eye.

The gratitude I experience, in this respect, towards the dancer lies in the fact that, thanks to him, my gaze does not appear and remains a lost object; the power of the dancer, like that of the witticism—and, perhaps, of art in general—is thus to annul the deadly power conveyed by the evil eye by which I am inhabited. The annulling of this petrifying power is the cause of an aesthetic *jouissance* that is antinomical with the obscure *jouissance* that is awakened in the spectator if the dancer stumbles or makes a false step.

What, in fact, is this cruel, uncontrollable laughter that takes hold of us when our fellow creature falls flat on his face? In what sense is this little misfortune so highly comical? Before pursuing this question, let us simply observe that this laughter, which has nothing to do with the laughter that follows a witticism, is of a deadly nature not only for the one who has just fallen flat on his face but also for the one who is laughing. Why does the fall of the dancing subject, which is related to the fall of the signifying support that sustained it, concern us? Because this disappearance of the symbolic support is our own disappearance. As spectators, we embody, do we not, for the dancing subject, that other place from which he was drawing support? If the dancer falls, we also fall, do we not, from that other place where we were, so to speak, absolute *Alter*?

By falling, the dancer takes us with him in his fall and, from absolute *Alter*, we are reduced to the altered state of Other, namely, the gaze. Our fall is signaled by the appearance of a sneering *jouissance* replacing the symbolic *jouissance* that was silently ours when the dancer was dancing, supported by the symbolic. The fall of the *jouissance* of the Other, *jouissance* of the *Alter*, into an altered state of *jouissance* is a fall through which the *jouissance* of the superego appears. It is linked to the fact that, at the very moment the dancer falls, the evil eye was able to free itself and to substitute itself for sight: ceasing to be seeing, we then become voyeurs or, at the very least, onlookers.

In the new place where we fell, there is an identity between the alteration of the subject who has fallen to the ground in his fixedness and the alteration that is ours, given that the appearance of our gaze is no other than the appearance of the "fixed," which thereby makes its return to us. The charm of suppleness resides in the establishment of a dimension in which the real is torn away by the symbolic from that which is monstrous when it shows the order of the "fixed." This monstration of the monster takes place on all the different levels that, from stiffness to jerky movements, are exploited by the directors of horror films to portray the fixedness that, inhabiting Frankenstein, gives a possible incarnation to the fixedness of our evil eye.

## B) FREUD AND THE SUPEREGO

Why is the superego the only concept of analytic theory for which neither Freud nor Lacan were able to provide a definitive theoretical explanation? Why couldn't Freud have said, like Lacan, "The only subject I have never dealt with is the superego"?[92] In my opinion, it is because they did not grasp the underlying articulation between the nature of the silent judgment conveyed by the gaze and the fact that a judgment also requires the dimension of the booming voice.

Now, the paradox of the superego is to incarnate the fact that "the eye hears" and that "the eye speaks," except that it does not hear in the same way at all as the ear does, nor does it speak in the same way at all as the mouth does: if it hears, it is in the mode of thought

---

[92] Jacques Lacan, seminar of March 10, 1971, in *Le Séminaire livre XVIII: D'un discours qui ne serait pas du semblant*, ed. Jacques-Alain Miller (Paris: Éditions du Seuil, 2006).

However, if Lacan did not treat the question of the superego systematically, throughout his teaching he insisted on the fact that the superego was a simulacrum of the law:

"...the obscene and ferocious figure that analysis calls the superego and that must be understood as the gap opened up in the imaginary by any and every rejection (*Verwerfung*) of the commandments of speech." Jacques Lacan, *Écrits: The First Complete Edition in English*, trans. Bruce Fink (New York: W. W. Norton, 2007), 298.

"A discordant statement, unknown in law, an enunciation pushed into the foreground by a traumatic event, which reduces the law down to a point with an inadmissible, unintelligible character—this blind, repetitive agency is what we usually define in the term 'super-ego.'"

Jacques Lacan, *The Seminar of Jacques Lacan, Book I: Freud's Papers on Technique*, trans. John Forrester (New York: W. W. Norton, 1988), 198.

"The superego is at one and the same time the law and its destruction." *Ibid.*, 102.

"The superego has a relation to the law and, at the same time, it is a senseless law, going as far as to become a failure to recognize [*méconnaissance*] the law." *Ibid.*

Later, Lacan will associate the superego with the imperative of *jouissance*. See, for instance, Jacques Lacan, *The Seminar of Jacques Lacan, Book XX: Encore*, trans. Bruce Fink (New York: W. W. Norton, 1998), 3: "The superego is the imperative of *jouissance*."

divination; and if it speaks, it is not by supposing a subject but by desupposing him. The confusion that takes hold of Robert when he encounters the woman's scornful gaze is precisely the moment when this gaze hears him and speaks to him: the fact that it can hear what he is thinking so well that he can no longer hide it is expressed by the fact that, by blushing, Robert admits that he can no longer hide anything. The fact that this gaze speaks to him while desupposing him is expressed by the silent judgment: "The fact that you are blushing shows that that is all you are, this blushing and silent thing devoid of speech."

Let us not forget that our question is the following: is this judgment irrevocable? Did Robert have no other possibility than to lend himself to incarnating this desupposing gaze, or—after an unconscious choice, on which we are meditating—could he have made a witticism? The specific difficulty in elaborating the superego is evident in the fact that Freud had to wait until the year 1923 to introduce, in *The Ego and the Id*, the term superego. In this text, he shows that the critical function thus designated constitutes an agency that has separated from the ego and seems to dominate it, as can be seen in pathological states of mourning or of melancholia, in which the subject feels criticized and devalued: "We can see," Freud writes in "Mourning and Melancholia," "how one part of the ego sets itself over against the other, judges it critically, and, as it were, takes it as an object."[93]

The question that we are going to have to ask ourselves resides in an attempt to grasp the origin of this critical judgment, which we will not consider, as Freud does, as being linked to a "part of the ego," but to that part of the subject which, dethroned from the symbolic, will return in the real in the form of a gaze entertaining certain affinities with hallucination. I have already referred in passing to this structural affinity between hallucination and the gaze of the superego, pointing out that, for Robert, it presented itself through the dimension of a "*déjà-vu*": the structural relationship between the uncanniness of this "*déjà-vu*," "the eye of conscience," and the delusional hallucination leads us to the heart of the signification of the superego's gaze and to the discovery that it is by reflecting on the origin of this gaze that

---

[93] Sigmund Freud, "Mourning and Melancholia" (1915), *The Standard Edition of the Complete Psychological Works of Sigmund Freud XIV* (London: Hogarth, 1961), 247.

## Chapter Two – The Three Superegos

we can grasp the nodal point where there is a fraternity of structure between neurosis and psychosis.[94]

This fraternity did not escape Freud: in his paper "Narcissism: An Introduction," he notes that the symptom of paranoid delusions and that of the transference neuroses have a point in common, namely, a psychic agency that "constantly watches the actual ego and measures it by that ideal.... Patients of this sort complain that all their thoughts are known, and their actions watched and supervised."[95] These words that come to Freud—"supervision," "watching," "thought-guessing"— to express the sovereign power of this agency are precisely those, are they not, that qualify the dimension of the effect of the gaze? And, insofar as Freud identifies this agency of "surveillance" with "moral conscience," I feel justified in speaking with the poet of "the eye of conscience," not only in its metaphorical, but also in its literal sense.

That this "eye" is not exactly a hallucination, but has structural relations with it, is very explicitly formulated by Freud when, two years before "Narcissism: An Introduction," he wrote in *Totem and Taboo*: "Moral conscience is the internal perception of the rejection [*Verwerfung*] of a particular wish operating within us."[96] This was a very bold hypothesis, to which psychoanalysts have paid little attention. According to Freud, what keeps us awake is the "anxious conscience" of a primordial foreclosure of the father. A foreclosed signifier of the symbolic makes its return into the real by presenting itself as the "internal perception" of this dimension of "*déjà-vu*" that is the eye of conscience. This eye looks at us, does it not, as if we were defendants that it had "already seen" somewhere?

That the "*déjà-vu*" and the "already heard" are inherent to the law of the superego, just as the dimension of the "never seen" and that of the "never heard" are inherent to the structurally astonishing function of the symbolic law, resides in the fact that the superego's

---

[94] It is this structural kinship—difficult to ground theoretically—that bestows on the superego of neurosis its excessive character. As J.-D. Nasio has pointed out—*Enseignement des sept concepts cruciaux de la psychanalyse* (Paris: Rivages, 1988), 202—the excess of the superego is deployed in three directions: exaggerated interdiction, exaggerated exhortation, exaggerated inhibition.

[95] Sigmund Freud, "On Narcissism: An Introduction" (1914), *The Standard Edition of the Complete Psychological Works of Sigmund Freud XIV* (London: Hogarth, 1961), 95.

[96] Sigmund Freud, *Totem and Taboo* (1913), *The Standard Edition of the Complete Psychological Works of Sigmund Freud XIII* (London: Hogarth, 1961), 68.

hold over the subject is effective because it is an act of ascendancy or mastery that is already expected. The opposition between the fixedness linked to the mastery of the "*déjà-vu*" and the surprise linked to the fact that the symbolic emerges each time as if it were the first time is related to the opposition between the two possible dwelling places for the signifier. Dwelling in the symbolic, the signifier is *never there* where one was expecting it, whereas, dwelling in the real, it is *already there* where one was expecting it. The question we are now faced with is this: How is it that "the terrifying eye" of moral conscience can manifest itself in a subject either as the agency of supervision to which the delusional subject prey to delusions of being watched is subjected or as the terrifying gaze to which Robert is subjected? If, in both cases, there is a structural foreclosure of the Name-of-the-Father, how is it that it presents itself as irreversible in one case but not in the other case?

To think about this differentiation that we had begun to look at in the analysis of the dream of the black point (see 62–66), it is necessary to account for the initial mechanism by means of which the *infans* substitutes for the disappointed expectation of the signifying gift an act of incorporation in which Lacan sees the origin of the superego: "It is to the extent that the reaction of oral incorporation is a compensation for the frustration of a 'yes' that the mold is provided for the incorporation of certain words... which are at the origin of what we call the superego.... What the subject incorporates is... the object of need, not insofar as it is itself the gift, but insofar as it is the *substitute* for the *absence of the gift*."[97]

In this very profound conception where the superego is what is substituted for the absent gift, Lacan goes beyond Freud's conception by introducing the dimension of a subject's unconscious choice that substitutes an object for the absence of a symbolic gift. The question that remains open is that of the structure of this symbolic absence: does it proceed from an irreversible act of *verwerfen* or from the act of *werfen* that, introduced by Freud in his article on negation, evokes the notion of a rejection that is not irreversible? I am led to understand that, where the subject was unable, owing to the absence of a symbolic

---

[97] Jacques Lacan, *Le Séminaire livre IV: La Relation d'objet*, ed. Jacques-Alain Miller (Paris: Éditions du Seuil, 1994), 175.

gift, to effect a *Bejahung* of the signifier, he incorporates the object of the gaze insofar as he substitutes it for what has not acquired significance. This gaze is all the more deadly (first superego) in that the symbolic absence is close to a foreclosure.

## C) ABUSE, INSULT, MALEDICTION

If we extend Freud's idea that puts a structural foreclosure of the father at the source of moral conscience, we arrive at the idea that this foreclosure is structural because there is no human saying without its companion, the *saying-badly*. In this respect, analytic experience teaches us that the destiny of a subject is woven by the effect induced in him by the portion of *saying-badly* that he receives in the original saying from his ascendants, generally unbeknownst to them. There he encounters a malediction that is the very source of his primordial fall.

That there is, at the origin of the term of living substance, the appearance of a decline, is already, is it not, what the first verses of Genesis announce insofar as they say, eloquently, how the world only appears through its companion, the domain of the abject: no earth without the formless void, no light without darkness. The structural conflict between the original darkness and the originary light of the symbolic, between what, in Freudian terms, is of the order of the primordial *Bejahung* or of the primordial *Verwerfung*, is echoed in man inasmuch as he is the effect of that which falls to the symbolic and what falls from it as real. In the type of response that the subject will give to the question posed by this rift between the term and the decline, an unconscious choice will manifest itself—that is to say, the choice of neurosis in which two types of antagonistic choice will present themselves clearly: either the desire to *become* or the malediction of a *jouissance*—originating in the superego—of *not becoming*.

I am going to try to show that this malediction of the superego is the expression of a *saying-badly* whose devastating effect is graduated according to the level at which the original foreclosure imposed on the subject operates. If, by definition, there is no word that can express what has fallen from the realm of symbolization, certain swear words nonetheless exist that language puts at our disposal, and that give us an idea as to which topological point was concerned by the foreclosure: abuse, insults, and blasphemy present themselves to us as translations of categories by which the *saying-badly* operates at different semantic levels that allow us to understand what the different superegos are.

*a) Abuse and Insult*

An abusive remark [*injure*] differs radically from an insult [*insulte*] because it says something false whereas an insult names a real that the subject is unable to contest: calling someone a "queer" or a "son of a bitch" has a completely different meaning depending on whether or not the person one is addressing is in reality a homosexual or the son of a prostitute. Thus, with the insult, the subject who is really homosexual is called a "queer," whereas a term of abuse, inasmuch as it treats a non-homosexual as a "queer" or a non-Jew as a Jew, *does not produce a nomination but rather significance*.[98]

Being treated as a "little idiot" is, in this respect, the kind of abusive remark that Robert regularly met with, without knowing why, from his classmates. The fact that it was an act of abuse and not an insult—he was in fact one of the best pupils in his class—constantly conveyed the following message to him: "The fact that you are the first in the class doesn't change in any way the fact that as an 'idiot,' you are not what you have become. It's pointless insisting and pretending that you have become something other than what you are."

Now, "Do not insist!" is precisely the translation of the silent message that Robert received from the outraged woman; if he agreed to blush, it was because he obeyed this commandment conveyed by the gaze: "By speaking to me you have tried to become other than what you are; but, by blushing, you yourself are confessing that you cannot become other than what you are. So drop it! Shut up! Don't insist!" An abusive remark is contrary to an insult insofar as it prejudges the future. It says: "There is no future for you." The insult, on the other hand, by treating the subject as a "shit," a "piss-head," or "snot," conveys a judgment concerning what he *has* really *always been*, namely, waste matter represented by piss, shit, and snot.

---

[98] In saying, "You are only what you are," the insult, through the nomination of being, refers to the first superego ("You are a grain of wheat"), whereas, by signifying, "You are not what you are," the abuse refers to the second superego (censorship).

## Chapter Two – The Three Superegos

If the wound inflicted by the insult is incommensurably greater than that of a term of abuse, it is because the "Don't insist!" of abuse is a question concerning the subject's aptitude for backing down or for not backing down, whereas the insult is not a question, but rather an affirmation. It does not preach, as abuse does, what is false in order to know if it is true that there is a subject in the process of becoming, because the very question of what is true and false does not exist for it; it only concerns, in fact, the nomination of that foreclosed part of the subject—that is to say, his cursed part. Whereas the statement, "That's all you are," is not addressed to a subject bestowed with speech, but rather to the subject fallen from speech, the "Don't insist!" shows that the subject has already taken a first step in speech, but contests that he is able to confirm this first word by a second.

It is an abusive contestation insofar as it conveys the message to the subject that he is a "failure" because his slip of the tongue shows that he *has* missed the path of wit.

The entire *Traumdeutung* shows that the dream, like the slip of the tongue, is a failed witticism, resulting from a compromise between the requirement of the subject of the unconscious and the requirement of censorship. The attempt to make himself transmissible through speech is only allowed to enter the manifest content of the dream because the subject who receives the dream, unlike the subject who receives a witticism, is not driven by this speech to make it his own by letting it insist that it becomes his. If the dreamer does not consider his dream as a witticism producing light, and if he is not spontaneously driven to *shed* light on his dream by interpreting it, it is because, at the same time as he receives the appeal contained in the dream, he receives a reminder not to insist from the censorship.

Among a thousand examples given by Freud, the following evokes eloquently the way in which the dream can transmute a witticism into a censored signifier. One of Freud's female patients, who felt divided in an ambivalent way between her admiration for the sublime aspects of Freud's thesis and her skepticism towards its ridiculous aspects, did not know how to tell him about this dilemma until the day when she had an obscure dream from which she recalled one incomprehensible word: the word "channel." With the help of her associations, she recalled the circumstances in which she had heard the following witticism told by a well-known French author at the expense of an Englishman: the latter quotes the phrase, "It is only a step (*pas*) from the sublime to the ridiculous," and the Frenchman replies, "Yes, *le Pas-de-Calais!*"[99]

The interpretation that Freud gives is the following: the witty dreamer made use of a witticism she had heard someone else tell to express to Freud what she had been unable to tell him, namely, her fear that he was ridiculous with his sublime theory. Between the sublime and the ridiculous, there is only one step, is there not, namely, the channel of the *Pas-de-Calais*? With this interpretation, the dreamer is led to recognize the level at which the censorship intervenes to interrupt the transmission of her message: it is not the message as such that is interrupted; rather, it is the subject's relation to her message given that the censorship acts by preventing, not the production of the message, but the assumption of the message by the subject.

If the dreamer had said to Freud: "It is only one step from the sublime to the ridiculous," the assumption of her desire of transmission would have been realized, and she would not have needed to produce the dream. The reason the dream is a failed witticism also lies in the fact that the dreamer consents to the "Don't insist" of the censorship. She abandons the idea of assuming her unconscious desire, which would have been affirmed in the following way: "There is a first voice in me that says that Freud is not sublime and there is a second voice in me that assumes responsibility for this first thought and that, by saying 'yes' to it, transmutes what has been thought initially into the fully assumed insistence of an 'affirmation of affirmation,' that is to say, of: 'I say, and I repeat, that Freud's theory is perhaps ridiculous.'"

The link that I am establishing between the infinitesimal moment during which the dreamer and Robert both choose not to make a witticism but instead, in one case, to have a dream, and, in the other, to make a slip of the tongue, is the moment that, called by the duty—the "*soll*"—of *well-saying*, they made the unconscious choice, for reasons peculiar to their history, of obeying the censuring commandment of the eye of conscience: "Do not answer 'yes' to your desire, retract what you said." We can see these two movements at work in Robert: in the first, he extricates himself from the influence of the archaic superego ("Not a word!") and expresses his desire to the woman, but,

---

[99] Sigmund Freud, *Introductory Lectures on Psychoanalysis* (1915–1916), *The Standard Edition of the Complete Psychological Works of Sigmund Freud VII* (London: Hogarth, 1961), 118–119.

subsequently, he falls under the sway of the second superego, namely, the censure, and can do nothing else but retract his words while blushing. At the very instant of this withdrawal, Robert understands that one cannot serve two masters at the same time: by obeying the commandment that says, "Don't insist," he gives up *ipso facto* the symbolic command to become and lends himself to what is an offence to him, "There is no future for your desire."

If, in this respect, the woman's scornful gaze was not purely fantasmatic, it was because she had really heard, as soon as Robert uttered his first words, even before his slip of the tongue, that he had spoken to her like a subject who was *already offended*—not believing that what he was saying could have any future—a subject who did not believe in this instance that the time of insistence of his desire could, by getting past the censorship, *confirm* the very fact that by speaking he had already got past a first superego.

### b) The Malediction: Oedipus and Polyneices

Insult and abuse seem to me, then, to translate the gap that I have identified between the first and the second superego. From this perspective, the silent message, "You are nothing but a grain of wheat," corresponds to the act of in-sulting, the effect of which, in short, is to foreclose the dimension of "ex-sulting"—that is to say, of the prefix "ex," which indicates displacement towards the Other.

When Lacan speaks of Oedipus agreeing or consenting to the malediction, strangely enough he only evokes the malediction of which Oedipus is the victim, without taking into account the malediction that he causes to fall on his son Polyneices. Now, while it seems true to say that a subject can agree to *being cursed*, is it certain that he can agree to *cursing*? Is there not, on the contrary, an absolute contradiction in the fact that a subject can both curse and, at the same time, accept responsibility for this malediction? Is not the act of cursing a *saying* that renounces the assumption of the signifier?[100] How are we to understand the fact that—just when Oedipus' destiny finally unfolds, when it is revealed to him that everyone, both the community

---

[100] The following pages are taken from Alain Didier-Weill, "Œdipe, Antigone et le Psalmiste," *Etudes freudiennes* 35.

of his Theban co-citizens and that of the Olympians, has abandoned him—he chooses not only to fully accept the malediction that is hanging over him, but also to perpetuate it by making it fall on his son, Polyneices?

In this respect, insufficient attention has been paid to the fact that, in the malediction with which his father burdens him, Polyneices hears something that goes far beyond the death wish, when Oedipus says to him: "Die by thy brother's hand." Indeed, as he says immediately afterwards to Antigone and Ismene, who are witnesses of the scene, he hears that his father has, in fact, condemned him to die without burial: "If his imprecations are fulfilled," he says to his sisters, "do not consider me unworthy of a tomb and funeral offerings."

"You are unworthy of a tomb" is the greatest malediction that a son can receive from his father, who thereby commits what Patrick Guyomard has rightly identified as a "sin against the mind": the famous "better not to exist" does not only refer to Oedipus, but also to his son, since it is the mind of his son that is condemned not to exist, not be reborn, if he is refused the piety of a funeral rite.[101]

When I say that Oedipus, at the very moment when he utters his malediction, makes a choice, the question that I am asking is that of the meaning of the choice: What is it, in fact, that Oedipus renounces by responding to the absolute state of dereliction in which he finds himself by uttering a blasphemy? In this moment when he is reduced to this state of human waste, showing that he no longer receives a word from the symbolic, he gives up the possibility of questioning the symbolic: he gives up, in this case, the possibility of saying "Why?," in saying, like the psalmist (Psalm 22:1), "My God, my God, why have you forsaken me?"

What is the signification of this "Why?" if not the expression of the possibility that man still has of calling in the night, when the Other specifies himself by not answering any call. By thus appealing to the tribunal of speech, the psalmist's choice is not to curse, like Oedipus, the reasons for the cessation of the gift of speech, but rather to maintain the question insofar as, by maintaining it, he makes speech rebound, which thereby becomes constituting for him once again.

---

[101] Patrick Guyomard, *La Jouissance du tragique: Antigone, Lacan et le désir de l'analyste* (Paris: Aubier, 1982).

Thus the tragic situation of man in the Bible is different here from Greek tragedy inasmuch as the psalmist tells us that when, during the night, God's absence does not manifest itself, as it does during the day, by silence, but rather by a silence that is more silent than silence ("...and the night season, I am not silent"), man nonetheless remembers the speech he received at the beginning as constituting. Preserving this memory makes it possible to affirm that the statements "there is speech" and "there is no speech" do not refer to two different Others, but to one and the same divided Other. The assumption of the fact that both the presence of the signifier and its absence spring from one and the same place removes the gnostic temptation of the subject to effect a split transference between a God who is creative and good and a God who is malicious and supremely wicked. The scope of the power of this supremely wicked Being invoked by Sade returns to the absolute hate that the psychoanalyst discovers, through the negative therapeutic reaction, at the root of the primordial masochism onto which the power of the most archaic superego is grafted.

This superego—which I interpret as being linked to the power of the signifier of the Name-of-the-Father insofar as it is foreclosed in the real—raises a radical question: is this foreclosure reversible or not? If it is reversible, the evil power of the superego will be inexorable, and its power of thereby putting to death the signifying cut that is the Freudian Thing will be irrevocable.

Why can the psalmist appeal by asking, "Why?" Because, in the tradition to which he belongs, the foreclosure is not irreversible. In this respect, there is a trace in Freud of this non-impossibility of the return of the foreclosed signifier. When he evokes the primal process whereby the ego expels (*werfen*) outside of itself what it is unable to introject, to justify this process of expulsion into the outside, Freud uses not the term of *verwerfen*, but that of *werfen*.[102] The suppression of the prefix *ver-* indicates an expulsion devoid of this absolute impossibility of return that can be imposed on a subject when, like President Schreber, he has been unconsciously cursed by his father or when, like Spinoza, he has been consciously cursed by his judges, according to the following ritual: "We anathematize, execrate, curse, and cast out Baruch de Spinoza... let him be accursed by day and accursed

---

[102] Sigmund Freud, "Negation," *op. cit.*, 235–239.

by night, let him be accursed in his lying down, and accursed in his rising up.... May the Lord never pardon him... and blot out his name from under the sky."[103]

We are thus led to contrast two types of foreclosure: set against the irreversible foreclosure of the subject by the Other (foreclosure of Schreber by his father) is the reversible foreclosure of the Other by the subject. Why, for example, is the wandering of a dead person among the living, namely, the ghost, not irreversible? Because certain symbolic rites allow this supremely wicked being, the dead person among the living, to leave this world where he is roaming and to gain access to the beyond where he can return as a living person who is dead—that is to say, as a signifier of the Name-of-the-Father.

Rites of return achieve, do they not, what the psalmist achieves through his prayer articulated by a "why?" Is not this "why?" the manifestation of the possibility for man to go back to his own primal act of *werfen* by means of which he had stripped the Other of his symbolic alterity? This "why?" is thus the path by which the psalmist separates from Oedipus: he does not freely accept the absolute malediction cast on him by the Other insofar as he is led to recognize that it was he himself who originally cast a malediction on the Other. Now this return by means of which man, in his dereliction, can invoke the Other is perhaps not accessible in the same way in Christianity, inasmuch as original sin—being insurmountable, at least from an Augustinian point of view—bars his return route.

A question arises here: By giving prominence, in his commentary on Oedipus, to the inexorable malediction that hangs over the subject, does Lacan not reconcile himself with the Christian conception of the definitive malediction that hangs over the subject owing to original sin? If Christianity was able to furnish itself with a metaphysical doctrine by grafting itself onto Greek thought, was it not, among other things, due to the fact that their encounter was made possible by their respective conceptions of the malediction? In the subterranean link that there is between psychoanalysis and Judaism, should we not, in this respect, take into account the consequences that can be deduced from the rejection of original sin by Judaism?

---

[103] Rite of expulsion from the Jewish community as translated in Robert Willis, *Benedict de Spinoza: His Life, Correspondence, and Ethics* (London: Trübner, 1870).

But, in truth, Lacan's conception of the malediction is not Catholic because, for him, it is not, as it is for St. Paul or St. Augustine, truly inexorable: his entire seminar on *The Ethics of Psychoanalysis* strives to demonstrate, on the one hand, that "the human factor will not be defined otherwise than in the way that I defined the Thing just now, namely, that which in the real suffers from the signifier,"[104] and, on the other, that "it is in relation to the original *Ding* that the first orientation, the first choice, the first seat of subjective orientation takes place, which I will sometimes call *Neuronenwahl*, the choice of neurosis."[105]

This choice that man is faced with lies in the solution that he brings to the question that is raised for him by the fact of miraculously being the bearer of the signifying cut by which the real in him suffers from the signifying mark.[106] The whole seminar consists in presenting the different types of destiny that the subject can attribute to the fact of being founded on the Thing and in showing that there is an alternative choice to the Sadean solution of the malediction of the Thing by the supremely wicked Being: the Thing can be this *Nebenmensch*, this fellow creature, by whom the true signification of the injunction, "You shall love your neighbor as yourself," beyond its impossible evangelical signification, is "that he make himself his own neighbor, as far as his relationship to his desire is concerned."[107]

How can the subject "assume," that is, accept, this proximate Thing, the cause of desire, in the mediation of the sexual object? How can he, in fact, assume the "impulse to find again" without confusing it immediately with the object that he perceives as lost?

This "impulse to find again"—which, for Freud, establishes the orientation of the human subject to the object—precedes the object logically and, as Lacan says, must be identified with the Thing and not with the lost object, for, "since it is a matter of finding it again, we might just as well characterize this object as a lost object. But although it is essentially a question of finding it again, the object indeed has

---

[104] Jacques Lacan, *The Ethics of Psychoanalysis*, op. cit., 124–125.
[105] *Ibid.*, 54.
[106] *Ibid.*, 282.
[107] *Ibid.*, 76.

never been lost."[108] The possibility that the subject has of sustaining himself by the pure "impulse to find again," without confusing it with the object that is found again, is the source of the sublime desire of Antigone, insofar as desire is defined by Lacan as being without an object. The expression of this desire, through which the beauty of Antigone is conveyed—beauty conferred by her close relations with the Thing—represents, for Lacan, the alternative by which the aesthetic function of the beautiful presents itself as "the true barrier that holds the subject back in front of the unspeakable field of radical desire insofar as it is the field of absolute destruction.... It stops us, but it also points in the direction of the field of destruction."[109]

How does Antigone's desire compare with that of Oedipus? In both cases, it is possible to speak of a wish to die; it is not, however, the same wish or desire. While Oedipus harbors a wish to die insofar as he wants to die and wants his son to die without a sepulcher, without that symbol that gives life back to the deceased, Antigone's wish to die is not, like her father's, a suicidal *death* wish. Hers is a desire oriented by the impulse to find the Thing again, which, for her, is symbolized by the enigmatic signifier that is Polyneices' sepulcher.

What are we doing when we are meditating in front of someone's grave if not invoking the presence of someone who is absent with whom we enter into the following dialogue: "You who are absent, you are present because I am speaking to you." This devotional "It's you" in which Lacan identifies the primordial invocation of the unforgettable and prehistoric Other, namely, the Thing, is the constitutive act by which the sepulcher is signified, going fundamentally beyond the signification of the hole that one finds in the cemetery. Its primary characteristic is that of being an internal topological site where the human being discovers, when he has lost everything, that he addresses himself by invoking—as if he were in front of a real sepulcher—an unforgettable Other: "You are the one who, independently of your absence, gave me these words with which I can say to you, 'You are the one, the absent one to whom I am speaking, who made me the present of this speech that speaks of your absence.'" This intrapsychic sepulcher was constituted by the intertwining of a double mourning: a

---

[108] *Ibid.*, 58.
[109] *Ibid.*, 216–217.

mourning of that part of the real of the subject that only suffered from the signifying cut because the subject had first been able to do the originary mourning of the signifier of the Name-of-the-Father. Freud teaches us that the most originary relationship to the signifier is one in which the ego—insofar as it carries out, in line with the pleasure principle, an operation of splitting whereby the signifier is introjected into the good inside, on the one hand, and expelled into the bad outside, on the other—creates a situation in which there is no affirmation of the mourning of the primordial Other. Mourning of the signifier of the Name-of-the-Father will only be realized in line with that which is beyond the pleasure principle, which, through the couple *Bejahung-Ausstoßung*, will symbolize this signifier as being both present and absent.

The following clinical case helped me understand what is involved in the process of mourning: a woman came to see me because, since she had lost her child a few months before, she had literally been unable to think for a single second about anything else than the absent child who was so present in her consciousness that it was impossible for her to find, even for an instant, the unconsciousness of sleep. The sessions stopped the day she told me that, the night before, she had slept and dreamt about the deceased. That the capacity to dream about the deceased was instrumental in restoring sleep was the sign that a process of mourning was underway. The dead person ceased to be an unforgettable dead person among the living and instead became a forgettable signifier of the child that could be remembered in a dream. Thus, when the subject has bestowed this symbolic sepulcher on the dead person at the level at which the real hole left by the absent one has transmuted into a symbolic hole, the subject is put in the position of being able to form a symbolic dialogue again with the absent one.

Why was it that it was when the dead person became symbolically present that the patient became alive again? Because this successful mourning enabled her to link up again with the originary mourning at the time when she herself had come into life. Originally, she had been able to convert the structural act of *werfen*, by means of which she had expelled the signifier of the Name-of-the-Father into the real, into a symbolic act. This created within her a sepulcher at the level of which the living dead person, namely, the foreclosed father in the real, had become a dead living person who, as the signifier of the Name-of-the-Father, could remain, as it were, *"ex-time,"* in an inside that was radically outside herself.[110] She could henceforth invoke its presence by saying, with reverence, "It's you"; its presence could be supposed once the subject was able to question its absence by saying, "Why have you forsaken me?"

What is the fundamental act realized by the subject when he invokes the Other as radically absent? He affirms, thereby, that the Other is so far away, so inaccessible, that he cannot touch the Other. In this respect, he does not run the risk of the supreme, deathly danger of violating the taboo that prohibits contact with the dead person.

The sepulcher is not only the constitution of the empty place where the real of the person's remains was transmuted into a living signifier; it is also the institution of that fundamental interdiction that establishes an impassable gap between the real and the symbolic, between the dead person among the living and the signifying dead living person.

A question arises here: what is the relationship between the taboo on contact with the dead and the interdiction to desecrate the burial place. I would say, in this respect, that the interdiction, just like the *dire*, is only a half-interdiction and that, consequently, it does not have absolute power to protect the sepulcher. I understand the taboo as the silent form that the prohibition takes when the *dire* that is the interdiction falters. This distinction between the taboo that exposes the subject to the mortal possibility of touching the dead person and the interdiction that raises the Other to a signifying place that is inaccessible to touch is at the heart of our reflection on this human thing that is *das Ding*. Indeed, is it not this Thing that cannot be touched on pain of death that constitutes that which is human? Touching the Thing to derive *jouissance* from it is, in short, the act of the superego *par excellence* by which the Sadean supremely wicked Being succeeds in showing that the Thing is not untouchable. From this perspective, we can say that the strength of the superego rests on the fact that primary masochism is characterized by the fact that it is not subject to the sway of the symbolic interdiction and is governed only by the dimension of the taboo, since the mere fact that the taboo prohibits contact means that this contact is not impossible. The subject prey to primary masochism is no longer under the sway of the symbolic inter-

---

[110] Expression of Jacques Lacan's contrasting with *"intime"* (intimate).

diction and manifests itself most clearly by the fact that the subject is put in the position of consenting to the malediction because he can no longer appeal to the symbolic tribunal of speech: he can no longer say, like the psalmist, "Out of the depths I cry to thee, Lord."[111]

What are these enigmatic depths, *de profundis*, from where Oedipus gives up speaking? The enigma lies in the plural that, evoking the "depths" and not "a" depth, makes the hypothesis that the human does not derive its source from a single origin, from a single beginning, but from two beginnings.[112] Beyond the beginning by which he comes into being as a subject determined by the depth of the law, there exists another depth that takes him back to that in him that does not belong to what is governed by the determinism of the law, but to that which subsists in him as a possibility beyond the causality of determinism. The dimension of this beyond raising the question of an earlier beginning than the beginning introduced by the law is introduced in the last session of Lacan's seminar *RSI*, in which he suggests that it is necessary to distinguish two phases in creation. Before the act by which the creator, in naming the things created, introduces the symbolic register of the law, there is the act of creation *ex nihilo* by which the commandment *Fiat lux*—which Lacan links up with the *Fiat hole*—makes the real emerge from a symbolic enunciation.

This *Fiat hole* "onto which is projected something beyond, something at the point of origin of the signifying chain," is the place where the inaugural hole of the Thing is established.[113] This is referred to by the psalmist as the beginning of beginnings, the depth of depths, where man can make a return that consists of rediscovering within himself the place and the moment when he responded to the *Fiat hole* by the earliest "yes" that led him to be a subject of the tree of life before being a subject of the tree of the knowledge of good and evil. Refinding this "yes" in which what was most real about him suffered from the signifier is the act on the basis of which he will later be able to appeal to the symbolic. This invocation will be accessible to the subject if, recalling the point at which his ego undid the original "yes" of the subject by a "no" of foreclosure, he can go back to his

---

[111] Psalm 130.

[112] See the commentary by Josy Eisenberg and Adin Steinsaltz in *Le Chandelier d'or* (Paris: Verdier, 1988), 47.

[113] Jacques Lacan, *The Ethics of Psychoanalysis, op. cit.*, 214.

first "yes" by choosing, this time, not to undo it but rather to make it insist by a second "affirmation-of-affirmation." The inscription in us of the sepulcher of the Other, namely, the Thing, is the inscription of an incandescent hole, of that ardent bush that Lacan interprets as Moses' Thing, at the level of which the real of our body is constantly being burnt, symbolized by the signifier. That part of the real that is our corpse to come never ceases, as long as life continues, not to show itself monstrously, as in melancholy, inasmuch as it is kept chained in a living way by the symbolic. That the function of this supremely wicked being, the superego, is to unchain what is chained by the symbolic in order to derive a certain *jouissance* from what becomes of the body when, ceasing to be symbolized, to be said well, he falls as an object that is badly said, cursed, is what is expressed through the malediction of Oedipus, who condemns the remains of his son to remain without a sepulcher in the real.

The analyst knows what traumatic effects can be produced in a descendant by the fact that the remains of his ascendants are thus condemned to wander in the real. Whether it is a child of the Shoah or a child whose father has decided to give his body to science, substituting a bottle of formalin for a tomb, the analyst is confronted with the effects produced by a living dead person whom it is impossible to mourn. In such a situation, the analyst's desire is a symbolic desire, through which the possibility can be given to these ghosts, suffering like Hamlet's father, of dying, of ceasing to persecute their descendants by their very suffering, by digging for them, in the analytic work, the symbolic hole of a sepulcher thanks to which a devotional dialogue can be substituted for the horror caused by the living dead person.

That is why, if Patrick Guyomard's commentary on Oedipus seems to be pertinent and fruitful when he shows that Oedipus is not so much someone who does not cede his desire as someone who renounces the symbolic call to speak well in order to consent to the deadly *jouissance* of speaking badly, Guyomard's commentary on Antigone, situating her as caught up in repeating her father's act, seems more questionable. Why does Antigone not seem to me, as she does for him, to be "a new Oedipus... as irreconcilable as him... the bearer of a tragic dimension that has nothing human about it any more... as spectral as Hamlet's father... and perpetuating a curse without hope of salvation..."?

Because with her the fatal repetition through which Oedipus has taken over in his own name on the curse of which he was the victim is interrupted: she is the one, is she not, who, having been the silent witness of the curse that her father put on her brother, will be led to rise up against this curse that dooms Polyneices to die without a tomb? By giving Polyneices a tomb, by rejecting the paternal blasphemy by which Oedipus perpetuates the prophecy of which he himself is the victim, doesn't she intervene in the blind cycle of repetitions whereby generations have been caught up in a fatality over which they had no control? This first act, in which speech pays tribute to the symbolic, brought a certain salvation to the possible future generations of the Labdacids.

In such an interpretation, Antigone's desire is not understood as incestuous desire for the dead brother, but rather as the desire of a subject who does not want to survive at any price: her wish to die does not mean that she desires death *as such*. She wants, through her death, to show that the price she accords to the fact of giving life again to the symbolic, put to death by her father, exceeds her desire to give life to a family descendance. That is why, from Oedipus to Antigone, it is not a case of repetition, but rather of the daughter getting beyond the impasse of her father, a transmutation whereby the discarded stone, Oedipus, has become the cornerstone of Antigone's desire for the symbolic.

This transmutation designates the very task of the analysand: he has to separate himself from the scene of the rebut that the archaic superego, with the complicity of his primordial masochism, has cursed by addressing to him this blasphemy coupled with an insult: "That's all you are, a grain of wheat without a signifying sepulcher." In this respect, we need have no hesitation in saying that this interdiction linked to the superego ("That's all you are") can be "forbidden by the efficiency of the symbolic interdiction, in such a way that the injunction, 'It is forbidden to forbid,' which we saw flowering on the walls in May 1968, is not necessarily paradoxical."[114]

---

[114] Sophie Colandin, "L'interdit, son énonciation," *Correspondances freudiennes* 34–35 (1991), 5.

*Chapter Two – The Three Superegos*

### III. The Third Superego: "Are You Going to Persevere?"

How can the subject who has entered on the path of insistence stay on it? Will he confirm this insistence by persevering or will he stand down?

To enter into the intelligibility of this question, let's draw on the support Freud gives us when introducing, for the first time, the term of *censorship*.[115] He proposes the following fable to help us understand its functioning: "Let us imagine a society in which a struggle is in process between a ruler who is jealous of his power and an alert public opinion. The people are in revolt against an unpopular official and demand his dismissal. But the autocrat, *to show that he need take no heed of the popular wish*, chooses that moment for bestowing a high distinction upon the official, though there is no other reason for doing so."[116]

The essential point of this apologue, which portrays the conflict between the subject (public opinion) and the superego (the ruler), lies in the fact of situating the censor as a presence that *must show that it need take no heed of the subject's opinion*. Freud helps us to appreciate clearly, thereby, that the power of the censorship is absolutely opposed to the power held by the Other when he is in the position of subject supposed to know. While the efficiency of the symbolic transference resides, for the subject of the unconscious, in the fact that the Other is supposed to know that he can come into being, the efficiency of the censorship lies, on the contrary, in the fact that it presents itself for the subject of the unconscious as an Other who fundamentally desupposes that he can come into being. In Freudian terms, the king must not let public opinion suspect that he supposes that the cry of revolt—"Down with the minister"—is, perhaps, going to insist. Insofar as the subject obeys the censorship by giving up his revolt, he proves that he has the capacity to subject himself to an Other who disavows him. Here we are confronted with the very enigma in which primordial masochism appears to be that alienation that, by setting the limit of human freedom, introduces the subject to the very meaning of this freedom.

---

[115] Sigmund Freud, *The Interpretation of Dreams* (1900), *The Standard Edition of the Complete Psychological Works of Sigmund Freud IV* (London: Hogarth, 1961), 144–145.
[116] Author's emphasis.

Whereas the first superego tends to reduce the subject to absolute silence, the second superego, the censorship, allows room for an act of speech: by saying, "Don't insist!," the censorship indicates that, though it has agreed to let *one* word through, it does not agree to this word being confirmed by a second one. To return to Freud's fable, the function of the censor that let through a first message, "Down with the minister," is thus to see to it that the subject's cry of revolt is without consequences, that is to say, without sequel. That the censor knows that an act of speech only begins to have consequences from the moment the subject is able to say, "I persist and I sign," is what explains its indulgence for anyone who makes the error of opposing it *once only*, for *errare humanum est*.[117] But this indulgence of the censor masks the condemnation that it will utter if the subject insists, for *perseverare diabolicum*.

What is the origin of the power of intimidation by which the censor to which Freud refers succeeds in preventing perseverance from emerging? The meaning of such intimidation was evoked one day by Robert, who recalled the following memory: when he was a child, around the age of ten, he was so terrorized by the little tyrannical leader of the gang to which he belonged that he had never dared, until then, to rebel against him. Nevertheless, he felt there was a strange bond between him and this young leader because the injustice of his tyranny curiously gave meaning to his life; he knew that one day—but he did not know when—he would rebel against it and let the whole world know that he was the one who had said "no" to injustice and "yes" to a possible justice.

"I will never forget," he said, "what happened on that famous day when I said 'no': he had kicked me in the playground in front of all our friends and I had called him a 'bastard.' I can remember the terrible silence that followed. It was almost as if a crime of *lèse-majesté* had been committed against him. Everyone gathered in a circle around the two of us and he said to me: 'Say that again and see what happens!' I knew that if I repeated the words, 'You're a bastard,' I would get a thrashing, because he was much stronger than me, but I know today that that wasn't the reason why I was so afraid to say again, after a long silence of hesitation, 'Yes, you're a bastard.'" This terrible fear

---

[117] In the Catholic confession, for example.

that Robert experienced during those few seconds of indecision before the decision to repeat what he had said was indeed related to something quite different from his fear of the thrashing that would ensue: it was related to the extreme position in which he was placed by the command of the censorship that, publicly, was saying to him: "Are you going to insist or desist?" If you desist, I will be magnanimous and forgive you. But if you insist, you will pay for it dearly!"

Actually, the price Robert paid for having repeated, "Yes, I said and I repeat that you are a bastard," was not that which he was expecting consciously. He discovered in the aftermath what the effect was of having substituted the superego's statement, "Don't insist" with the symbolic enunciation, "I insist." By substituting the symbolic order for the order of the superego, the situation of intimidation that he had been in until then vis-à-vis the censor ceased to be in the forefront, allowing feelings of angst to emerge that reflected a new relationship between the subject and himself. While, before, he had been living on intimate terms with this personal persecutor in the form of the censor, he now had to face the void created by the censor's sudden absence, insofar as the command, "Don't insist," had been invalidated by the expression of his insistence. Before the ordeal of the angst induced by this absence of the superego, he did not know that this personal persecutor, the censor, while burdening him with guilt, had exempted him, by virtue of its function as a stop-gap, from the experience of angst. It was only by detaching himself from the censor that he discovered the reason why he had been so attached to it: through its inhuman commands, the censor had hitherto transmitted to him a persecuting law whose unjust character had given the following meaning to his life: "I am the one who will fight against injustice one day."

The angst that took hold of him after he had said, "I said and I repeat that you are a bastard," may thus be interpreted by the sudden invalidation of what had given meaning to his desire. As his desire was no longer be directed by a struggle against the internal enemy, where was he to find a new support to goad it? In other words, what conditions were necessary for the subject, who had been disoriented by the absence of the censorship, to find his bearings again and reorient himself at the level of speech?

There is a world of difference between taking up again something one was saying that had been cut by the presence of censorship and having to take up something one was saying that had been cut, *stunned* by the sudden absence of censorship. In this respect, if we return to the fable with which Freud opposes the revolt of the people and the censor, we can distinguish three logical phases that can be differentiated in the act of speech constituted, for instance, by the cry of popular revolt, "Down with the censor!"

1) *The first cry* of revolt is, I would say, an innocent cry insofar as the censor, as Freud points out, only has to frown for the revolt to die out immediately.

2) *The second cry. By repeating the cry of revolt*, "Down with the censor!," the subject's first insistence can be heard; in short, like Robert, he says: "I said and I repeat...."

This insistence, insofar as it implies a transgression of the command, "Don't insist!," suppresses the situation in which the subject is face-to-face with the censor, leaving him instead face-to-face with "himself": it is, therefore, in this moment when the subject is called upon to derive his authorization "from himself" that the ordeal of *"being stunned"* emerges.

Michelet (1798–1874) shows in his *Histoire de la Révolution française* that he understands very clearly this moment of *"being stunned"* when he evokes the staggering silence that descended on the people of Paris for several hours as soon as they learned that their censor had fled to Varennes.

Among other things, this moment of *sideration*, the silence of the people induced by the sudden absence of power, signifies this question: will the insistence of our cry of revolt cease to insist or not now that there is no longer any censorship? Will it find the place of perseverance?

3) *The third cry*. If we want to grasp the ultimate signification of this anguished silence that takes possession both of the people of Paris and of Robert, just at the moment when they encounter the absence of power, we need to understand that what, in fact, is being enacted is the most overwhelming situation possible for a subject. An extreme situation in which the latter, because he is no longer subject to the influence of the command of the censorship, is led to cross a threshold that leads him, in fear and trembling, to consider this question: "You, who have said twice, 'Down with the censor!,' will you be able to go on insisting now that you no longer have to resist censorship? Will you be able to free yourself from the state of being stunned, so as to accomplish the moment of perseverance by finding the third cry of revolt?"

What does it mean to find the path of *"de-stunning"* if not to find the path that leads the subject to the *desiderium* that is "desire." To desire, in the strong sense of the term—that is, etymologically, *de-siderare*, i.e., an act of *de-stunning*—introduces us to a conception in which the essence of desire is realized beyond insistence in its perseverance. Henceforth, I understand this being stunned as the moment of indecision in which the subject, having decided to pass beyond the second superego, namely, the censorship, has not yet decided how he will respond to the Other, when, suddenly, the latter asks him if he is going to take responsibility or not for desire in its dimension of perseverance. In this demand that comes to him from the Other in the form of a *Che vuoi?*—"What do you want?"—we note the third moment in which the superego, ceasing to be an *injunction* against saying one or two words, becomes a *question*: "Will you find the third word of perseverance?"

By sustaining persevering desire in response to the challenge of the question, "What do you want?," desire is articulated beyond the source that causes it, as a resource that the subject has for choosing. Will he take on board the interrogative form of the superego or will he prefer to return to the superego of censorship, which does not question but prescribes? Beyond relating to the object of desire, the question, "What do you want?," is about the relationship of desire to itself. This "What do you want?" also signifies: "How do you desire your desire?"

"Now that, by saying 'yes' twice to your desire, you have uprooted it from innocence, will you be able to take responsibility for the insistence of your 'yes-of-yes' by converting it into a persevering vocation of a 'yes-of-yes.' 'The conquest of this third "yes" makes you tremble, for you already know that it is costly: you will have to pay with your "flesh."'"

How will the subject of unconscious desire make the discovery of this third "yes," of this third word by virtue of which the point of incandescence—which Lacan writes S (𝐴)—through which he derives his support, his authorization, only from himself, is articulated? The enigma posed by such desire is the enigma of the type of certitude that it induces.

How is it that even though he is alone against the world in his certitude, there is something in Freud that tells him that in truth he does not err? How can he not yield to the pressure of the collective superego, how can he not resist the temptation of reconciling himself with the censorship that he has transgressed?

This was the question that Robert asked himself for a long time, when he was trying to understand in his analysis the reason why he was led, after he had said, "I say and repeat that you are a bastard," to retract what he had said instead of persevering.

If he backed down, it was because the act of speech in which he had gone beyond the censor had immediately put him in the position, vis-à-vis his friends, to assume the consequences of what he had said by accepting to become himself the leader of those who were revolted by the tyrannical style of the little boss. Now, to the extent that he did not want to assume this responsibility, the following question arose: Was he taking flight from his responsibilities? Had his cry of revolt been nothing more than a careless blunder? What he understood years later, while he was chewing over this story on the couch, was that being capable of rebelling against the injustice of the censor did not require the same desire as that which was demanded by the question of the *Che vuoi?*: "Are you going to persevere?" Persevering implied, in effect, finding a *third* wind that was certainly necessary for the struggle against injustice, but far from sufficient. To sustain itself, this third wind could no longer draw on an internal persecutor whose *injustice* had to be denounced, for it had to find and accept, in the void left by the absence of the censorship, the symbolic rectitude of the stunning signifier.[118]

It is only through the assumption of this signifier that desire endowed with perseverance can be articulated, desire that does not withdraw. This definition of the persistence of desire leads us to interpret certain mutations that are introduced into the thought of some men as being linked to the way in which their thought can be clothed by a movement of withdrawal, driving them one day to say "no" to something to which they had initially said "yes."

How are we to understand the structure of the "yes" that analysts like Kris, Hartmann, and Lowenstein had given one day to the Freudian unconscious inasmuch as, a few years later, their theory of the "autonomous ego" consisted in a certain way of saying "no"

---

[118] See further on my analysis of the subjective position of Saint Paul, 183–192.

to this unconscious? Should we consider that this "no" signifies the withdrawal of an original "yes," or should we understand that the first "yes," already, was not the fundamental assent or acquiescence that characterizes the *Bejahung*?

"Are you giving me your assent in full knowledge of the facts or have you let yourself be carried along by argumentation and habit into giving me your assent so quickly?" This formidable question that Freud could, no doubt, have put to Hartmann is, in fact, one that Plato had already put literally in *The Sophist* to his disciple: how did the "yes" that the young Theaetetus gave to his argumentation differ from the "yes" that the sophists knew how to extract from young people through their argumentation?[119] This question immediately expresses the major difference that exists between the "yes-of-yes" linked to the insistence of desire and the "yes-yes" that the censor expects from the "yes man."

We may assume that, confronted by his mentor with this double structure of the "yes," Theaetetus must have been stunned. It clearly did not occur to him that his assent might not be sufficient in itself and that not being recognized by his mentor as a "yes" necessarily would have repercussions. It did not occur to him either that it was impossible for the subject to say "yes" and at the same time to give the guarantee of this "yes": when the subject believes that this guarantee can be given because the ego announces that it will be possible, like a "yes man," to vouch for his first "yes" by a mere repetition, this means that he has already given up the idea of taking responsibility for himself as a subject of the unconscious, because, like the heretic, he has strictly no other guarantee to give than the enunciation of a "yes-of-yes."

We can interpret the theory of the "autonomous ego" in two different ways: if the first "yes" given by Hartmann to the Freudian unconscious had the structure of the "yes-yes" of a "yes man," his subsequent theory did not retract his first "yes."

But if his first "yes" had the structure of the "yes-of-yes" of insistence, we have to say that the later theory clearly shows that the existence of insistence does not guarantee—as Robert discovered one day—the passage to perseverance; the angst linked to the experience

---

[119] Plato, *The Sophist*, 236c.

of being stunned connotes the psychic moment in which the subject of the unconscious is faced with the unconscious choice of half-saying or of retracting what he has said.

In his meditation on the fall *of Dasein*, Heidegger, anticipating in a divinatory fashion the Lacanian theory of the division of the subject, is led to discover that *Dasein* corresponds to primal or originary angst in two antinomical ways. On the one hand, the subject falls into significance by representing the nothing by a signifier (the *Da*) that represents it for that other signifier, which Heidegger names *Sein*.[120] On the other, he tends to fall from significance by filling the hole of the nothing $S(\bar{A})$ with the cork that is "the prince of this world," the prince of temptation. It is owing to this fall—in which the subject betrays his own authenticity by succumbing to the temptation of the world—that the subject must insist so that the "existence of being" does not fall into oblivion.

The fact that this insistence can fail or lapse and give way to a withdrawal, to a flight of *Dasein* from itself, is precisely what Heidegger bore witness to the day when, by ceasing to contest his fall in order to attest it, he succumbed to "the prince of this world, by crying out to him, in the ambient 'one,' 'Heil Hitler!'"

\* \* \*

With three knocks on the door—Knock! Knock! Knock!—speech announces that it has crossed the threshold of the silence that reigns behind the scenes and that the subject that it represents is going to walk onto the stage: if such a rhythmic beat is needed for the enunciation to surge forth, it is because the genesis of the *Verb* requires the generation of a rhythm in three times.

---

[120] [*Signifiance* is a process through which the "subject" of the text, escaping the logic of the ego-cogito and engaging in other logics (those of the signifier and of contradiction), struggles with meaning and deconstructs itself ("loses itself"). And this is what immediately distinguishes *signifiance* from *signification*: it is not the work by which the subject tries to master language (for example, the work of style), but rather that by which he explores how language works and how it defeats him once he enters it. It is, if you wish, "the endlessness of possible operations in a given field of language." *Significance* will therefore be used in this context, in reference to the above definition.]

We will come to understand that this generation of human time is the diachronic effect of a synchronic conflict between the symbolic law and the law of the superego: it is because speech has to cross three thresholds to accomplish itself in the symbolic that we are justified in saying that it beats according to a rhythm in triple time, as if it were dancing to the rhythm of the waltz.

# CHAPTER THREE

# THE QUESTION OF THE STUNNING COMMANDMENT

## I. Freud and the Commandment of Verblüffung

### A) BEWILDERMENT AND ILLUMINATION: FREUD AND WITTICISM

What happens if, in the drone of everyday chatter that gives rise to an uneventful exchange between two interlocutors in which each one finds that his or her sense of permanence and continuity is confirmed, the "stunning" signifier suddenly appears? A *Verblüffung* occurs, interrupting all possibility of pursuing this eternal exchange in which the *ego* and its *alter ego* communicate through a dialogue of this sort:

"Good morning, how are you?"
"I'm well, thanks, and you?"
"Very well, and how are things at home?"
"Everything's fine, thank you."

What is the function of this dual exchange? It is to establish the places in which each person feels assured that nothing untoward will be said that will interrupt the to-and-fro of a symmetrical exchange of words. This rite, designed to avert anything being said that is out of place, reminds us of what has to be avoided, namely, the emergence of speech containing a third dimension, endowed with a power of scansion that is comparable to that of a stunning shot in tennis. With this tertiary speech there appears the dimension of what Freud identified as the *dritte Person* [third person] in his work on jokes.[121]

In a note at the bottom of the first page of his *Jokes and their Relation to the Unconscious*, Freud refers to a book by Theodore

---

[121] Sigmund Freud, *Jokes and Their Relation to the Unconscious* (1905), *The Standard Edition of the Complete Psychological Works of Sigmund Freud VIII* (London: Hogarth, 1961), 144–5, 150, 173, 181, 185, 207, and 222.

## Chapter Three – The Question of the Stunning Commandment

Lipps, *Komik und Humor* (1898), about which he says:[122] "It is this book that has given me the courage to undertake this attempt as well as the possibility of doing so."[123] What is there that had the power to give Freud "the courage" and "the possibility" of undertaking his work on jokes? If the question is worth asking, it is because Freud's debt towards Lipps seems to be very slight. Each time Freud refers to Lipps—on twenty-two occasions to the best of my knowledge—it is not in connection with the latter's long analyses of the mechanisms of witticisms, but rather in relation to a pair of words set in quotation marks, which provides Freud with the spark that enables him to grasp the very foundations of witticisms. This pair of words (bewilderment and illumination) furnished Freud with the fundamental idea around which he constructed his work on jokes.[124] "The word that is the vehicle of the joke appears at first simply to be a wrongly constructed word, something unintelligible, incomprehensible, puzzling. It accordingly bewilders. The comic effect is produced by the solution of this bewilderment, by understanding the word.... It is only this second illumination, this discovery that a word that is meaningless by normal linguistic usage has been responsible for the whole thing—this resolution of the problem into nothing—it is only this second illumination that produces the comic effect."[125]

We shall see later that these categories—the enigmatic, the unintelligible, and the incomprehensible—are just approximate words that come to Freud's mind for translating the effect of an encounter with the inaccessible.

We are therefore faced with the following enigma: a word only acquires the dignity of a witticism if it passes through two very different logical moments, that of "bewilderment" and that of "illumination." This passage from one to the other is not automatic; at the beginning of Chapter Six, Freud makes the following remark: "I have an impression that my *Interpretation of Dreams*, published in 1900,

---

[122] See Philippe Koeppel, "Lipps, référence freudienne," *Apertura* 4 (1990) and his translation of Théodore Lipps, "Sidération et illumination dans le trait d'esprit," on pages 187–190.

[123] Sigmund Freud, *Jokes and Their Relation to the Unconscious, op. cit.*, 9.

[124] Marie Bonaparte translated the two words into French as *"sidération"* and *"lumière."*

[125] *Ibid.*, 13.

provoked more 'bewilderment' than 'enlightenment' among my fellow-specialists."[126]

The question we are faced with—what is it that enables a subject to overcome this state of bewilderment and to gain access to illumination—requires us to elucidate a preliminary question: what is bewilderment? What is this power whereby language is able to abolish itself in such a way that the meaning it conveys is replaced by a non-meaning that Freud construes as the appearance of the bewildering dimension of the unintelligible, the incomprehensible, the enigmatic?

Among several examples that Freud gives of a bewildering witticism, here are two, figuring the eternal pair of the bridegroom and the marriage broker, in which the former asks the latter to find him the fiancée of his dreams.[127] This pair is particularly interesting for us insofar as the bridegroom, the one who asks for a bride, evokes the position of the analysand vis-à-vis the analyst. The analyst defers this demand, on the one hand, and a punctuated session, on the other. The witticism with which the marriage broker concludes the dialogue is to be understood, in effect, as an example of scansion of the analytic dialogue.[128]

"The bridegroom was most disagreeably surprised when the bride was introduced to him, and drew the broker to one side and whispered his remonstrances: 'Why have you brought me here?,' he asked reproachfully. 'She's ugly and old, she squints and has bad teeth and bleary eyes....'—'You needn't lower your voice,' interrupted the broker, 'she's deaf as well.'"

"The bridegroom was paying his first visit to the bride's house in the company of the broker, and, while they were waiting in the salon for the family to appear, the broker drew attention to a cupboard with glass doors in which the finest set of silver plates was exhibited. 'There! Look at that! You can see from these things how rich these people are.'—'But,' asked the suspicious young man, 'mightn't it be possible that these fine things were only collected for the occasion—that they were borrowed to give an impression of wealth?'—'What an

---

[126] *Ibid.*, 159.
[127] *Ibid.*, 64–65.
[128] Alain Didier-Weill, "La question de la formation du psychanalyste pour Lacan," *Revue internationale d'histoire de la psychanalyse* 2 (1989), 371–372.

idea!,' the broker protested. 'Who do you think would lend these people anything?'"

*Sidération* is the term proposed by Marie Bonaparte to translate the German word *Verblüffung* into French.[129] Before evaluating the pertinence or non-pertinence of this translation, let us explore the complex semantic crossroads articulated in the German language by the term *Verblüffung*. Three directions seem to impose themselves in the course of such an investigation.[130]

The first signification is that by which the subject who is *verblüfft*, affected by something surprising, an imposing landscape, for instance, expresses how he feels by saying: "*Das ist ja verblüffend* [That's absolutely stunning or staggering]," which can only be translated, as in negative theology, in negative terms: "It's unheard-of, it's unbelievable, it's incredible!" The loss of the use of language is what appears with the second aspect of *Verblüffung*: in this new mode of bewilderment, there is an intensification of the subject's feelings, such that he remains speechless. In line with this, Grimm gives the following citation from Kelle: "My attitude left her *verblüfft*: she was quite unable to reply.[131]" The emphasis is placed, then, on the notion of a subject who is torn between his emitting function and his receptive function: he receives the speech *of* the Other, but is no longer able to emit speech *for* the Other. The stunning nature of what the subject has received is such that he is deprived of any possibility of responding; he can no longer name what is happening by saying at the same time, as in the example before, "It's unheard-of, it's extraordinary!"

To produce such a suspension of speech, the stunning event must, like thunder, be sudden and unforeseen. The temporary character of this suspension of speech is specific to astonishment that is fleeting, for its duration resembles that of a spark; it is destined not to last and to leave only the memory of a "blank," of an ephemeral instant in which the subject has been disinhabited by speech. It is different, in

---

[129] See footnote 3.

[130] I am indebted to Michèle Wague, and I would like to take the opportunity here to thank her for having guided me in discovering this semantic crossroads, which she has explored principally with reference to the dictionaries of Trübner (Trübners Deutsches Worterbüch (Berlin: De Gruyter, 1954–1957), 8 vols.) and of Grimm (Deutsches Worterbüch (Leipzig: Hirzel, 1854–1971), 17 vols.).

[131] Grimm, *Deutsches Worterbüch* [German Dictionary] (Leipzig: Hirzel, 1854–1971), 17 vols.

this respect, from the first aspect of *Verblüffung*, in which the subject has not lost speech, and from its third aspect, which we must now consider.

It is sometimes the case that the latent phase of the experience of bewilderment is not temporary and that the absence of repartee on the part of the subject tends to take on a more permanent character. The subject then experiences a loss of speech that he cannot overcome and that, consequently, no longer corresponds to the reversibility that is characteristic of astonishment. The subject, who can thus no longer return to "square one," is in a situation of stupor and perplexity. The cutting of speech that appears in states of perplexity and stupefaction does not tend, as in the case of astonishment, to resuscitate speech, but, on the contrary, to perpetuate silence. From this point of view, Trübner cites Kant: "He has lost his composure; he is no longer himself, he is bewildered [*verblüfft*]!"

The citation from Kant that states that the subject is no longer himself, that he has lost his composure, clearly indicates, with the use of the present perfect, that a certain fixedness has set in that might well be definitive. Kant does not say that he is *not* himself, that he loses composure, but that he is *no longer* himself, that he *has lost* his composure. Whereas losing one's composure proceeds from an ephemeral experience that does not mortgage the future, the fact of having lost composure compromises the process of becoming. In this respect, it raises the question of what becomes of the subject when, invaded by the signifier, he succumbs to what Lacan called the *jouissance* of the Other. The essential testimony of the mystics, who abandon themselves to this *jouissance*, consists in saying that "they experience it but know nothing about it."[132]

The state of bewilderment appears as the subjective phase through which the signifier, by proving to be the "cause of *jouissance*,"[133] translates such a spiritual trance or *raptus*,[134] an experience

---

[132] Jacques Lacan, *Encore, op. cit.*, 76.

[133] *Ibid.*, 24.

[134] Térèse d'Avila, *Œuvres complètes*, French text Marcelle Auclair (Paris: Desclée de Brouwer, 1964), "Le château intérieur [The interior castle]," "Sixièmes demeures [Sixth mansion]," 977: "...this sudden spiritual trance (*raptus*) is such that the mind really seems to take leave of the body."

## Chapter Three – The Question of the Stunning Commandment

that is familiar to the mystic—for instance, Teresa of Avila, evoking her "silliness" and her ignorance.[135]

Grimm gives the following example of the impact of the *jouissance* of the signifier: "It doesn't take much to pull the wool over the eyes of a *verblüfft*, weak-headed person." He also gives this citation from Heine: "When man arrived, the giants left the country, completely *verblüfft*, for their big heads don't contain much in the way of brains."[136]

The *Verblüffung* designates a mode of entry into *jouissance* that has the specific characteristic of facing the subject with a choice of direction. Either he will stay in this *jouissance* and abandon himself to the mystical position of an absolute relation to nonsense or he will extricate himself from the *jouissance* of the Other. This will allow him to gain access to that other form of *jouissance* that is the dimension of unconscious meaning, the dimension of the illumination or light of the witticism, where what I shall call the "fragmentary" *jouissance* of "*j'ouïe-sens*" emerges.[137]

Does the word *sidération* with which Marie Bonaparte translates *Verblüffung* account for these two semantic directions?

By transmitting the idea of a cause coming from the beyond (from the sidereal) that flabbergasts the stupefied subject, the signifying connection between the beyond with life here below is happily made.

But, above all, the interest of the word "*sidération*" lies in the fact that its etymology gives us a key for understanding the lock that makes it possible to pass from the state of bewilderment to that of light. The pair "*sidération-lumière*" ("bewilderment-illumination"), teaches us two things:

1) If there is light, there has necessarily been a passage through an ephemeral state of sideration. The necessity of passing through a state of sideration before the light of meaning can emerge implies

---

[135] *Ibid.*, "Premières demeures [First mansion]," 878: "Anyone who reads me will need patience, as I need it to write what I *do not know*; for, it is true, I sometimes feel completely *silly* taking a piece of paper."
This citation, like the one in the note above, is taken from Marie Pesenti-Irrmann's remarkable article in *Apertura* 10 (1994).

[136] Grimm, *op. cit.*

[137] [There is a double word play here: "I can hear meaning" and "I derive enjoyment from meaning."]

an inner liberation through which the subject manages to extricate himself from the state of sideration, to un-stun (*de-sideré*) himself now. *De-sideration* (un-stunning) is precisely the etymological root of the word "desire." From *sidus-sideris*, which designates the astral constellation, is derived *considerare*, which means "to examine with respect," and *desiderare*, which means "to stop seeing" and "to regret the absence of...,"—hence, "to desire."[138]

As Denis Vasse points out, desiring indicates the movement that frees or releases the subject from astral sideration and that introduces him to a new type of encounter with the Other.[139]

2) Conversely, a state of sideration may set in without there being a transition to a state of un-stunning, that is to say, to unconscious desire. Non un-stunning is expressed by the appearance of that psychic inhibition that is the state of stupor of a mystical kind. Thus the obligation in which the subject finds himself of having to go through a state of ephemeral sideration in order to articulate the time of unconscious desire is the expression of a commandment that the subject may or may not obey: this obligation conveys a signification to which the subject may give his consent, or he may prefer—for reasons I shall explain further on—to remain in the *jouissance* of the Other.

The point we will have to consider is this: if the passage from sideration to un-stunning is not automatic, if it shows that the subject of the unconscious can say "yes" or "no" to this passage, the question raised is that of the unconscious choice between a "yes" and a "no."

Astonishment is the path by which I say "yes" to un-stunning inasmuch as I have agreed to the obligation that has been transmitted by the stunning message. How is this obligation to be understood?

The analysis of sideration makes it clear that this obligation consists of two interwoven messages: one is an interrogation; the other is an injunction.

The question that is put to me, in the ephemeral instant of astonishment, is this: "What do you discover now that speech has been suspended, now that you are astonished to find that everything that you already knew, all the knowledge that you had stored up hitherto,

---

[138] A. Ernout & A. Meillet, *Dictionnaire étymologique de la langue latine* (Paris: Klingksieck, 1917).

[139] Denis Vasse, *La Chair envisagé* (Paris: Éditions du Seuil, 1988), 7.

## Chapter Three – The Question of the Stunning Commandment

is of no avail to you for making contact again with the speech that you have just lost?"

This question implicitly contains the other signification—injunctive—of the astonishing message: "Since all your knowledge cannot fill this hole that is shown by the interruption of your speech, forget what you *already* know and allow what you *still do not know* to come into being: a new speech."

We can understand the reason, then, why a stunning message has the effect of a scansion: by calling the "*j'ouïe-sens*" into being, it interrupts the *jouissance* of the Other and waits for a new speech to come into being that substitutes the "not yet known" for the "already-known."

But it is important to distinguish between two types of interruption of speech: one is a deadly interruption aimed at extinguishing speech, for it is the effect of the agency or "instance" [*instance*] of the superego; the other is a living interruption that, caused by a transitory state of sideration, is aimed at getting speech going again.[140] By means of this stunning interruption, which interrupts the authority of knowledge, the paradoxical injunction to authorize himself to speak is transmitted to the subject: can an act of freedom—even if unconscious—be the response to a commandment? Can I manifest the freedom of becoming speech if I obey the obligation of an injunction that says to me: "Where it was, speech becomes! [*Là où c'était, devient parole!*]"?

The signification of this "duty" of speech, of this Freudian *soll*, is linked to the division of the subject between the pleasure principle and the beyond the pleasure principle: whereas, in the name of what is beyond the pleasure principle, the subject tends to hear the insistence of the call to speech, he tends, on the contrary, in the name of the dulling homeostatic power of the pleasure principle, to become deaf to this call. The awakening power of the stunning signifier, which reminds the subject of the call commanding the advent of speech, is thus opposed by a sleep-inducing power whereby man, rendered drowsy by the forgetting of the mind, is delivered up, without delay, to the reign of common sense. Thus, with the question of *Verblüffung*,

---

[140] Jacques Lacan, *Encore*, op. cit., 3: "Nothing forces anyone to 'enjoy [*jouir*],' except the superego. The superego is the imperative of *jouissance*—Enjoy! [*Jouis!*]"

*Chapter Three – The Question of the Stunning Commandment*

Freud discovers the function of a signifier that has the power to introduce a rupture in the discourse that presents itself to the subject as an injunctive call to change his discourse, to make a shift—to take up a fundamental contribution of Lacan—from the university discourse, by which we are all inhabited, to the analytic discourse. In this respect, we can say that the famous scansion promoted by Lacan had already been discovered by Freud in his book on jokes and, as we shall see, in his *Interpretation of Dreams* and in his *Psychopathology of Everyday Life*. But, having identified the function of scansion, Freud, unlike Lacan, did not introduce it into his recommendations on conducting the treatment. It may even be pointed out that, having opened up this path, Freud let it close again. In this connection, I will be led further on to formulating certain hypotheses on the signification of this abandonment in which, to the best of my knowledge, he was followed by his close pupils. As for the path by which Lacan was led to rediscover the question of the stunning scansion, it seems to me to be specific to his own singular evolution: on this subject, he does not seem to be indebted to the Freudian question of *Verblüffung* insofar as it was through his original work on "Logical Time and the Assertion of Anticipated Certainty" that he discovered the question of scansion, which he subsequently introduced into his psychoanalytic practice.[141]

## B) SIDERATION WITHOUT LIGHT

### a) Freud and the 11$^{th}$ Commandment of Censorship: "Don't Let Yourself Be Verblüfft!"

#### 1. The Repression of the Signifier

##### α) The Two Provincial Travellers

If Freud's work on jokes shows that the sudden appearance of the light of meaning occurs in the form of a liberation whereby the subject frees himself [*dé-sidère*] from the effect of sideration, *The In-*

---

[141] Jacques Lacan, "Logical Time and the Assertion of Anticipated Certainty," in *Écrits*, *op. cit.*, 161–175.

*Chapter Three – The Question of the Stunning Commandment*

*terpretation of Dreams* discovers, on the contrary, that the dream is a failed witticism because an agency [*instance*]—which Freud discovers to be the censorship—has the power of censuring the effect of the stunning signifier and to prevent the subject from achieving this work of liberation towards desire.

According to Freud, censorship operates in two different ways to bring about the repression of the stunning signifier: either it has the power of "stripping" the affecting signifier of its "high degree of psychical importance" or it has the power of inducing a displacement that makes it possible to forget this stunning signifier in such a way that attention is directed towards an indifferent signifier (the "waking residue").

Freud gives a comic example of the possibility for the censorship to strip the stunning signifier of its astonishing charge.[142]

A provincial traveller, he tells us, had come up to Paris to listen to a speech at the Parliament on the very day that a bomb planted by anarchists exploded nearby. On being asked for his reaction, he replied that he had thought that it must be customary in Paris to fire a cannon shot after the speech of a deputy.

Why does the repartee of this provincial traveller make us laugh? Because it incarnates the blunder that someone inevitably makes when, in the face of all opposition, he claims to have an answer to everything. Having an answer to everything is possible on one condition: that one is incapable of being astonished, that one no longer consents to the crippling of intelligence that occurs when, through the voice of the cannon, the stunning clap of thunder reminds us of the ascendancy of the real over knowledge. Someone who wants to master the real by having an answer to everything makes us laugh owing to the kind of erring, the kind of error, into which he is led: he errs because he does not want to be duped by the real,[143] he does not want to be duped by the stunning effect of the signifier.[144] He wants the other

---

[142] Sigmund Freud, *The Interpretation of Dreams* (1900), *The Standard Edition of the Complete Psychological Works of Sigmund Freud IV* (London: Hogarth, 1961), 498.

[143] Jacques Lacan, *Les non-dupes errent*, unpublished seminar.

[144] Jean Charmoille interprets the fascination that the perverse individual has for the neurotic by saying that the first does not lend himself to being stunned ("Le surmoi du psychanalyste et le discourse pervers," Day of Study, *Correspondances freudiennes*, 1993).

person to know that he is someone "who cannot be taken in." When this other person laughs, showing him how comical his pretension is, he is suddenly stupefied and understands that he was in fact mistaken even though he thought he wasn't. He believed he had been walking briskly along a road where doubt was inconceivable, since what is doubtful—the real—was excluded from it. This exclusion was achieved by the choice he had made to repress the signifier that acts as a *passer* of the real, the signifier of *Verblüffung*.

In short, it is as if the signification of this choice obeyed the commandment: "Don't let yourself be *verblüfft*!"

I was astonished in this respect to discover in the semantic network with which the German language condenses, at the level of the word *Verblüffung*, diverse significations, the appearance of a link between the recognition of *Verblüffung* and a *commandment* manifesting a horror of that said *Verblüffung* and prescribing the rejection of it.

The German language teaches us that this commandment is even raised to the level of the 11th commandment that God supposedly forgot to dictate to Moses. Hence, we find in Trübner the following citation from Herder, exhorting his son in the following manner: "*Keep the 11th commandment, don't let yourself be* verblüfft*!*"

Why does the formulation of this 11th commandment—"Don't let yourself be *verblüfft*!"—interest us so much? Because it is one of the most pertinent translations possible of the commandment of the agency that Freud discovers at work in the displacement in dreams, which he calls the "censorship."

What does he tell us about the mode of action of this censorship? Its function is to withdraw the subject from the power of the "signifier with a high degree of psychical importance" by means of which, the day before the dream, he was affected to the point of being deprived of speech, of being *verblüfft*.

How can the subject be withdrawn from this power of the stunning signifier? By the mechanism that Freud calls "displacement": at the very point where the subject has been pinned down, as it were, by the stunning signifier, where he is flabbergasted, unable to respond, and suddenly devoid of all the knowledge that he thought he had, a mechanism comes into operation by means of which he is able to extricate himself from this highly signifying place in order to occupy a new place characterized by its signifying benignity, by its indifferent

## Chapter Three – The Question of the Stunning Commandment

character.[145] The "indifferent" signifier that makes it possible to articulate this new place will be found by the dreamer in what Freud calls the "day's residues."

So the censorship is what allows the subject to escape the strange commandment transmitted by the signifier that is foreign to unconscious knowledge, namely, the signifier of *Verblüffung*. In opposition to the commandment of this stunning signifier—a *passeur* of the real, which reminds the subject that, in order to gain access to meaning, he must go through the *pas de sens* of being stunned—the censorship proposes a different commandment: "Don't let yourself be *verblüfft!*"[146]

In short, it is as if the censorship "knew" that, by censoring the moment of being stunned, the moment of the "light" of meaning would be censored retroactively.

The censorship has a second means of acting upon the signifier of *Verblüffung*: in addition to the possibility of repressing it, it also has—according to Freud—the power to "suppress" the affect caused by the stunning signifier, to "strip" it of its affecting power. The example of the provincial traveller who has an answer to everything, according to the process of secondary elaboration, illustrates the censorship's power to suppress affect: because he does not accept the real, our traveller finds himself endowed with a way of thinking whose rigidity is, in fact, the product of his intensity.

We will now examine, in some detail, how Freud is led to break with the ethics of censorship. The discovery of the unconscious is, in fact, not only the discovery of a man who was passionately curious about the truth: first and foremost, it is the achievement of a man who had the audacity to conceive of an *ethic that is entirely different from that of censorship*.[147] In order to tackle this question, let us consider

---

[145] Sigmund Freud, *The Interpretation of Dreams, op. cit.*: "an experience [with] a high degree of psychical importance," (174); "psychically significant experience," (176); "intensely cathected ideas," (176); "the true source of the dream," (177); "the true source of the dream," (178); "real meaning of the dream," (178); "the instigating source of a dream," (179).

[146] *Pas de sens*: see footnote 15.

[147] This entirely different ethic is, in my view, that which is transmitted by the stunning commandment insofar as it reminds man that, apart from the fact that the ten commandments tell him what he must not do, he is not acquitted of the obscure duty—obscure because it is not inscribable—of accomplishing what is required of him by humanity, for

*Chapter Three – The Question of the Stunning Commandment*

the famous and inexhaustible example of Signorelli with which Freud begins his *Psychopathology of Everyday Life*.

## β) The Determination Not to Change and False Thinking

Freud is travelling: he had caught a train in Ragusa that was taking him to a station in Herzegovina, and on the train he was conversing quietly with his travelling companion.[148] Freud was telling him what one of his colleagues had told him about the customs of the Turks in that region, which he had experienced as a result of practicing among them. The discussion seems to be quite subdued when, at a given moment, a signifier that Freud has innocently introduced into his discourse becomes loaded with a strange and stunning presence that radically changes the course of Freud's discourse. This signifier, "*Herr* [Sir]," introduces itself so easily into Freud's discourse that he seems to have no reason to be personally concerned by it: he takes care to point out—by using quotation marks—that this signifier "*Herr*" did not crop up in his own discourse, but rather in that of a colleague, whom he is merely citing. This citation, moreover, is a second-hand citation, since, for the benefit of his travelling companion, Freud cites the formulation his colleague had used to show how these Turks of Bosnia-Herzegovina reply to the doctor when he makes a fatal diagnosis: "*Herr*, what is there to be said? If he could be saved, I know you would have saved him."

No sooner has this citation been communicated to his companion than Freud is disturbed: suddenly, the quotation marks with which the signifier "*Herr*" had been exorcized lose their protective function and, owing to an unexpected signifying connection, "*Herr*" emancipates itself, escapes Freud's control, and imposes itself on him like that absolute master that is death. Just as Freud was going to follow up his first citation with a second (that of a Turkish patient suffering from sexual impotency who had once said to Freud's colleague, "*Herr*, you must know that if *that* comes to an end, then life is of no value"), he

---

which he is responsible. In this respect, it is extremely interesting that André Glucksmann—*Le XIe Commandement* (Paris: Flammarion, 1991)—has been led to call the "eleventh commandment" not the commandment of censorship, but rather what corresponds to my stunning commandment.

[148] Sigmund Freud, *Psychopathology of Everyday Life, op. cit.*, Chapter 1.

suddenly breaks off the communication of the said citation. He breaks it off due to the transfiguration acquired by the signifier *"Herr,"* which suddenly embodies the unthinkable connection between death and sexuality. Freud is thunderstruck by this realization because he is preoccupied at the same time by the recollection of a recent piece of news that he had received at Trafoi: one of his patients had preferred to put an end to his life rather than put up with an incurable sexual disorder.

That the signifier *"Herr,"* on account of the equivocation that it suddenly conveys, acquired the brutal power to interrupt Freud's speech makes us appreciate the significance of the euphemism he resorts to. Instead of telling us that he *was* interrupted in his communication, he tells us that *he himself* interrupted it; in other words, it was Freud who decided not to name this *"Herr,"* this absolute master, this signifier of death. In the same vein, a few lines further on, he tells us that he had "intentionally" forgotten the topic of death, whereas he should have said that it was he, Freud, who had forgotten himself, who had lost his mind under the gaze of this stone guest.[149] In fact, the path that Freud takes is not unrelated to the second phase of the *"politique de l'autruche* [Ostrich politics],"* which Lacan identified as one of the three logical times that order the subjective positions of the protagonists of Poe's short story.[150] He thinks he has diverted the attention of his traveling companion from the Turks of Bosnia-Herzegovina towards the fascinating subject of Italy, having turned the discussion towards the subject of travel in Italy by means of a displacement. Innocently, because his companion (like the king with the queen) is completely blind, Freud thinks he has also become as invisible with regard to the signifier *"Herr,"* as he was for his traveling companion. The rest of the story shows us how he has never ceased, in fact, to remain under the gaze of the signifier *"Herr,"* as a result of which,

---

[149] The Stone Guest (Russian: Каменный гость, Kamenny gost) is a poetic drama by Alexander Pushkin based on the Spanish legend of Don Juan.

[150] Jacques Lacan, "Seminar on the 'Purloined Letter,'" in *Écrits, op. cit.*, 16. "In order to get you to grasp in its unity the intersubjective complex thus described, I would willingly seek patronage for it in the technique legendarily attributed to the ostrich [*autruche*] when it seeks shelter from danger. For this technique might finally be qualified as political, distributed as it is here among three partners, the second believing himself invisible because the first has his head stuck in the sand, all the while letting the third calmly pluck his rear. We need but enrich its proverbial denomination by a letter, producing *la politique de l'autruiche*, for this technique in itself to finally take on a new everlasting meaning."

## Chapter Three – The Question of the Stunning Commandment

to use Lacan's expression, he will "have the feathers on his backside plucked."[151] On the nature of this gaze, I would not say that it is dumbfounding—for a dumbfounding gaze is seen as such—but rather, it is bewitching, in that the bewitched subject does not know who, in the shadows, is looking at him.

Of this second phase of the *"politique de l'autruche,"* we can say that it is a negating position. We can imagine Freud saying to the signifier: "You see, it's not you who decides what I have to say; it's me. I'm cutting you out, I'm excluding you, and I will discuss whatever I want." Naturally, at the very moment when Freud proclaims to the signifier that he is emancipated and free in the choice of his discourse, he contradicts himself and (this is where he has a flash of genius) shows that he is capable of recognizing it. In the very choice of Italy that he has made, in changing the conversation in order to avoid *"Herr,"* Freud is as irresistibly attracted as he would be by a magnet—it's very much love that is involved here—by the idea of speaking about Orvieto and the famous frescos painted by....

At this point, he interrupts himself: not like the first time because of anxiety, but rather because the word fails him. And, of course, it is this word that fails him, this "Signorelli," this *signor*, this lord and master, this *"Herr,"* that comes back to his mind, thereby showing him that at the very moment when, in order to avoid it, he had chosen the route of Italy, the game was already over without his realizing it. Freud had chosen nothing at all; he had simply followed the *path chosen by* "Herr" to bring Freud back to *"himself"* (it's worth noting, in passing, the ambiguity that language confers on this *"himself"*).

What has happened? Owing to the unexpected appearance of *"Herr,"* Freud, who is suddenly stunned, deprived of all the knowledge he possessed, is called upon to "change his discourse," to abandon what he knows *already* in order to gain access to what he does *not yet know*; however, at the same time, he finds the means to avoid this call by forgetting the signifier *"Herr,"* which is the cause of his state of bewilderment. In this respect, we are led to consider repression as the response to the following choice that is offered to the subject: "Will you accept, initially, to be stunned so that subsequently you can free yourself from this state of being stunned? Or will you obey the

---

[151] *Ibid.*, Lacan evokes the "dumbfounding force" of this gaze.

11th commandment of the censorship: "Don't let yourself be *verblüfft*! Don't let yourself be stunned! Forget the metaphorical place to which the signifier '*Herr*' is calling you and move metonymically!"

I am thus led to propose as one of the possible readings of the division of the subject the fact that a subject is under the sway of two antinomical commandments. The first is the commandment that is given to me to become Other than I am, to come to that Other place of this unconscious knowledge of which Lacan says: "Unconscious knowledge is what changes, what causes to change, what can reduce the '*sinthome*.'"[152] The second commandment, that of the censorship, which tells the subject, "Don't let yourself be stunned!," tends to give consistency to a form of knowledge, which, as Lacan pointed out in the same seminar, is first and foremost "a will or determination not to change."[153]

## γ) *Falsified Thought and the Ethics of Psychoanalysis*

The way Lacan qualifies this knowledge that does not want to change as "anti-knowledge" should be set alongside what Freud says about the knowledge of our provincial traveller that is not open to being astonished.[154] Freud qualifies it as "falsified thought," the mode of thinking that appears when the subject, choosing to evade the call of the signifier of the *Verblüffung*—a signifier beyond the pleasure principle—embarks on a path governed by censorship that is in competition with the pleasure principle.[155]

Some manage to pursue the voyage that they are making in this world without ever being astonished by anything at all. Given that they *must not be without* an answer to everything, when the real thunders beside them they will not be astonished. They will draw immediately on the stock of their *already constituted* knowledge. For them, it is a question of erasing the very possibility of the unforeseen by means of the *"ready made."*[156]

---

[152] Jacques Lacan, seminar of December 15, 1977, "L'insu que sait de l'une-bévue s'aile à mourre," unpublished seminar. (See further on, 225.)
[153] *Ibid.*
[154] *Ibid.*
[155] Sigmund Freud, *The Interpretation of Dreams, op. cit.*, 603.
[156] English in the original.

*Chapter Three – The Question of the Stunning Commandment*

This question is of the highest concern for analytic ethics. Will the analyst's relation to his knowledge be comparable to the provincial traveller's relation to knowledge? Will he be capable of being affected by the real transmitted by his analysand or will he receive the stunning signifier as a signifier that, stripped of its virulence, will have fallen to the rank of what Freud identifies as an "indifferent," benign signifier?[157]

According to Freud, the acquisition of such benignity is the very principle of repression, one of the major effects of which is to displace affect, to transmute the indigestible, "affecting" signifier into a neutral signifier, digestible with any kind of sauce. The price of this digestibility is, of course, high, since it is that of this "falsified" thought with which our good provincial traveller interprets the unforeseeable detonation of the real as a detonation that is purely a matter of protocol.

Twenty years after the *Traumdeutung*, Freud gives an idea of the nature of the unconscious mechanisms that are at the origin of this "falseness of thought": it is a mode of thinking that distinguishes what is false from what is true in relation to the criterion of pleasure and unpleasure.[158] Insofar as what is false is that which is bad, it must be expelled outside, while that which is true is "good" and can thus be symbolized. The true and the false are divided up according to the spherical topology of the "good inside" and the "bad outside." The essential point of this simplistic distribution resides in the crucial fact that it is not because, by virtue of the pleasure principle, the quality "good" or "bad" is attributed to a signifier that the signifier is recognized as existing. Our provincial traveller gives the demonstration of this impossibility of the judgment of existence.

If you got our good provincial traveller to talk, this is roughly what he would say to you: "You won't make someone like me, who knows what he knows, believe for more than a second that there is something that exists that defies my knowledge. I am ready to admit that I cannot always find, on the spot, the explanation for what's wrong, but, in the end, I can always find the explanation for what seemed unexplained to you. With everything that I *already* know, no one can pull the wool over my eyes. The passing astonishment at what I do not know, on the spur of the moment, is nothing other than a

---

[157] *Ibid.*, 173–178.
[158] Sigmund Freud, "Negation," *op. cit.*

## Chapter Three – The Question of the Stunning Commandment

mere lack—which is all too human—of information. You see, I can't be fooled; I am not taken in by what astonishes you."

It's a fact: our good "non-dupe" will never be caught off-guard, for he is always guarded. Guarded by what? By the signifier, which, in its metonymic aspect, substitutes itself for the appearance of discontinuity. When things are out of tune, when the signifying chain is interrupted by this absolute *Alter* that is the signifier of the real, metonymic displacement re-establishes a semblance of continuity by "stripping" the signifier of "high psychical importance" of its virulence and by substituting for it an "indifferent" signifier that defers the encounter that might change the subject. If the non-dupe "errs," it is, of course, because he is the last person who is capable of realizing that his thought is "falsified," owing to his inability to change, to be staggered.[159]

"It's staggering all the same! It's unbelievable!," several of us heard Lacan exclaim one day, after the interview that he had just conducted in front of us with a patient he was presenting. Lacan had this aptitude to be astonished, whereas, for us, as auditors and pupils, it seemed that what we had heard that day about the patient in question illustrated precisely the knowledge articulated by Lacan's theory concerning the questions that this patient seemed to have raised.[160] At that moment, Lacan resembled Freud when he said to his pupils: "With each new case, forget everything you already know!"

The forgetting of which Freud speaks is not the forgetting of secondary repression; on the contrary, it is a subjective disposition in which the subject, eluding the 11$^{th}$ Commandment ("Don't let yourself be *verblüfft*!"), creates the conditions for being astonished, for being staggered as Lacan was, on that day, to the point of forgetting everything he knew. If what the analyst learns from his practice is not monotonous, it is because the very nature of what is transmitted to him by his analysands does not correspond exactly (like "The Purloined Letter" with which Lacan, in his *Écrits*, inaugurates his teaching) to

---

[159] [*Non-dupe erre* is homophonic with *nom du père* (Name-of-the-Father).]

[160] In his "Letter to Jacques Sedat," *Littoral* 41 (November, 1994), Marc-Francois Lacan spoke of this relationship to the real as follows: "My relationship to my brother is situated at the heart of this quest that implies the refusal of knowledge as a means of access to this real. Our life-long friendship was always based on the mutual recognition of two persons in search of the real."

the description of a form of knowledge whose efficacy consists—and I am citing Dupin—of being "fully sufficient in the circle of its specialty."

Someone, like Poe's Prefect of Police, who is searching in the signifier for something that "corresponds to the description," has the power to exclude from his investigation any possibility of surprise and astonishment: either because he will not find the object and will consequently be irritated or because he will find it but without having been astonished by it because the object lies within the circle of his specialty. The analyst, however, for structural reasons specific to the object of his research, will not be able not to being apt for the function of astonishment.[161] When speaking of astonishment, it is important to maintain the distinction that we have been led to make between astonishment and stupor: for if astonishment is defined by a transitory and ephemeral experience of bewilderment, stupor, on the contrary, is a subjective position in which the subject, who is unable to emerge from this state of sideration, cannot gain access to the de-sideration of desire. In this respect, Edgar Allan Poe reveals to us that when Dupin gives the Prefect of the Parisian Police the purloined letter, thereby confronting him suddenly with the stunning signifier, the latter does not react with astonishment but with stupor. Poe gives the following striking image: "He seemed absolutely thunderstruck. For some minutes, he remained speechless and motionless, looking incredulously at my friend with open mouth and eyes that seemed starting from their sockets...."[162] Then the narrator alludes to the Prefect's "dumbfounded and vacant look" and to his "agony of joy"—which is reminiscent of a certain form of feminine *jouissance*.

When, a moment later, the Prefect "rushes at length unceremoniously from the room, without having uttered a syllable," we can guess that he is still utterly dumbfounded. This gives us immediate insight into the clinical picture of a subject who has been, as it were, "thunderstruck," but has been unable to emerge from this state of sideration: since he has not agreed to be "fooled" by the signifier, he has been unable to find the solution of desire—*de-sideration*—and remains in this form of "erring" that is stupor bordering on stupidity.

---

[161] In *Un psychanalyste pour quoi faire?* (Paris: Jacques Grancher, 1988), 166–167, J.-J. Moscowitz writes: "By virtue of this astonishment, the analyst is faced with a fundamental doubt."
[162] Edgar Allan Poe, "The Purloined Letter," *op. cit.*, 501–502.

*Chapter Three – The Question of the Stunning Commandment*

His "dumbfounded and vacant look," his perfect "agony of joy," are evocative, are they not, of the happy imbecile?

This "Purloined Letter" with which Lacan opens his *Écrits* is the astonishing signifier to which the subject can only be receptive if he pays a certain price. That such a price—and we will see later that it is the price of symbolic castration—must be paid implies the sanction of a certain angst. This signifier is qualified by Freud, in *The Psychopathology of Everyday life*, as a "disagreeable signifier" and, in *The Interpretation of Dreams*, as a "signifier of high psychical value," as a "powerfully cathected idea," or as a "psychically significant fact." The paradox of the signifier of *Verblüffung* is that it requires the subject to carry out a work of symbolization by sending him back to the state of not-knowing that he was inhabited by without realizing it. This "unknown" has a double signification: on the one hand, it is unknown because it has been forgotten due to the veil of knowledge; on the other, it is related to the radical being incognito of the subject of the unconscious, the specific characteristic of which is that of not knowing that it exists. This incognito is promoted by the stunning signifier insofar as it presents itself as the presence that allows us to suppose the existence—unknown to itself—of the subject of the unconscious. The very fact that astonishment is the bearer of the Freudian commandment, "Where it/id was, become!," implies that a subject who does not know himself is called upon to be sustained by a desire whose cause is radically unknown to him.

But this desire X—which is what the analyst has to offer to the analysand—is fundamentally fragile to the extent that, although it has its sources in sexual not-knowing, it may perish when knowledge takes the place of the commandment.[163] The analyst's relationship to knowledge must be one of "*gai savoir*," for he is not expected to speak knowingly about desire, but rather to speak *with* desire *about d*esire.[164] That he can speak *with* desire *about* the analysand's desire,

---

[163] J. Clavreul, *Le Désir et la loi* (Paris: Denoël, 1987), 69: "We may ask ourselves if, as he gets older, the psychoanalyst does not let go as far as desire is concerned, falling more in love with knowledge, which he then puts in its initial place, that of a commandment. When university discourse holds sway, social life is facilitated but desire is suffocated."

[164] *Ibid*. *Gai Savoir* is the French translation of Nietzsche's book *Die fröhliche Wissenschaft, la gaya scienza*, published in English under the title *The Joyful Wisdom: or The Gay Science*.

*Chapter Three – The Question of the Stunning Commandment*

that is to say, that he can produce an interpretation structured like a witticism, implies that during the treatment the analyst can forget analytic theory. It is owing to this forgetting that he is not in the position of a master, or of a father, but in the position of one who occupies a topological site from which a potential subject can be supposed.

We will see that with some of his disciples—Ferenczi in particular—Freud was prevented from occupying such a place because he could only occupy the place of the father of doctrine. Chauki Azouri has made a very thorough study of this superego position, the persecuting effects of which pushed Ferenczi, after others, to break off from Freud.[165]

If we were dealing with psychoanalytic splits, we would have to recognize that these splits do not proceed—other than exceptionally—from theoretical divergences, but rather from the effects of the persecutory impact produced by the collective superego of the group. If the law governing an association is so frequently superego-based, it is because the analyst-member tends to renege on the mourning he carried out towards the end of his analysis. Having mourned the loss of the Other who is supposed to know, the institution then re-establishes, for him, the Other who had initially been deposed.[166] It is probable that the malaise prevailing in certain institutions is the effect of how analysts *may be unable to forgive themselves* for being led to give up what they had conquered on the couch, in particular, the feminizing effect linked to the assumption of speech.[167]

---

[165] Chauki Azouri, *J'ai réussi là où le paranoiaque a échoué* (Paris: Denoël, 1991), 209: "Freud puts Ferenczi in the position of a son/analysand, while occupying himself the position of father/master, without, however, being Ferenczi's analyst.... Where Ferenczi has an insatiable demand for truth, Freud, owing to an imaginary filiation, tells him he must repress."

[166] Jean-Pierre Winter, in *Fin d'une analyse...*, *op. cit.*, 317–318, writes: "We cannot fail to notice the extent to which we remain dependent, not on the object *a*, the cause of desire, but on the Other who is incarnated, after the analysis, as a subject who is supposed to know.... To say, as if it were obvious, that "the Other does not exist" can only be understood as a denial, especially where it is constantly being incarnated.... What acts as a tie between analysts when they come together in groups—and it is Lacan's expression—is to 'commune without communicating.' ... This feeling, which is knowledge in a pathetic form, is called hate.... Institutional transmission does not take place from ego to ego, but from superego to superego."

[167] Mathilde Troper, in *Fin d'une analyse...*, *op. cit.*, 332: "In relation to the exclusion of the feminine in discourse, is the way in which psychoanalysts speak about themselves... linked to this exclusion of the sexual and related to self-hatred?"

That said, we also need to recognize that the malaise that exists in analytic societies is linked to the fact that these societies, insofar as they are structured by a democratic law arising from the humanist ideology of human rights, cannot take into account the transcendent dimension of the symbolic law as it is promoted by psychoanalysis.[168]

## 2. The Murder of the Stunning Face and the Foreclosure of the Signifier

The example of such an event that I am going to give now is an opportunity to grasp what can happen in a subject who, having said "yes" to the stunning commandment of speech, can free himself from this state of astonishment by going back on his "yes," by retracting what he had said.[169] The scene takes place in Beirut: a man, who later defines himself as a terrorist, has received from his superiors the order to shoot anyone who crosses the road that he has to watch. A woman carrying a child appears, and she clearly intends to cross this road. She sees the machine gun pointing at her and looks silently at the man.

How long did this gaze last? A second? A quarter of a second? It is of little importance. It brought these two human beings face-to-face. As a result of being contemplated without hatred, the man was taken back to an experience of being stunned. Time, having been interrupted, he was suddenly taken back to *an ahistorical* time, a time when a subject within him, who was still indeterminate with regard to the choice between good and evil, could be brought to life again. The effect of being stunned deprived him, during an enigmatic moment of latency, of his ordinary determination to obey the orders of his superiors. *Was he going to shoot or not?* Why did this man, who ordinarily obeyed orders without considering the matter, have the fleeting experience on that day, not of indecision, but of a hole in the act of deciding?

---

[168] G. Haddad, "Loi et Liberté," *Pardès* 17 (1993), 46: "The experience of this century has provided ample demonstration of the failure of humanism and of the ideology of human rights. Can the law be founded on a mutual agreement between men, on collective good will? This is the tragic question for psychoanalysis that affirms a transcendental linguistic dimension of the law."

[169] The next five pages are taken from the text "Dire oui ou dire non au visage?," *Les Nouveaux Cahiers* 117 (Summer 1994).

## Chapter Three – The Question of the Stunning Commandment

Why was he led, in the end, to free himself from this state of being stunned by deciding, without really assuming responsibility for it, to shoot and to sign the death warrant, which he believed to be definitive, for this face that was looking at him?

For several months, he was haunted by the face of this woman who continued, relentlessly, to look at him. Eventually, deprived of all possibility of sleeping, he decided to consult a psychoanalyst, my friend, Dr. Houbballah, who told me about this case.

My hypothesis—and on this point I can only agree with the extraordinarily illuminating analysis that Levinas gives us of the signification of the message communicated by the human face—is that, during the infinitesimal second when the terrorist was stunned by the woman's face, it was revealed to him, in the strong sense of the term, that "the face speaks."[170] In addition, through this speech, the dimension of the "absolutely other" inhabiting his fellow creature was revealed to him.[171] This transcendental dimension violently reminded him that the "idea of the infinite," which was sleeping within him, had suddenly been awakened, asking him the question that no human being can forget, in spite of his efforts to the contrary.[172] The question God raised to the first man: "Where are you? Where in you is the 'thou,' that human thing that I gave you that is speech, which I entrusted you with so that you would not forget that it is the guardian of the infinite from which it proceeds?" That this question cannot be received without fear lies in the fact that, as soon as it is put, man can no longer ignore the fact that he is no longer master of himself. It is revealed to him that this idea of the infinite deposited in him is not a reminiscence according to which "it is impossible *to put* an idea into a thought without it already having been found there,"[173] but rather is that by means of which "what this idea aims at is infinitely greater than the act through which one thinks it."[174]

In this respect, even if he is not aware of it himself, we cannot fail to recognize the astonishing proximity between Levinas' thought

---

[170] Emmanuel Levinas, *Ethics and Infinity*, op. cit., 87.
[171] Emmanuel Levinas, *En découvrant l'existence avec Husserl et Heidegger* (Paris: Vrin, 1988), 172.
[172] Emmanuel Levinas, *Ethics and Infinity*, op. cit., 91.
[173] *Ibid.*, 92.
[174] *Ibid.*, 91.

## Chapter Three – The Question of the Stunning Commandment

and Freud's discovery, insofar as Levinas is led to assert: "A thought that thinks more than it thinks is desire. This desire is unquenchable not because it answers to an infinite hunger, but because it does not call for food. This desire without satisfaction thus takes cognizance of the alterity of the other."[175] As a transmitter of the infinite, the light of the face is the incarnated trace of the light of the first day which is transmitted to man both as a commandment, "Let there be speech," and as a prohibition, "It is forbidden to kill speech." Here, where I inevitably agree with Levinas, who interprets the message of the face as meaning "Thou shalt not kill!," the nagging question arises once again. Why did the terrorist, whose state of being stunned showed that he had fully received this message, kill out of fear? What was it that finally made him say "no" to this commandment when, as a subject of the unconscious, he had said "yes," in the space of a momentary flash, to the light of the face? How was it that this first "yes" was unable to insist, as "yes-of-yes," as a double affirmation, and declined its responsibility. Here we are touching on the relation of man to the fear induced by the proximity of transcendence. It is one thing to encounter, when fear takes hold of us without asking for our opinion, the dimension of the absolutely unforeseen. It is quite another to give in to this fear by fully accepting, through a second "yes" lending insistence to the first "yes," what it requires of the subject of the unconscious. If the "yes-of-yes" to the face is radically different from the first "yes" given to the face, it is because the first "yes" with which the terrorist acquiesced to the message, "Let there be speech," was a signifying "yes" acknowledging that "he" had received the message. But the fact that this "he" had been brought into existence by recognizing himself as the receiver who had been seriously affected did not mean, however, that this "he" was ready to accept the cost of the message received, namely, that of ethics.

The subject knows, without having to learn it at school, that the price to be paid for this "yes-of-yes" is what the psychoanalyst recognizes as symbolic castration, that which costs "flesh."[176] By agreeing to interpret the stunning message, he is led to discover what it is that costs "flesh." He is introduced to the ethical signification of the act whereby he must cease to be the receiver saying "yes" to the message

---

[175] Emmanuel Levinas, *En découvrant l'existence avec Husserl et Heidegger*, op. cit., 172.

[176] [*Coûte "chair"*: a pun on *coûter cher* (to cost a lot, to cost dearly).]

## Chapter Three – The Question of the Stunning Commandment

addressed by the Other and become instead an emitting agent extending his first "yes" into a "yes-of-yes" addressed to the Other.

The enigmatic time of the psychic latency of being stunned is thus the unconscious moment of a possible choice whereby the subject is in a position either to "assume" his first "yes" as a "yes-of-yes" or to withdraw this first "yes" with which he acknowledged receipt of the message of the face, turning himself into its accuser and choosing to put it to death.

To grasp how the subject finds his way out of the state of being stunned, we need to understand that he is led to interpret, in the stunning message of the face, a profoundly subversive message, insofar as it involves a commandment that requires him to go against the very movement that brought him into existence. Why? Because the subject, in order to become a speaking subject, had to carry out the strange psychical operation known as "primal repression," which consists of forgetting that he is only an emitter of speech, since he is first a receiver of this speech that comes to him from the Other.[177] The delusional hallucination of the psychotic is there to show us what happens to the subject who, having been unable to carry out this operation of forgetting, is reduced to experiencing himself as a pure receiver of an unforgettable Other. Just as, to be able to write, you need a blank page, to be able to speak, you need an act of forgetting, a blank, an absolute silence of the Other, without which speech cannot resonate.

It is because man constructs himself as forgetful and disloyal being that the message of the face presents itself as a stunning subversion of this originary forgetting. In order to persevere in his being, he needs to ignore his symbolic debt towards the Other place from which speech comes to him. The face, as an unforgettable trace of the Other—comparable, but not identical, in this respect, to a hallucination—now suddenly makes this constitutive forgetting impossible by conveying this message to him: "Don't forget that you forgot me in order to come into being." This commandment, which may be translated equally well as, "Where are you, you who are constantly forgetting me?," is traumatizing. It calls into question the foundational forgetting of existence, and man, in the moment of deliberation, can choose in

---

[177] See 288ff.

accordance with the pleasure principle to answer "no" to it or, by virtue of the beyond the pleasure principle, to answer "yes."

To conclude, I would say that this terrorist, in the time of latency of unconscious deliberation, took two decisions. On the one hand, he chose unconsciously to obey the commandment of censorship: "Don't let yourself be stunned!" On the other hand, once this decision to forget the stunning face had been taken, he was led to the more originary choice of killing the speech transmitted by the face. The murder of the face was made possible because he forgot the link associating the originary "yes" to speech to the originary "no" to speech. Owing to this act of unlinking, the injunction of the superego, "Not a word!," was able to take control of the originary foreclosure—because it was no longer bound to the originary *Bejahung*—and was able, through the murder, to act upon it.[178]

## b) The Subject Remains Stunned: Stupor and Stupidity

The "open mouth," the "dumbfounded and vacant look," that Edgar Allan Poe shows us in his Prefect who is stunned by the sudden encounter with the purloined letter express eloquently a profound state of stupor.[179] This moment of stupefaction is by definition ephemeral: it does not last because it tends to be swept away by the sparkle of the mind. However, if, for certain reasons, the unconscious process of the mind does not occur, the subject may remain in a state of being stunned and what was only acute stupor may tend to be transformed into a chronic state.

This abdication of thought can follow very different paths. One of them, the most dangerous, is that which was observable in the type of inane enthusiasm that could be heard, for example, in the voice of fascism. The abdication of all discriminating thought aroused by a persistent state of being stunned by the signifier "*Führer*," created the opportunity for the enthusiasm of a Brasillach,[180] of a "supreme bedazzlement" in the face of those "great poets," Mussolini and Hitler:

---

[178] See 291–294.

[179] See 131.

[180] Robert Brasillach (1909–1945) was a French author and journalist. Brasillach is best known as the editor of *Je sues partout*, a nationalist newspaper that came to advocate various fascist movements and that supported Jacques Doriot. After the liberation of France

*Chapter Three – The Question of the Stunning Commandment*

"The various forms of fascism succeeded because they were marvelous stimulants to national poetries. When Mussolini spoke to the Italians of the native soil, he was a great poet, in the tradition of those of his race; and Hitler, who invented the nights of Walpurgis and the feasts of May, who mixed into his walking songs the Romanticism of the forget-me-nots, the forest, the young girls with blueberries, engaged to lieutenants of assault sections, was a poet, too, a German poet."[181]

*c) Anticipatory Expulsion of the Stunning Signifier: Drugs*

What is the drug addict saying when he spits out this statement, which is his emblem, "I don't give a damn about others!," if it is not that drugs plunge him into a state of anesthesia that prevents any possibility of aesthesia for the Other. Anaesthetized and withdrawn from the stunning power of the Other, the drug addict thus feels he is unreachable and invulnerable to others insofar as he has stripped them of the alterity that might have altered him ("I don't give a damn about those idiots!"). The choice of hebetude, which, by making him frigid to the Other, *protects him from being stunned*, is the strategy of the drug addict.

## C) THE FORECLOSURE OF THE STUNNING SIGNIFIER

The case that I am going to describe gives us the opportunity to understand the mechanism whereby a foreclosure is established not, as in the case of the terrorist, in the aftermath of an experience of being stunned, but, on the contrary, to ward off the very possibility of being stunned by the signifier. The subjective connotation of the sideration that is involved in this case observation is that which is described, in the Bible, as an experience of "fear."[182]

---

in 1944, he was tried and executed following Charles de Gaulle's express refusal to grant him a pardon.

[181] Robert Brasillach in *Je suis partout* [I am Everywhere], January 30, 1937.

[182] It is upon this notion of the "fear of God" that Lacan draws to back up his conception of the *"quilting point"* (*point de capiton*) between the signifier and the signified. Cf. Jacques Lacan, *The Psychoses, op. cit.*, Chapter 21 "The Quilting Point."

## Chapter Three – The Question of the Stunning Commandment

A woman analysand who was asking herself questions about the psychotic destiny of her daughter was reminded one day by a dream of the traumatic memory of giving birth to her. When the child had just emerged, and was still out of her field of vision, she turned her head towards the obstetrician and asked him this question: "Who is that?" By way of a response, the obstetrician took the newborn baby and, without further commentary, placed the genitals of this child in front of the mother's eyes.

Thirty years later, on the couch, this woman was led to progressively recognize the signification of the trauma she had suffered as a result of this event. She was expecting the obstetrician to say something, but instead received a monstration which proved monstrous for her, for the silent irruption into her vision of the infant's genitals—it was a girl—seemed to her like the pure real of a hole endowed with a gaze by which she felt permanently fixed.

The characteristic of the gaze of this eye was this fixedness incarnating that dimension of the real, which, by always returning to the same place, has the power to impose an absolute fixedness. This analysand thus came to recognize that, in the years following the birth of her child, she had been unable to remove herself from the unique place assigned to her by the fixedness of the eye of her daughter's genitals, in such a way that, when she looked at the child, she had the feeling that it was she herself who was being looked at. What was particularly trying for her when she looked at the child was the feeling that she was devoid of any mystery under the gaze that fixed her, and that this gaze itself—inasmuch as it appeared to her as something "strangely familiar"—was devoid of any form of stunning alterity.

To understand the origin of this fascinating gaze, we need to go back to what happened in the initial scene, when the mother appealed for a foundational act of speech that did not come at the moment she was expecting it. What was she asking, then, when, turning towards the obstetrician, she put the enigmatic question to him, "Who is it?" Was she asking for information about the child's sex? Certainly not: it was something else entirely.

It was because the obstetrician, like a deaf and dumb person, was neither able to hear this "other thing" nor to respond with wit that she was unable to find the signifying support that would have allowed her to find in herself the point of alterity from which she could have looked at the infant's nudity with the "painter's eye."[183] Should we see the mother's impossibility of making the assumption of the signifier of the Name-of-the-Father, at the very moment when she was calling it, as the beginning of the process of foreclosure inducing the psychosis that subsequently manifested itself in the child?

### a) The Witticism and the Call

The signification of the call transmitted by the mother's question, "Who is it?," becomes clearer if we see how it can be situated within the general framework of the transference as it comes into play in the process of telling a joke. The joy derived from it consists in the sudden cessation of the radical dissatisfaction that the subject usually experiences because the Other never responds to his absolute demand. With the suddenness of a flash of lightening, an intercessor (the one who produces the witticism) has found the means to make the *dritte Person*, that absolute "He" in which Lacan recognizes the unconscious, emerge from his retreat. The success of a witticism is the transference by means of which, in the space of a flash, the person producing the witticism is the stand-in for the Other onto whom the listener has been able to transfer his quest, which is at last satisfied, for this *dritte Person* that is the Other.

We will thus be led to compare the invocation with which the mother asks, "Who is it?," with the silent invocation with which each subject, without even realizing it, constantly asks, "*Who is it* that will tell me if there is some evidence of the Other (*y a de l'Autre*)?"[184] In this respect, the fundamental demand of the subject to his partner is perhaps the demand of receiving a witticism from him, the witticism that has the power to make the *dritte Person* emerge from his silence, making him resonate.

With her question, "Who is it?," the mother was asking for something altogether different from information about the infant's sex. Similarly, the auditor of a witticism asks of an intercessor the question, "Where is he?," with which he invokes, without realizing it, a "He" to whom, not being a mystic, he does not address himself directly by

---

[183] See further on, 144.
[184] See footnote 48.

saying, "Where are you?" Our mother was expecting the obstetrician to make the significance of this "He" transmissible to her, as if, with her question, "Who is it?," she had entered into an absolute invocation. She was addressing whomever it may concern—the signifier of the Name-of-the-Father—so that this absolute stranger, namely, the new, recently born subject, may be symbolized.

The ambiguity on which Lacan plays between the barred $ and the "Is it?" signifies that the new subject emerges fundamentally as an absolute question. However, this question is different from all the other ones that a subject can ask inasmuch as it is, *par excellence*, a question that he can certainly ask, but without posing it to *himself*. He cannot, because if there is no intersubjectivity between two subjects of the unconscious, it means that a subject can no more suppose that he exists than he can suppose the existence of another subject. In this respect, the critique that Lacan made of the term "intersubjectivity" came after the notion of "subject supposed to know," which he had already introduced to speak of the analyst. It would have been more precise, in relation to his own thought, to speak of the analyst, not as a *subject* who is supposed to know, but as an *Other* who is supposed to know.

It is thus such an Other, such a third party, that is evoked by the mother so that her question, "Who is it?," might be heard. Who is supposed to know that there is a subject? This question requires three unconscious minds: that of the newborn, that of its mother, and that of the obstetrician insofar as the latter symbolizes a function that, as we shall see, corresponds to the function Lacan defines as *l'Un-père*, A-father.[185] The non-transmission by the obstetrician of the symbolic third dimension invoked by the mother produces in her the impossibility both of "assuming" this third dimension and of transmitting it to the *infans* to enable her, in her turn, to assume it.

Thus, the possibility of assuming the signifier of the Name-of-the-Father requires three logical times that can be differentiated. These three times (that of the obstetrician, that of the mother, and that of the *infans*) correspond analogically to the *three times of the witticism*: the first time is the production of the witticism, which is transmitted in a

---

[185] [*Un-père* translates as *One-father* and *A-father* at the same time. This creates an equivocation between the start of a numeric series and the call for, or the designation of, a father.]

second time to the listener (the mother), whose laughter transmits, in a third time, the passage of the Name-of-the-Father to a third person (the *infans*).

The exigencies of this triple assumption indicates the existence of two types of "foreclosure": if the possibility of assuming the Name-of-the-Father is not granted to the *infans*, it is either because—as in our example—the mother does not receive from the father the signifier that she calls for or because she does not "pay attention" to the signifier that has been transmitted to her by the father.

## b) Lacan's A-Father [l'Un-père] and the Question of Procreation

### 1. The Foreclosure of the Mother's Call

Meditating on the case of Schreber—and discovering how the desire of Schreber's father had prevented, to the point of foreclosing it, the transmission to his son of the symbolic law—Lacan was led to ask himself what it is in the paternal function that allows for the transmission of this *dritte Person* that is the signifier of the Name-of-the-Father. He was led to suppose the existence, beyond the function of the symbolic father, of a new function, that of "A-father."

This supposition would lead him to criticize the notion of the oedipal triangle insofar as the paternal third element must necessarily be *divided* between the symbolic function of the Name-of-the-Father and the dimension by which the Name-of-the-Father, "in order to be operative, must be incarnated" in the "quarter element"[186] that is "the A-father."[187] This distinction was announced in 1953, in the article "Le mythe individuel du névrosé," where the categories "real, symbolic, and imaginary" appear not as nouns, but as adjectives, insofar as they appear as real father, symbolic father, and imaginary father. It is in this fundamental text, where three paternal functions are dissociated, that Lacan conceptualizes the function of a "quarter element," which would make its return in his teaching, more than twenty years later,

---

[186] Jacques Lacan, "Le mythe individuel du névrosé," *Ornicar?* 17–18 (1953).
[187] Jacques Lacan, "On a Question Prior to Any Possible Treatment of Psychosis," in *Écrits, op.cit.*, 480–482.

in the form of a fourth loop of string, bound up, in my view, with the function of "A-father."

The essential element that Lacan contributes on the distinction between the symbolic father and "the incarnation of the symbolic function" relates to their fundamental discordance. "This overlapping of the symbolic and the real is absolutely ungraspable.... In a social structure such as ours, the real father is always, in some way or another, a discordant father in relation to his function, a deficient father.... There is always an extremely sharp discordance between what is perceived by the subject at the level of the real and at the level of the symbolic. It is in this gap that lies the something which means that the impact of the Oedipus complex, far from being normative, is often pathogenic."[188]

This problem of the deficient father and of his pathogenic role, which leads on to the notion of the perversion of the father, raises the following question: "How can we define, as rigorously as possible, the task of the real father?" If his function is to "incarnate" the symbolic function, what does such an incarnation require from him? To the extent that the real father is not a sort of tape recorder that records the law as faithfully as it has heard it, what is the share of betrayal that is produced in his translation? Another question: Why is the mother—who, as a subject, has already received the law—not in the same position as the real father to "incarnate" it?

The novelty introduced by positing that "the A-father" designates a function whereby the father intervenes in the transmission of the symbolic law is that the causality of psychosis is no longer attributed exclusively to the mother, as is so frequently the case in psychoanalytic circles. We frequently hear, do we not, the expression "mother of a psychotic child" being used as if it explained everything concerning the origins of psychosis?

The question, in fact, is more complex: why, if a caricature of the "mother of a psychotic child" exists, does a caricature of the "father of a psychotic child" not exist? The profile of the "mother of a psychotic child" can easily be caricatured, as it shows patently the extent to which the obstruction of the transmission of the symbolic is visible. The profile of the "father of a psychotic child" escapes caricature for

---

[188] Jacques Lacan, "Le mythe individuel du névrosé," *op. cit.*

structural reasons, for the father's mediating function is invisible and much less identifiable.

The example of our mother and her obstetrician allows us to clarify things by highlighting the following point: when a child is born, the mother does not have the immediate power of gaining access to the signifier that could give her the possibility of symbolizing the child, of seeing him or her through what I have called the "painter's eye." This signifier must be transmitted to her by an intercessor who is capable both of receiving her call—"Who is it?"—and of passing it on, in the manner of the witticism, to its true recipient: the signifier of the Name-of-the-Father. If this signifier can only be delivered from its withdrawal if it is called by whoever has the right, what is the presence that can legitimately call it?

In his commentary on the case of Schreber, Lacan answers this question as follows: "By nothing other than a real father, not at all necessarily by the subject's own father, but by A-father."[189] The fact that "A-father" and the signifier of the Name-of-the-Father both stand in a relationship to the symbolic ternary raises a complex question which was discussed by Lacan in 1957 and then taken up again twenty years later in his seminar on Joyce.[190] The difficulty consists in situating one in relation to the other, the function of the symbolic father and that of the "the A-father." "It must be admitted," Lacan continues, "that the Name-of-the-Father redoubles in the other's place the very signifier of the symbolic ternary, insofar as it constitutes the law of the signifier."[191] This reduplication of the symbolic would be taken up again in 1975, in the seminar on Joyce, as a division of the symbolic into symptom and symbol. In this seminar in which the function of the father as "*père-version*" is introduced, the real father is considered, in line with the text of 1958, as giving his "version" of the symbolic father—that is to say, in my view, as an intercessor who translates the symbolic while betraying it. The whole question would be one of dissociating ***structural perversion***—linked to the fact that the real father is structurally discordant in relation to the symbolic father insofar as he cannot express "the whole of" the symbolic law—from the perversion inducing foreclosure, when "the A-father" does not introduce the symbolic but

---

[189] Jacques Lacan, "Treatment of Psychosis," *Écrits, op. cit.*, 481.
[190] *Ibid.*
[191] *Ibid.*

### Chapter Three – The Question of the Stunning Commandment

rather interrupts its transmission, as the obstetrician did, for instance, in our clinical example.

Through the notions of "reduplication" or of "division" of the symbolic third element, Lacan encountered the question of the "double path" required by the *vocation* of the signifier of the Name-of-the-Father. Has this vocation—whose enunciation may be translated as a "*Fiat hole*, let there be speech!"—been taken over by the subject, as it becomes "his" own vocation as a speaking being?

In order for this human vocation to come into being so that speech can announce itself as "I," between the big "He" that is the Other and the big "I" that is the subject to come, there must still be the intercession of a "you." "The A-father" is that presence which, receiving the call from the Other—"You will be the one who will be father"—interprets it as, "You will be the one who will be my son or my daughter."

For the time being, I shall define foreclosure as the process whereby the call that a father can receive to position himself as a "you" who is able to "assume" the mandate, "You will be the one who will be father," is foreclosed.

Illustrating in an exemplary manner the fact that the delusion of President Schreber was caused by the sudden appearance in his existence of the question of paternity, Lacan evokes a case of psychosis in which the delusion was triggered a few days after a woman had announced to the subject: "You are going to be a father."[192] The signification of the assumption or non-assumption of this call puts in perspective a "yes," a *Bejahung*, which must be produced at the level of each of the three generations. For the newborn to be able to say "yes" to the speech that will constitute him, the mother must be able to "be attentive," that is, must be able to say an unconscious "yes" to the speech of "A-father." But for her to be able to "attribute importance" to this speech, "A-father" still has to transmit to her a constituent speech, constituted by the fact that she has already said "yes" to the signifier of the Name-of-the-Father.

We can see, then, that the *Bejahung* is a complex requiring the knotting of three "yeses." Understanding the process of foreclosure, that is, the process whereby the subject is unable to make the primordial assumption of speech, calls for an examination of what has been

---

[192] Jacques Lacan, *The Psychoses, op. cit.*, 306.

interrupted in the process through which speech has been transmitted to his ascendants.

## 2. Assumption or Foreclosure of the Call: The Question of Fear

If the transmission of the signifier of the Name-of-the-Father by the mother depends, as Lacan points out, "on the importance she attributes to his speech—in a word, to his authority—in other words, on the place she reserves for the Name-of-the-Father in the promotion of the law," she still has to receive, or ask for, a speech to which she can "attribute importance" or not.[193]

Our clinical example shows us that the mother is ready to "attribute importance" to the speech of the one who is in the position of "the A-father," because she asks him: "Who is it who will be able to call on the signifier of the Name-of-the-Father so that this signifier can emerge from silence and call the newborn baby to be born to speech?"

Why could the signifier of the Name-of-the-Father, insofar as it already inhabited this woman's unconscious, not be convoked directly by her? Why was the intercession of "the A-father" necessary so that this signifier, in relation to which she had already made the *Bejahung* at the dawn of her existence, might be encountered once again? How, indeed, are we to understand that she does not possess this signifier that "one day" was passed down to her by her ascendants, to the point that she is unable to gain access to it herself and to help her newborn gain access to it?

This question leads us to realize that the signifier of the Name-of-the-Father does not sojourn *in* the unconscious in the same way as a repressed signifier. While a repressed signifier, insofar as it is *in* the unconscious, can make its return to the speech of the subject provided the censorship is lifted, the transmissibility of the signifier of the Name-of-the-Father does not depend, as in the return of the repressed, on the permeability of the censorship. In this respect, it is unlike the unconscious signifier *in* the unconscious of the subject, from where it could be made available to the subject if the censorship authorized its return.

---

[193] Jacques Lacan, "Treatment of Psychosis," in *Écrits, op. cit.*, 482.

## Chapter Three – The Question of the Stunning Commandment

That the *dritte Person* is not available to the subject is the fundamental teaching, is it not, of the witticism? Why, indeed, can a subject not make a witticism by himself and laugh at it? Why is he unable both to produce the witticism and to receive it? Likewise, why is one absolutely unable, by singing a melody that one likes, to reproduce the effect created by hearing this melody sung by another voice? Precisely because *alterity suits the signifier of the Name-of-the-Father so much* that, to be transmissible, it must go through the alterity of the Other. Neither singing the melody that I like nor learning it by heart can make up for the medium that is the real of the alterity transmitted by another voice. If, then, a quaternary structure is needed so that the signifier of the Name-of-the-Father can be transmitted to the *infans*, it means that, just as a subject cannot produce a witticism for himself, the mother cannot produce by herself the spirit of the paternal metaphor. She can transmit it insofar as she receives it from the one from whom she awaits the password that will be needed to transmit the spirit of the *dritte Person* to her. It is to the extent that she can derive enjoyment from this password, just as one can derive enjoyment (without necessarily laughing at it) from a witticism, that the signifier of the *dritte Person* will be transmitted to the newborn infant, who is a witness to this unconscious *jouissance*.

Thus the path that leads to the emigration of the signifier of the Name-of-the-Father from the place of the Other to "the A-father," then to the mother and to the *infans*, consists of four stages. The intercession of "A-father" is necessary between the mother and the Name-of-the-Father because, as a mother, she has no immediate relationship of a mystical order (as she can have, for instance, as a woman) with the signifier. The signifier of the Name-of-the-Father is conveyed, in fact, for her, as a mother, by the fact that what makes her a mother is not, as it is for the Virgin Mary, the spirit of the Name-of-the-Father, but rather the phallus of the child's real father. That the phallus of the real father must express the law to symbolize this procreation is the task of "the A-father." But, for the obstetrician to have been able to answer the call that was made to him, he would have had to agree to pay the price required so that the *dritte Person* might be delivered from his withdrawal: that is to say, the price of not avoiding the fear and trembling by which every real father cannot fail to be gripped when he has to answer the call of the signifier of the Name-of-the-Father.

## Chapter Three – The Question of the Stunning Commandment

This function of fear as a subjective translation of the stunning signifier is strongly isolated by Lacan in his seminar on the psychoses.[194] He gives the example of the encounter, in Racine's *Athalie*, between Abner and the high priest, Joad; Lacan notes that the whole scene turns on the subjective reversal whereby Abner, who was initially a supporter of Athalie, becomes a supporter of Joad at the very moment when the latter transmitted to him, through his discourse, the "fear" of God. If this dimension of the "fear" of God, which is omnipresent in the Bible, attracts Lacan's attention so much, it is because it seems to be a vehicle of that major structural function of being that establishes in a subject what Lacan called, at that time, the *"quilting point"* between the signifier and the signified, which, precisely, is absent in psychotics.[195] We are thus led to understand this fear of the "One" as the price to be paid if this *"quilting point"* is to come into being. Subsequently, it will become a Borromean knot by means of which the creation of a hole in the symbolic (*Fiat hole*) creates the conditions of possibility of speech.

In this respect, the fear of the "One" has nothing to do with the fear of the ancient gods: "The fear of the gods from whom Lucretius wants to free his little friends is something altogether different, a multiform, confused feeling, one of panic...."

"The fear of God, on the other hand,... is the principle of wisdom and the foundation of the love of God.... To have replaced these innumerable fears by the fear of a unique being who has no other means of manifesting his power than through what is feared behind these innumerable fears is quite an accomplishment. You will say to me—*that really is a curate's idea!* Well, you're wrong. The curates have invented absolutely nothing in this genre. To invent a thing like this, you have to be a *poet or a prophet*, and it is precisely insofar as this Jehoiada[196] is one to some extent... that he can use as he does this major and primordial signifier."[197]

This split between Joad and Abner helps us to understand, analogically, the nature of the split between "the A-father" and the real

---

[194] Jacques Lacan, *The Psychoses, op. cit.*, Chapter 21.
[195] *Ibid.*
[196] [Jehoiada is the name that appears in the English version of the Old Testament in place of "Joad" in the French version, and in Racine's play.]
[197] *Ibid.*, 266–267. Author's emphasis.

father. "The A-father"—insofar as he is, in a similar way to Joad, in a position that Lacan refers to as "prophetic-poetic"—incarnates that part of the subject that hears the call of the signifier of the Name-of-the-Father. This is opposed to that other part of the subject that does not hear but that, like Abner, can be dragged out of his deafness, provided that the intercessor that is "the A-father" renders the stunning signifier of the Name-of-the-Father transmissible for him through fear.

We are entitled to suppose that our analysand, with her question, "Who is it?," is putting the following question to the obstetrician: "I am appealing to the prophetic-poetic function that is in you: will this function of 'the A-father' make itself heard—as Joad was able to make himself heard by Abner—by the one who, in you, is deaf?" The answer that the mother received to this invocation addressed to the obstetrician was, in short, the following: "There is neither a prophet nor a poet in me: there is only the presence in me of an Abner, who, because he has not yet met Joad, remains deaf to any fear of the signifier." What would have happened if, on that day, the poet Joad who was lying dormant in the obstetrician had woken up? He would have dragged the deaf Abner out of his foreclusive deafness and put him in a position to fully accept his function—allotted to the real father—as an agent of castration.

To come back to our analysand, I would say that through her "Who is it?"—which poses the triple question: "Who is the signifier of the Name-of-the-Father?," "Who is 'the A-father'?," and "Who is the real father?"—she obliges the psychoanalyst to think of the foreclusive process solely in terms of the quaternary structure in which the function of intercessor of "the A-father" is related (1) to the mother, (2) to the real father as an agent of castration, and (3) to the signifier of the Name-of-the-Father.

It seems to me, for example, that if, in the remarkable study he made of "l'Aimée de Lacan,"[198] J. Allouch comes to the conclusion that "there is no question here of foreclosure," it is because he envisages the death of Marguerite's elder sister only as an infanticide that, perpetrated by the mother on the child, does not call into question the foreclosure of the father.[199] But this act—by which "the still-born

---

[198] J. Allouch, *Marguerite ou l'Aimée de Lacan* (Paris: EPEL, 1990).
[199] *Ibid.*, 398.

child... was killed by its mother *in utero* because it would have been unnamable and thus humanly unviable"—could have been interpreted in terms other than those of infanticide if one had taken into account the mother's relation to "the A-father."[200] In this instance, if the child was unnamable, it would have been pertinent, would it not, to have examined the type of foreclosure that prevented the mother from receiving the metaphorical function and the naming function from the father.[201]

## D) THE APRÈS COUP LIGHT:[202] THE FREUDIAN TIME OF INTERPRETATION[203]

The movement that led Freud to invent psychoanalysis was undoubtedly linked to his passionate curiosity for truth. But it also came from quite another direction, namely, Freud's relationship to ethics. The moment he discovered that, in the unconscious, there is a signifier that transmits a commandment calling the speaking subject into being was decisive for him.

The possibility of coming to a deeper understanding of the signification of this commandment is within our reach provided we grasp the fact that this signifier, which is the "cause of sideration," is related precisely to the signifier that Freud identifies—in his *Interpretation of Dreams*—as the one that is the "source of the dream." The "source of the dream" is not, in fact, as is generally thought, the realization of infantile sexual desire: dreams are caused by a signifier that, during the day preceding the dream production, had the power to traumatize the

---

[200] *Ibid.*, 336.

[201] On the distinction between the procreative function and the naming function of the father, see Lacan's *RSI* (unpublished seminar), and in particular the session of May 13, 1975.

[202] ["*Après-Coup*" (literally: "after the shot/after the coup") is a commonly used French expression usually rendered into English as "in the aftermath," "afterward," or "a posteriori." In the analytic vocabulary, *Après-Coup* translates the concept *Nachträglichkeit*, constitutive of Freud's understanding of the logical time proper to psychic causality. *Nachträglichkeit* indicates the temporal scansion whereby an earlier experience is invested with meaning in the light of a fresh experience: what happens after gives a significance to what preceded. The concept of *Nachträglichkeit* has been erroneously translated into English as "deferred action," suggesting the wrong idea of a stimulus-response gap.]

[203] What follows was published as "La passe de Freud," in *L'Ethique de la psychanalyse et la Question du coût freudien* (Paris: Evel, 1984), 84.

subject by leaving him speechless, dumbfounded. What Freud teaches us is that the subject will find the means to overcome this state of being stunned thanks to unconscious *sexual desire* that will express itself in the dream. In this respect, sexual desire is not the *source* of the dream, but the *means* by which the subject will manage to displace himself. It is because this displacement is of a *metonymic* rather than a *metaphorical* order that Freud would be led to say that the dream is a failed witticism.

Do we have the means of translating this symbolic commandment?[204] We will see gradually that, although it is characterized by the fact that it is transmissible to the subject, it is not, however, inscribable: inaugurating meaning, it exceeds it with an untranslatable overabundance. We will not be surprised to learn that this excess is related to the abyss that is opened up by the question of debt and of the signifier of the Name-of-the-Father.

In the dream called "The Botanical Monograph"—where Freud introduces, for the first time, the question of censorship and of the signifier that is the cause of the dream—we learn that sideration is introduced by the symbolic debt. We already knew that the symbolic debt can be stunning from what we have learned from the witticism: is not the movement of recognition that carries me towards the one who was able to make me laugh a recognition of debt?

In what way is Freudian psychoanalysis innovative? Insofar as it introduces us to the fact that the subject of the unconscious stands in such a dependent relationship to the signifier that the notion of debt, according to which tradition has always recognized that a subject is indebted to his biological parents, is renewed. Freud helps us to discover, in fact, that beyond being indebted to the author of his days on earth, the subject of the unconscious is indebted to a much more elusive author, namely, the signifier of the Name-of-the-Father.

If Freud breaks radically with all the existing discourses prior to him, it is because he finds a way to answer the question of the symbolic debt in a manner that is different from the universal answer of the

---

[204] In a recent article—"Le temps d'un avènement," *Che vuoi?* 1 (1994)—Jacques Hassoun shows the same concern for accounting for the stunning encounter insofar as it takes the subject back to his most inaugural point of departure. The translation that he proposes for the signifier of the stunning encounter is linked to the significance of "death, negation, difference, time."

pleasure principle, where each subject finds himself answering in the form of a dream or in a symptom. I would suggest, then, that it is the fact of paying in another way than through the dream or the symptom that puts Freud in the position of naming the unconscious. It is what it costs him not to respond to this symbolic debt in accordance with the pleasure principle that requires from him the very different cost in the form of the signifying *après-coup*, and which results in the fact that, between cost and signifying *après-coup*, Freud passes psychoanalysis to us. Before discussing how and by what path Freud is led to demonstrate what the recognition of this symbolic debt costs, let us see briefly what the different positions are by means of which a subject sustains himself with the words: "I am not indebted to the signifier."

The master says: "How could I be indebted to the signifier since I 'am' the signifier itself?"[205] The academic within the university discourse says: "I have acquitted my debt towards the master, for I have devoted my life to erasing my enunciation in order to announce, without betraying him, the name of my master." As for the hysteric, his speech, as in the case of the madman with the king, is of no consequence. The truths that he announces are merely alibis in order to make the king laugh, which has the effect of acquitting him of his impertinent remarks.

What I want to draw our attention to is how Freud breaks with these different discourses through which the symbolic debt is deferred. This rupture can be identified in a logical "time of *après-coup* (*Nachträglichkeit*)" in which Freud ceases to respond to the signifier of the symbolic debt with a dream, raising his response to a level at which he makes himself the *passant* of psychoanalysis. But why is the moment of the *pass* necessarily a "time of *après-coup*"?

Since analytic discourse does not master the signifier, it finds itself dependent on it: this dependency requires a path that is specific to the law of the signifier. When the subject is no longer under the sway of this dependency, he can advance along the straight line of the university discourse insofar as he is unaware of the specific constraint of the signifier.

---

[205] These three discourses are drawn from Jacques Lacan, Jacques Lacan, *The Seminar of Jacques Lacan, Book XVII: The Other Side of Psychoanalysis*, trans. Russell Grigg (New York: W. W. Norton, 2007).

## Chapter Three – The Question of the Stunning Commandment

It was this signifying constraint that Freud would encounter before he was in a position to let the discovery of the unconscious pass into the dimension of *après-coup*. We are going to see how, owing to this constraint, he was obliged to pass, along a zigzagging path, through a certain number of signifying places, each of which corresponds to one of the specific ways in which the subject can encounter the question of the symbolic debt. These places, which are four in number, describe a sort of mathematization of Freud's *pass*.

Of the first of these places, we can say that it designates the point at which the subject is overwhelmed by the symbolic debt. Of the second, that it is the point at which he is placed in an impasse. Of the third, finally, that it is the sleight of hand whereby the subject settles his account, helped by the pleasure principle, with the symbolic debt.

What I am particularly interested in here is how Freud breaks the vicious circle passing through these three points by introducing a fourth place, which, for its part, is by no means an innocent return to the symbolic debt. Since I claim that this trajectory, whatever dream in the *Traumdeutung* we are referring to, is always the same, I could simply give the mathematized skeleton of these constant places. However, I have chosen to incarnate this trajectory in one of the dreams Freud expanded on the most: the dream of "the botanical monograph."[206]

### a) First Logical Time: The Subject Is Overwhelmed

One evening, Freud is conversing with his friend Königstein, who, in the course of the conversation, tells a joke that unsettles him, takes his breath away, leaving him suddenly speechless. This witticism corresponds to a reproach that Freud gives way too easily to his fantasies. It corresponds to what Freud would call, several days later, "the psychical representative of a high psychical importance."[207] This representative appears, then, to Freud as the signifier that was "the true source of the dream."[208] From this perspective, Freud is led to see the dream as a resumption of a message that was interrupted by the "sig-

---

[206] Sigmund Freud, *The Interpretation of Dreams, op. cit.*, 169–176 and 281–284.
[207] *Ibid.*, 174.
[208] *Ibid.*, 177.

nifier that was the source of the dream," which, in a certain way, has the function of a traumatic signifier.

In a first approximation, the enigmatic power that the signifier of "high psychical importance" possesses to interrupt the discourse is that of the effect exerted on the speaking subject by the troubling reminder that, in spite of everything he has done, he cannot do whatever he likes because he remains dependent on the signifier, he remains indebted to it. This is Königstein's general reproach, intimating to Freud that he tends to think he can do whatever he wants, that he should not give way to his fantasies. What Freud is being asked to do here is to recognize his debt: a symbolic debt according to which the more he embarks along the path of the signifier, the more he becomes indebted to the signifier without realizing it. If this signifier of the symbolic debt thereby acquires such a "psychical value," "charged with emotion," it is because, notwithstanding the arguments of mastery that he possesses ("I am not in debt; I am the one who was at the origin of the discovery of the anaesthetizing properties of cocaine thanks to which it was possible to operate on my father"), the reminder of this debt persists, as if it were suggesting that it was not susceptible to this sort of bargaining. The fundamental problem is that, by virtue of this reminder, Freud encounters the dimension of the impossible: indeed, Königstein's assertion, "You are in debt," proves, at least initially, impossible to reject, impossible to deny, impossible to repress. In this respect, how are we to understand that the purpose of the pleasure principle, which is to avoid unpleasure through repression and denial, is thus rendered impossible by the action, which, after all, is sovereign, of the signifier "of high psychical importance"? Indeed, if the pleasure principle played its repressive role, the troubling, not to say traumatic, question, of the symbolic debt would be reduced to silence. But this question is not silenced by the pleasure principle: quite to the contrary, it is this question that silences the subject of the pleasure principle by cutting him at the level of his speech.

*b) Second Logical Time: The Subject at an Impasse*

This first moment in which the subject is overwhelmed by the cutting power of the signifier of the symbolic debt is followed by a second moment of time that confirms the impasse that the subject is at with regard to his speech. This impasse is particularly apparent to

## Chapter Three – The Question of the Stunning Commandment

Freud in that not only has his speech been cut by the signifier of "high psychical importance," but it also finds itself in the—at least transitory—impossibility of rising from the ashes.

1) For example, it does not even spring to life again in the context of ordinary paranoiac reaction, authorized by the pleasure principle, which would have allowed Freud to say something like: "It's not me, it's you," or "But, sir, you don't know who you are speaking to."

2) Nor is it able to find a new lease of life by using what it already knows: indeed, the knowledge already acquired proves to be of no avail when it comes to facing the question of the signifier of "high psychical importance." Insofar as Freud finds himself deprived by this signifier of what he thought he possessed, it may be said that this signifier that has the power of putting constituted knowledge to one side is a *passeur* of the real.[209] It is a *passeur* of the gaping hole of the signifier that opens up in him when he is left flabbergasted, "open-mouthed." This gaping hole of knowledge is a lack of knowledge, a fault of the signifier that is nothing other than "the" fault. In this respect, the guilt linked to the fact of remaining stunned resides in the fact that *the subject is guilty of the real*.

3) This impasse could be overcome if the subject of the unconscious found for the question of the symbolic debt the answer of a new signifier, a signifier X by means of which Freud's symbolic desire would be metaphorized according to the structure of the witticism. But this new signifier was not found. Consequently, as the real by which Freud is inhabited can no longer be supposed by the symbolic (R/S), it becomes unbearable and, at the same time, provides no support for the imaginary (I/R), which collapses. Clinically, this is translated by the fact that the subject, who is transitorily stripped of his specular image, feels he is exposed, transparent, under the absolute gaze of this stone guest, which is the signifier of the symbolic debt.

The fact remains that Freud cannot stay indefinitely in this position of desubjectification. Owing to the withdrawal of the signifier, as a result of which the subject cannot be represented as "I," the subject will be driven to reposition himself rather than remaining forever fixed by the gaze of the stone guest. Under this pressure, the subject will reposition himself and take flight, this time from the question of

---

[209] See footnote 11.

## Chapter Three – The Question of the Stunning Commandment

the "signifier of high psychical importance." This flight will take place with the participation of the censorship and of the pleasure principle, which regain their rights, having been temporarily excluded, by constituting a dream. By this sleight of hand, the signifying support—articulated metonymically—of the dream of the botanical monograph is given back to Freud.

### c) Third Logical Time: The Sleight of Hand

The sleight of hand that will be employed consists in substituting the words "I am in debt" with the words "I am not in debt." The repression thus realized is a compromise of the desire for symbolization, which has withdrawn in the face the signifier of high psychical importance. If that had not been the case, Freud would not have needed to have a dream a few hours later to take up the discourse again at the point where it had been interrupted. Anyway, the function of this dream is to give the means to take flight from the traumatic signifier. This flight will take the form of a displacement that substitutes a metonymic response for a metaphorical response: that is why Freud says that the dream is a failed witticism.

The moment of desubjectification by the traumatic signifier leads to unknotting of the real, the symbolic, and the imaginary. I propose that the dream be understood as a reknotting of the R.S.I., but a reknotting with four knots, with the help of a signifier that Freud qualifies as an "intermediate common entity" and which turns out to be a plant of an indeterminate species. Of this "intermediate common entity,"[210] Freud also says (a "premonition," Lacan might observe) that it is the signifier that forms the "nodal point of the dream."[211] In order to evaluate how this hypothesis is defended, let us join Freud again at the point of *fading*, when, unsupported by the signifier, he rediscovers the means to sustain himself by discovering a new signifier: the signifier "botanical."[212]

We left Freud reduced to silence in front of Königstein, who embodied, for him, during this moment of subjective destitution, the

---

[210] *Ibid.*, 282.
[211] *Ibid.*, 283.
[212] In English in the original.

## Chapter Three – The Question of the Stunning Commandment

agency of the *Che vuoi?*. How would this silence be lifted? When the encounter between the two friends was interrupted by the unexpected arrival of Professor Gärtner and his pretty wife, whom Freud compliments on her "blooming" looks. So it was with this apparently trivial word that Freud *was able to speak again* and, without knowing it consciously, he found the idea that enabled him to rearticulate—in the form of a sexual desire—the desire that had abandoned him. What reawakens his desire, in the sequence "blooming *Frau* Gärtner," is less *Frau* Gärtner than her "blooming looks," that is to say, the signifier "flower" that she is carrying. With "flower," Freud has found a *parry* to the signifier of "high psychical importance." This parry consists in a displacement that allows him to abandon the question of the symbolic debt, substituting it with a signifier articulating the fact that the subject Freud is not in debt. He is not in debt because a flower (cocaine) had given him the opportunity of making an important discovery (that of its anaesthetizing properties), thanks to which his father was able to undergo an operation for glaucoma. Furthermore, flowers and botany serve as supports for his infantile sexual desire: incestuous desire is evoked by references to pulling the artichoke apart, to worms eating away at books in the library, etc.

There are thus four categories of heterogeneous signifiers in this dream:

(1) The signifier of the symbolic debt, which I understand as the signifier that functions as a *passeur* of the real.

(2) The "botanical" signifier of unconscious desire, which appears to me to be the signifier of the unconscious symbolic chain.

(3) The indifferent signifier of the "day residue," providing the idea of the dream, which is the couple "blooming-cyclamen."

The reason why the idea of the dream can only be provided by a chance encounter occurring the day before the dream has astonished me for a long time. Why, indeed, can the subject not find the idea with which to constitute a dream among his own signifiers? On this point, Freud is categorical and asserts that a signifier can only serve its purpose if it has not had time to link up with the unconscious chain. The day residue cannot belong to the unconscious signifiers because, Freud says, it must be indifferent, which is why it must be "less than a day" old, otherwise it would lose its freshness.

Freud's line of reasoning, which distinguishes the day residue of the signifier of high psychical importance (the first must be indifferent, that is to say, of low psychical importance) from the unconscious signifier (it must not belong to the unconscious chain) leads me to think that this signifier (the day residue) introduces what Lacan called "the imaginary." The support of this identification comes once again from the fact that the function of this signifier is not to be a-semantic, but rather to provide the idea of the dream.

4) My hypothesis—according to which the "knot of the dream" is a signifier that, in the proper sense of the word, knots the three unknotted RSI rings—is backed up by the fact that there is no common link between the three, except for one, and only one, which is precisely this "nodal," or "intermediate common entity" signifier ("indeterminate species of plant") with which the signifiers, "You are in debt" (real), cyclamen (imaginary), and cocaine (symbolic) are articulated one by one. The signifiers supporting the real, the symbolic, and the imaginary can thus converge with this signifier "intermediate common entity" ("botanical monograph on an indeterminate species of plant"). It seems to me that what Freud calls "the idea of the dream" consists in finding the idea that *allows* these heterogeneous signifiers to be *brought in relationship* with each other: is not this linking up of the heterogeneous signifiers by the "intermediate common entity" signifier what allows them to be knotted in the dream? In this respect, these three types of signifier each maintain relations of metonymy or metaphor with the signifier "indeterminate plant."

(1) By virtue of a metaphorical displacement, the signifiers of unconscious desire (cocaine, artichoke, page of a book) converge with the signifier ("an indeterminate species of plant").

(2) By virtue of a metonymic displacement, it is:

A) The day residue, the signifier "cyclamen," which is articulated with the signifier "indeterminate plant." The signifier "cyclamen" is not found as such in the manifest content of the dream, which introduces not the idea of a plant but rather the literalness of a signifier, "indeterminate species of plant";

B) The signifier of the symbolic debt, the source of the dream, insofar as, by a sleight of hand, the subject Freud succeeds in repressing this "signifier of high psychical importance" by moving into more benign territory. Though Freud could not reposition himself because he could not find a new signifier to symbolize the real while supporting it (R/S), he rediscovers the possibility of repositioning himself thanks to a "knot" signifier. It will support the real, even though there has not been any true symbolization of this real, which is why Freud says that the dream is a failed witticism.

In the situation in which Freud, the dreamer, finds himself, we can say that his subjective position has not changed at all: though it is astute, the idea of the dream has in fact put itself in the service of his determination not to change his discourse. In this regard, what does not change is that, thanks to his dream, Freud maintains his ego-resistance to the question of the symbolic debt: "I, Freud, am the unrecognized author of the discovery of the virtues of cocaine, who is not accountable to anybody."

### d) Fourth Logical Time: Freud's "Pass"

But it so happens that Freud is not just a dreamer. Something pushes him, the day after his dream, to sit down at his desk, to analyze his dream, and to operate, in this "time of *après-coup*," a return to himself from which, through a rupture of discourse, the transmissible recognition of the unconscious will emerge.[213] Owing to this return to himself, where he discovers that the burgeoning of signifiers linked to botany is the effect of a sleight of hand whose function is to conceal, to repress, the signifier that is the "source of the dream," Freud does not seek, this time, to avoid the gaze of the signifier of high psychical importance. On the contrary, he is the one who looks at it, but from a completely new perspective. This is not purely and simply a return to square one, which would merely be a repetition, because he returns to himself with another subjective position.[214]

Why, in this "time of *après-coup*," is he able to look squarely at this signifier of high psychical importance without dying of shame? Because, this time, it is not with shame that he encounters the real, but rather with astonishment. Why, in this respect, are shame and astonishment so antinomical?

Shame is the movement of *fading* that the subject experiences when, under the gaze of the Other, he feels unmasked and transparent.[215] If the moment of unmasking is so painful for the subject, it

---

[213] The signifier "Freudian cost" [*coût freudien*] is the question of what this moment of "*après-coup*" costs [*coûte*].

[214] The commandment "where it was, become!" implies "where it was, come back!".

[215] This unmasking of a usurped identity has been discussed by Oscar Mannoni.

## Chapter Three – The Question of the Stunning Commandment

is because it appears to be a sort of confession that the subject was hiding the fact that he was living in a state of imposture. Which imposture? He does not know, for he has forgotten the fact that he was indebted to the signifier and that *it is this act of forgetting that he pays for, subjectively, with the persecutory feeling of being an impostor.*

The astonished subject is in a converse position; accepting to be recognized as in debt towards the real, he does not repress the signifier of the real and what is consequently required of him—namely, to forget what he already knows so that what he does not yet know may come into being. This entails a reversal of the situation that corresponds to the return of the drive, whereby, from accepting that he is recognized as being in debt to the real, the subject changes into a subject who is grateful to the signifier. Recognizing a debt that he recontracts without guilt, he breaks, at that moment, with the morality of the censorship, which is a morality of compromise with the signifier. In doing so, he agrees to become even more indebted to the signifier by responding with the production of a new signifier, a different signifier.

What is a "different signifier"? It is a signifier that does not defer the a-semantic dimension of the real and that, in this respect, differs from the signifier of the day residue, whose function is always to answer this question: "How can the symbolic debt be deferred?" The articulation of such a different signifier requires a desire that is different from the desire of the dream and that introduces the desire of the analyst Freud: the price of this different desire is what has to be paid so that the subject's desire is not structured only by the pleasure principle.

If we want to get an idea of this desire, we must recognize that in the analyst there is a presence that acquiesces to the recognition of the signifier of high psychical importance. This acquiescence is not self-evident; indeed, we have seen that Freud could utter a "yes" of gratitude towards the signifier of the real without entailing any consequences provided that this "yes" which coincided with the state of sideration was followed subsequently by a withdrawal, a repression.

But the acquiescence that the signifier of the real receives from Freud in return is no longer an innocent "yes," but rather a "yes-of-yes," a second acquiescence whereby the act of enunciation of the subject Freud ceases to be separated from his utterance. It is the articulation of such a different desire that allows Freud to look, in this "time of *après coup*," at the signifier of high psychical importance without being stunned. At this moment, he makes a third and last displacement, which puts him in the position of taking a step further than that which consists of looking, without flinching, at the signifier of high psychical importance. He produces a signifier that transmutes the insistence of the "yes-of-yes" into the perseverance of a "yes-of-yes-of-yes." At this level, we can say that Freud, who, in our first logical time, had made himself the *"passeur" of the real*, here makes himself the *"passant."*[216]

The novelty of the signifier that his unconscious desire now allows him to articulate resides in the fact that Freud, for the third and last time, has moved towards a fourth place (that of the barred Other, in Lacan's graph), from which he succeeds in making psychoanalysis transmissible. Knowledge about the unconscious is transmitted if this knowledge lets the fourth place from where he is speaking pass, as in a witticism. From this new place, Freud, recognizing his symbolic debt, is in a position to name the heterogeneous places that he has passed through and recognized. Those of the "signifier of a high degree of psychical importance," of the signifier of a low degree of importance (the day residue), and of the signifier "intermediate common entity." As for the concept of displacement, which appears to be the movement pushing Freud to pass through the four subjective places that we have differentiated, it is a key concept of *The Interpretation of Dreams*, rendered transmissible by the interpretation of the dream of the botanical monograph. The power of transmissibility that Freud was able to give to this word—which is the reason it has come down to us—lies in the virulence of the knowledge that it transmits. This virulence is conferred on it by the fact that, at its level, the three organizations that knowledge receives from the real, the symbolic, and the imaginary are knotted, namely, conscious knowledge, unconscious knowledge, and sexual not-knowing.

Freud's *pass* is the movement that makes him pass from a first position to a fourth, a position from which his knowledge about the unconscious is knotted in such a way that it can be passed down to us. The virulence of this passage lies in the fact that the knowledge transmitted has the structure of a half-saying.[217] It half says the symbolic,

---

[216] See footnote 11.

[217] Philippe Julien, *Le Manteau de Noé* (Paris: Desclée de Brouwer, 1991), 74: "The *bien dire* founds a different ethic, one which 'supposes that we take into account another dimension of language, that which renews the inexhaustible power of the poetic power of

half says the real, and half says the imaginary. If Freud is the *passant* of psychoanalysis, it is because his half-saying is of a nature to receive, from his good listener, a retroactive effect of symbolization (note the analogy with the emitter receiving from the receiver his own message in an inverted form).

From this perspective, a *passant* of psychoanalysis is anyone whose unconscious desire X (desire of the analyst) is knotted to its signifying elaboration in such a way that—like the witticism—it has the power to induce, in the one who receives it, an effect of symbolization.

It is on the basis of this effect—which is identifiable *après-coup*, at the level of the Other—that we are justified in recognizing that there was a subject functioning as a *passant*.

*II. Sideration beyond the Pleasure Principle:*
*The Question of Unconscious Choice*

A) FREUD AND THE QUESTION OF THE UNCONSCIOUS CHOICE

Sideration may be viewed as an astonishing experience of a time that, eluding historical determinism, imposes itself as beginning when the real is approached *as if it were for the first time*. At this point, the subject is taken back to the way he once accepted the pre-historical contract by which he is linked to the law of the Other. Does the stunning ascendancy of this partner, who imposes himself on the subject without asking for his opinion, signify that this subject has no "self-possession" and is in a state of absolute passivity in relation to the Other?

We are justified in answering this question by saying that the state of the stunned subject, contrary to that of the traumatized subject, is not passivity, but rather *capacity*. As we have seen, the stunned person is liable to unconsciously choose these three solutions, which are inhibition, symptoms, or anxiety.[218] Whereas it seems possible to interpret inhibition as being linked to the impossibility of overcoming

---

language.... It promises an ethical discourse that does not content itself with saying [*dire*] the good or the law. It is that of a *bien dire*....'"

[218] Sigmund Freud, *Inhibitions, Symptoms, and Anxiety* (1926), *The Standard Edition of the Complete Psychological Works of Sigmund Freud XX* (London: Hogarth, 1961).

the state of being stunned and symptoms as the effect of the repression of the signifier, anxiety seems to be what is produced when the subject remains in no man's land, suspended between the realization of being stunned and the non-realization of being un-stunned. As for the realization of desire, this seems to me to be the effect of this fourth solution, which is made possible when the subject accepts the stunning signifier, as is the case in the process of the witticism (being stunned, followed by light).

Can we identify the existence of this moment of unconscious choice in which the subject chooses one of these solutions rather than another? After the titanic debate between Erasmus' *"de libero arbitrio* [On free will]" and Luther's *"de servo arbitrio* [On the bondage of the will]," how can psychoanalysis maintain, against someone like Sartre, this aporia that is raised by the unthinkable existence of an unconscious choice?[219] Inasmuch as we have noted the existence of such a choice, the path that we will take now to prove its signification involves the attempt to translate the stunning message. The signifier that is the source of the dream is not purely and simply that which, as Freud says, affects the subject. Insofar as it is that which transmits a certain unconscious message to him, we can understand to what this subject is saying "yes" or "no."

The difficulty we come up against immediately is that, insofar as it exceeds any signified, the stunning signifier defies every attempt to translate it. In his *Traumdeutung*, Freud does not help us to overcome this difficulty; he simply observes that this signifier is "of a high degree of psychical importance," without asking himself what the meaning of this "importance" is. In other words, he confirms the existence of a particularly "affecting" signifier, as if the reference to affect exempted him from seeking to translate the significance of the message transmitted by this signifier inducing scansion. It is only in his subsequent work on jokes that he attempts a translation of the stunning or bewildering signifier, suggesting that it relates to what is unintelligible, incomprehensible, and enigmatic. We have to recognize that the experience of not-knowing, to which the *fading* subject is brought back, tells us nothing about the cause of the *fading*. The subject can no longer say anything or think anything on this point except that he has encoun-

---

[219] Martin Luther, *Œuvres V* (Geneva: Labor et Fides).

## Chapter Three – The Question of the Stunning Commandment

tered a highly "affecting" signifier. What will be instructive for us, then, is to examine the logical moment in time in which the subject of the unconscious, Freud, succeeds (by means of the dream of the botanical monograph) in eluding the signifier of high psychical importance by repressing it. This movement of avoidance is, in fact, the consequence of an unconscious psychical debate in which the unconscious thoughts of the subject attempt to reject, with the aim of repressing it, the message of the signifier that is the source of the dream. It is thus possible to reconstitute, with the help of the dreamer's rejecting thoughts, the logical moment of an unconscious choice where one can understand, on the spot, the subject's decision to refuse, for certain alleged reasons, to say "yes" to the question posed by this signifier. It is on the basis of the analysis of the bad faith of the dreamer, whose thoughts tend to justify the repression of the signifier, that we will be able, retrospectively, to deduce the meaning of the message that the dreamer's latent thoughts resist.

What do we learn from the latent thoughts of the dream of the botanical monograph? In Freud's own words, it is a "passionate plea" in which Freud discovers that, as in the dream of Irma's injection, he is led to justify himself and plead his case. But this plea diverts attention from what is really at stake. Freud positions himself as one who has been *accused*, yet he has only been *called into question* by the stunning signifier. Why substitute an accusation for a calling into question?

Let us return here to the conversation with Königstein that moved Freud so much. Why does Königstein's remark—"Aren't you yielding too much to your fantasies?"—acquire, for Freud, the power of a signifier of a "high degree of psychical importance"? This question makes Freud recall an event that happened when he was seventeen years old. At the time, he had opened an account with a bookshop and was unable to settle his debt. This debt, which was in fact unpaid, and which his father found inexcusable, made Freud think of another type of debt, namely, the symbolic debt.

How can we be sure that the appearance of the signification of the symbolic debt is the true source of the dream? Freud's very defense, which tends to reject the idea that he is in debt, was: Is it not he himself (having taken part in the discovery of the anesthetic properties of cocaine for the eye) who had allowed his father to undergo an operation for glaucoma?

## Chapter Three – The Question of the Stunning Commandment

The first question that this defense raises is why, when the discussion with Königstein raised the question of the symbolic debt, following Freud's recollection of his outstanding debt with the bookshop, was Freud unable to justify himself in front of his friend Königstein with the same talent that he deploys in the latent thoughts of the dream? True, his conversation with his friend was, he tells us, interrupted by the arrival of the "blooming" Frau Gärtner, but a certain confusion is maintained here between a subjective and an objective cause of the interruption. If the cause of the interruption was "objective," why was the conversation between the two friends not taken up again by Freud after the arrival of the blooming Frau Gärtner? Because the signifier of the debt that interrupts Freud's discourse goes well beyond the person of Königstein: indeed, it incarnates the a-semantic signification of this *dritte Person* who can appear when, for example, the signifier *"Herr,"* ceasing to refer to the little other that is the fellow human being, has become that absolute master of death, which is the signifier of the barred big Other.

What do we learn from making a parallel between the state of *Verblüffung* experienced by Freud when he encountered the signifier of the symbolic debt through a remark made by his friend Königstein and that which he experienced as a result of a remark he himself made to a travelling companion? We learn that, when the signifier of the symbolic debt appears, it is not contested because, at that particular moment, it seems to convey a question that the subject recognizes to be *incontestable*. What is important here is to grasp the subject's relation to what he contests retrospectively. How is it that the subject who, in the first logical moment, accepts without astonishment, and as unquestionably fair, the question that has been put to him by the signifier of the symbolic debt is led, subsequently, to correct himself, to reverse the situation, to change his position by contesting what he had earlier accepted, namely, his debt?

In the logic of this reversal that Freud makes, there is a genuine turning away from the question that he has received from the signifier of the Name-of-the-Father. Indeed, in his unconscious defense, Freud behaves as if he had already been accused, and this is where the real complexity of the message transmitted by the stunning signifier begins. During the moment of *Verblüffung* in which Freud was interpellated, he was *not accused* but *only questioned* by a question the receipt of which he had acknowledged. *Acknowledging receipt is not the same as being accused*; why is Freud led, then, to turn the meaning of a question into that of an accusation? What gain does he derive, as a subject, from this diversion whereby he chooses to substitute for a question that he accepted as being unquestionably fair an accusation that he is led to contest as unfair?

This gain is the regaining of a certain use of speech: it is as if Freud's speech, reduced to silence by the aptness of the question, could only emerge from this silence *if he ceased to be fairly called into question in order to be unfairly accused.*[220] With this sleight of hand, he substituted for the existence of a calling into question that left him dumbfounded the existence of an accusation whose injustice triggered the possibility of a "passionate defense." Expressing his extreme indignation, Freud put his finger on the existence of two antinomical laws. The first questions the subject about the justness of his evolution as a subject in respect to saying well, whereas the other, the law of the superego, does not present itself as a question about the problematic advent of the subject, but rather as a sanction that reveals to the subject that he is guilty.[221] The great difference between these two laws resides in two points.

First, the law of the superego has the power to accuse the subject by announcing the injustice of which he is guilty, whereas the symbolic law does not accuse but rather solicits the existence of the aptness of a *saying*. The difficulty that results from these two laws is this: the law that solicits the subject's becoming is received as licit, but gives no indication about how to find the apt *saying*, whereas the law that sanctions specifies where the injustice of which the subject has been proved guilty lies. In so doing, it gives him the possibility of evading the unconscious choice of the pertinence of the *well saying*.

---

[220] See further on concerning St. Paul's words: "Say no to injustice rather than yes to justice" (183ff).

[221] We shall see later that this confusion that Freud makes between the symbolic law and 'sin' [*faute*] proceeds from a readiness to take upon oneself the sins of the father that must be kept hidden. The analysis provided by M. Balmary of the attempt made by Freud's father to admit to his son, in the enigmatic dedication written in the Bible that he offers him, which sin he had committed is fascinating ("La Bible brisée de Jakob Freud: où Jakob, sous les traits d'un roi d'Israël, avoue sa faute à son fils, postface à S. Freud," in *L'Homme aux statues* (Paris: Le Livre de poche, 1994).

## Chapter Three – The Question of the Stunning Commandment

This avoidance confronts us with the second fundamental aspect of the difference between the symbolic law and the law of the superego. Should we not understand Freud's indignation at being unfairly accused by the law as being linked to the fact that he has repressed the stunning signifier that was the source of the dream and to the fact that he *cannot forgive himself* for having reduced to silence the pertinence of the question asked? Thus, when he reacts indignantly, he is overlooking the fact that, by repressing the call of the symbolic debt, he was the one who chose to submit himself to a censorship that he could easily denounce later as unjust. This mechanism, which Freud analyzes retrospectively with exemplary courage, is universal. Is it not the case that many virtuous indignations obey this process? The very fact of feeling indignant at injustice allows many people to see themselves as being just.

Think, for example, of people who, without being paranoiacs, see themselves as upholders of the law because they denounce injustice. And when these same people denounce the Machiavellianism of the "He" ("'He' takes us for idiots...," "'He' won't get us..."), are they not behaving like Freud in his dream? The enigma is this: why does man seem to prefer this persecutory *"He"* to the *"He"* of the *dritte Person?*

For me, the answer is clear: this universal preference for the persecutory superego proceeds from an unconscious choice for a law, which, by persecuting the subject, paradoxically bestows on him a certain good conscience ("It's the law that's wrong") and enables him to avoid the unconscious choice to which the stunning signifier threatens to expose him, insofar as this signifier does not say to him, "*Where is the injustice?*," but rather, "*Where is the fairness?*"

Further on, I will be examining the question of whether the universal repercussions of St. Paul's doctrine do not lie precisely in the fact that he knew how to turn this universal preference for guilt to his advantage. The point on which Freud takes issue with Pauline doctrine is that, according to Freud, man's guilt is not attributable to original sin, but rather to a failure of his own responsibility towards the duties inherent in the exercise of speech.[222]

---

[222] Even though he defends the doctrine of original sin in *Moses and Monotheism*.

## Chapter Three – The Question of the Stunning Commandment

Since Freud, we know that the subject of the unconscious is responsible for the choice of producing either a dream, a symptom, or a witticism. Below, I have provided a list—established by Annick Feissel and Max Bensasson—of the instances where Freud discusses this problem of the unconscious choice of neurosis:

| Gesammelte Werke | English Translations[223] |
|---|---|
| I, pp. 180–183 | "Miss Lucy R.," *SE 2*: 122–124 |
| I, p. 414 | "Heredity and the Aetiology of the Neuroses," *SE 3*: 149 |
| I, pp. 451–454 | "The Aetiology of Hysteria," *SE 3*: 214–217 |
| V, p. 154 | "My Views on the Part Played by Sexuality in the Aetiology of the Neuroses," *SE 7*: 276 |
| VII, p. 456 | "Notes upon a Case of Obsessional Neurosis," *SE 10*: 241 |
| VIII, p. 237 | "Formulations on the Two Principles of Mental Functioning," *SE 12*: 225 |
| VIII, pp. 442–452 | "The Disposition to Obsessional Neurosis: A Contribution to the Problem of Choice of Neurosis," *SE 12*: 317–326 |
| XI, p. 396 | "The Common Neurotic State," *SE 16*: 382 |
| XIV, p. 61 | *An Autobiographical Study*, *SE 20*: 36 |

This question, which comes back insistently in Freud's texts, is one of the threads of my own research, weaving its way through my work and returning with perseverance in each of the five chapters:

| | |
|---|---|
| Choice between a slip of the tongue and a witticism | p. 35, 198 |
| Silence of darkness and silence of the abyss | p. 44 |
| Fascinating gaze and dumbfounding gaze | p. 62 |
| True secret and false secret | p. 74 |
| "Why have you abandoned me?" | p. 96 |
| Taboo and prohibition | p. 97 |
| Insistence or perseverance? | p. 101 |
| *Jouissance* of the other or "*j'ouïe-sens*" | p. 118 |

---

[223] I have given the corresponding English references here for the French translations listed by A. Feissel and M. Bensasson.

## Chapter Three – The Question of the Stunning Commandment

Saying "yes" or saying "no" to the face — p. 134
Assumption or foreclosure of the call to the mother
    by "the A-father" — p. 143
Accusation or calling into question? — p. 167
"That's all I am" or "I am not only that" — p. 207
Can the analyst choose to look at the Medusa? — p. 274
The traumatic dilemma — p. 278
Passivity or capacity of the subject — p. 285
Possibility or impossibility of a choice of the originary pact — p. 290

    From the standpoint of the philosophy of freedom, the notion of an unconscious choice is an absolute contradiction, since for philosophy freedom is the privilege itself of conscious being. Among the philosophers, Heidegger is undoubtedly the one who came closest to the paradox that we need to reflect on: if the subject is radically determined—insofar as he is fundamentally indebted to speech—can he escape this absolute determinism? A whole chunk of Heidegger's meditation seems to accept such a determinism inasmuch as he recognizes the authoritative character of the call by which the voice of consciousness—very similar to Lacan's *Che vuoi?*—presents itself as an absolute ad-vocation for *Dasein*.

    But, in a very subtle manner, by considering the response of *Dasein* as a mark of authenticity with regard to oneself, Heidegger privileges the dimension of responsibility towards oneself to the detriment of moral responsibility towards the alterity of the law. Whereas a psychoanalytic conception leads us to recognize that a beyond determinism is only possible if there is an uncompromising assumption of determinism, Heidegger's reflection comes up against the difficulty of accepting the ascendancy of the Other; this ascendancy is not recognized by Heidegger as an ethical dimension of obligation, but rather as a dimension of "mastery"—*Botmässigkeit*—to which *Dasein* must not succumb if it wants to affirm the freedom of an authentic "will-to-be."[224] We can see how Heidegger, discovering the harrowing determinism of "being-in-debt," escapes this existential anxiety that he

---

[224] See Jean Greisch, *Ontologie et Temporalité* (Paris: Presses Universitaires de France, 1993), 166.

describes so lucidly, while draping himself in the concern for authenticity of a *Dasein* that is only responsible unto itself.

For us psychoanalysts, if there is a function of freedom, it exists, as Lacan recognizes, insofar as the subject is radically subjected to a primordial signifier that "kills all meanings," that has the power to institute us as subjects who are alienated from meaning and to relieve us from this alienation.[225] The signifier not only has the capacity to cancel out, as in the witticism, the meaning of the code, but is also the building block that can be substituted for detritus: where the real that has not fallen within the scope of the symbolic has fallen into decline, the signifier can, if the subject of the unconscious chooses to be taken in by it, return to pick up again what, at one time, it had dropped. The subject is faced with an unconscious choice: either he must consent to the *jouissance* of the Other's superego or he must consent to the *"j'ouïe-sens."*

## B) BEYOND THE FREUDIAN CONCEPTION OF BEYOND THE PLEASURE PRINCIPLE

Clinical experience of being stunned allows us to take the question of an unconscious choice further than Freud did, for it is in this way that the subject can be freed from that blind repetition compulsion that led Freud, in 1920, to put forward the hypothesis of a beyond the pleasure principle.

The differences that can be observed between the diabolic repetition brought to light by Freud and the repetition whereby the signifier transforms itself insistently in order to stun can lead to confusion, clinically, but they must be radically distinguished. The confusion lies in the vagueness of the term "unpleasure" with which Freud refers to the subjective effect of the compulsion to repeat. "Unpleasure" masks the fundamental difference that exists between the traumatic return of the latent real that entraps the subject in the compulsion to repeat and the return of the stunning signifier in the real, causing unpleasure. This confusion on Freud's part is the effect of a failure to distinguish between two parameters that are combined in traumatic repetition.

---

[225] Jacques Lacan, *The Four Fundamental Concepts, op. cit.*, 252.

### Chapter Three – The Question of the Stunning Commandment

This diabolic repetition of which Freud speaks refers not only to the coarseness of an immediate commemoration of the traumatic real, but also, at the same time, to the repetition of a paradox with which the subject has been faced in the traumatic situation. The subject entered the traumatic experience because it was revealed to him as a result of maternal privation. Even though the presence of the signifier was suddenly absent for him, he was able to come through the trauma because he received from the Other a message that, by signifying to him the existence of an *"y a de l'un,"* confronts him with the paradox of two contradictory messages: "there is" and "there is not."

The unconscious ego and the subject of the unconscious respond in a contradictory manner because the ego tends, owing to its repressing power, to say "no" to the "there is not," while the subject of the unconscious is required to answer "yes" to the signifier of the "there is." It is because Freud did not distinguish *the unpleasure to which the ego says "no"* from *the unpleasure experienced by the subject saying "yes"* to the stunning signifier that a confusion arose. On the one hand, there is the terror of the ego that is unable to repress the unbound stimuli, thereby threatening the protective shield (*Reizschutz*); on the other, there is sideration insofar as the subject does not come into existence harmoniously by saying "yes" to the signifier of the Name-of-the-Father, but rather in a catastrophic experience of stunning subjectification.[226] It is not impossible that the Biblical notion of "fear" should be included in such a primordial experience.[227]

This distinction that I am establishing between the terror characteristic of the unconscious ego and stunning fear, which is characteristic of the subject of the unconscious, leads us to distinguish what the affect of unpleasure linked to repetition tends to confuse, namely, the two antinomical sides bound together by what is beyond the pleasure principle.

1) The first side is that of the compulsion to repeat. Freud attributes a diabolical character to it because it teaches the subject how he is inexorably subjected to a determinism that leaves him no choice. The trauma of this structuring experience, through which the real

---

[226] Translated as "protective shield against stimuli" in *Standard Edition XVIII*, 27.
[227] On the relation between the "fear of God" and the "quilting point," see 148.

shows its ascendancy over the symbolic, demonstrates that the sole recourse that remains for the subject is to sustain himself with the signifier of the Name-of-the-Father, not in order to forget the real of the lack of a signifier—which is impossible—but to transmute this real lack of a signifier into a signifier of a symbolic lack.

2) The operation whereby "there is some signifier (*il y a du signifiant*)" is substituted metaphorically for "there is no signifier (*il y a pas de signifiant*)" corresponds to this other side of the beyond the pleasure principle. In it, the action of a subject, constituting itself in primal repression as the signifier of a lack of a signifier, replaces a traumatizing passivity. Through this act, by means of which he evades the blind determinism of the traumatic real insofar as he can say "yes" (*bejahung*) to the signifier of the Name-of-the-Father, the subject shows that he has the power to enter significance by an act that moves away from pure determinism. From this point of view, we can understand that the stunning signifier is transmitted as a reminder of the originary call in which the traumatized subject heard the Other say to him: "*y a de l'Un*"—even if the trauma indicates the contrary.

If psychoanalysis has the power to put a check on the compulsion to repeat, it is because it offers the analysand the opportunity, one day, to hear that, at the very heart of the traumatic repetition of the same, intertwined with it, is the presence of the voice of an alterity that says: "*y a de l'Un*." This insistent vocation of the Other to make himself heard teaches us that the compulsion to repeat is not, as Freud suggests, only the effect of a pure diabolic exogenous manifestation: it is also the effect of an exogenous manifestation whereby the symbolic Other presents himself to the subject as a voice transmitting to him the alterity of a radical question that Lacan, for his part, translates by his stunning *Che vuoi?*.

The subject is faced with an unconscious choice: Will he yield to the compulsion to repeat as if it were a diabolic and blind determinism, condemned to repeat itself, identical to itself until the end of time? Or will he choose not to obey the 11th commandment of censorship in such a way that, by acquiescing to the signifying power of the "*y a de l'Un*," he will have the stunning experience of a subjective dispossession? Uprooting him from the repetition of the same, dispossession will brutally bring him back to square one, to the absolute point of origin of primal repression where it is no longer a question

*Chapter Three – The Question of the Stunning Commandment*

of repeating the identical—for, at this point, there is no model—but rather a question of *recommencing* differently.[228]

If it is possible to recommence differently, it is because, by the very fact of being stunned, the ego is suddenly stripped of its negating activity by virtue of which it was able to claim: "The Other, the signifier, does not know where I am!" This gives the ego the illusion of mastery, which leads him to believe that he actually is in the place where he is hiding from the gaze of the Other. Insofar as the hiding place is sufficiently consistent—for example, by virtue of titles or social emblems—the ego can claim to know where it is, where its speech is, and where its body is.

But what happens if the question of the Other reaches this ego that is so well-hidden? What does Adam, for example, discover when, hidden behind his fig tree, he hears the stunning question: "Where are you?"[229] Two things: the first is that in the eyes of the Other he is not as invisible as he thought; the second, much more troubling, consists of the fact that the Other asks him, "Where are you?," even though he can see him perfectly well. This second aspect of the question not only signifies to him that his negating activity is suddenly invalidated, but also that the existence of an Other place is supposed, one that is not topographical, but rather topological, from which he can reply by finding the words that are equal to the question.

What is the reason for Adam's anxiety at the very moment when he hears this question about the hidden place from which he could come into being? His anxiety is a result of the fact that the specular hiding place where he was hidden only derived its consistency from its negating ignorance: "Because I do not want to change, I do not want to know that the Other can suppose, beyond my ego, the existence of an Other subject; if the Other does not know where 'I' am, I may stay where I am hidden." The determination not to change is effective as long as the Other can be denied by saying: "He does not know where I am."

---

[228] J. Hassoun, "Le temps d'un avènement," *Che Vuoi?* 1 (1994): "Could there be a time in analysis, a virtual time... which is, as it were, suspended—something literally unheard of—during which the representation of what *is not* seems to come into being?... There is a stunning encounter that marks a veritable turning point in the subject's existence.... This passage could be represented by a signifier that attests to the repetition of an inaugural moment that is subject to a radical forgetting...."

[229] Genesis 3: 9.

*Chapter Three – The Question of the Stunning Commandment*

But if the Other, owing to his manifestation in the real, ceases to be deniable, becoming instead undeniable, undeniably *the one who knows where I am*, then, like Adam, I am uprooted from the hiding place of my ego and I suddenly no longer know where I am. My disorientation is thus both of a temporo-spatial and of an ethical order: I no longer know where good and evil lie (this is the question of the real); I no longer know where my body is insofar as it has become transparent under the gaze of the Other (this is the question of the imaginary); and I no longer know how to respond aptly to the Other (this is the question of the symbolic). In this moment of sideration, then, we are witnessing the unknotting of these three dimensions of the real, the symbolic, and the imaginary.

The way in which the real, symbolic, and imaginary are knotted will depend on the position I take in relation to my speech; will I change my discourse by articulating speech that has its source in this "Other place" supposed by the question: "Where are you apart from your denial?" Genesis teaches us that Adam will not change his discourse, will not leave behind the register of guilt and denial, because he is content to put the blame on his fellow creature: "She's the one who's guilty! That woman!"[230] In short, for Adam, it is as if there had been a moment of hesitation, of indecision, when he had been supposed by the Other to be capable of passing from one discourse to another discourse.

Why is it that when a subject is asked the question, "Where are you?," he is unable, at that particular moment, to deny the fact that he is supposable as a subject who can sustain himself with another discourse? How are we to understand the fact that this questioning commandment is undeniable, unquestionable?

Although experience teaches us that, in the aftermath, the subject may, like Adam, return to his position of denial, that still does not explain why, at the very moment of being stunned, the pleasure principle is paralyzed by a principle that is situated beyond it. This question brings me back to the following hypothesis: being stunned is the effect of the vocation of that originary voice, which, by questioning the subject ("*Che Vuoi?*," "Where are you?"), temporarily strips him of that in him which resists the transmission of the signifier. It is owing

---

[230] Genesis 3: 10.

to this temporary eclipse of the ego—which reveals the ascendancy of the beyond the pleasure principle over the pleasure principle—that the subject is reduced to a point zero (primal repression), where he is put in the position of being able to choose again: will he choose to assume the stunning signifier or will he choose, once again, to repress it, thereby exposing himself to the risk of falling under the yoke of the law of the superego?

On this point, we need to establish precisely what the difference is between the clinical experience of sideration, which refers to the ascendancy of the signifier, and that of the compulsion to repeat, which refers to the ascendancy of the traumatic real of which the gaze of the superego has taken possession. What, indeed, does the clinical experience of sideration teach us? It teaches us that the subject undergoes an experience of dispossession in which he loses not only the support of speech, but also the support of his image and of his own body.[231] If such a loss is comparable to what occurs repeatedly for him when, under the sway of the gaze of the superego, he loses his speech, his image, and his bodily mobility, it is not, however, identical to it. Whereas the subject who is fascinated by the gaze of the superego is reduced to the state of waste matter, abandoning himself to the law of gravity, showing his blushing face, or letting an absolute silence be heard, the subject who is stunned by the signifier is not a heavy body, but rather an immaterial body. He is not a blushing face, but rather, like Hamlet faced with the ghost, a pallid face. He is not silence that lets nothing be heard, but rather silence that lets the unheard-of be heard.

The dualism between the clinical experiences of fascination and of sideration is reminiscent of another dualism. The beyond of the pleasure principle simultaneously incarnates the principle that blindly determines a de-subjectification while eliciting quite another type of de-subjectification beyond everything that is determined. The difference between these two states consists in the fact that, under the gaze of the superego, the subject is objectivized, since he is stripped of any lack, whereas the stunned subject is taken back to a state of absolute subjectification, for he "is," then, pure lack. That he can, in the present, be absolute lack (colorless, weightless, speechless) is due to the fact that he is *no longer* related to lack, that he is no longer

---

[231] See further on, "Primal Repression as an Originary Metaphorical Pact," 288ff.

## Chapter Three – The Question of the Stunning Commandment

determined by desire, and that, consequently, he is reduced to a state of indetermination pre-existing the time of unconscious choice. In order to have any kind of relation to the missing object—the cause of desire—the subject must be divided between two signifiers that introduce him to the half-saying of truth. At the level of the signifier $S_1$, he appears as meaning, whereas at the level of the signifying Other—a binary signifier—"he is manifested as *fading*, as disappearance."[232] This disappearance of meaning is linked to the fact that the binary signifier $S_2$ "constitutes the central point of the *Urverdrängung*," the point at which, in the enigmatic time of primal repression, the significance has fallen.[233]

The subject is desiring because, owing to the very fact of his division between $S_1$ and $S_2$, he *has* a causal relation with the fall of meaning that is incarnated by the signifier $S_2$ and symbolized by the object *a*. However, the stunned subject loses his causal relation to lack because, as he ceases to *represent* through the intermediary of $S_1$, the binary signifier of absolute lack, he *presents* this lack. He incarnates, then, that prehistoric time when he was only one signifier: the signifier of primal repression.

Sideration may thus be considered an event of temporal regression in which the subject again comes into contact, fleetingly, with "that moment when the subject as X only constitutes himself from the *Urverdrängung*, from the necessary fall of this first signifier."[234] But if he constitutes himself around the *Urverdrängung*, he cannot, as Lacan points out, "substitute anything for it as such—since this would require the representation of one signifier for another, whereas here there is only one, the first."[235]

What I call desideration is thus the humanizing act whereby, in this period of latency between sideration and illumination, the subject will not subsist at the level of a single signifier insofar as he conquers his division between two signifiers. By finding the signifier $S_1$, he finds

---

[232] Jacques Lacan, *The Four Fundamental Concepts.*, *op. cit.*, 218.

[233] *Ibid.*, The writing of the S2 can lead to confusion given that Lacan sometimes uses this acronym to designate unconscious knowledge (that is to say, the symbolic) and sometimes the primal repressed (that is to say, the real). I suppose that, if Lacan used the same letter to designate the real and the symbolic, it was because he was concerned to render their intersecting relationship (the real hole in the symbolic) transmissible.

[234] *Ibid.*

[235] *Ibid.*, 251.

## Chapter Three – The Question of the Stunning Commandment

the signifying light, which, by representing him to the signifier of the lack $S_2$, distances him from this lack. Ceasing, from thereon, to *be* the lack, he will not cease to *have* a relation to the lack, which will institute him as desiring, as liberated from the state of sideration. As long as he lives in desire, the subject will be able to ignore the fact that his desire is the effect of a primal fall of meaning. He will be reminded of the fact that this fall is procreative of a real causing his desire each time he is stunned. Each time he is brought back to the absolute point of origin of primal repression, he will be led to commemorate the fact that absolute subjectivity can—without yet being so—be oriented by desire. It is this absolute subjectivity, which Lacan writes as "S," "where it is," that must become a relativized subjectivity between two signifiers.[236]

One of the theoretical difficulties we are faced with is this: in the dialectic of the symbolic and the real, of meaning and no meaning, where is the precedence? Commenting on Lacan's last formulations on foreclosure (such as, "The orientation of the real forecloses meaning, a foreclosure that is more radical than that of the Name-of-the-Father"),[237] Claude Rabant suggests that "foreclosure makes the very existence of meaning possible."[238] The hypothesis implied by this formulation is one of a *possible*, rather than a *necessary*, relation to meaning, of a possible primal choice with which primal subjectivity, which precedes the division of the subject, is faced.

This primal division is the effect of a "yes" and a "no" given to the symbolic, which Freud, in his text on negation, translates by two pairs of words expressing different significations: to the pair *"introjizieren-werfen,"* governed by the ego and the pleasure principle, he opposes the pair *"Bejahung-Austoßung,"* which are brought into play by the beyond the pleasure principle and the subject of the unconscious. That the "yes" to the signifier is only possible because the subject says "no" to it at the same time shows us that the subject's relation to speech excludes the possibility of saying "the" truth. By saying "no" (*Austoßung*) at the same time as "yes" (*Bejahung*), he can only say badly and say well *at the same time*. Being, thus, a being who simultaneously takes and breaks an oath, the subject is primordially confronted with the following choice: how can he, who has broken his

---

[236] Jacques Lacan, "The Freudian Thing," in *Écrits, op. cit.*, 347.
[237] Jacques Lacan, seminar of March 16, 1976, in *The Sinthome, op. cit.*
[238] C. Rabant, *Inventer le réel* (Paris: Denoël, 1984), 240.

oath by proceeding to an originary foreclosure of the commandment of speech ("Let speech be"), nonetheless sustain this commandment that he receives to become a "speaking being"? Can obedience to the Ten Commandments—which Lacan defines as a law without which speech could not exist—offer him a guarantee of respecting the originary commandment of speech?[239] No, and that is why the harrowing question raised by the stunning signifier is pertinent here: "Does the fact that you have not disobeyed the interdiction necessarily mean that you have obeyed the unwritten law of my saying?"

By virtue of the stunning commandment, the subject who is sent back to the originary time that precedes the time of the interdiction is thus put back into an originary position where, as the law is not there to tell him where good and evil lie, he has to make an act of discrimination between good and evil that must be understood as an authentic creation on his part; for, in this situation of being stunned, there is no ready-made thought available to orient him ethically. In this respect, it is not exceptional to meet a subject who is oriented in his life by an ideology that militantly tells him where good and evil lie, but who may then suddenly be disoriented by a stunning event that violently dispossesses him of his ideological bearings.

## C) THE FALL OF THE SIGNIFIER OF THE NAME-OF-THE-FATHER INTO THE REAL: *AUSSTOßUNG, VERWERFUNG, WERFEN,* AND *VERBLÜFFUNG*

While Freud did not isolate, as Lacan did, the role of the signifier of the Name-of-the-Father in triggering psychosis, we discover that through the three canonical books in which the unconscious was revealed to him in its inaugurating freshness, he was led, in fact, to recognize—though under different names between which he did not necessarily make a connection—the different manifestations of what Lacan would call the signifier of the Name-of-the-Father.

It is as though Lacan had been led to name this signifier by identifying in psychosis the effects of its deficiency, and as if Freud, who for his part was led to identify the different names by which this signifier

---

[239] Jacques Lacan, *The Ethics of Psychoanalysis, op. cit.*, 68–69.

*Chapter Three – The Question of the Stunning Commandment*

can act concretely (signifier of the *Verblüffung*, signifier of debt, signifier that is the source of dreams, signifier of high psychical importance, *dritte Person*), had not succeeded in naming it as such because he had failed to grasp the oneness behind its diversity of metaphorical actions.

We will try to grasp later on the subjective reason for which Freud was unable to conceptualize the psychosis of Schreber in the light of what he had implicitly discovered in his first books.

In fact, Freud's difficulty in articulating the manifestation of the symbolic father in neurosis and in psychosis is symptomatic of his fluctuating position towards the real: these fluctuations, which I will comment on at a later point, are revealed by the fact that he uses at least four different terms to refer to the notion of the fall of a representation into the real: *Ausstoßung*, *Verwerfung*, *werfen*, and *Verblüffung*.

### III. An Attempted Translation of the Stunning Commandment

This attempted translation faces us with an almost impossible task, for, as we know, the effect produced by this signifier defies comprehension by exceeding any signified; it leads us to the risk of erasing the specific efficacy of this signifier, since, just as the oral law takes charge of what the written law cannot say, the stunning signifier takes charge of what is un-inscribable. In this respect, it is to be feared that the translation of the stunning signifier only fulfills its vocation by acting preventatively against this sideration. In truth, there is no definitive vaccination that permits its preventative repression.

If the subject wants to avoid being *verblüfft*, each time he will have to find an idea that allows repression to forget the stunning signifier. This work of repression will have to be repeated each time this signifier insists again; for, unlike sexual repression, which can act once and for all, the repression of the stunning signifier does not act once and for all. It has to be repeated because its institution cannot prevent the stunning signifier from insisting, from making its call heard again and again (*encore et encore*).[240]

---

[240] Jacques Lacan, *Encore, op. cit.*, 4: "Again (*Encore*), is the proper name of this gap, in the Other, from which comes the demand of love."

## Chapter Three – The Question of the Stunning Commandment

One of the fundamental tasks of psychoanalysis is to enable the subject to save the effort he puts into repressing the "signifier of high psychical importance." In this respect, it builds on the gigantic act whereby Freud, having done everything to repress the voice of the signifier that he did not want to hear, succeeded in returning to himself so that he could finally hear and assent to his vocation. By virtue of this return, Freud ceased to displace the question raised by the signifier "source of the dream" and assumed the new place, which was foundational for psychoanalysis, where he agreed to be stunned by the a-semantic message of which I am going to try to give a *partial* translation, given that it is untranslatable.

The translation with which I propose to render signifiable this reminder of a transcendent significance unfolds in three directions:

1) "What is your debt?"
2) "Where are you?"
3) "That is not all you are!"


A) WHAT IS YOUR DEBT?

*a) The Justness of the Question*

Speech allies the paradox of being at once something that has been given to me freely and of teaching me, by uprooting me from my innocence, that in fact this free gift has a price that I have to pay. This is where angst appears: it is a price that no instruction manual can tell me how to pay. If I knew how to pay it, I would do so readily; but, as I do not know, I remain in a state of angst that I can only get out of in two ways. Either I manage to extricate myself from the extreme state of solitude I am in—owing to the fact that the Other has abandoned me by not telling me what I must do—by finding within myself the support that potentially enables me to authorize myself to produce a saying well, or I effect the sleight of hand that Freud called "displacement." I displace the meaning of the stunning question in giving it a completely different meaning by which I feign to be accused, when in fact I was only called into question.

Why am I able to derive benefit from this displacement? Because the fact of being accused implies an unjust accusation that leaves me with many more opportunities to respond than a question pertaining to what is given to me and that I recognize as just, especially if I do not know why I recognize its justness. That it is easier for me to speak when the purpose of my speaking is to say "no" to the injustice than to speak in order to say "yes" to justness resides in the fact that saying "no" to injustice, even if its is a praiseworthy moral act, is not the equivalent of saying "yes" to justice. Replying "yes" to what is just in the revelation of the symbolic debt by the stunning signifier implies being able to tolerate what I do not understand: the state of not-knowing I am in with regard to how to acquit myself of this debt.

This "yes" therefore implies resisting the temptation of substituting the possibility of tolerating this not-knowing with the possibility of acquitting myself of the debt by embarking on the path of guilt induced by the superego—a path on which I could cease to be ignorant of that of which I am guilty. Analytic experience teaches us in this respect that, in order to escape the question of not-knowing, the subject is all too ready to accept the fact that he is really accused, even though he does not know exactly what the charge is. It is not exceptional to see a subject commit a real mistake in order to be brought into relationship directly with the law that ceases to manifest itself as questioning and instead becomes purely sanctioning, stating clearly what the offence is and what price has to be paid for it.

These two types of law—questioning law and sanctioning law—never cease to manifest their antinomy throughout the course of a psychoanalytic treatment. If the analyst is not aware of the meaning of this, referring the signification of guilt back only to the oedipal fault-line—that is to say, to a fault-line linked to what actually occurred, in act or in fantasy—he exposes the analysand to a reductive relationship to guilt.

This reduction, which finds expression in forgetting the question posed by the stunning signifier, shifting the emphasis onto oedipal guilt alone, is translated by the fact that the analysand agrees to keep his symptoms. He has now "understood everything," all his misfortunes stem from his oedipal guilt and he cannot forgive himself for having wanted to put daddy in the tomb and mummy in bed.

## b) The Forgetting of the Question: Saying No to Injustice Rather than Yes to Justness; Paul of Tarsus

We have already had the opportunity of seeing how the process of repression of the "signifier of high psychical importance" revealed itself to Freud: this repression resulted in an ardent plea contesting his guilt. The subject of the unconscious, Freud, chose to displace the question of the symbolic debt posed by the "signifier of high psychical importance." Instead he employed a sleight of hand to place himself on the terrain of superego-induced guilt—that is to say, on the terrain of an accusation whose flagrant injustice could not fail to provoke in him feelings of legitimate indignation.

That the subject is able—precisely where he did not succeed in responding to the justness of the stunning question—to choose to respond by rebelling against the injustice of the law of the superego is a universal solution. The universality of this law, according to which man persuades himself that he has been brought into a relationship with justice because he says "no" to injustice, is perhaps one of the reasons that may account for the speedy universal repercussions that the message of Saint Paul had. How can one fail to be sensitive to the legitimate indignation that drives him to interpret the Biblical law as a prison, since it is "bringing me into captivity to the law of sin which is in my members"?[241] Who can deny that such a prisoner does not have the right, and even the duty, of rebelling in order to regain his spiritual freedom thus lost? Who would dispute the fact that a law depriving man of his inner freedom is fundamentally unjust?

But the problem is more complex than that, for the real question is the following: by being legitimately indignant, is Saint Paul really speaking to us of the Biblical law? Is it not the case that this suffocating law of which he speaks has become so for him because, without even realizing it, he has not paid the price that would have enabled him to receive the spirit of it through the letter? Is this letter of the law, deserted by the spirit, not the very effect of the repression that left Paul deserted by the spirit of the law?[242]

---

[241] Romans 7: 23.

[242] This desertion is the consequence, in my view, of the repression of the Biblical "fear" of God, which Lacan interprets as a subjective effect of the establishment of the quilting point between the letter and the Spirit (see 148).

If this is the subjective position of Paul, then what we discover in him is a mixture of lucidity and blindness. On the one hand, he is lucid: what free mind would not denounce a law that, depriving the subject of all his inner freedom, is no longer symbolic but rather governed by the superego? On the other hand, he is blind, because he does not recognize that "the" law he is referring to is not the law of the Bible, but rather what this law becomes when, deprived of its symbolic dimension—through which speech is supposed—it falls to the level of a law that is strictly under the domination of the superego and that imposes silence on the subject.

What Paul does not know when he denounces the injustice of the law of the superego is that the promotion of this injustice is the very effect of the movement whereby he abandons any attempt to recognize that the law is first and foremost given *for the just*. For him, in effect, the law is given *for delinquents*. From the point of view of a superego law, does he in fact have a solution other than that of decrying the injustice of the law and calling for the justice of a redeemer?[243] The fact that he has no other solution is an astonishing reversal for someone who was the pupil of Gamaliel, since Paul gives an interpretation of Biblical law that breaks radically with the tradition of the Pharisees, distinguishing the written law and the oral law. The necessity of this distinction was introduced in the Pharisean world owing to the increasing awareness of the reason why the written law cannot be read and applied without interpretation.

What would happen if there were no interpretation? Well, the law would be comparable to a rule in a game that it would suffice to obey, without having to interpret it, in order to know how to play each shot, in order to win the game that is life. Now, if life can be compared to a game of chess, they are not identical. A game is characterized by being able to designate without ambiguity who the winners and losers are. The contract established by the rules of the game between the subject and the Other harbors no secret, no shadowy zone. In this respect, the referee is there to make sure the rules of the game are respected unequivocally. The very fact that these rules are unequivocal implies that they can be applied by the player without his having

---

[243] Timothy 1: 9: "The law is not laid down for the just but for the lawless and disobedient, for the ungodly and sinners, for the unholy and profane, for those who strike their fathers and mothers, for murderers, fornicators, and sodomites...."

to interpret them. The tennis ball is either in the court or it is not; the discussion that this can lead to does not raise the question of interpretation. A sufficiently sophisticated machine will settle the matter in the case of a dispute.

If, on the other hand, a machine will never be able to determine if the life of a subject is a success or a failure, it is because the law to which he is subjected, from the moment he is linked by a contract with it, contains a shadowy zone, a point of ignorance. Moreover, this is what haunts the jurist when he says: "No one is supposed to be ignorant of the law." What happens when the referee of the game (be it football, tennis, or whatever) sanctions the transgression of a player? In general, the player gets angry, accusing the referee of having missed something, of having made a mistake. Now it is the exact opposite that occurs when the subject, under the gaze of the big, invisible, and silent arbiter that is the big Other, feels accused. Not only does he find that he is not in a position to accuse the Other of having made a mistake, but also, under this gaze, he feels and recognizes that he is deceitful. It is in discovering the dimension of a flouted truth that truth is brought into perspective for the subject owing to the emergence of guilt that teaches him about the existence of an extremely paradoxical pact with the law. It is as if he had forgotten the existence of this pact, which he has transgressed without realizing it. At the same time, it is as if this pact were in fact unforgettable, for, even though he does not know what it stipulates, he recognizes, owing to feelings of guilt, that he is not innocent in relation to it.

It is this point of inaccessibility that means that the law is not the rules of play. Would such a set of rules be what they are if they were not entirely thinkable and entirely accessible to the player? If they did not give him, simultaneously, both knowledge about the signification of the game to be played and knowledge about the way in which the player is in a position either to stay within the framework of the game or not? The law is therefore deficient compared with the rules of the game, for, quite apart from what it specifically prohibits, it is inhabited by a silence at the end of which it does not yield its definitive instruction manual, so that it does not give man the guarantee of knowing how to go about things in such a way that this game that is life is played in accordance with it. There is, in the law, a fundamental point of silence that teaches the Jewish man that, on this point, he is in a state of absolute solitude from which he can only emerge by venturing to speak precisely where the law remains silent, and to interpret it where it does not yield the key to its meaning.[244]

From this point of view, one can say that the Jewish conscience, unlike the Christian conscience, which thinks of creation as a triumph of the Word ("In the beginning was the Word"), never ceases to take into account the fact that the originary creation involves the appearance of an abyss and a formless void. That the silent abyss thus has precedence over the world of speech, which can at any instant founder if man does not take care of it, predisposes the Jewish man to what Buber called "Jewish holy insecurity." This is expressed, on the one hand, by the fact that the Jewish man has to tolerate the silence of the law and, on the other, by the further fact that, at the very moment he interprets this silence, he has no guarantee, once again, that his interpretation is sound.

But if the act of interpretation does not preclude fundamental insecurity, it produces, as a partial response to the stunning question posed by the silence of the law, a subjectifying effect on man, who, through the act of speech itself, defines himself as a subjectivity that *becomes* and is endowed with a possible future. This faith in becoming is perhaps the point at which the Freudian commandment, "Where id/ it was, become!," comes closest to Judaism and breaks with Pauline Christianity: indeed, for Paul, the symbolic law of speech, put at the disposal of man, cannot contribute to his salvation, since only the redemptive Son can save him from original sin.[245]

The first consequence that a Christian conscience infers from the fact that, without Jesus, man is unable to accomplish this return to God is as follows: a man who is saved by receiving the grace of God through Christ is no longer in the holy insecurity that weaves Jewish subjectivity. But something dreadful takes the place of this insecurity, namely, endless guilt. The fact that this guilt is attributed to original sin prevents it from being attributed to its true cause, to the fact that the subject is unable to forgive himself for having given up the idea of responding to the stunning commandment that still faces him, even

---

[244] Armand Abéccassis (unpublished lecture, December 4, 1995): "In a Jewish family, the father must have the *courage* [my italics] to interpret the law so that it can be assumed by the child."

[245] On the production of the French verb "*s'être*," expressing the mode of absolute subjectivity, see Jacques Lacan, "The Freudian Thing," in *Écrits, op. cit.*, 347.

though he has repressed it, with an unsettling question. "By claiming that the sin that is in you is devoid of any possible becoming, are you not trying to avoid the stunning terror of the infinite symbolic possibility that, as you know, is at your disposal to help you evolve towards something other than original sin?"

This is how Paul, *by seeking to avoid insecurity*, encounters inexpiable guilt: by substituting man's aptitude for becoming indignant about the injustice of the written law for man's aptitude to be stunned by the accuracy of a question that requires an infinitely interpretative act of creation.[246] He confines man within the prison of the superego and *shuts the door* that, for a moment, had been opened by the stunning signifying call.[247]

*c) The Quarrel with the Law*

How was it possible for Pauline doctrine to take over what is universal in guilt? The reason is that this doctrine makes it possible to rationalize, by giving it a name, the guilt experienced by man when he agrees to obey the 11th commandment of censorship: "Don't let yourself be stunned!" The most patent expression of this guilt is the rage Paul expresses against the injustice of the law. Forgetful of the fact that since he flouted it this law has become persecuting, superegoistic, he is constantly quarrelling with it.

What is a domestic scene? This scene has the privilege of portraying two plaintiffs, each of them reproaching the other in a manner whose fundamental monotony, owing to its very repetition, reveals to us the existence of immutable suffering governed by the sway of the persecutory law. The partner of each of the protagonists is designated here as the bearer of a law that one cannot trust or have faith in,

---

[246] Marc-Alain Ouaknin, returning to the Talmudic commentaries in *Lire aux éclats* (Paris: Lieu commun, 1989), 83–84, helps us to understand how Abraham is not deaf to the stunning call that he receives from the Other when, for example, he hears the following words uttered on the subject of his descendance: "This man will not be your heir, but he that shall 'come forth out of thine own bowels' will be your heir" (Genesis 15: 4). Insofar as *mea*—the bowels—comes from the word *ma*, which signifies "what?," Abraham receives the following stunning message: "You will have a child, the fruit of your questioning."

[247] Christian guilt, in my view, stems from the fact that the Christian cannot forgive himself for having shut this door again, like Paul.

## Chapter Three – The Question of the Stunning Commandment

inasmuch as he is apprehended fundamentally as being "of bad faith." The context in which I am led to reproach the other for his bad faith is always, in one way or another, one of debt: this reproach is generally the way in which I reply to the other person when he or she reproaches me for not recognizing the debt that I have towards him: "I've had enough; I am doing all the housework, cleaning the kitchen, while you are reading the paper!"

The response to this accusation is generally one of accusing, in turn, the accuser of bad faith: "What? I work like a maniac from morning to evening to bring home money for us to live on, and I'm not allowed to read the paper?"

Why does this dialogue of the deaf inevitably go round in circles? Because its interruption will not be achieved by an act of speech containing something unexpected, but by an act of speech containing an expected violence. If the two partners of the domestic quarrel are caught in this vicious circle, it is because the type of discourse they are engaged in leaves no opportunity for astonishment to appear. Actually, the obscene speech of the domestic quarrel does not only lose its surprising power. On the contrary, it also conveys the least surprising message there can be, namely, one that I was expecting and anticipating: "Not only do I think that you are a bastard, but I also think that you think that yourself: I think that you think that I think that you think that."

Here we are touching on the fundamental nature of the prison in which one can be confined by guilt: it is a prison I cannot hope to escape from, for the law in the name of which I am, on this point, guilty, is a law that deprives me of the possibility of appealing; whatever I say, in this context, will be rejected. What does this bad faith of the two plaintiffs consist in? In what respect do they no longer have faith? In *Totem and Taboo*, Freud gives this very apt definition of moral conscience: "To put forward any reason for this [condemnation] would seem superfluous: anyone who has a conscience must feel within him the justification for the condemnation...."[248] The guilt that this quarrel arouses is based on justifying a law even though it does not need justifying. So in attacking the law of the other who accuses me of being guilty, by accusing them of being in bad faith, I only get more tangled

---

[248] Sigmund Freud, *Totem and Taboo, op. cit.*, 68.

up, since I am the one who justifies this law—without knowing why—and accepts that it does not need to justify its condemnation.

The paradox is as follows:

1) I am accused by this law in a manner that I feel is unjust.

2) But this injustice does not need to be justified. So, when I plead not guilty, I am in denial. I pretend to rebel against an unjust accusation that, in fact, I accept unconsciously. In doing so, I am like Freud when he pleads not guilty, affirming that he is no longer indebted to his father since he has had the merit of participating in the discovery of cocaine. We have seen that the very fact that he pleads not guilty, even though the question that was put to him was not related to guilt, showed that the subject preferred to choose the path of guilt rather than encounter the signifier of alterity.

We are touching on the first distinction that I am establishing between the metaphoric commandment and the superegoistic one. While the first asks, without judging, "Are you justified in your speech?," the second emits a judgment that does not question, but accuses: "There's no justification for you to speak." The first commandment, which the subject considers to be just—without knowing why—implies that this subject has a choice in how he responds. Will he accept a question that does not judge him? It is a terrible choice; for, if he accepts, he will be immediately confronted with the terrifying abyss of the question of his freedom.

How are we to understand the irrepressible tendency that drives certain subjects to feel they are constantly being judged in an essentially negative and unjust manner? Should it be seen as an attempt to escape anxiety? By renouncing this inner freedom, the subject is then led to fight for his freedom, except that it is no longer the same freedom. He will fight against the superegoistic judge who deprives him of his freedom by rebelling against his unjust judgment. In so doing, he will be led to cry out against the injustice of a master that he has himself instated and will demand the freedom that he did not want when he had the opportunity of taking it.

It is against his own choice of a law that does not ask him to choose, but to obey, that the subject rebels: this rebellion is justified, for, at the moment when the subject chose this path, he abdicated his possibility of choosing the law of alterity that the arbiter in him had at his disposal. Owing to this abdication, which introduced him to the prison of guilt, the subject is infuriated with himself without realizing

## Chapter Three – The Question of the Stunning Commandment

it. In his attempt to get out of this prison, he hates the law that he has given himself, not realizing that the more he rebels against it the more he gives it consistency. His rebellion has the effect of *reinforcing the forgetting* of the act whereby he chose the commandment of the superego in order to avoid subjecting himself to the metaphorical commandment of the stunning signifier.

The impossibility of overcoming guilt is inextricably linked to the subject's incapacity to deliberate when he agrees to receive the commandment of the superego: the immediateness of his response to the superego manifests itself, for example, in his instantaneous blushing under the gaze of the master that is the superego. This instantaneity stands in radical contrast to the non-instantaneity of the response of the one who is stunned by the commandment of the stunning signifier.

This time of sideration is a *time that is proper to the subject*. When he shows that he is *capable of not responding instantaneously* to the commandment received, the inner arbiter intervenes. The inner arbiter, who has the freedom to say "no" to the stunning signifier by repressing it, or to say "yes" to it.

Things are quite different with the commandment of the superego where there is *no such period of latency* in which the subject can deliberate between the "yes" and the "no": his obedience to the superego is not really obedience, but rather the impossibility of disobeying. The example of blushing manifests this impossible disobedience. The fact that I blush shows that I accept immediately, without *deliberating*, the sanction that says I am guilty. By blushing, I do more than confess to a mistake whose meaning I do not understand. I show, with my flesh, that I agree to subject myself to a law that sanctions me, for I have abandoned the idea of making an appeal before the tribunal of the symbolic. If, in this respect, the domestic quarrel is a vicious scenario, it is because neither of the two protagonists is able any longer to incarnate for the other the symbolic Other to whom it would have been possible to appeal. The obscene verbal exchanges of the domestic quarrel are, from this point of view, as unacceptable as the breast for the anorexic child. He cannot accept milk, which is a vehicle of so much guilt: "What I want," says the anorexic to her mother, "is not your milk, but a way of giving it to myself."

Is this gratuity of the gift not what is brought into play in witticisms? Why does someone who listens to a witticism laugh so joyously?

## Chapter Three – The Question of the Stunning Commandment

Because the gift of the signifier that is made to him is doubly gratuitous. On the one hand, someone who makes the gift of a witticism does not obey a law of the superego prescribing a gift; and, on the other, someone who receives a witticism receives the signifying gift without any obligation in return. Moreover, it is because he accepts it freely—that is to say, neither as a courtesan nor as a partisan—that it is an authentic gift by which the receiver is raised to the level of this "third" person, of this *dritte Person* who alone has the power of authenticating the witticism. In this regard, we need have no hesitation in saying that the newborn baby accepts the maternal milk all the better in that it is given like a witticism: what he incorporates first and foremost through this milk is the presence of this symbolic third that is the *dritte Person*.

That the domestic quarrel dramatizes the behavior of two anorexics in this way helps us to understand the meaning of the accusation of "bad faith" that each of them makes of the other. My bad faith signifies that, in fact, I have lost faith in the existence of the *dritte Person*, of that absolute and incomprehensible alterity, which, when it can be recognized in my fellow creature, confers on him that alterity that uproots him from proximity. By recognizing that, although he is my fellow creature, he is at the same time inhabited by a dimension that is too distant to be my specular semblance, I discover that, not knowing him as much as I thought I did, I am led to detect in the other the surprising presence of the stunning signifier in relation to which I accept to be in debt, except that this recognition of debt requires something utterly different than my guilt: it *obliges me freely*.

Therein lies the paradox of the metaphorical commandment: it is because I recognize its character as a free gift that I am freely obligated towards the stunning signifier. It is the freedom of this obligation that makes me recognize, paradoxically, that there exists a symbolic debt in relation to which I am not free. This recognition is identical to that which the auditor of a witticism is obliged to feel for the author of this witticism, and to that which the analysand may feel for the analyst provided the latter has known how to be the mediator of the stunning signifier. By virtue of the intervention of this signifier, the subject can reconsider his choice of symptom and choose differently: he can choose to no longer accept being accused at the level of his guilt, instead agreeing, this time, to be called into question by the *stunning* signifier. He will be able to give this assent if he has sufficient trust in the analyst to allow him or her to be a witness to the anxiety he is preparing to face at the moment when he renounces a law that says to him: "You are guilty," adopting instead one that says, "You are not innocent."

The big difference between these two commandments is that the first sends the subject back to an interdiction that he has already transgressed, whereas the second sends him back not to an interdiction, but to a saying, to a prescription confronting him not with what he has already done, even if it was in a dream, but with what he has not yet done. If we have so much difficulty in translating such a metaphorical commandment with words, it is because it is uninscribable. As a result, it puts the legislator in the position of being unable to make a written law of it that, by giving the subject the possibility of obeying, could vouch for the fact that the subject, through his obedience, is innocent.

Nonetheless, we will try to translate in the following partial way the meaning of the question of the symbolic debt that the stunning commandment transmits: "You who chose, when I questioned you about your debt, to turn away from my commandment and to turn instead towards guilt, know that you can make a different choice: you can renounce superego-induced guilt by returning to your symbolic duty."

B) "WHERE ARE YOU?"

*a) The Revelation of the "Where"*

*1. Adam*

The first aspect of the stunning question, "In what respect are you justified in speaking?," contains a second question concerning the place from which speech must come so that it can be received by the subject not as a semblance, but legitimately as his own. This question, "Where are you?," is the first question that, in a state of sideration, the first man receives from God, and it introduces us to the signification of the difference between the two types of guilt that can

## Chapter Three – The Question of the Stunning Commandment

take hold of man. Is Adam guilty towards the tree of the knowledge of good and evil for what he did and should not have done, or is he guilty towards the tree of life in relation to what he did not do, but should have done?

Why is Adam disoriented and anguished by the question God suddenly puts to him, "Where are you?" Because, thinking that he knew "where" he was, he learns that he is not where he could be. Whereas he thought he was where he had hidden, behind his fig tree, he discovers in anguish two things: on the one hand, that this hiding place is not in fact one under God's gaze and, on the other, that in spite of the gaze that tells him, "I know where you are," God still asks him, "Where are you?" This question leads him to understand the error he has made. While he thought he had escaped guilt by hiding silently in a place where he thought he was invisible, God calls into question the structure of this "where" by addressing a double message to him: "I am not asking you where you are hidden; I am asking you 'where you are' when you think that you are hidden. By seeing you, I am indicating to you that the place 'where' you think you are hidden is not a place where you are incognito. By speaking to you, by asking you '*where* you are,' 'where you are with me,' I am letting you know that there exists in you a point of freedom, even though I still do not know 'where' it will engage you. Though I know, by looking, where the specular, topographical hiding place where you are hiding is, I do not know—since I am asking you the question, 'Where are you?'—'where' the metaphorical place is, which only you can find by yourself, from which you can answer me without fleeing."

This exegesis of these verses means that God supposes that there exists a place of which he knows nothing from which the speech of Adam can be born. How is it possible, for the omniscience of the one who knows everything, that there exists a place of which he knows nothing?

It is to this formidable question that the hypothesis of the subject of the unconscious replies: the Other knows nothing of the subject of the unconscious insofar as the subject, because he is unconscious of himself and does not know that he exists, offers no hold for knowledge. Where mastery through knowledge is impossible, two antinomical positions exist for apprehending the subject of the unconscious: the first is that of the Other who, owing to the fact that he is not omniscient—that he is, as Lacan writes, a barred A—is put in the position of

### Chapter Three – The Question of the Stunning Commandment

supposing what he does not know.[249] The question "Where are you?" transmits such a supposition for, if it indicates to Adam that the Other knows where his specular hiding place is, it tells him at the same time that the Other supposes that there exists a non-specular "where," where Adam could be hidden in quite a different way.

The second position is that of the ego: it is expressed by a will not to recognize the existence of the subject of the unconscious. The strategy of this misrecognition is as follows: whereas the Other addresses the subject by asking him, "Where are you?," it is the ego that answers for the subject by hiding, as in the game of hide-and-seek, and obeying the logic of negation: "The Other does not know where I am." What the ego wants to remain ignorant of, by using this strategy, is that in hiding from the gaze of the Other it is hiding from itself the fact that there exists a thing [*das Ding*] that it does not need to hide in order for it to be hidden. That the Other does not know where I am gives the ego the illusion of mastery whereby it believes it is actually "there" where it is hiding from view. Insofar as the hiding place is sufficiently consistent—for example, behind titles or social emblems—the ego can pretend to know where it is.

But what happens if the question of the Other, "Where are you, you who are so visible behind your tree?," reaches this ego that is so well hidden? This question lets him know not only that his activity of denial is suddenly null and void, but also that the existence of another place is supposed, topological rather than topographical, to which he could hope to gain access.

Why is Adam so anxious when he is asked this question about the hidden place to which he could gain access? Because the specular hiding place where he was dissimulated only derived its consistency from his denying misrecognition: "It is because the Other does not know 'where' I am that I can stay where I am hidden." But when the Other, by manifesting himself in the real, ceases to be deniable and, undeniably, becomes instead the one who knows where I am, then I am uprooted from the hiding place of my ego and suddenly no longer know where I am, for I have not gained access to the place where I am called to be.

---

[249] [Rather than translate "barred A" as "barred O" (A derived from *Autre*; O from Other), we opted to retain Ⱥ, since Lacan utilized it, as well as others, as mathematical symbols.]

## Chapter Three – The Question of the Stunning Commandment

The disorientation that then takes hold of me is the very manifestation of what we have identified as the state of sideration that is as much of a temporal-spatial as of an ethical order. I no longer know where good and evil lie (this is the question of the real); I no longer know where my body is insofar as it has become transparent under the gaze of the Other (this is the question of the imaginary); and I am no longer able to reply to the Other (this is the question of the symbolic).

At the very moment when the ego loses its hiding place, by losing its faculty for denial, the question of the Other, "Where are you?," acquires its truly stunning signification: "It is now that you have given up hiding in a hiding place that was at your disposal that you are able to recognize that there is something radically hidden in you that does not need to hide itself to be secret, since it does not even know itself that it is hidden from itself. It is only now that you have lost the false secret that was at your disposal, only now that you think that you have lost everything by losing it, that you can discover that deep down within you there is 'that': the true secret at whose disposal you are."

If we want to define what the structure of this "false secret" corresponds to, we have to explain what this secret is. It is structured by the interlocking of a triple misrecognition: that of the ego, that of secondary repression, and that of primal repression. The misrecognition of the "Es" [id], which, owing to primal repression, does not know itself, is increased by the unconscious misrecognition of secondary repression and the conscious misrecognition of denial in such a way that we can formulate the false secret in the following way: "I don't know that I am hiding the fact that it is hidden."

The reordering brought about by the state of sideration stems from the fact that, in the aftermath of the fall of denial, a new articulation appears in which the true secret that is *das Ding* is revealed: "I cease not to know that I was hiding the fact that it is hidden."[250] This revelation is the act whereby, when all the veils have fallen, an ultimate veil, that of nudity, both physical and psychical, appears as that which is constantly re-veiling itself. When the veil that is the piece of clothing falls, revealing the underwear that is the *cache-sexe*, the subject is at the threshold of the radical veil that is nudity, whose most profound

---

[250] Jacques Lacan, *The Ethics of Psychoanalysis, op. cit.*, 46: "What one finds in *das Ding* is the true secret."

*Chapter Three – The Question of the Stunning Commandment*

meaning is to reveal an absolute secret in the face of which the knowledge of the subject discovers its absolute deficiency.

Lacan speaks of this deficiency in the following way: it is what makes it possible to "specify the human being as being, not the masterpiece of Creation, the awakening point of knowledge, but, on the contrary, the seat of an *Unerkennung*, not only a non-recognition, but an impossibility of knowing what has to do with sex."[251]

## 2. Music

We should have no hesitation in saying that the vocation of a subject is linked to the way he responds to the voice that asks him: "Where are you?" This voice is not necessarily stunning; though it follows the path of music, it turns out that the baring of the "true secret" can occur without angst being present.

What happens to you when you hear a piece of music that touches you? What is the magic with which this other message has the power of inducing in you a metamorphosis? Initially, you have the feeling, as a listener, that you are listening to music. But inasmuch as you are, as we say, "touched" by it, you discover that it is not you who is listening but that it is the music that hears you, that hears a presence whose existence you had forgotten, and that, by virtue of being heard, starts to live again and to be given to you. If this presence is "given" to you, it is because you cannot give it to yourself: it is not at your disposal. It is at the sovereign disposal of the Other, who is the only one who is able to free it from its retreat and to deliver it to you by revealing it to you. Each time it occurs this revelation is astonishing, for you cannot get used to this presence: it is, *par excellence*, the thing that can only be received in a state of surprise. Why does this surprise dispense joy? Because it has the power to dissipate the doubt that you had about your existence.

If, when hearing music, we cease to respond to the doubt about our existence by saying to ourselves, "*Cogito, ergo sum*," it is because this "*sum*" revealed by music is no longer in doubt. Why is that? Because the subject has found the possibility of the faith to which La-

---

[251] Lacan's reply to a question by M. Ritter, June 26, 1975, *Lettres de l'école freudienne* 18 (April 1976), 11.

can refers in the seminar on ethics.²⁵² Lacan also remarked that Freud himself had observed that it was impossible for the paranoiac. But the question immediately arises: What are we to do with this existence once it has been revealed to us? In effect, this existence revealed by the Other is not self-sustaining for, as it is inhabited by traumatic experience, it continues to contain a deficiency exposing it to the risk of its own disappearance.

How can one pass from this deficiency of the Thing to its possible efficiency? How can the subject receive the gift of the existence of the Freudian Thing in spite of the fact that he cannot make use of it and that his knowledge gives him no control over it? Can he only recall the astonishment caused by the "blue note" and trust in what this astonishment has given him a glimpse of? What is this faith? From a certain point of view it is an act of faith in the recognition of an identity between the existence of the Thing revealed and the existence of the music that revealed it. This identity is enigmatic: it does not correspond to any of the three identifications designated by Freud. It is a metaphorical identification between the synchronic structure of the subject—revealed by the blue note—and its diachronic structure revealed by the rhythm of the melody. This affinity between the intimate nature of the timeless structure and external temporal diachrony corresponds to an "ex-time": the notes of the diachronic melody represent the subject in relation to the timeless dwelling place that is the Freudian Thing—*das Ding*—insofar as the "blue note" can make it fleetingly resonate.²⁵³

From where does this thing get its property of being at once *that which music causes* to sound and *that which makes* music sound? And why does this sound make us hear something that is no longer the A flat that is being played but a sound that its signification transcends? Because the place that is made to resonate by the music, by the interposition of the unthinkable conjunction between the temporal and the timeless, between the rhythm and the blue note, produces the commemoration of a place that is literally unheard-of, a place to which the Other, owing to primal repression, withdrew into a silence from which he escapes any possibility of hearing.

---

[252] Jacques Lacan, *The Ethics of Psychoanalysis, op. cit.*, 54.
[253] *Ibid.*, 101.

*Chapter Three – The Question of the Stunning Commandment*

Before music made it resonate, what was this place like? It was abandoned to its radical destiny of being forgotten, waiting to be delivered from the absolute subjectivity of the "there where it was" by the aptness of a note providing the key to its deliverance. The gift of the artist, which permits him or her to give us this key, reminds us of an ethical duty: must we not, for our own sakes, find the word that will give us the access key to this other signifier before which we have to represent ourselves? This ethical reminder that we receive from the artist takes us back to the call of the stunning commandment insofar as the artist shows us that he is the one who has been able to answer the question of the symbolic debt. The moment when he found the right note, the blue note that makes the "ex-time" sound, was the moment when he succeeded in no longer displacing the stunning question by finding the exact place from which to answer it in the light of the discovery of a *saying well*. The subject is called upon to make this discovery by this commandment: "The forgotten part that is in you has already been created by an author who is not you. You, you must be the second author who can 'authorize himself' to give insistence to what the first author brought into existence."

*b) The Forgetting of the "Where Are You?"*

*1. Witticism or Slip of the Tongue?: The Question of Shame*

Freud remarks that one cannot make a witticism with just anyone; for the witticism to come off, one has to belong to the same parish. How is this parishioner who has the capacity to evoke the presence of wit in me to be defined?

The clinical example of Robert puts us on the right track: if a woman can have stunning power over a man, it is because the man is led to hear in the silence of this woman the force of the silent question that he hears being put to him: "Where are you?" Why does a woman expect a man to prove himself to be a man of wit? Because she expects him to be in a position to reply to her question by telling a joke that reveals that he knows where he is, where the cause of his desire is.

But why is the slip of the tongue, which is also the admission of a hidden desire, nevertheless not a witticism? An important point, one that Freud overlooked, helps us to answer this question: when

## Chapter Three – The Question of the Stunning Commandment

the witticism has been authenticated by the laughter of the listener, it puts the author of the witticism in the position of being able to laugh in turn, responding with his own laughter to the listener's. But there is nothing of the sort in the slip of the tongue; the author of the slip of the tongue is not led to laugh with the listener, for he is gripped by a very particular sense of shame. Is the signification of this shame linked to the fact that the subject has revealed his desire? No; is not such a revelation precisely what the witticism achieves?

The difference is that, in the witticism, the subject reveals "himself" whereas, in the slip of the tongue, he "is" revealed. If in the witticism the subject agrees to let it be understood "where" he is, in the slip of the tongue he does not allow himself to show where he is. In spite of himself, he shows "where" he is by blushing, thereby addressing himself not to an ear that might be able to hear him, but rather to a gaze for which his blushing is destined.

If we want to interpret the shame encountered in the slip of the tongue, we must understand what happens in the moment of unconscious deliberation when the subject is stunned. If there is deliberation it means that the subject is in a position to answer "yes" or to answer "no" to the stunning commandment that asks him: "Where are you?" My hypothesis is that, if he accepts the question, if he agrees to make a *Bejahung*, an affirmation, of it, he then puts himself in a position to be able to overcome his state of sideration and to encounter the cause of his desire. If, conversely, he denies the existence of the stunning signifier, if he acts, for example, like Freud, who chooses, initially, to repress the signifier *"Herr,"* he creates a situation where the stunning signifier ceases, insofar as it is repressed, to be a questioning presence and becomes instead a gazing presence.[254] Just as Freud remains, without knowing it, under the gaze of the *"Herr,"* even though he thinks he has escaped it by switching the discussion to the subject of Italian painting, the subject remains, without realizing it, under the gaze of the Other. He only becomes aware of this gaze when he makes a slip of the tongue, when his blushing reveals that his speech no longer has any hope of finding the supposing listening of an Other, since it is already addressed to the de-supposing gaze of a superegoistic Other.

---

[254] Sigmund Freud, *The Psychopathology of Everyday Life, op. cit.*, 3–4.

## Chapter Three – The Question of the Stunning Commandment

The de-supposing efficacy of the gaze is translated by the fact that the one who is being looked at does not have this deliberating possibility that manifests itself in the moment of sideration: insofar as he is not stunned, but fascinated, the subject who feels ashamed under the gaze replies instantaneously, without any deliberation, by blushing. But what is he ashamed of? Why, at the very moment when he blushes, is he unmasked, in the manner of an impostor? And if he feels he has been unmasked, what had he been covering up without realizing it?

That is where the true enigma begins, for, the point is, he does not know. The only thing he knows is that he is led to interpret this masking as the masking of a lie, but which lie? The paradox is as follows: whereas the fact of confessing a lie implies an admission of the truth, the subject who blushes painfully discovers that it is not because he has confessed to lying that he admits the truth. Why? Because the truth requires to be said, whereas blushing is a silent act that does not require a listener but rather a gaze. If, at the moment of speaking, I blush, I am seized by shame because I realize that I am doing something quite different from confessing: I am disavowing myself. By the very fact of silently showing my intimate color, I am disowning my possibility of demonstrating through speech that I am a "speaking being" [*parlêtre*], a being whose paradox is one of both being determined by speech and determining through his speech. That there is a realm in this "speaking being" beyond the one governed by the determinism of the pleasure principle signifies that the subject has the enigmatic capacity of a choice: the choice between the commandment of the superego that radically determines him and the symbolic commandment, which appeals to what remains undetermined in him, inasmuch as it is linked to the "beyond" of the pleasure principle. The shame of blushing is, in this respect, nothing other than the psychic pain induced in the subject by the fact of having disavowed himself: in choosing to obey the commandment of the superego, the subject knows that he has disavowed the possibility that the symbolic commandment supposed he had of authorizing himself not to be determined only by the superego.

The question that inevitably arises at this point is the following: If indeed such an unconscious choice exists, how are we to understand the subject's frequent preference for the solution of superego-based guilt? Insofar as the Other, immediately after having made himself heard through the voice of the stunning signifier, withdraws and falls back into the silence from which he had emerged, the subject remains radically alone with the question that has been put to him. Owing to this absence of the Other, the subject can no longer rely on him and falls back on the enigmatic "of himself" from which he is able to authorize himself when the authority of the Other has vanished. This eclipse of the symbolic Other may be contrasted with the gaze of the superego as a mode of presence, which, not knowing how to make itself absent, imposes itself with the persistence of an absolute authority. Beyond the psychic pain that accompanies the shame of blushing, there is also the encounter with a secondary benefit that the subject may be unwilling to give up. The fact that he suffers is compensated by the fact that his very shame puts him in contact with the alterity of a gaze whose persistence ensures him that it is indeed possible to have dealings with an Other who, at least, *will not let him down*, will not go absent. If there is something irremediable in masochism, it is that the subject may prefer the path of guilt that puts him in contact with an unbarred Other to that of the angst that arises when the Other, by absenting itself, commemorates the radical forgetting of primal repression.

The scandal introduced by the stunning signifier lies in the fact that it reveals to the stunned subject the existence of a symbolic law that is paradoxical: on the one hand, it has the power to remind the subject that he is indebted to it, but, on the other, it does not seem to have the power to tell the subject what he must do in order to acquit himself of this debt. What can we say about this symbolic law that does not provide any instructions on how it is to be used except that it is utterly different from the rules of a game? Would the rules of a game be what they are if they did not give the player both the means of knowing that the game he is playing is only possible because there is a basic set of rules and the knowledge that he can continue to play as long as he remains within the framework of the rules?

Such an assurance, as we have already seen, is provided by the existence of the umpire.[255] It is true that a mistake can be made: saying that the ball fell outside the limits of the court when the player saw that it was in. However, the essential point is that the umpire theoretically has the possibility of not making a mistake: eventually, the view

---

[255] See 185.

## Chapter Three – The Question of the Stunning Commandment

of a photoelectric cell could settle the matter and decide, scientifically, whether the ball was in or out.

That life is not a game like other games lies in the fact that it is governed by a law the exact formulation of which its agent, the subject, does not possess, any more than he possesses the instructions on how to use it. Is there no arbiter, then, who can tell the subject if the way he is playing the game that is his life is adequate or not in terms of the symbolic law?

Yes! This arbiter exists, but he manifests himself in a completely different way from that of the umpire of a tennis match. Whereas the player who has committed a fault is tempted to accuse the umpire, under whose gaze he stands, of having made a mistake, the subject who is under the gaze of that arbiter, the big Other, finds he is not in a position to accuse him of having made a mistake. As a subject who is being watched from a place that he cannot see, he himself feels, without understanding how or why, like a cheat who has been exposed. Why would he be such a cheat? Because, as he does not have the means of knowing, since the symbolic law has not given him its instruction manual, if the act with which he has inscribed himself in life corresponds to what this law expects of him, he is put in the position of being the defendant at a trial who knows neither what he is accused of nor what the verdict is. Is he guilty or not? He does not know; he only knows one thing, that he is under the gaze of an unusual examiner, for it is an examiner who demands a response without, however, being required to say if the examination has been passed or failed.

We sometimes hear an analysand translating into the following terms his transference onto the *stunning* signifier of which we, as analysts, are the transitory repository: "In the waiting room I was waiting for you anxiously. Why was I feeling anxious? Because you expect something of me and I don't know what it is: I don't know if I will be able to do what is required of me to pass this examination." In short, it is as if the subject, without having read Freud, was translating as follows the silent question that he assumed was being put to him by the examiner that the analyst sometimes is: "Where it was, have you become?"

Thus, without the subject knowing what this "speaking being" that he must become is, and without knowing how to bring this "speaking being" into existence, he nonetheless knows that he must make it exist because the simple question, "Have you become?," makes him tremble with angst.

## 2. The Conformist

What is conformism if not a subject's desperate attempt to subject his life to a set of rules that permits him to forget the insistence of the stunning commandment? The law that the conformist wants to obey is structured like the rules of a game in such a way that his acts can be judged by a judge who possesses the same guarantees as those of the umpire in a tennis match. Just as the umpire has the possibility of knowing if the ball is in or out of play, likewise the reference to the law by which the life of the conformist is sustained gives him the possibility of positioning himself in relation to an arbiter who knows the civil code well enough to judge whether each of his acts is out of play or not.

But does this judge to whom the conformist submits possess the power that the latter supposes he has of telling him if he is a winner or loser in his life? No: the day inevitably comes when he discovers the extent of the alienation he has exposed himself to by rejecting the frightening dimension of a law that contains a shadowy zone. If life is not a game like other games, it is precisely because it is governed by a law of which a part is inexpressible because it is non-inscribable. The paradox of this veiled part of the law consists in the fact that this veil presents itself as what knowledge cannot fail to be ignorant of while, at the same time, presenting the enigmatic commandment, "No one is supposed to be ignorant of the law."

That no one is supposed to be ignorant of that of which he is ignorant is what the conformist wants to overlook. Thanks to this willful ignorance, by forgetting what is forgotten in the written law, he may have the illusion of mastering the fits and starts of his life just as he may master the moves in a game of chess. However complex a game of chess is, none of the moves, however unexpected they may be, escape the set of rules that prescribe the strictly determined way in which each piece is to be moved. If the madman could suddenly forget the obligation to move his pieces diagonally and instead moves them vertically, the game would be interrupted immediately, for it would no longer be a game of chess.

What would this other game be, then, in which a new agent would appear that ceases to move in accordance with the written law? This new game gives us a glimpse of what life is insofar as it is subject to a law, which, because it does not say "everything," determines a

## Chapter Three – The Question of the Stunning Commandment

place of not-knowing that is precisely the place where the subject is called upon to authorize himself by moving in an unforeseen way. The following Jewish story of the deer humorously illustrates the question of that other scene where the subject must be able to jump like a deer in order to come into being as a subject of the unconscious. That such a leap necessarily eludes any sort of movement foreseen by the rules of the game is the crux of this story, which involves a dialogue between the two eternal compères of Jewish humor.

Itzik asks Moishé: "The deer must cross the stream but there is no bridge; it can't swim and doesn't know how to jump either. What should it do?"

After thinking a little, Moishé replies: "If it really can't jump or swim, there's no solution."

Itzik: "Yes, it can jump!"

Moishé: "What? You told me that a deer couldn't jump!"

Itzik: "What are you saying? A deer doesn't know how to jump over a stream?"

What will happen, inevitably, one day or another, to someone who, like our conformist, is determined to ignore the possibility that there is another movement that would enable him to jump over the stream? He may be gripped by what I shall call the angst of semblance: he suddenly discovers that the more he conforms to what he wants to conform to, the more this conformity appears to him to mask a lie; and he feels all the more guilty about this lie insofar as he does not understand what it consists of. It is certainly not an ordinary lie, for he knows very well that he is capable of lying, in certain circumstances, without feeling guilty about it.

Why is this lie not comparable with the lie of that deceiver *par excellence*, Satan? Because Satan's fundamental error is to be the ape of God, one who does not create but imitates divine creation. Now the lie that the subject feels he is guilty of under the Other's gaze always relates, in one way or another, to the fact that he simulates the fact of existing. He even dissimulates the fact that he simulates because it is so important for him that the Other should not know that he is simulating.

Why does he simulate his existence? Because he sees that it is deficient, that because it is pierced by the hole of the *"troumatism,"* it does not have the consistency of a thing that has come into being

## Chapter Three – The Question of the Stunning Commandment

by virtue of a definitive creative act.[256] Why can he not accept this semblance of existence without feeling guilty? Because the more this semblance of being phallic resembles the idea that he has of the phallus, the more he has the sense of stealing this phallus and of being illegitimately associated with it. This illegitimacy that makes him feel as if the insignia of power that he displays (his decorations, titles, diplomas, etc.) are an imposture brings him back to the question of the law. What, then, is the clause of this law that he does not obey, and which takes its revenge by suggesting that his titles seem illegitimate to it? And yet, from the point of view of the written law, of the civil code, his titles are perfectly legal. So beyond what the law reveals of itself, there is an unknown part of which he is ignorant, but whose truth he recognizes even though he does not understand it. While he does not know what this guilt that he does not understand is related to, it is as if he does in fact know which unknown decree he has not respected.

The comedian is, *par excellence*, someone who knows how to measure the gulf separating the rules of a game from the law. The paradox, which he is faced with by the rules of a game that are imposed on him, is that of discovering that it is possible to bring the dimension of truth onto the stage by playing at being someone else. Why is he able to be so natural, so at ease, when he borrows the words of the Other, whereas, when he has to speak off the stage, on the stage of his life, with his own words, he discovers the painful feeling of feigning, of no longer being in the truth? While he feels real when, on the stage, he has to feign or pretend, he finds he is inhabited by the feeling of pretending when, off stage, he is no longer required by the rules of the game to assume the semblance, but implicitly required, by the law, to assume his truth. Why is the comedian, who has all his gifts at his disposal when the rules of the game require it, so dispossessed of them when it is the law that requires it?

Because the law has the power, which a set of rules does not have, to ask him a question that arouses his angst, namely, the question of the fault to which he is exposed on account of the enunciation

---

[256] [A neologism proposed by Lacan during the meeting of February 19, 1974, during the seminar *Les non-dupes errent*. Where Freud insistently articulated trauma in relation to an event (real or imagined), Lacan, through this neologism, makes it understood that it is language that, in making a hole (*trou*), is responsible for *troumatisme*. Language is that against which the subject struggles without being able to surpass it.]

of a prescription that he cannot disregard, even though this prescription is non-inscribable. How is this failing, this moral fault, linked to semblance? Because, when he is in the semblance of being, he "is playing" at life, behaving as if life were a game governed as such by a set of rules that he knows just as well as he knows the rules of a game. The fault thus lies in the lack of distinction between the law and the rules of the game and in the confusion between the law and the rule, in the fact of giving himself the possibility to believe that, having acquitted himself by obeying the written law, he has paid the symbolic debt required by the law.

What does the fact of acquitting oneself of this symbolic debt lead to? It leads one to adopt what Lacan identified as a "discourse that would not be a semblance."[257] This proceeds from a relation to language that has the power to rediscover, beyond the false secret that the subject wants to have at his disposal by dissimulating the fact that he was simulating, the true secret at whose disposal he is. What is this true "secret" in which Lacan identifies the agency or "instance" of *das Ding*? It is a secret that does not need, like a semblance, to be veiled in order to have consistency. On the contrary, it is a secret that consists precisely in the fact of being unveiled: the unheard-of dimension that music allows one to hear, the immaterial dimension that the dancer reveals, and the invisible dimension that the painter shows, are all manifestations of this secret that only has consistency by emerging from its latency.

The false secret articulated by the semblance is an open secret; like that of Edgar Allan Poe's "Purloined Letter," it tends to disappear as soon as the hiding place where it was covered up is brought to light before the eyes of a Dupin, from whom nothing that is in the order of an imaginary hiding place can be hidden. The true secret does not fear the light of day, but rather it demands to be brought into broad daylight in order to reveal itself.

The gratitude that we feel towards the artist is addressed to his faculty for making us recognize the point of alterity, radically invisible to all knowledge, that is foundational to what we call our existence. The debt that we owe him consists in the fact that, having been able

---

[257] [The expression refers to Lacan's seminar *D'un discours qui ne serait pas du semblant*, 1971.]

to pay the price that is required to gain access to the invisible, to the unheard-of, to the immaterial, he reminds us that we in our turn must pay it to access our triple incognito. The paradox of this is that the subject only gets the measure of it at the moment he loses it. It is when he blushes and thereby loses what in him was invisible to the Other that he discovers that he has lost that dimension of invisibility that was one of the parameters of the true secret.

It is when he is transfixed by the gaze of the Other that he discovers what his body has lost: something that could make him dance, the secret dimension of his immateriality. It is when the superegoistic Other knows "everything" about him, and when he has nothing more to make the Other hear, that the subject discovers the "unheard-of" dimension that had inhabited him before he lost his speech. The dialectic of the false secret and of the true secret is related to the fact that the subject, doubting the secret that he "is," strives to substitute it with a secret that he could have. The doubt that he opposes to the accession to that in him which is inaccessible to the pleasure principle (the unheard-of, the invisible, the immaterial) is related to the doubt that he has, as a conformist, about being able to accede to the inaccessible dimension of the law.

## C) "THAT'S NOT ALL YOU ARE!"

### a) *Being and Existence*

The subject, torn between a superegoistic commandment that says, "Renounce yourself!," and a symbolic commandment that signifies, "Become!," is the locus of a deliberation that pushes him to make a choice between being and existence: either he will choose to "be" what is outside or beneath the realm of speech or he will choose to exist through speech.

The choice of "being" is the choice whereby he will agree to reveal what "being" he is made of if he renounces speech: the lifting of this veil will reveal, through the act of blushing, for example, that silent thing that is the intimate color of the fallen object of speech, namely, the object *a*. Why does this fallen object qualify what the philosopher has called "being"? Because it refers to nothing else than itself: the fallen object only shows itself when, having lost its connection with symbolic alterity, which brought it into existence in the symbolic, it drops as stripped of any relation with alterity, and is purely identical to itself.

Experience teaches us how we are reminded of this originary fall on a daily basis: a "swear word," that is, a word that renounces its symbolic power, is all that is necessary for the latent dimension of the human wreck to become obvious; if language puts words like "pissy," "snotty," "shitty," and "bastard" at the disposal of the speaker to de-subjectivize a subject, it is because these words have always contained a superegoistic knowledge concerning the cursed part of the subject. The real question posed by the insult—much more profoundly than that of the aggressiveness of the person who proffers an insult—is that of the reason why being is fundamentally insultable. If the insulted person is rooted to the spot, can no longer ex-sult, can no longer make that leap which takes him out of himself, it is because, deprived of the linguistic possibility of displacement, he henceforth knows only one place: that of the absolute being that he is when, denuded of existence, he falls as waste matter.

How can the subject choose between being and existence?

## b) Forgetting the Question: The Tramp

Experience teaches us that the subject can choose, albeit without being mad, the "being" of degradation. This can be seen from the person who is referred to as a "tramp": even though he chooses to show the monstrous aspect of the human wreck, he is still our brother. He reminds us that to the prescription, "Become where it was!," it is possible to reply, "I will not become." What gives us the possibility of choosing not to be a tramp? Is it that we can choose to avoid this possibility by standing up? What is the force that can lift us up and tear us away from this human wreck that we are fundamentally?

It is linked precisely to the efficacy of the stunning commandment: while a possible translation of the superegoistic commandment transmitted by the insult could be stated as, "That's all you are, just a piece of waste matter," the translation of the stunning commandment could be stated as, "You are not only that [*Tu n'est pas que ça*]."

The enigma of this commandment lies in the fact that, if it informs me of what I am not, it does not, however, inform me of what I am. By saying to me, "You are not only that," it reminds me that I am "something else" than that—something of which I have no possible knowledge, but the recognition of which is bestowed on me owing to the fact that it is supposable by the Other. The fact that recognition is not knowledge leads us to the signification of what the supposition is: where the Other is barred, he cannot know, but can recognize, a supposed subject.

If the analyst is supposed to know that there is a subject, it is because he has been able to transmit to this subject that he was supposable. Otherwise this subject, because he is unconscious, does not know if he exists. Without the transmission of this supposition, the transference on to the analyst is unwarranted and the question of analytic imposture is raised.

### IV. Question to Lacan and Question of Lacan
### "He knows (that I know (that he knows (that I know)))"

In order to present the reasons why a theory of sideration proved necessary for me in the course of theorizing the analytic process and its conclusion, I must show how this necessity gradually became concretized in the course of a private and public dialogue with Lacan.

The question that I put to Lacan at the time of his seminar, "L'Insu que sait de l'une-bévue s'aile à mourre" (1976–1977), was this: The process of symbolization encounters on its path two specific obstacles that are, on the one hand, the superegoistic obstacle of the statement "He knows" and, on the other, the negating obstacle of the statement "He does not know." How can we account for the unconscious reorganization that allows the crossing of these two thresholds that tend to interrupt the symbolic progress of an analytic treatment? However different these two obstacles—the superego and the act of negation—are, they nonetheless have one point in common: owing to their intervention, the "He" that is the signifier of the Other is stripped of its stunning power of "high psychic importance" over the "I" that is the subject of the unconscious.

The negation tends to prevent the subject from rediscovering the "yes" of the unconscious of the *Bejahung*, which constituted him originally. As Freud points out, when the subject has become aware of his "no" and wants, in good faith, to annul it by saying "no" to his negation, he is discouraged to discover that this "no-of-no" does not have the power to go back on the repression by affirming the founding "yes" of the *Bejahung*. Inasmuch as the fundamental sense of negation is to signify, "I know that 'He' does not know," how can this objectified and objectifying "He" rediscover the subjectivizing power that, for example, it acquires when it rediscovers, in the moment of a witticism, that function which Freud identifies as that of the *dritte Person*?

It was from this point of view that I proposed to Lacan that the reorganization necessary for the "He" to cease to be objectified by negation and instead to be objectifying as superego involved a reduplication of the statement "I know that he knows." The division of the subject and the division of the Other are necessarily to be written as: "he knows (that I know (that he knows (that I know)))."

The hypothesis of the need for such a reduplication seems justifiable to me in light of the following three observations.

A) THREE OBSERVATIONS INVOLVING THE STATEMENT "HE KNOWS (THAT I KNOW (THAT HE KNOWS (THAT I KNOW)))"

*a) First Observation: A Rejection of Sideration*

Why am I suggesting that, in order for a state of sideration to occur, a reduplication of the "I know that he knows" is necessary? As in the witticism, a transferential unveiling of the "He" takes place for the subject of the unconscious. Without this reduplication binding the division of the Other and the division of the subject, the subject of the unconscious remains under the sway of negation.

The following observation shows how the articulation of knowledge, if it remains at the level of the three sequences, "I know (that he knows (that I know))," without attaining the four sequences of the reduplication, remains under the yoke of negation. It was in middle school that a teacher had given us an essay to write on the subject, "Give an account of your holidays." When the teacher gave back the copies, he kept one and told us that he had one excellent essay that he was going to read. The teacher then read us the account of the holidays related by the boy in question—I will call him Moutarde—and we gradually recognized that in fact it was one of the *Letters from My Mill* by Alphonse Daudet. The giggles that it produced in the class were

## Chapter Three – The Question of the Stunning Commandment

accentuated by the fact the teacher pretended that he had not noticed that he was reading from Daudet.

It was obvious to everyone that Moutarde was in the position of being able to say to himself: "I know that they know that I have lied." The problem was that Moutarde resolutely denied the fact that he had lied. He recognized that there was in effect a coincidence that he, too, found extraordinary; but he nonetheless maintained, in spite of everything, that he was the author of the text in question: "I admit," he said, "that it is an incredible coincidence, that there was a chance in a million of my writing the same thing as Alphonse Daudet, but every week, in the national lottery, someone is designated as the beneficiary of a coincidence that is just as incredible."

What is fascinating in this situation is to understand what makes a subject continue to deny something when he knows perfectly well that he is fooling no one. One can only assume that we, his classmates, were really fascinated by his obstinacy. The passion with which we tried for a long time to make him own up to his lie was, in itself, a question: why, indeed, could we not tell ourselves that Moutarde was, quite simply, an obstinate liar? Why were we completely captivated by the question that we asked him over and over again: "Since we know that you copied, and since you know that we know that you know it, you might as well admit to us, your friends, that you are lying!"

The fact that he never admitted it and that he always stubbornly maintained that the text was his own teaches us that his aim was not to make us believe his lie. Rather, it was to show that, even though he was not mad, he had the capacity to defer the appearance of the division to which he would have been exposed if he had owned up. The reason why every real confession—for example, a confession of love—involves pain that has to be overcome is that it is not the transmission of an objective piece of information. It is a subjective transmutation whereby what is at stake is not *what* the subject says but *that he* is saying. While Moutarde's confession would have taught us nothing, since we knew it already, his confession would have confronted us, not with knowledge, but with the intimate relation that he had with the truth.

The fact that the bursting out of the confession of truth has the dimension of "I know that (he knows that (I know that (he knows)))" is a situation that an author like Marivaux was able to exploit by bringing onto the stage the different logical times necessary for producing a declaration of love. First time: The sweetheart learns from a confidant

## Chapter Three – The Question of the Stunning Commandment

that the person she loves also secretly loves her, but does not dare to declare himself. Second time: The confidant reveals to the lover that he has divulged his secret to the sweetheart.

The position of the lover is thus one of knowing that she knows that he loves her. But as *she doesn't know* that he knows this, he still does not declare himself; this is the first negative formulation. Third time: The lover catches the confidant divulging to the sweetheart that the lover knows that she knows that he loves her. The new subjective position of the lover is therefore more complex, for he knows that she knows that he knows, while he is still able to deny his love without declaring himself, sustaining himself with the second negative formulation: "She doesn't know (that he knows that she knows that he knows)." In this way, the subject can remain silent and the story of the play shows us that, as long as the lover does not speak, admitting, finally, that yes he knows that she knows (that he knows that she knows) that he loves her, nothing happens.

What Moutarde, like the lover, was avoiding was to recognize that he knew that we knew (that he knew that we knew). The following observation shows us how the unfolding of these four phases can produce a state of sideration that the subject cannot overcome.

### b) Second Observation: A State of Sideration without De-sideration

It concerns a recollection of fainting that came back to an analysand in a particular context of his analysis. He was five years old when, in the company of his little sister, aged four, and of a nurse, they were playing hide-and-seek. He and his little sister were hiding behind a tree and the nurse was looking for them. In fact, he realized—after noticing that she had seen them—that she was pretending that she was still looking for them. He whispered to his little sister, "She has seen us," and, out of complicity with him, his sister remained hidden next to him in such a way that both of them could see the nurse, who was pretending that she was looking for them.

In this situation, the nurse does not know that he knows that she knows where they are. Next stage: His little sister comes out of her hiding place and runs towards the nurse; he sees her whispering something to her in her ear. He is now in a position to suppose that his little sister has told the nurse: "We know that you have seen us." However, the nurse chooses to continue to pretend that she is searching

## Chapter Three – The Question of the Stunning Commandment

for them so that he now finds himself in this new position: She knows that he knows that she knows where he is.

Why does he nonetheless, from this moment on, continue to feel he is hidden to the point of being able to persevere in the game? For the ultimate negating possibility persists: "True, she knows that I know that she knows where I am, but my position has still not been exposed because I have the advantage of being one stage ahead of her—an advantage that remains a secret for her: she does not know that I know it."

What difference is there between the situation of this subject, who, hidden behind his tree, hears the other calling out to him, "Where are you?," and the situation of Adam, who, hidden behind his fig tree, hears God's words: "Where are you?" Why does Adam live in fear and trembling, insofar as he is radically exposed by God's gaze, whereas our subject sees himself as still being hidden? Because Adam is dealing with an Other to whom he cannot say both "yes" and "no," for it is a unique Other, whereas our subject, owing to his negation, is dealing with an Other who is split between two forms of knowing: on the one hand, he says "yes" to the nurse insofar as she knows where he is; and, on the other, he says "no" to her insofar as she does not know what he knows about what she knows.

But the moment comes when this negation that allows the game to continue will no longer be tenable. This moment comes when, suddenly, the nurse leaps into his hiding place alongside him, crying out, "You are there." It is at this precise moment—when he can no longer maintain that "she does not know that I know that she knows that I know"—that the subject faints.

"What did this 'You are there' mean?," the analysand asked himself thirty years later. Why, by fainting, did I not accept to be "there," when I knew from the beginning of the game that she knew that I was "there." With this question this analysand distinguishes a form of knowledge in the real, affecting the subject, from "intellectual" knowledge, which, governed by negation, has no consequences and does not affect the subject. This split between intellect and affect that Freud identifies as an effect of negation finds its motive force here. As long as the ego can deny the Other, positing him as a "he"—or a "she"— who knows *and* does not know, he masters the situation, so much so that the knowledge that the other has does not affect him. If what the nurse knows about the place where he is hidden is of no consequence,

## Chapter Three – The Question of the Stunning Commandment

it is because the nurse's knowledge, insofar as it can be objectified by thought, is referable to a "she" that is thinkable. It is only at the moment when this "she," ceasing to be the support for two objectively different kinds of knowledge, becomes a unique, unthinkable signifier that it becomes the support for a stunning form of knowledge that is of consequence. It then acquires the power to call—by supposing it—for the arrival of the subject of the unconscious, who is the real subject who is supposed to know.

In this respect, the major difference between the absolute knowledge of the superego and the absolute knowledge of the symbolic is that the first de-supposes the subject, whereas the second supposes him. The paralysis of the madman in front of the hen—whose knowledge conveys the message to him, "That's all you are, a grain of wheat"—is quite different from the state of sideration produced by the nurse's stunning words, "You are there." The statement, "That's all you are," means: "You are nothing more than a fallen object, deprived of speech." The words, "You are there," mean: "You are in a place where, as you can no longer deny that you encounter my speech, you can no longer deny your own speech either. You now realize that by trying to escape from my power you were in fact only escaping from the power of your own speech that you were keeping repressed."

By virtue of the signification of this stunning message, the subject is taken back to the logical moment when he was led to make the unconscious decision to repress his speech. He is placed once again before the choice that had been his when he was faced with a traumatic situation: Will he make the same choice of repression again or will he choose another solution?

The example of the child who faints is a compromise: by fainting, he shows how, although he has gained access to the ultimate hiding place where the nurse can no longer see him, he nonetheless declines to insist upon the existence of the subject of the unconscious. This insistence could have happened if the subject had found the means to extricate himself from his state of sideration by finding the path of de-sideration, of unconscious desire. For this to happen, he would have had to reply to the affirmation, "You are there," proffered by the Other, with the following act of affirmation, of *Bejahung*: "Yes, I am here, here, in a duration that I can endure without fainting."

The difficulty whereby the subject must assume the "I" supposed by the "you" is what we must examine. The angst in which this difficulty has its roots may not be "assumed" in diverse contexts. It may be at the moment when the anxiety reveals itself, as in the case of the child who faints. Or, as in the case of Moutarde, it may be in anticipation of the situation, insofar as he probably sensed that an admission would have made him experience such anxiety.

What is the cause of this angst? The first cause is linked to the fact that the dissolution of the negating function introduces a dissolution of the ego-image, which Lacan pointed out in his optical schema, in which he makes the mirror tip over from the vertical plane to the horizontal plane.[258] The second is linked to the emergence of unconscious guilt, whose signification I am going to identify. Insofar as, in the moment of sideration, the subject realizes in the present that, up till then, he did not know that by hiding from the gaze of the other he was in fact hiding from himself, he is led to recognize that before being stunned he was in the following position of *méconnaissance (misrecognition)*: "I did not know that I was hiding." There are thus two "I's" of different structures, whereby the "I" of negation ("I didn't know") is articulated with the "I" of secondary repression ("I was hiding").

The virtue of negation is to introduce, as Jean Hyppolite says, an *Aufhebung* of the repression.[259] The "I was hiding" of repression is in this respect uprooted from its radical solitude by the ego's negation inasmuch as it introduces the dimension of knowledge about the existence of repression: there is no fundamental difference between saying, "'I know' that I am hiding," and saying, "'I don't know' I am hiding," for, in both cases, it is signified that something hidden is linked to knowledge. If the formulation, "I know that I am hiding," represents progress in relation to, "I don't know that I am hiding," this progress is in fact limited because it does not result in the lifting of the repression: wanting to go beyond the negation by denying it only leads to an intellectual "yes" that is not the equivalent of the unconscious "yes." Since the moment of sideration is one in which the repression is lifted, this moment is not definable by the formulation, "I know that I

---

[258] Jacques Lacan, "Remarks on Daniel Lagache's Presentation: 'Psychoanalysis and Personality Structure,'" in *Écrits, op. cit.*, 543–574.

[259] Jean Hyppolite, "A Spoken Commentary on Freud's 'Verneinung' by Jean Hyppolite," in Jacques Lacan, *Écrits, op. cit.*

was hiding," insofar as it is compatible with the maintenance of the repression.

What, then, is the translation that should be adopted to define the reorganization of the unconscious knowledge by which negation falls? I will tackle this point by asking a new question: Why, when the negation is lifted and it is revealed to the ego that "$he_1$" knows that "$he_2$" is hiding, does terrifying guilt appear? It is because the ego considers it is not free to hide and *must account* for its act of repression.

Before which presence must it give an account of itself, if it is not before the subject of the unconscious, that is, before a presence that is all the more hidden in that it does not know that it is hidden? Insofar as the ego knows that it is hiding, it can conceive of what is hidden as relating to an act that is its own and to which it can go back to when, for example, there is a return of the repressed. It cannot imagine that there is something hidden that does not depend on it and over which it has no hold, since it is a hidden element, which, not knowing itself, can in no way give access to knowledge. As long as I know where I am hiding, there will always be a Dupin who will be able—however ingenious the place where the "purloined letter" is hidden may be—to gain access to the knowledge that I have of what I have hidden. But if, in a similar way to the child who faints to avoid knowing where he is hidden, I faint as a subject of the unconscious, without even knowing it, then the ego loses all possibility of being able to think about "where I am hidden."

This is the reason why the ego's fundamental attitude is this activity of misrecognition [*méconnaissance*] whereby it does not want to know that, beyond what it is hiding, there is something hidden whose radical nature resides in the fact that it does not have to *hide itself* in the shadows to *be hidden* in full daylight. The formula of sideration is thus not only the revelation made to the ego that a first "I" did not know that a second "I" was hiding, but also the revelation made to the ego that there is within it a second misrecognition, beyond the misrecognition whereby "it" does not want to know (denial) that "$he_2$" is hiding (secondary repression). It does not want to know that there exists a third "I"—the subject of the unconscious—that does not need to hide from the ego in order, owing to primal repression, to be hidden.

The complete formula of sideration thus reveals that "$I_1$" *did not want to know that* "$I_2$" *was hiding the fact that an* "$I_3$" *was hid-*

*den*. This formula knots three "I's" that can be differentiated in Borromean terms. The first "I," which is negating, draws support from the imaginary function of the ego; the second "I," which brings into play secondary repression, draws support from the symbolic; the third "I," brought into play by primal repression, draws support from the real. This formula allows us to begin to understand the fear of guilt that is deployed, for the following reason, in the moment of sideration. The strategy with which secondary repression creates something hidden by veiling speech is to be understood as a symbolic fault in relation to the stunning command, which is a *call for the originary veil of primal repression to be unveiled in speech*.

The error in relation to the symbolic consists in substituting for the existence of this true secret of primal repression, according to which there is *a forgetting, a hole in the symbolic* (the subject of the unconscious), the pseudo-secret of secondary repression, according to which there is a *forgetting of the symbolic by the imaginary function of the ego*. It is as if the ego preferred to be accused of being guilty of introducing hidden knowledge rather than to acknowledge the fact that, in the symbolic, there is a bar at the level of the subject, a radical deficiency of knowledge *for which the ego is not responsible*. This imputation of guilt directed at the ego has the effect of saving the Other by affirming that he is innocent, that it is not him but the ego that is responsible for the existence of an original lack of knowledge. That the Other lacks consistency, is deficient with regard to knowledge, is related to a supreme horror that the ego, in order to preserve its consistency, prefers to veil by making itself the cause of a deficiency of knowledge. *Guilt is the means chosen by the ego to avoid facing the angst* that would be involved in recognizing the existence of a hole in the Other for which it is not responsible.

The symptom has the function of substituting for the dimension of a truth that is hidden from the ego the dimension of an ego hiding the truth. This situation can be observed in certain cases of lying involving children, where it turns out that the child, inasmuch as he has constituted himself around a radical avoidance of saying certain things (for instance, he has not been told that his father is not his father), chooses to lie in order to position himself as the cause of the lie, whereas, in actual fact, he is only the effect. The following dream of an analysand illustrates, in its own way, the same process: "Someone has died in a mysterious way. A piece of white cardboard has been found on his body on which there are two letters, "bm," and people are wondering if it might be the visiting card of a killer who has left his initials like in certain detective stories." The associations to the dream suggest that "bm" refers to *"belle mort"* (nice death), and so this raises the following question: If the subject died a nice death, why suspect a killer?

Once again we are faced with the substitution whereby the mystery that is death, insofar as it is a manifestation that is inaccessible to knowledge, is substituted by the hypothesis of an inaccessible mystery, insofar as it is reduced to the level of the detective's hypothesis of a mysterious killer. The dream substitutes the question of angst in the face of death with that of the guilt of a killer, who, by taking upon himself the fact that death has a comprehensible cause, saves us from having to look squarely at what is incomprehensible when death is the effect of no other cause than itself. Through his dream, the dreamer has thus learnt that dying his nice death was for him more terrifying than dying at the hands of a killer.

That the ego must be able to let go of this guilt and to accept, while looking at it squarely, the angst of not knowing is the condition on which the subject can go beyond the state of *sideration*.

### c) *Third Observation: A Case of Sideration Followed by De-sideration*

The clinical example I will give to illustrate a case of sideration followed by de-sideration is that of a man who is led to question himself, retrospectively, about the conditions under which he was led to recognize a state of paternity that he had been denying. This story of recognition involved a birth resulting from adultery: he was the lover of a married woman who gave birth to a son; and this woman informed him that he was the father. He did not want to recognize the child owing to his rationalizations based on denial because he did not want the husband who, moreover, was a friend, to learn that he had been deceived.

So the child grew up taking the deceived husband for his father, until the day when he learnt from his mother, around the age of twenty, who his real father was.

Different dialectical times of a de-negating resistance to the revelation of the truth then unfolded between the mother, the son, and the child's biological father. The mother told her lover that she had just confessed to her son that he was his real father and that the young man wanted to have a meeting with him so that he could tell him, face-to-face, that he had learnt the truth. But he declined to meet the young man because, though he knew that the son knew that he knew that he was his father, he felt incapable of going back on the original negation that made him reject this paternity.

Things remained unchanged for several years until, one day, by chance, when telephoning to the woman who was still his mistress, he encountered, on the other end of the line, the denied son, who was at his mother's that day. Against all logic, the son answered the telephone with the words, "*Il y a personne* [There's no one at home]."

Hearing in this statement the words, "*Il y a père sonne* [There is father ringing]," the subject said he had been stunned before bursting into laughter, thereby confirming that his son had just succeeded, unwittingly, in making a magnificent witticism.

How are we to understand that it was by virtue of laughter that this man, who had so fiercely denied his paternity, had been led to take responsibility for and assent to what the stunning ambiguity of the phrase had led him to hear: "A father is ringing." This laughter is, in fact, the unconscious enunciation by which he admits: "Yes, it is really me, your father, who is ringing."

My hypothesis is that the joy that is signified in this laughter is both joy at being able to escape from the ego's negating power and joy at not escaping, on that day, from the commandment that resonates through the witticism: "You will be the one through whom the father rings." By his laughter, the father agrees, for the first time, to say "yes" to the fact of being called to the place of "A-father," and the fact that his son laughed in turn, intermingling his laughter with his father's, signifies that, for the first time, something other than the objective knowledge about the father that he had received from his mother had been transmitted to him: namely, the recognition of his filiation insofar as it could only be transmitted to him, as an unconscious message, by "A-father."

How was it that the father was able to indicate to his son, during the ephemeral space of a second, that he had done more than consent to the stunning commandment to be a father? With his laughter, he had revealed how he had assumed this state of sideration by converting it into de-sideration, into the unconscious desire to be a father.

Life teaches us that highly symbolic acts, like this laughter through which a father admits his guilt, can occur in extremely fleet-

*Chapter Three – The Question of the Stunning Commandment*

ing moments, whose transience stands in strange contrast with the permanence of the effect produced. As analysts, we sometimes learn that subjects have been able to emerge from a traumatic situation thanks to a small detail—a smile, a glance—that reminded them that, beyond the traumatic disorder, the signifying order could continue to persist. That this small detail, the signifying gift, is what can keep us alive, just when our life is in the process of falling to bits, is something that the poet knows how to express particularly well when, for example, he says, in his *Chanson pour l'Auvergnat*: "This song is for you, the Stranger who, unceremoniously,... smiled to me when the police caught me...."[260] If there is a connection between the transience of the Stranger's smile in the song and the transience with which the father of our observation gave his laughter to his son, it is that of the force of the instant, endowed with a redemptive power that the historical duration of time does not possess.

The work of Rozenzweig is instructive for us in this respect.[261] By opposing the Christian conception of Hegelian time, conceived of as time revealing the dimension of Redemption in historical duration, it shows that the Jewish conception of time is one in which pure synchrony is endowed with the power to break with historical diachrony in order to shatter, through the instant, the possibility of encountering a grain of poetic eternity dispensing Redemption.

Is it not the attribute of the signifier of the Name-of-the-Father— one of the Biblical names of which is "the Eternal"—that the father of our observation encountered when he was "stunned" [*sonné*], by which his son named for him the signifier of the Name-of-the-Father: a "father who rings" [*un père qui sonne*]? We suppose that, for this father, the dimension of the absolute alterity of the signifier of the Name-of-the-Father couldn't be brought into perspective except through this particular nomination, concerning which his son, for a reason that is unknown to us, had unconscious knowledge. The fact remains that it was through such a nomination that this radically alien signifier—the signifier of the Name-of-the-Father—ceased to be alien for the father and that it was able, for him, to ring like a stunning commandment that enabled him to constitute himself as a good listener.

---

[260] [A song by Georges Brassens (1955).]
[261] F. Rozenzweig, *L'Etoile de la Rédemption* (Paris: Éditions du Seuil, 1982).

### Chapter Three – The Question of the Stunning Commandment

In music, there is not this gap between hearing badly and hearing well, inasmuch as the subject who dances or sings does not have to create, in order to sing or to dance, any other music than that which he hears. However, the subject constituted as speaking speaks not only with the speech of the Other. If he speaks, it is because he elects to speak and not because he takes it up as he has received it, as with music. Insofar as speaking implies expressing oneself in a language (that of the unconscious) that is foreign to our maternal language, two successive times are involved: first, that of decoding the message of the Other (time of translation into the mother tongue), then that of encoding through the maternal tongue (time of translation into the foreign tongue).

As soon as we speak, we are confronted with these two times, the distinction of which is not required when we dance inasmuch as the processes of decoding and encoding are then simultaneous. The phase of latency required by sideration and de-sideration is the time the subject needs to decode the speech received as speech that can be coded by him. For the signifier "rings" [*sonne*] to be integrated into the unconscious chain of the subject, he must be able to forget that he is "stunned" [*sonné*] by this signifier. Indeed, as long as he is stunned, it means that he has not found the means of decoding. To do so, he must find within himself the signifying element that—comparable to the day residue that permits the dreamer to find the idea of the dream—will give him the access code to unconscious meaning. This secret code will be the signifier "son," which, by entering into contact with the signifier "*sonne*," will create a metaphor causing the meaning of filiation to sparkle poetically inasmuch as it is linked to what in the father "*sonne*" [rings]: the *sonnerie* [sounding] of the shofar.[262]

Whereas the man who dances experiences no gap between the instant of decoding the music and that of encoding, since the dance step of which he is the agent is in perfect synchrony with the music that moves him, the man who speaks is torn by this gap or discrepancy, thereby revealing the sense of human time. A period of time is needed, that of de-sideration, for the subject to be able to decode—with the help of the signifier "son"—the signifier "rings" [*sonne*] and

---

[262] ["Son" is in English in the original.]

## Chapter Three – The Question of the Stunning Commandment

to assume, by encoding it, the new metaphorical signification that is produced. As long as the unconscious decoding has not been realized, the subject remains in suspended time. The stunning signifier resounds in him like the shofar, like a signifier that, open to all meanings, calls out to all meanings while waiting to find one. As long as this potentiality of infinite meaning remains supposable by the Other, the latter presents himself as one who possesses stunning absolute knowledge about what could, but has not yet, come into being. It is when the subject agrees to renounce this excess of possibility by choosing one way of decoding among all the possible decodings that a transport of metaphorical meaning will occur, in this case, by decoding the signifier "*sonnerie*" [ringing sound] by the signifier "son" of filiation.

The fundamental point is to understand that it is at the precise moment when the father finds within himself, in his own unconscious signifiers, the unconscious signifier "son" that he removes himself from the power of the stunning signifier. It was absolute as long as it referred to all the meanings possible, making them all resonate at the same time, rather like a note of music that makes its multiple harmonics resonate. For example, we could imagine that, during the time of sideration, the subject—insofar as he had a certain relation to illness—had the unconscious possibility of choosing between "son" and signifiers like "Adison," "Parkinson," etc., in order to find the path of a possible metaphor, which could also have raised the question of paternity from the angle of death.

The discovery of the signifier "*son*" thus made of it the *passer* signifier that transmuted the signifier *passed* to the subject by the Other—"*père sonne*"—into a *passing* signifier of the subject.[263] It is this passage from the signifier passed *to the subject* to the passing signifier *of the subject* that represents the conquest whereby the time of the subject is substituted for the time of the Other. This is how, by finding within himself this *passer* signifier, the subject passes over to the side of the unconscious and becomes aware of the following paradox: it is insofar as he becomes a subject of the unconscious that he derives the authorization from himself alone to laugh.

Can he authorize himself if he does not know that he is authorizing himself? To understand this paradox, we need to return to the

---

[263] See footnote 11.

## Chapter Three – The Question of the Stunning Commandment

decisive moment in the transference when the speech proffered by the Other for a supposed subject suddenly becomes speech proffered by the subject for a supposable Other. If, in this process, the Other ceases to be a stunning emitter and becomes instead a supposable receiver, it is because the subject only becomes a speaking subject from the moment the Other falls into radical silence, which will be the empty space within which speech can emerge. This silence results from the fact that the subject, who is no longer in a state of sideration, has forgotten the Other and can henceforth only suppose him unconsciously; if, indeed, he does not know that he is speaking when he speaks, or that, when he speaks, he is addressing the Other, he is nonetheless addressing him, as Freud discovered by discovering the transference. It is precisely because the Other is silent, because he does not answer, even if the subject curses him for this silence, that the subject is unable, as in dance, to derive his authorization from the Other, but only from himself. The signification of this enigmatic "from himself" [*de lui-même*] becomes clear if we grasp the fact that it introduces us to a relationship of fidelity between the subject and the act that constituted him. This "from himself" does not refer the subject to a "himself" that would signify an identity with oneself implying the exclusion of all alterity; if the exclusion of alterity is characteristic of the ego, given that its peculiarity is to strive for identity with itself, the assumption of alterity, the "yes" to the Other, is, on the contrary, the primordial act for which this "from himself" of the emerging subject came into being.

In fact, this "from himself" does not refer directly to the Other, since he is forgotten, but rather to the unforgettable memory of the act whereby the subject succeeded in forgetting the primordial "yes" that he gave to the Other. In short, it is as if the subject had forgotten the Other in order to be able to speak, but *did not forget*, however, *that he had committed this act of forgetting*. The paradox of this forgetful subject is that he responds to an act of infidelity that pushes him to forget the primordial act with which he turned away from the Other with an act of fidelity that drives him to return to his primordial forgetting by maintaining it as *unforgettable forgetting*.[264]

---

[264] See 281.

## Chapter Three – The Question of the Stunning Commandment

The structure of this "not-forgetting of forgetting" is complex, for not only does it not yield a recollection that could succeed in making up for the act of forgetting, but it also accentuates this primordial forgetting inasmuch as it commemorates it as irremediably actual. This "not-forgetting" of the primordial loss is the stuff of which human desire is made, insofar as it is caused by an object commemorating the unforgettable forgetting of the primordial loss.

A question arises here: How should we understand the difference between the desire caused by a sexual object and the desire caused by a sublimated object? The difference between sexual desire, caused by the nudity of the body, and the desire of the painter, caused by the nude that he is painting, resides in the fact that sexual desire is caused automatically, within the framework of the pleasure principle, without the subject needing to be stunned. The painter's desire, which comes under the aegis of the beyond the pleasure principle, is the fruit of an experience of de-sideration that necessitates the prior experience of sideration. If, with the desire of sublimation, the subject of the unconscious is sent back to this dimension of fidelity according to which he derives his authorization only from himself, sexual desire does not refer the subject to this subjective dimension of fidelity to oneself. The unforgettable object of sideration is therefore never acquired once and for all, as the object of sexual fantasy is. Unlike the object of fantasy, which reveals itself each time in the same way, the sublimated object does not need to be unveiled, but rather to be revealed as being different from itself each time: the same *A* flat will never sound twice in the same way.

Why is the desire of sublimation, which I shall call desire X (which has the same sound in French as "*ics*" [ucs.]), so difficult to articulate? Because it articulates two antinomical dimensions that, traditionally, are irreconcilable: that of the intellect and that of the affective.

The intellectual "yes," devoid of affecting power, is radically opposed to the unconscious "yes" that the father in our observation rendered really affecting by his laughter, the unconscious message of which was, "Yes, you are my son!" If this "yes" resulted in subjective transformations for both the father and the son, it is because a third dimension was introduced by it, with the result that the pair "signifier-affect" ceased to be opposed in a dualistic way. This third topological point is the point of sublimation, where affect ceases to be a noun—affect—opposed to the "signifier" and becomes instead a verb of which the signifier is the agent.²⁶⁵ By ceasing to oppose "the" signifier to affect in order to posit the signifier as *that which affects*, sublimation restores to the signifier the dignity that had been contested by repression.

By signifying to his son, through his laughter, "Yes, you are my son!," the subject produced a signifier that affected, for life, two people: the father and his "son."

## B) THE SEMINAR OF FEBRUARY 15, 1977

It was to defend the hypothesis that the end of an analysis could take effect when the analysis, or the analyst, produced a signifier with the power to stun both the negative "he doesn't know" and the superegoistic "he knows," that I was led, at Lacan's request, to propose, in the seminar of February 8, 1977, the fiction of a special analytic moment of time.²⁶⁶ The analysand—"Bozeff"—had the experience of reduplication whereby, through this "he knows (that I know (that he knows (that I know)))," the "he" was restored to its symbolic function of *dritte Person*.

The reduplication of the "I know that he knows" will have an inverse effect on negation and the superego. It will withdraw the negative knowledge of the subject due to the fact that it is "only intellectual." Inscribing it in the real will withdraw the absolute knowledge of the superego because it is only a "he knows" inscribed in the real, so that a "he knows" that can be inscribed in the symbolic may come into being. Indeed, as long as the absolute knowledge of the superego presents itself as this "He knows that I am only a grain of wheat," the subject is unable to say to the psychiatrist anything but this hopeless truth: "For my part, I know that I am not a grain of wheat, but 'it' [the hen] does not know that." The hope of truth will only be restored to the subject if the dumbfounding "he knows" of the superego can be substituted by a stunning "He knows." Through this "He," which has become symbolic by virtue of our reduplication, he will be supposed as a subject who can say "yes" to this second "He."

---

²⁶⁵ On the subject of this dualistic conception of affect and the signifier, see André Green, *The Fabric of Affect and Psychoanalytic Discourse*, trans. Alan Sherdian (London: Routledge, 1999).

²⁶⁶ Transcriptions in *Ornicar? Analytica* VI (1977).

### Chapter Three – The Question of the Stunning Commandment

Lacan replied to my hypothesis in the seminar of February 15, 1977, saying that there was one point on which he agreed and another on which he disagreed. The point of disagreement concerned the fact that I proposed to give a name—"Bozeff"—to the subject who was stunned by the stunning "He." The point of agreement concerned the necessity of recognizing that analysis derives its status of reduplication from the "I know that he knows." "The objectification of the unconscious," Lacan says, "requires a reduplication, that is to say, an 'I know that he knows that I know that he knows.' It is on this condition alone that analysis holds on to its status."

In this seminar, Lacan lays much stress on the fact that the negation expresses itself as knowledge with which the ego produces an "I know" concerning the unconscious, which is knowledge of a "he." "What significance can this 'I know that he knows' have," Lacan asks, "apart from objectifying the unconscious?" This objectification of the unconscious belongs to knowledge of consciousness, which "is very far from being knowledge because what it lends itself to is quite precisely falseness. 'I know' never means anything except that what one knows is false, *but* is sustained by consciousness, the characteristic of which is precisely to support this falseness with its consistency. To the point that it could be said that one should look twice before accepting something that seems obvious, and that is why I said that it was necessary to empty out ... the obvious."[267]

Lacan extends the idea of what the obviousness of an unemptied knowledge is by evoking a personal recollection: "an 'I know' that is conscious, that is to say, not simply knowledge but the will not to change; something that I experienced very early on with someone who was close to me, someone I called at that time 'my little sister'—I was two years older than her—she is called Madeleine and that day she said to me, not 'I know,' because the 'I' would have been too much, but 'Manène knows.'" Through this "Manène knows," Lacan raises the

---

[267] [Jacques Lacan, seminar of February 15, 1977, *Seminar XXIV*, unpublished seminar: « Je sais » ne veut jamais rien dire, et on peut facilement parier, que ce qu'on sait est faux. Est faux, mais est soutenu par la conscience, dont la caractéristique est précisément de soutenir de sa consistance, ce faux. C'est au point qu'on peut dire que, il faut y regarder à deux fois avant d'admettre une évidence, qu'il faut la cribler comme telle, que rien n'est sûr en matière datièrefaut et c'est pour ça que j'ai énoncé qu'il fallait évider lvider fall que c'est de lque c'est que lque c'est relève.]

## Chapter Three – The Question of the Stunning Commandment

question of the absolute knowledge whose ravaging effects we are aware of as analysts. The analysand is so often led to recognize how far his destiny is marked by his alienation from such an absolute commandment, inasmuch as he may dedicate his life to trying to accomplish it. In one way or another, the general formula of such absolute knowledge is received by the child as knowledge that concerns his being and is expressed as: "You are only that."

The content of this "only that" is of little importance—an idiot, a clot, a moron, an imbecile—the essential issue lies in a seizure of the being that, limited to being "only that," is excluded from its power of becoming. The question is thus: how can the subject be protected from the malediction of such absolute knowledge, whose effectiveness is naturally evocative of that of those evil oracles that the bad fairies of children's tales proffer to the newborn in his cradle. Such an oracle conveys unconscious knowledge sustained by a "he" or a "she" ("he, or she, knows what is going to happen to me"), which is articulated with the conscious knowledge of the ego ("I know") in such a way that "Manène knows" is in fact an "I know that she knows," through which the conscious and unconscious are articulated. "I have always had to deal with consciousness," Lacan says in this connection, "but a form that was part of the unconscious, since ... the person in question put herself in the third person by calling herself 'Manène,' in a form which was part of the unconscious, since it is a 'she' who, as in my title for this year, an *elle qui s'ailait à mourre*, pretended to be a bearer of knowledge."

"'He' or 'she' is the third person, it is the Other as I define it, it is the unconscious...." Lacan responded in the following way to the hypothesis that this "He," in order not to be objectalized, should be redoubled if it is to find its symbolizing capacity "to change something, to reduce the sinthome." "The objectification of the unconscious necessitates a redoubling, namely, the 'I know that he knows that I know that he knows.' *It is on this condition alone that analysis holds onto its status. This is what creates an obstacle to that something that, by limiting itself to 'I know that he knows,' opens the door to occultism and telepathy*." It was owing to an insufficient grasp of the status of anti-knowledge, that is, of the anti-unconscious, in other words of that pole which is consciousness, that Freud allowed himself from time to time to be titillated by what have since been called "psy phenomena."

*Chapter Three – The Question of the Stunning Commandment*

The interpretation of the appearance of the "He," insofar as it can depose the absolute knowledge of the superego, raises a question that I have tried to answer without knowing if I have succeeded. The efficacy of the stunning "He" resides in the fact that it can manifest itself as a knowledge that returns, not in the symbolic (which would indicate a return of secondary repressed material), but in the real. The notion of the inscription of knowledge in the real poses a problem because it implies distinguishing between two types of absolute knowledge. The knowledge *inscribed* in the real by the stunning signifier is antinomical to the knowledge that has *fallen* into the real, incarnated by the superego or hallucination, insofar as one supposes the subject and the other de-supposes it. The knowledge that is inscribed as an unconscious "I know," at the moment of sideration, is not of the same order as the inscription of the superegoistic "he knows." In this respect, the "I know that he knows (that I know (that he knows (that I know)))" cannot be referred, for Lacan, to a subject who can be named, insofar as it could only be formalized in the way that it is by the "parenthesis of parentheses" of the *Écrits*.

This was precisely the point, when I was led to name the incarnation of the stunning absolute knowledge ("Bozeff"), at which Lacan directed his critique. "Bozeff is not something that deserves to be named ... it is not nameable ... this absolute knowledge, I [bluntly] insisted on it, namely, that the whole appendix that I added to my writing on *The Purloined Letter*—that is to say, what goes from page 52 to page 60 in my *Écrits*—to which I gave the title "Parenthesis of parentheses," is precisely what is substituted for Bozeff." Lacan is thus led to oppose two types of knowledge in the real: an absolute knowledge supposing an "I," which, as "I know that she knows that I know that she knows," is not nameable, and a de-supposing absolute knowledge supported by a nameable "he" or a "she," in the example he gives on this occasion, "Manène knows."

Lacan referred to this question again in a letter addressed to Soury two days later, on February 17, 1977: "I am racking my brain over this question: is the real writing of 'I know' conceivable? Or is there only the 'he knows' or the 'Manène knows'?"[268]

---

[268] Published by Michel Tomé.

*Chapter Three – The Question of the Stunning Commandment*

## C) THE END OF AN ANALYSIS: UNKNOTTING AND RE-KNOTTING

This question of a real inscription of knowledge is fundamental for imagining the end of an analysis. Does the analysand's psychic reality only derive its real consistency from the intermediary of the "He" from which the signifier of the Name-of-the-Father draws support or can this consistency be obtained from an unconscious articulation whereby the "I" of the unconscious is able to do without the father?

If we take into account the final contributions of Lacan on the Borromean knot, the question can be reformulated as follows: insofar as the three rings of the real, the symbolic, and the imaginary are knotted by the intermediary of a fourth ring, whose paternal function of nomination is to give Freudian psychic reality consistency, should we consider that this knot with four rings is the one that is produced by the end of an analysis? This question—which became an object of controversy between René Major and Philippe Julien during a day of *Études freudiennes*, organized by Conrad Stein—deserves to be taken up again today.[269]

Philippe Julien's position consisted of recognizing that, for a long time, the consistency of psychic reality was assured by the transference, owing to the presence of the fourth ring of a knot, that is to say, the "nominating *saying*" of the analyst.[270] However, the conclusion of the analysis was characterized by the fact that the analysand managed to do without this "nominating *saying*," insofar as, at the end of the analysis, there would be "a consistency which could one day support itself without this fourth ring."

What makes possible such a passage from the knot with four rings to the knot with three rings? According to Philippe Julien, it is a certain know-how of the analyst, who, knowing how to make his own name fall to the rank of the most common name, puts the analysand in a position to "mourn" or let go of his transference onto the enunciating function of the name. The example Philippe Julien used to demonstrate this possibility is the one employed by Lacan in his seminar *The Sinthome*. He concluded it on February 10, 1976, with these words: "You must have had your fill of it and even your *jaclaque*, since I could

---

[269] "Lacan lecteur de Freud," *Études freudiennes* 33.
[270] That is, the fourth ring of the Borromean knot.

### Chapter Three – The Question of the Stunning Commandment

just as well add to it a *han!*... I thus reduce my own name to the most common noun."[271]

The pertinence of this example gives us an idea of what the know-how of an analyst must be, but it does not tell us what the unconscious know-how of the analysand must be if his psychic reality is to come into being according to a Borromean knotting. To give ourselves the means of understanding that this event is not magically obtained by the fall of the analyst's proper name, we need to take into account the existence of two logical times in this operation. The first moment appears to me, as it does to Philippe Julien, to be introduced by the stunning intervention of the analyst, who, by causing his own proper name to fall, puts the analysand in a transferential relationship with this anonymous "He" of the unconscious, which was concealed by the patronym. But this moment of sideration, by means of which the *dritte Person* emerges from repression thanks to the introduction of the "He knows (that I know (that He knows (that I know)))," does not seem to me, as it does to Philippe Julien, that of the knotting of the knot but, on the contrary, a moment of subjective destitution in which the sudden inconsistency of an unknotting occurs.

The notion of the existence of such a process of unknotting was the idea that René Major was led to defend when commenting on the following statement by Lacan in his seminar, "*L'insu que sait de l'une-bévue s'aile à mourre.*" "What I put forward in my Borromean knot of the Imaginary, the Symbolic, and the Real led me to distinguish these three spheres, and then, subsequently, to re-knot them. I enunciated the Symbolic, the Imaginary, and the Real in 1954, titling an inaugural conference with these three names, which have become, in short, through me, what Frege calls proper nouns. Creating a proper name is something that elevates your own name a little bit. The only proper name in all of that is mine. It is Lacan's extension of the proper name to the Symbolic, to the Imaginary, and to the Real, that allows these three terms to find their consistency."

René Major then asked this question: "If it is impossible to speak of real-symbolic-imaginary, without citing, in so doing, the name of

---

[271] ["Han!" is an interjection expressing relief. *Vous devez en avoir votre claque, et même votre « Jacq'Lac », puisque aussi bien j'y ajouterai le « han ! » qui sera l'expression du soulagement que j'éprouve avoir parcouru aujourd'hui que je réduis mon nom propre au nom le plus commun.*]

## Chapter Three – The Question of the Stunning Commandment

Lacan, does it mean, without the name of Lacan, the trilogy would lose its consistency?" Major answered his own question by suggesting that if there was a consistency in the enunciations of Lacan, it was insofar as his own name could fall into a *"désistance,"* a "desistance," with the effect of introducing an unknotting that would create the conditions of resignifying what had been de-signified.[272] It seems to me that the debate between Philippe Julien and René Major about knotting or unknotting the knot is an effect of structure. The end of an analysis is, in my view, to be understood neither as unknotting *nor as* knotting, but rather as unknotting *and* reknotting. What is particular about the stunning unknotting of the knot is that it is not—as in psychosis—permanent, but rather inscribed in the pulsating of a time of unknotting that is awaiting a time of reknotting, which is effected, in my opinion, not by the "nominating *saying*" of the father, but by the "nominating *saying*" of the analysand.

Is this "nominating *saying*" that inscribes itself in the real as an "I know" conceivable? This question, as we have seen, is the very question that Lacan put to Soury two days after his seminar of February 15, 1977: "Is the real *writing* of 'I know' conceivable?"[273] The reason I am led to take a more affirmative approach to what remains for Lacan in a state of questioning is the consideration I have given to the nature of the articulation in the real produced by the unconscious know-how of the artist. It seems to me in this respect that if the artist succeeds in transmitting the unheard of, invisible, and immaterial character of the real, it is because he manages to articulate as "I" the nomination of one of the three first Names: the musician names the symbolic; the painter names the imaginary; and the dancer names the real.[274] The artist may thus be considered as the one who intervenes with respect to what is knotted as a Borromean knot by primal repression, by making the unpronounceable real transmissible.[275] By taking into account the real in the face of which the word keeps silent, art shows what

---

[272] [*Désistance* is a neologism based on the verb *désister*, to withdraw, step aside, stand down; there is also word play here with *insistance*.]

[273] [*"l'ecriture réelle du 'je sais' est-elle concevable?"*]

[274] Jacques Lacan, seminar of March 11, 1975, *RSI*, unpublished seminar.

[275] Jacques Lacan, seminar of January 14, 1975, *RSI*, unpublished seminar: "This knot ... is nothing less than the *Urverdrängt*, primordial primal repression."

cannot be demonstrated by revealing—by means of a note, a color, a movement—what is radically concealed.[276]

The monstration of the unprecedented, the invisible, and the imponderable is, in a certain way, a recreation of the originary act by means of which the real of the *Fiat lux* was brought into existence by the nomination "day." The difference between the nominating *saying* "day," with which God brings into existence what he has created by his *Fiat lux*, and the nominating *saying* of the artist consists in the fact that the latter does not create the word, but rather takes charge, by showing it, of the part of the real that "sists" without ex-sisting, because it has not been brought into existence through nomination.[277]

Whereas the nominating *saying* of God the Father corresponds to the fourth ring of the symbolic nomination by means of which occurs a real *writing* of the "He knows how to deal with the real," the nominating *saying* of the artist is, in my view, the *writing* of an "I know how to deal with the real" that replaces the knotting of four rings by the "He" with a knotting of four rings by the "I" of the unconscious.[278] From this point of view, we can say that, at the end of analysis, the analysand becomes, if not an artist, at least a poet. From the discovery of the unconscious syntax that governed his demand, he can drop the prose with which he spoke, leaving speech instead to the poem that inhabited him—a poem that he can inhabit from now on.

In this transfer from the prosaic to the poetic, the analyst ceases to incarnate for the analysand the presence of a "you" for whom the immediacy of his demand is intended. Lacan lets it be supposed that he can then become the mediating support of this big absent one that is the "He." In the seminar of February 7, I had suggested that the moment in which the "I" chooses to speak should be understood as a moment in which the subject emerges from the state of sideration effected by the "He" by replying "It's you"—that is to say, by naming it in the second person. Lacan replied, in the following seminar, by interpreting this "It's you" as a "you know," that is to say, as a "you" raised to the level of the third person.

---

[276] [... *devant lequel le mot fait 'motus.'*]
[277] [Lacan translates *Fiat lux*, as we have already seen, as *Borromean Fiat hole*.]
[278] Jacques Lacan, seminar of May 13, 1975, *RSI*, unpublished seminar.

# CHAPTER FOUR

# THE TIME OF THE OTHER: MUSIC

For Claude Lévi-Strauss, Gilbert Rouget, and Billie Holiday.

> "The function of music shows that it cannot be reduced to any translation of it into a verbal form. It exerts itself beneath language and any form of discourse, were it to emanate from the most inspired commentator, would never be profound enough to explain it."
> Claude Lévi-Strauss[279]

> "'In the beginning was the Word.' The Word was sound."
> Gilbert Rouget[280]

## I. Untranslatability[281]

Why, in the very moment I hear music, am I delighted by it? Because something happens that I am not prepared for. When I am speaking with someone, experience teaches me that I only receive the speech of my interlocutor through an internal deliberation that requires me to make a decision about the message heard ("Will I say 'yes' to it or will I say 'no'?"). When I hear the sound of music, I discover each time, with equal stupefaction, that I cannot but say "yes" to it. What is strange about this "yes" is that it is a radical "yes" that is not derived from an internal deliberation that has made me choose not to say "no"; this absolute "yes," which cannot conceive of "no," puts us

---

[279] Claude Lévi-Strauss, *L'Homme nu* (Paris: Plon, 1971), 580.
[280] Gilbert Rouget, *Musique en Jeu* 12 (October 1973), 105.
[281] The first two sections of this chapter were published as "La musique dans l'intraductible" in *Io* 5 (1994).

### Chapter Four – The Time of the Other: Music

on the tracks of the real sense of the *Bejahung*. The simplicity of this "yes" does not signify, however, that it is simple to understand: on the contrary, it is incomprehensible.

What, then, am I saying "yes" to? A subjective transmutation that turns—in a way that is always astounding each time it happens—my position as a heard subject into that of a hearing subject. While I thought that I was in the process of listening to music, I suddenly discover, at the very moment it sounds, that it is the music that hears me.

What does it hear? That I heard, in what it had given me to hear, a call that I answered with a "yes" whose extreme simplicity is matched only by its enigmatic character: indeed, I do not know either *to whom* I said "yes" or *who* said "yes." The most I know is that, by virtue of this "yes," an articulation occurs between a receiver in me who has received the call addressed by the music and the appearance of an emitter who addresses himself to the music in order to call it. With this "yes," I am saying both, "Yes, I am called by you," and, "Yes, I am calling you."[282]

It is in this mutation whereby an invoked subject becomes in turn invoking that we can identify, in this urge to say "yes," the invocatory drive. If music has a particular relationship with this drive that is "the closest to the experience of the unconscious," it is because, in transmitting itself as the good hearer of a "yes" that did not know itself, it frees the enunciator of this "yes," that is, the subject of the unconscious bringing it into existence.[283]

How can we conceive of this urge to say "yes" that music has heard? Does it come from an unconscious "I" that had always been there, waiting to be recognized, or is this "I" of the unconscious, on the contrary, sovereignly created by music? Is it the bar of the divided subject that sustains the Other's desire—incarnated by music—or is it the Other's desire that creates *ex nihilo* the subject of the unconscious? These two positions are one and the same if one considers that the call that is in music does not require an ego that is already there, but rather a subject who is not yet there, indefinitely susceptible to coming into being.

---

[282] This absolute "yes" is evoked by C. David (*La Beauté du geste, op. cit.*, 160, § 20): "The answer is yes."

[283] Jacques Lacan, *The Four Fundamental Concepts, op. cit.*, 104.

## Chapter Four – The Time of the Other: Music

Thus music teaches the ego a thing or two by uprooting it from the innocence that had led it to misrecognize the intimate urge intimating the existence of a subject. It teaches the ego that this urge is not unfamiliar to that radically exterior stranger, the Other. In this encounter between the most intimate and the most exterior, the subject learns that he is not constituted, according to the Freudian conception, by a discontinuity between inside and outside, but rather according to the Moebian concept, by a continuity between the intimate and the exterior, which Lacan baptized with a neologism: "ex-time." This continuity between the Other and the subject of the unconscious does not signify that the Other, by acquiring a place in the subject, is in a conquered land: not only do I not experience the presence of music as an intrusion characteristic of being raped, but I discover, on the contrary, with the most extreme certitude, that, in this place acquired in me, the Other is at home.

Could this lack of distinction between "mine" and "his," where the subject no longer knows if he is the agent or acted upon, be subject to the principle of that famous mystical fusion of the oceanic feeling that Freud wrote to Romain Roland about, suggesting that it was merely the effect of a regression to a state of maternal fusion? Freud's reference to maternal regression seems to me to be an indication, beyond Freud's phobia for music, of the fact that his positivist conception of mysticism, in which he sees nothing but obscurantism, hindered him from grasping the logical relations between the invocatory drive and mystical invocation.[284] This hindrance is evident in Freud's theory of identification where, in distinguishing three types of identifications, he overlooks a fourth type of identification that opens up the question of a metaphorical identification between the Other and the subject of the unconscious. This fourth identification, which corresponds to the Lacanian theory of the paternal metaphor, raises the question of the identity between the subject and the Other via the notion of a double negation: *the subject is no stranger to this stranger that is the Other*. This necessity of a double negation to evoke the kinship between the subject and the Other can, for instance, be seen in the fact that we may feel the urge to travel. Why do we like to go abroad if it is not

---

[284] See the article of J. and A. Caïn, "De l'incompatabilité de la psychanalyse avec la musique," in *Dixième Rencontres psychanalytiques d'Aix-en-Provence* (Paris: Les Belles Lettres, 1991).

because we then experience an identity that is impossible to experience when we are "at home"? In discovering that we are no stranger to this strangeness that we encounter in a foreign land, we discover that there are two ways of feeling "at home." The feeling that I have of being "at home" in the country where I live confronts me with an identity between me and my surroundings that is fundamentally different from the identity acquired by the fact of not being a stranger when in a foreign land.

As a result of this omission, Freud is unable to conceive of the metaphorical identity between the $ and the being of alterity. In spite of having broken radically with the metaphysical misrecognition of alterity, he discretely returns to it: hence his reductive position towards music, insofar as it conveys an absolute alterity. (Two major exceptions to this metaphysics of being should be noted: the first is that of the Platonic idea of Good beyond "Being"; and the second is the Cartesian idea of the infinite.) If, in this respect, reading the writings of Derrida, Levinas, and Jankélévitch is instructive for the analyst, it is because these authors, without being influenced by psychoanalysis, constantly return to the path along which the dimension of alterity tends to shatter, to deconstruct, the metaphysics of the same.

At this juncture, I have no hesitation in suggesting that a theoretical reflection on music is one of the possible ways of understanding the most primordial relation of the subject to the Other. The power of music is the power of commemorating the primordial time when the subject, prior to receiving speech, receives a stem, a root, upon which speech will subsequently be able to germinate. In this original stem, which I think of as the effect—not memorable, but com-memorable—of a primordial inscription, without the mediation of the imaginary, of the symbolic in the real, we are led to recognize the unary trait of Lacan.[285] This leads me to identify in the unary trait the emergence of the "simplest" musical element, that is, a chanted note. In my view, the *infans* perceives this note in the music of the mother's voice before he perceives the meaning of phonemes. The simplicity of the musical element *does not yet represent* the subject, but *names* what he possesses of the real. It is this through which a rhythm is transmitted, in-

---

[285] Jacques Lacan, seminar of February 21, 1962, *L'identification*, unpublished seminar.

carnated in a melody whose diachrony only acquires meaning because it is sustained by the synchronic structure that is harmony.

Why am I asserting that musical experience relates to an authentic mystical experience that the *infans* undergoes? Because the Thing [*Chose*] in him, which has been called, invoked by music, will, by virtue of a reversal, become an invocatory Thing that will start him moving—by singing or dancing—in response to the invocatory drive.

How are we to conceptualize the question of the source of the initiation of movement through which the subject, by dancing, will enter into the invocation of the Other?[286] What gets the subject moving in dance, without his having to make any particular effort, is the fact that the displacement he is engaged in uproots him from a place where he can no longer stay. He cannot stay there because, from the moment the music sounds, the new position he finds himself in ceases to be limited by the temporo-spatial orientation that it had received from the symbolic law and suddenly acquires the characteristic of a place inhabited by the amplitude of limitlessness. As soon as he encounters this limitlessness, he is no longer able to stay in place, for he has to move in order to inhabit this new space, henceforth metamorphosed into the fourth dimension by the rhythm and the music.

Was this limitlessness his own or does it belong to the Other? It belongs to both without being the property of either, for it rejects every owner. It is insofar as the subject is the subject of this limitlessness, and insofar as this limitlessness is something that is inaccessible to any form of knowledge, to any form reasoning that would turn him into an owner, that the subject commemorates it through his dance. In dancing the pure excess that is limitlessness, the subject discovers what he is not. He ceases to be limited by the specular law (he becomes invisible); he ceases to be limited by the law of gravity (he becomes immaterial); and he ceases to be limited by the symbolic interdiction (he becomes unheard-of).

How are we to understand this beyond meaning to which the dancer gains access? This a-semantic beyond, at the level of which no signified whatsoever is allotted to the signifier, is strangely reminiscent of what Lévi-Strauss is led to say in his preface to Marcel Mauss concerning *mana*. *Mana*, he says, is the manifestation of a real that sud-

---

[286] See 249, the question of the invocatory drive.

denly emerges in a social group when this group is led to encounter a point of real that, because it exceeds any possibility of being supported by a signifier, incarnates, for Lévi-Strauss, "the zero point of significance."[287] This leads me to put forward the idea that this zero symbol of a signifier without a signified is to be understood as a "first Name" whose power is to create *ex nihilo* a primordial real that can have consistency without being *covered* by the naming power of language. If "light" can have consistency without a nameable name ("day") being given to it, it is because "light" refers indissolubly to an intersection between the symbolic and the real: the intersection between a first creating Name and a pure created real.[288]

What is the difference between the first Name "light" and the second name "day"? The first, comparable to a proper name, is untranslatable, whereas the second Name is translatable ("day," etc.), in such a way that we can make the following hypothesis.[289] The first Name "light" is of the same structure as music, since a note of music (an A flat, for example) is strictly untranslatable by another note. Conversely, "day" can be translated as *"jour,"* for it refers to a translatable signified, whereas A flat does not refer to a signified, but rather to a pure real. In the passage from "light" to "day" there is thus a double movement that involves both an acquisition of meaning and a loss of meaning, since the untranslatable part in "light" cannot be taken in hand by the name "day."

The excess that cannot be covered by speech persists in music: if the dancing man can go beyond his spatiotemporal limits, it is because *he is dancing to what exceeds the field signified by speech*, to that part of clarity which, transmitted by "light," is untranslatable by the word "day." That this "untranslatable" real is dissociated from the real that is translatable by "day" poses to us a problem: Why, at the very moment when "light" is created, is there not a simultaneous creation of the name that would make it exist at the same time as "day"?

---

[287] Claude Lévi-Strauss, "Introduction à l'œuvre de Marcel Mauss," in Marcel Mauss, *Sociologie et Anthropologie* (Paris: Presses Universitaires de France, 1973).

[288] The light that appears with the *Fiat lux* (Genesis I: 3) pre-exists the fact of being named "day" (Genesis I: 5).

[289] Claude Lévi-Strauss, *Le Cru et le Cuit* (Paris: Plon, 1964), 34: "Music is a language, since we understand it, but one whose absolute originality, which distinguishes it from articulated language, resides in the fact that it is untranslatable."

If that were the case, if these two times introducing discordance between the translatable and the untranslatable did not exist, we would be living in another world where language would not be split between speech and music. The problem is that the world we are living in is permeated by the split between a first nomination and a second nomination and thus disposes us to a double relationship to the real. The first Name—which Lacan, in his seminar *RSI*, defines as "first Name insofar as it names something"—is comparable with a note of music that creates *ex nihilo* a "light" that we can dance even though we are not yet able to speak it.[290] We can only speak it when its translation into "day" bestows on us a tempered clarity that allows us to forget, thanks to meaning, the excess of semantic clarity whose pure light, as a zero signifier of significance, would dazzle us.

The question we are immediately faced with is the following: Insofar as this zero signifier of significance is what we encounter both in music and in the moment we are stunned by the signifier, where does the difference lie? This difference is fundamental, for it introduces us to the essence of our relationship to time. The subject who is in a state of sideration goes through the experience of a psychic time of latency in which he remains dumbfounded as long as he has not found the unconscious translation towards meaning (translation towards what should be—*soll ich*. The subject who hears music, on the other hand, has the experience of a subjective transmutation whose most astonishing characteristic is that it is *instantaneous*, for *it does not know this latency caused by sideration*. As soon as the subject hears music, he is in a position to instantaneously convert what he hears into a dance step, without there being, as there is with sideration, the shadow of a gap between the reception of the message heard and the emission of the message to which he responds by dancing. The great mystery of music resides in this *absence of diachrony* between the Other and the subject, such that the dancing subject is in a relationship of absolute synchrony with the Other: what he hears is converted, without temporal deliberation, into a dance step. If we try to account for this singular phenomenon, we discover that this strange possibility bestowed on the subject by music consists precisely in the fact that the subject *does not have to translate* what he hears. If he is not required to make

---

[290]Jacques Lacan, seminar of March 11, 1975, *RSI*, unpublished seminar.

## Chapter Four – The Time of the Other: Music

a translation it is because the music resounds as an untranslatable first Name with which he who, in speaking, "names himself without knowing it, without knowing with which name," finds himself finally named.[291]

Because music presents itself as this first Name reminding him of the originary time when what is most real in him received the immemorial name of "light," the subject becomes aware of the fact that the more he speaks, the more he commemorates the fact that he names himself with a name of which he knows nothing. The remembering of this forgotten name induced by music is especially cruel in that it reminds him of the fact that its translation, by his own first name and family name, simply confirms the fact that his first Name exceeds all possible translation. The first Name is thus forged, as Lacan asserts, by the pure inscription of a "unary trait" in the real.[292]

I understand this inscription as the origin that, because it is rooted in the sound of musical significance, will provide the stock from which speech will subsequently germinate.

Throughout Lacan's teaching—even though he did not speak specifically of music—we find these two logical times opposed. There is an absolute time of commencement with the inscription of the first Name of this originary "step," the unary trait, and a subsequent time of the origin of the speaking subject who constitutes himself by erasing the "trace of this step." The substitution, through primal repression, of a "no trace" [*pas de trace*] for the originary "trace of a step" [*trace de pas*] is thus the effect of the radical erasure of the primordial inscription of the first Name—the price to be paid if the enunciation of speech is to come into being.

Here is an example of how Lacan speaks of this logical phase of a commencement of creation: "The unary trait is before the subject. 'In the beginning was the Word [*Verbe*]' means: in the beginning is the unary trait."[293] That the unary trait appears to refer to the element that is contributed by the musical phenomenon—no doubt through the mediation of the voice of the parents—is a point that was not envisaged by Lacan, who, like Freud, had very little interest in music. In this

---

[291] Jacques Lacan, seminar of January 10, 1962, *L'identification*, unpublished seminar.
[292] Jacques Lacan, seminars of December 20, 1960 and January 10, 1962.
[293] Jacques Lacan, seminar of November 29, 1961, *Anxiety, op. cit*.

*Chapter Four – The Time of the Other: Music*

respect, if one is willing to take into consideration contemporary studies on the relationship of so-called "primitive" societies to madness, it is difficult to spare ourselves the effort of examining the underlying relationship between music and madness.[294] All these societies consider that letting a delusional person listen to certain kinds of music has the power to reverse the foreclosure of the unary trait that is generative of delusion. Insofar as "primitives" may not have forgotten the structural affinity between the unary trait and the rhythmic trait of a note of music, we are justified in asking ourselves if there is not a fact of universal structure involved here.

This affinity leads me to extend the hypothesis that the support of the originary language in which the originary commandment was transmitted, the *Fiat lux*, was no other than the medium of music. Is it not because this originary language, music, is untranslatable, that it is universally audible? If the biblical myth teaches us that God dispersed man at Babel, making him speak in different tongues, might this not be an allusion to the fact that the originary language that they spoke prior to the dispersion had the capacity to be universalizable because it was an untranslatable musical language?

I take this hypothesis seriously in order to try to understand the reason why the treatment of madness seems universally, in primitive societies that are unknown to each other, to have required the mediation of music. Without going into the multiple differences in the rituals through which the followers of Dionysos, or those of Voodoo, care for the patient suffering from madness, I will simply indicate the common denominator of all these rites that are structured around a dance of therapeutic possession. The common point is organized around a belief that constitutes a social bond: the delusions of the madman are a punishment administered by a god who is angered by the fact that the

---

[294] Gilbert Rouget, *La Musique et la Transe* (Paris: Gallimard, 1980). Marc Moralli, "De l'interprétation musicale à l'interprétation psychanalytique," *Apertura* 4 (1990); "Diva, une passion de la voix," *Apertura* 8 (1992). Jacqueline Assabgui, *La Musicothérapie* (Paris: Jacques Grancher, 1991). Marie Daraki, *Dionysos* (Paris: Arthaud, 1985). Henri Jeanmaire, *Dionysos* (Paris: Payot, 1970). Marcel Detienne, *Dionysos à ciel ouvert* (Paris: Hachette, 1986). France Schott-Billmann, *Possession, Danse et Thérapie* (Paris: Sande, 1985); *Le Primitivisme en danse* (Paris: Chiron, 1989). Mélèse, "J'ouïr," *Musique en jeu* 9 (1972); E. Lecourt, "Compte rendu des séminaires de musicothérapie," *Revue de musicothérapie* 4 (1984); P.-P. Lacas, "Questions aux musicothérapeutes," in *ibid.* F. Bismuth, "L'Ecoute musicale," DESS de psychologie clinique (1992–1993).

## Chapter Four – The Time of the Other: Music

subject has committed a major symbolic error in relation to him. As these societies are polytheistic, the first task of the shaman is to identify the god who is vexed. The second task is to address an appropriate ritual invocation to this god, asking him to withdraw his malediction and to form a new symbolic pact with the subject. These tasks are accomplished through the mediation of musicians who, working together with the shaman, play different kinds of music, each of which is the specific insignia of a god. When the music corresponding to that of the vexed god sounds, the god may agree to let himself be identified by descending on the ill person and taking possession of him in a recognizable way. The patient then begins a dance of possession that is not anarchic but strictly coded, making it possible to recognize, through specific and identifiable movements, which god is riding his mount.

So it is through this act of dance, namely, the trance, that the "transported," "enthusiastic" subject can find again, by virtue of a symbolic act, the god from whom he had separated himself by breaking a pact that resulted in the god being rejected and foreclosed in the real where he subsisted in anger.[295] That music, through the medium of the trance, can create the conditions for a reversal of foreclosure raises the following question: Does music have the power—a power that speech does not have—of creating the conditions in which the subject can return to what was foreclosed? This simply confirms what we learn from our clinical experience: while interpretation has the power to dissolve the repression that is the source of a neurosis, it is generally powerless in relation to delusion; that a word is unable to deliver from its retreat the signifier that is foreclosed in the real is due to the fact that the foreclosed signifier is not translatable by another word with which it could, as in the witticism, equivocate. This signifier would have been translatable if the subject of the unconscious had been able, before repressing it, to "assume" it according the unconscious "yes" of *Bejahung*.

Let us take this example of a repression of the signifier of the Name-of-the-Father insofar as it gives rise to a possible translation. The father of a family consulted an analyst, in a state of anguish, for the fol-

---

[295] On the subject of Dionysian enthusiasm, see the work of H. Jeanmaire, M. Daraki, and M. Detienne, cited in the footnote above.

## Chapter Four – The Time of the Other: Music

lowing reason: when he played with his young son, saying to him, "*Tu n'es qu'une vilaine asperge* [You are just an ugly asparagus]," his son would reply, "*Non, je ne suis pas vilain, je suis beau, je suis ton beau fils* [No, I am not ugly, I am beautiful, I am your beautiful son]."[296] In fact, the son of this man was not his real son, but this truth had always been concealed from him. This father had consulted the analyst because he was asking himself: Was it the coincidence of a play on words that made the child say, "*Je suis ton beau fils* [I am your stepson]," or had he used this word-play to let his "father" know that he had always known that he was his stepson?[297]

This clinical case, which was reported to me by Charles Melman, shows us in an exemplary manner how, since the repression of the signifier of the Name-of-the-Father is not a foreclosure, translation takes place. By enunciating the message, "*Tu es une vilaine asperge, un vilain fils*," the father was conveying a double message. With the signifier "*vilain*," he was unconsciously translating the signifier "*beau*," which qualified him, for the good hearer that the child was, as "*beau-père*" [stepfather]. By saying, "*Tu es un vilain fils*," he was also signifying that he had—beyond the word "*vilain*" that bore the repression—assumed, according to the primordial *Bejahung*, the signifier "*fils*." As the signifier of the Name-of-the-Father was not foreclosed but repressed, the son was thus able to make an assumption of the signifier of the Name-of-the-Father. Understanding that this signifier had been transmitted to him by means of a repression, he had been able to translate it perfectly by sending the message ("*tu es vilain*") back to its emitter in its inverted form ("*je suis beau, je suis beau-fils*").

The relationship of unconscious refusal of this "A-father" towards the child was thus radically different from the foreclusive position of the psychotic. It could be said that the delusional subject's impossibility of assuming the Name-of-the-Father introduces a rupture of the pact with this signifier, with the consequence that a stupefying gaze makes its return in the real. Speaking in the terms of primitive man, one could say that this gaze is the very manifestation of a god

---

[296] ["You're just an ugly asparagus"—"No, I'm not ugly, I'm your beautiful son." In French there is a derogatory expression, *Quelle asperge*! (What an asparagus!), to describe someone who is gangling.]

[297] ["*Beau fils*" may mean "beautiful son" or "stepson."]

## Chapter Four – The Time of the Other: Music

angered by his foreclosure. What power does speech have to resume a dialogue with this angered god whose stupefying gaze is the expression of a silent, absolute knowledge imprisoned by the real? Insofar as this signifier is in the real and not in the unconscious, how can the analyst's speech, which addresses itself to the unconscious, reach a signifier in the real? This question may leave an analyst feeling helpless: If the tool of his work is the transference, what can he do with a signifier that, being foreclosed, is necessarily a signifier that escapes the power of the transference?

This formidable question—one that has no doubt always intrigued man, for, ever since he conquered his humanity, he has been aware that the price of this conquest is also that of madness—is answered by primitive man as follows. It is not impossible that the signifier in the real that is the angered god will allow himself to be transferred into the symbolic, if we address ourselves to him through that strange vehicle which is music. If it is not impossible for the angered god to let himself be swayed by the rhythm of a note of music, rather than by a good word, it is because music is the language of the gods. Music can reach them because it is made of a fabric similar to theirs. Human language arouses the wrath of the god when it is no longer able, or no longer willing, to use its power to proclaim that which goes beyond human meaning. Music is precisely the zero signifier that absorbs this excess of meaning that, because speech is unable to absorb it, condemns speech to only half-saying the truth.

Does this mean that music expresses *the* truth? No: it only expresses the real, insofar as it brings it into existence. In this sense its power is at once superior and inferior to that of speech. It is superior because the real that it brings into existence disposes man—as well as the angered god—to respond with an absolute "yes" that is incarnated in a dance. Through it this man, and the god who rides him, enter into a relationship with each other. But it is inferior to speech with regard to truth because it is only with speech that the question of truth and of ethics arises. It is not because music, by virtue of what it makes man hear, is capable of moving him to the point of reducing him to tears that it confronts him with the question of good and evil; no sooner had the Nazis left a concert where they had wept listening to romantic music than they returned conscientiously to the accomplishment of their program. If we want to explain, with a minimum of rigor, what the transference induced by music has that is specifically different from the transference brought into play by the act of speaking, we need to distinguish the two ways in which music acts on the unconscious. The first is linked to the fact that music has the power of making one hear, simultaneously, the melodic diachrony played by the right hand on the piano and the harmonic synchrony played by the left hand. When we are speaking, we hear the diachronic flow of speech, engaged in the unfolding of time, without hearing, at the same time, the harmonic synchrony—that is to say, the unconscious code that confers on our speech its own resonance. Whereas, when we enter into the world of music, we hear *both* the melody and the synchrony, so that if a pianist were to hit a false note with his right hand he would hear it immediately. On the contrary, if I am speaking, I can be led to say something that contradicts my unconscious knowledge without hearing the falseness of what I am saying. If what I am saying is not in tune with the unconscious chain, I will not hear the dissonance, the distortion of the truth that results from it. By definition, I cannot hear my unconscious structure as long as there is no symptom.

The tension that music creates, by letting us hear the melody at the same time as the harmony, produces a specific expectation of a particular note: the "blue note." This note incarnates the human hope for a possible solution for the unsurpassable antinomy that exists between the synchronic structure and diachronic time.

The second way in which music induces a specific transference is, as we shall see, that of the mystery of rhythm.

## II. The "Blue Note"

Music requires two subjective positions: a first position in which I wait for the return of the rhythm that supports the movement of the dance; and a second position, of an ecstatic order, which leads me to wait for the call of a certain note that is not yet there, but whose tension, produced by the encounter between the harmony and the melodic notes already played, leads me to suppose that I am not waiting in vain.

This capacity to wait for this note seems to me to fundamentally correspond to what is called "hope." Except that it is not a matter of having hope in something whose content is already known to me—hope in the "great evening"—but of having hope in something that I know to hope for, even though I absolutely don't know what it consists of. If the way a musician plays is such that it sometimes enables me to hear this "blue note," I learn that my hope was not in vain.[298] In this respect, the blue note differs from the witticism that, when it is produced, necessarily catches me unawares, since, when the blue note sounds, I was already aware of the hope of hearing it.

The recognition that I have for it, if it resounds, lies in the fact that the state of rapture it puts me in is literal. It uproots me from the specular world I was in and makes me cross a threshold that I would otherwise probably not have ventured to cross—the threshold of a world whose extreme novelty is that in it the power of the "unheard-of" reigns. The power to wake me up, teaching me that everything sensible that I had been able to hear hitherto was, without my realizing it, under the ascendancy of the unheard-of.

The transference to this absence that is the blue note is thus linked to the expectation of a signifier stripped of all meaning, in relation to which all the other articulated notes represented the subject that I was unaware of being. Can such a signifier be heard through psychoanalytic interpretation? Lacan broached this question in his last seminar, "*L'insu que sait de l'une-bévue s'aile à mourre*," by asking himself how a signifier could be introduced that "awakens" the subject: "a new signifier... which would have no meaning whatsoever... which would open us up to what I call the real...." In this respect, he opposes science to poetry: "Science," he points out, "provokes an awakening, but an awakening that is difficult and suspect." Referring to poetry a few lines further on, he says: "It is only poetry that allows for interpretation... poetry which is an effect of meaning [*effet de sens*] but equally an effect of hole [*effet de trou*]." The reference to poetry is the path by which Lacan appeals to music, insofar as poetry embodies the possibility of language to transcend prose and to make us hear the untranslatable character of the musical of which words are potentially a vehicle.

---

[298] Alain Didier-Weill, intervention at the seminar of Jacques Lacan of December 21, 1976, "L'insu que sait de l'une-bévue s'aile à mourre," unpublished seminar; "De quatres temps subjectivants dans la musique," *Ornicar ?* 8 (Winter 1976–1977); "Point de vue psychanalytique sur la musique," *Revue de musicothérapie* 4 (1984); "Brève remarque psychanalytique sur la musique," *Revue de musicothérapie* 6 (1986).

Represented by the melodic chain in relation to the blue note, the subject, in an ecstatic moment, is uprooted from historical time so that he encounters the grain of eternity from which the temporal rhythm receives its true breath.[299] There can be no rhythm if there is no note—this blue note—that has the absolute power of abolishing rhythm, letting us hear instead a fundamental silence. Of this silence, overabundant with meaning, a melomaniac also once said that, in the brief silence following the end of a performance of Mozart, it was "'Mozart' that could then be heard."

But this instant of eternity that a note brings forth only has one time. It is limited by something that is imposed on the subject that will introduce a totally different type of transference in him: a pulsating transference caused by the beat of rhythm.

### III. Rhythm, the Invocatory Drive, and Dance

#### A) DANCE AND THE GENERATION OF TIME

I agree with Lacan that "the invocatory drive is the closest to the experience of the unconscious," inasmuch as this drive is most particularly activated by music.[300] Just as every drive is characterized by a movement back and forth, whereby a reversal causes a new subject ("seeing-being seen," "eating-being eaten") to appear, the invocatory drive initiates such a reversal of the subject with the difference that, as it is not a partial drive, the subject invoked becomes invoking without the support of a partial object.

Let us try to understand the signification of the subjective experience by means of which the drive reversal is initiated, in this trance that dance can be, thanks to which the new subject, the invoking subject, comes into being. I have already spoken of the first mutation produced in a subject who, under the assault of music, discovers with astonishment that, though he thought he was listening to music, he is

---

[299] On the subject of this experience of immortality, see the article of J. Rousseau-Dujardin, "Génération de la musique," in *Dixièmes Rencontres psychanalytiques, op. cit.*

[300] Jacques Lacan, *The Four Fundamental Concepts, op. cit.*, 104.

## Chapter Four – The Time of the Other: Music

the one, in fact, who is being listened to. The music hears him, hears in him a call of which he knew nothing, that is, a call to become what, as yet, he is not.

If, again and again, the subject can hear this call, it is because in the unconscious there is an irreducible gap that the subject, in spite of his attempts to forget it by filling or stopping it with the cork that is the sexual object, is unable to forget. This unforgettable "again" is, as Lacan says, "the proper name of this gap in the Other from which the demand for love stems."[301] It is because the subject is structurally unable to forget the demand for love that he remains indefinitely permeable to the auditor that is music, which invokes him: "I who hear your call, I ask you to allow it to be."

What is strange about this command is that the subject receives it as a command that requires not his obedience, but rather his freedom. If, indeed, the word "freedom" has a meaning, it is that which is dispensed to the subject at the very moment when, by engaging in the act of dance, he "freely" accepts the command: "Dance!" This command will be realized because the subject who is invoked to become will no longer be able to stay in place; as soon as he has received the invocation to dance, he is invoking the existence of the Other. So he has to move in order to accomplish his first dance step. Through it he will let emerge the signification of the new subject that he has become since the moment he was no longer simply the one who *was called* by the Other to uproot himself from the place where he was, but the one who *uprooted himself* from this place by making a leap. During this displacement that frees him from the earth's gravity, he is suspended in space for an ephemeral period of time, waiting to fall back down again from this new place, which is that of the Other. This initial step whereby he accomplishes his passage into the unconscious is different from that of the child who hesitates to take his first step, knowing that he must do it alone and that he may fall. However, the dancer does not launch himself completely alone: he has faith that he will be accompanied by music. This faith in the fidelity of music will be expressed as follows: "Having called me to leave the ground and to rise up towards you, are you now going to abandon me or will you be there when I fall back to the ground? To you, who said to me: 'Leave your earth and

---

[301] Jacques Lacan, *Encore, op. cit.*, 4.

become something other than what you are,' I am asking you, just as I am about to come back to earth, to be present with me. What I am saying to you is: 'Come back.'"

What does this invocation "Come back" signify other than the fact of asking music to be there at the very moment when the subject comes back down to earth? Music consents to this invocation at the very moment when the subject gets his feet back on the ground. The rhythm of music welcomes him through this act of presence that says to him: "You see, it was not in vain that you placed your hope in me by saying, 'Come back.'" This reversal whereby the "become" addressed to the subject by the Other is transmuted into a "come back" addressed by the subject to the Other is *what founds the tempo*, the first time of rhythm, whereby the subject has the dual experience both of being freed from the law of gravity, at the moment when he takes off, and of falling again under the influence of this law. It is not really a question of two distinct phases in which the subject first has an experience of weightlessness, followed by an experience of returning to gravity. What is profoundly enigmatic is the fact that, when the dancer touches the ground again, it is as if the earth ceased to be the locus of the centripetal force governing falling bodies, becoming instead a centrifugal force that can make the subject rebound, like a trampoline.

To understand what is mysterious about the way a body symbolizes, or not, the law of falling bodies, it suffices to observe two young girls playing with a jump-rope. How are we to understand that, despite the fact that they have the same weight, each time that the first girl lands on her feet we hear the repetitive sound of "boom-boom," whereas, when the second lands, we hear no sound at all? Is it that the one who bounces without making any noise has stronger muscles than the other? No, her capacity lies in the fact that, for her, the earth is endowed, for a mysterious reason, with an elastic power such that she does not need to make any muscular effort to take off. This mysterious reason is no other than that of the transference through which the subject, if he manages to get in touch again with the musical rhythm that is in him, is put in contact with the power that the Other possesses to pull him away from the ground, saying to him: "Become other than you are, other than this body subject to the real of gravity." If the subject is able to consent repeatedly to this commandment, it is because, for his part, he enters into the rhythm by responding to the "become" with a "come back." This conversion is the double pulsation

## Chapter Four – The Time of the Other: Music

that founds the commencement of the rhythm by which the subject, uprooted from his originary place, was propelled, in the first phase of the invocatory drive, between two places, between heaven and earth.

Let's describe the second phase during which the invocatory drive takes charge of the subject, who, having made a first displacement, must now make a second, bringing him back to square one. There can be no dance, in effect, if there are not two steps, one of them articulating a beginning and the other a conclusion, thereby creating the conditions of beginning again. At the moment when the subject touches the ground again, the dialogue he entertains with music is modified: the latter no longer says to him, "Become," but rather, "Become again," since with his first move he has in fact come to this new place where it was waiting for him. Up until that precise moment, music had shown its aptitude to give its inaugural "become" the dimension of insistence through which the signification of the rhythm appeared. This time, when it says, "Become again," to the subject, music is asking him to provide evidence, in his turn, of a possible "insistence." It tells him to forget what has become, what has already begun, and to conquer a second place, the place of square one from where everything must begin again.

The difference between the "become again" that music addresses to the subject and the "come back" that the subject addressed to music, in the earlier phase, consists in the fact that the "come back" was a demand signifying, "Don't let me fall," whereas the "become again" signifies, "Don't fall; find again in yourself, and by yourself, the first burst of energy which made you take off when I said to you, "Become." Becoming again, the subject will take off for the second time, but this second taking off will not be a repetition of the first, elicited by the "become." Indeed, thanks to the second leap, which takes him back to square one, he knows that he is going to hear, for the second time, the initial commandment "become" with which the instinctual movement will begin again, but he does not apprehend this "become" in the same way as did the first time. Why? Because the "become again," insofar as it precedes the "become," has the effect of an interpretation, making him discover that, if he has become again, it is due to an insistence of which he knew nothing before it had been revealed to him by music. This insistence of which he knew nothing, is that of the demand for love, of that weak point which insists in order to say to the Other: "Come again!"

## Chapter Four – The Time of the Other: Music

The Other's power to reveal to the subject that he can become has its source in the fact that, without knowing it, the subject had been invoking the Other with a "come," even before the Other addresses him. The subject only fully assumes the fact that he can insist by becoming again. Then he is able to draw not only on the "become" of the Other, but also on the point where, in his originary *dire*, an objectless desire insists whose enunciation is: "Come."

The dancing cycle of the invocatory drive completes when the subject, having in a first moment become, in a *second moment* is relaunched by the insistence of the Other insofar as he returns, in a third moment is solicited by the Other's perseverance that says, "Become again," and then finds in the *fourth moment* the point of insistence where the enigmatic desire of a demand for infinite love "comes."

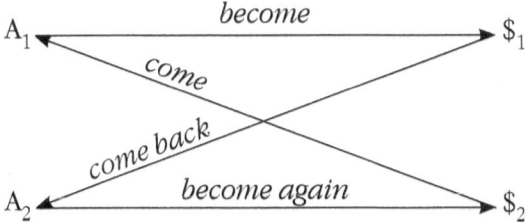

By saying, "Come," and not, "Come back," the subject appeals to the first manifestation with which the Other inaugurates the absolute time of a first phase of the *tempo*. It will constantly return insofar as it is engendered by the fading of the second, which the subject will welcome from now on by tapping his foot or his hand in time to the rhythm. This time measure through which he gets himself to *swing* is how the subject discovers that the greatest happiness that can be given to him is quite simply linked to the fact of gaining access to the perception that time can pass. He is able to do this insofar as he is a passenger who, by returning from the second to the first moment, creates the conditions of recreating infinitely the return to the first step.

Chapter Four – The Time of the Other: Music

B) FORECLOSURE OF TIME

For some psychoanalysts, it would seem that there is nothing mysterious about time: it is considered as existing "in itself," and as owing nothing to human creation. On this view, it is a scientific object that is quantifiable and measurable by an adequate tool: the clock. In this respect, the clock is what gives its support to this objective conception of time; by making it possible to cut up time into slices of varying degrees of thickness, it gives man the possibility to consider it as a measurable and controllable quantity.[302]

When this conception is shared by the psychoanalyst, he is quite "naturally" led to consider that in exchange for the quantity of money he receives from the analysand, he must give a measurable quantity of time. In this type of exchange, one quantity is equivalent to another quantity: "Time is money." This equivalence, full of good sense and bourgeois morality, means that the question of the qualitative structure of what is specifically human time is quite simply eluded. Man, in fact, does not dwell "in" time; he only exists insofar as he is inhabited "by" time, for, fundamentally, he is inhabitable by it. "Inhabitable" signifies that the habitat will occur if something has made it possible for the graft of time to take. This "something" that sustains the invocatory drive, upon which the unconscious pulsates, can be absent. My contention is that psychoticizing foreclosure is precisely a foreclosure of this graft of time.

The clinical experience of neurosis has already taught us that human desire is linked to the perception of temporal rhythm, which, without being foreclosed, can slow down. The first sign of depression, along with the appearance of boredom and monotony, is the oppressive feeling that time does not pass quickly enough, and that this slowing down of time is accompanied by a slowing down of the body, which suddenly becomes heavy and difficult to move around. The fact that time can slow down is the sign of a possible catastrophe: indeed, this slowing down can continue until time purely and simply comes to a stop. The melancholic (when melancholia manifests itself in its fully developed form of Cotard's syndrome) is someone who is familiar with the

---

[302] Ilya Prigogine and Isabelle Stengers, *Entre le temps et l'éternité* (Paris: Fayard, 1988), 19: "Time, which is our very life, does not set us in opposition to an objective world; on the contrary, it translates our solidarity with the real."

extreme experience of an extinction of time interpreted as an extinction of all life in him. From this point of view, when he affirms that he is no longer alive, but a "living dead" person, he is speaking the strict truth.

What can reverse the tendency for time to slow down, which is the first sign of depression? Is it interpretation? No: in depression interpretation has no effect. The depressive does not want to know what the meaning of the symptom is. He wants to encounter the radically a-semantic, incredible presence that can check the slowing down of the temporal rhythm and make it beat to the rhythm of desire. He wants, in short, to encounter the enigmatic scansion that, by "punctuating" time at its right rhythm, will make of him a being who transcends the real of his body. If this body is crushed by depression, it is because the pressure of gravity, having ceased to be symbolized by the rhythm of the invocatory drive, has taken hold of this body, reducing it to its most real aspect: its weight.

When the weight of the body is released, what does the body do if not show that occulted thing that is the heavy corpse that we carry potentially within us? The corpse that the living dead person, namely, the melancholic, lets fall out of the window; for, to find his tomb, he need do no more than trust in the law of falling bodies.

How are we to conceive of the way in which foreclosure has transmuted a body "living for death" into a "living dead" body? The above description of the different phases of the invocatory drive has made it possible to identify, in the dialectic of the subject and the Other, two moments of *Bejahung* whereby the subject is led to make two types of assumption of the Other. In order for the most fundamental "yes" that the subject is disposed to give to the Other to be assumable, the Other must be able to give meaning to the subject's primordial call, "Come," by manifesting that he has heard the subject's "come" and that what he has heard has consequences. By saying "Become," the Other proves to the subject that he has heard his "come," in such a way that the "come the become" and the "become the come" can be conjoined. By answering "yes" to the "become," the subject intimates to the "come" of which he was the vehicle to tear itself away from its intimate dimension and to export itself through an initial step that sets it in movement towards the outside. It is in this conjunction articulating the intimate and the outside that the "ex-time" occurs in which both of them, saying "yes" to each other, incarnate the success of the primordial *Bejahung*.

## Chapter Four – The Time of the Other: Music

It is because this success is that of the paternal metaphor that we can consider that the therapeutic trance succeeds in persuading the signifier of the Name-of-the-Father to come back from the real where it had remained foreclosed, and to "ride" symbolically the subject with whom he renews the pact that had been broken.

The first *Bejahung* may thus be understood as the success of the most originary pact whereby the subject, through the intermediary of the medium of music, ceases to be a stranger for that stranger that is the Other. In this respect, music has strictly no other meaning than that of being the mediator of a purely logical articulation between the Other and the subject.

The question we need to ask about music, then, is this: If it alone has the power to renew the pact that has been broken, are we not justified in supposing that it was by virtue of it alone that this original pact was formed? If that is the case, we can only suppose that the *infans*, immersed in parental speech, only communicates with it through the medium of the music that he hears through the intermediary of the rhythm punctuating the melody of the maternal voice. The most radical foreclosure would thus refer to the rupture of the primordial pact with the unary trait, which I conceive of as the untranslatable but inscribable part deposited in the signifier, that does not yet represent the speaking subject but names him with a "first Name" that is unpronounceable. If the first possibility of foreclosure is related to the disavowal of the pact by which the Other and the subject are linked together in the metaphorical scansion "come-become," the second possibility for foreclosure to occur unfolds as an interruption of the second time of the pact brought into play between the Other and the subject, insofar as what is then foreclosed is the conquest of this second scansion, "come back again-become again," by which time that began can begin again. The difference between these two metaphorical times [*temps*] lies in the difference between what is affirmed and what is confirmed. The Other may indeed have given the *infans* the possibility of *affirming*, while recusing himself at the particular moment when the child, just as he is ready to take his first steps in life on his own, feels the need to know if the Other will *confirm* the first affirmation by which he was sustained primordially.

It is this appeal for confirmation that we see when, for instance, the child who is on the point of performing a great feat, like getting across a ditch or jumping into water, keeps calling out to his mother,

## Chapter Four – The Time of the Other: Music

"Look!" What is the child saying with this "Look!" if not: "You who gave me the means to jump, will you be there when I actually do it?"

It is not exceptional for a mother to be unable to confirm what she had previously affirmed; indeed, her capacity for attention may be less sustained from the moment the child no longer elicits from her the enunciation "become," but rather the enunciation "become again," with which she invites him to give insistence to what she has contributed to bringing into existence.

How can we differentiate between the effects produced by a foreclosure pertaining to the Other depending on whether he says, "Become" or "Become again"? For the time being, we will leave this question open.

### IV. The Trauma, Speech, and Music

The human unconscious is apt to be traumatized by the collapse of maternal consistency, insofar as it lacks a signifier, because the subject has already made the assumption, through the intermediary of musical rhythm, of the presence "one" of the unary trait. It is because, primordially, there is "*y a de l'un*" that the *signification of the -1 can appear retroactively*. But it is not because the One, rendered transmissible by music, introduces the possibility of giving signification to the trauma that it affords the possibility of resolving the traumatic ordeal. For the subject to be able to come out of the trauma into which he has entered, quite another dimension than that of music is needed, namely, that of speech, inasmuch as it alone can take charge of the trauma.

Music and speech are thus opposed insofar as the first gives access to entry into the trauma, whereas the second gives access to the way out of it. Music introduces the *Bejahung* and stands in opposition to speech, which introduces primal repression.[303]

In a certain way, music is a hypocritical consoler. It is the great consoler because, under its power, by encountering a trustworthy Other who is present when needed, man forgets the traumatic dimension of the Other who is absent when needed. But it is a contradic-

---

[303] See 281.

## Chapter Four – The Time of the Other: Music

tory consoler because it is by virtue of the Other's intervention that absence acquires meaning. The contradiction lies in the difference of structure of the absence to which the subject is introduced by music, on the one hand, and by trauma, on the other. Whereas music induces the subject to discover the absence *of* the Other who, so that he may return, goes absent rhythmically, the trauma leads the subject to encounter the absence *in* the Other.

Music prepares us for thinking about a reversible absence situated in temporal diachrony, whereas trauma introduces us to a synchronic absence that is irreversible insofar as it is not inscribed in temporal pulsation. In this respect, the real trauma is not the absence *of* the mother, but the absence *in* the mother. Faced with the mother's absence, the child is not absolutely without recourse because he can cry out "Help!" to make her come back. On the contrary, when he is confronted with the real hole of maternal privation, he is deprived of the recourse of speech. The state of fascination into which this hole plunges him reduces him to silence, thereby showing that any possibility of calling for the help of any Other whatsoever is forbidden to him.

How could he call for the help of an Other when the "*troumatism*" reveals to him that the Other, in whom he thought he could trust, has ceased to be a locus giving sense to the world and has become instead a locus of non-sense that is generative of repulsion? Analytic theory does not sufficiently measure the extent to which the subject interprets this signifying deficiency of the Other as an act of betrayal whereby the Other lets him down and abandons him. Insofar as the subject cannot justify this abandonment, the originary meaning of injustice becomes apparent to him. Traumatic distress is thus the means by which the question of truth and ethics is posed: insofar as the subject interprets the traumatic bankruptcy of the Other as a rupture of contract, he lives this rupture in relation to truth and justice.[304] The dimension of truth is discovered by virtue of the fact that the Other is apprehended as a *deceiver*, and that of justice by virtue of the fact that this deceiver is *unjust*.

If music is the great consoler, it is so because we know that it will not deceive us. The silence that exists between two notes is not

---

[304] See further on, "Entering the Trauma," 265ff.

the terrifying absence of trauma, for it is a silence bearing a promise the fidelity of which we believe in. "I am leaving you for a moment, the fading note says to us, but I will come back shortly in the form of another note which will return in time; you can count on my tempo, it won't let you down." As a matter of fact, the subject who is dancing will not fall when his feet touch the ground again, for there is no misunderstanding with rhythm, which guarantees the exactness of a successful meeting with the Other. This precision with which the dancer, even if he or she has not learnt to dance, executes a step is something profoundly enigmatic. You only have to watch a very young child who has never learnt to dance and, what's more, who has never seen anyone dance, and you will see that he immediately executes with his body movements that interpret the music perfectly accurately.

The man who is speaking only advances in speech with faltering imprecision and slowness, because there is an intermediate time of inner deliberation between the moment he receives speech and the moment he speaks, which is necessary in order to decode the received message and encode the emitted message. The rapidity and precision of the man who is dancing lies in the fact that he *does not need to be aware of* this period of latency between what he hears and what he says in response. The man who speaks, insofar as he is subjected to the three aspects of the law, namely, the legislative power, the judicial power, and the executive power, may be contrasted with the man who dances and who is topologically situated in a place at the level of which these distinctions are abolished. The speaking subject only engages in the execution of speech (executive power) after having interpreted (judicial power) the symbolic law that he receives from the Other (legislative power), while the dancing subject concretizes *in the same synchronic moment* the fact of hearing, interpreting, and executing. The presence or absence of this temporal latency is paradoxically the means by which music introduces the subject to the dimension of justness *that cannot aspire to justice*, whereas speech is the means by which the question of justice is introduced insofar as it does not possess the power of justness which would make it possible to tell "the" truth.

Why can speech only half-tell the truth? Because the fundamental act of speech is the act whereby the subject has to be able to *make an act of presence at the traumatic point where the Other proves to be absent*. Up until then the subject was not without having symbol-

## Chapter Four – The Time of the Other: Music

ized the absence of the Other, but it was an absence that had presented itself to him through the teaching that he had received from the invocatory drive, insofar as it was inscribed in a temporal succession in which the Other confirmed his fidelity rhythmically, becoming present again after having gone absent.

With the trauma, the Other, ceasing to be *alternately* present and absent, poses the unthinkable paradox of being simultaneously both present and absent. This paradox of an absence in presence is, in a certain way, present in the first verses of Genesis, which teach us that light and darkness, which are separated in the third verse ("And God divided the light from the darkness"), had not been divided before the separating act. The fact that they were indistinguishable in the beginning gives us the idea of a "darkened" light, that is to say, of a simultaneity of presence and absence. It is at the moment when the trauma substitutes the alternation of the presence and absence of day and night with the synchronic simultaneity "light-darkness" that the subject, losing the support of the rhythm *of* the Other, has to become capable of creating his own rhythm as a support on which he can lean.

How will he find this support with speech? By an act of unconscious interpretation—which the dancing subject does not have to produce—whereby, through an act of primal repression, he will substitute a real hole in the symbolic for the symbolic hole in the maternal real. By means of this substitution, the subject, who is now lacking, oriented by the permanence of the missing object, the cause of his desire, will be led to forget the rhythm of the appearance and disappearance of the Other. But this forgetting of the Other is not radical: if, in acquiring speech, the subject forgets that it comes to him from the donator that is the Other, speech nonetheless remains the unforgettable witness of the existence of a donation.

With speech, there is a split between the consciousness of a given and the unconsciousness of a donator that does not exist in music. The man who speaks is in a state of solitude with which the man who dances is not familiar. With each note that he hears, the dancer is consciously connected with the Other, whereas the speaking subject does not consciously know that he is connected with the Other by the speech that he receives from him. This is because, ever since the trauma, he has ceased to be instantaneously in phase with him, and it is owing to this experience of being out of phase with him that henceforth he will need time—the time of sideration—to rediscover this Other. This time of translation is the reason why the half-saying of the truth exists. When he speaks, the subject, without even realizing it, translates, and in so doing betrays in such a way that he cannot help but translate well and translate badly, say well and say badly.

Are we devoid of any criteria for distinguishing the *well saying* and the *badly saying*? Not entirely: am I not in a position to hear, when a subject speaks, what he cannot hear himself, namely, whether or not his speech is inhabited by the accent of truth? What is the accent of truth associated with if not with the fact that the presence who speaks either gives or does not give its assent to what it is speaking about?

Is it not possible to hear a subject stating an objective truth, while hearing, at the same time, that his enunciation contradicts what he is saying? That it is possible to hear a speaking subject not say "yes" to what he claims to be saying resides in the fact that his relationship to speech, before being occupied by "the" truth that he claims to be defending, is sustained by the act of *Bejahung*, of primordial assumption, with which he said "yes" to the speech he has received from the Other. Saying "no" to the Other encourages him to believe he is the owner of what he is saying, while forgetting that speech is the property of the Other. This repression of the Other allows the subject to speak without being affected by the place or locus from which the speech comes. That speech can thus be *frigid* is what happens each time that a subject, renouncing the idea of authorizing himself, can only speak when sustained by the guarantee obtained from the authority of a master. If, in this respect, frigid speech does not permit the *well saying* of the accent of truth to be heard, it is because it is impossible to be faithful to a master without being unfaithful to oneself, that is to say to that which constituted us as speaking, namely, the Other.

Inasmuch as music is a presence that reminds us that, in our attempt to forget the Other, we are obliged to encounter a point where the Other, eluding our determination to forget, manifests itself as something unforgettable and undeniable, and inasmuch as speech is, conversely, a donation of meaning by a donator whom we tend to deny, the question of human ethics may be defined as follows. Could it not be defined as the path by which man must be capable of receiving from music the affecting power that it derives from its recognition of the Other, *in order to knot it* with the meaning of speech—which the ego tends to isolate insofar as it represses, so as not to be affected by it—this beyond meaning that is the Other?

Such an ethic implies that the rapport of justness without justice of the dancing subject and his music can be reconciled with the rapport of justice without justness of the speaking subject and his Other.

CHAPTER FIVE

THE TIME OF THE SUBJECT OF THE UNCONSCIOUS: SPEECH

(Theory of Primal Repression and Originary Bewilderment)

*I. Originary Bewilderment and the Way out of Trauma*

A) ENTERING THE TRAUMA

Why does the law humanizing man only intervene in discontinuous fits and starts rather than through an intervention that would take effect once and for all? Because it is not sovereign in relation to the real: in order to "let itself be," this real imposes on it the existence of certain logical times through which it has a specific efficacy.

I have put forward the hypothesis that what uprooted the newborn from this primordial real that is the "formless void" was not the law of speech articulated as such, but rather a law whose specificity is to introduce into the inertia and timelessness of the primordial chaos the dimension of the pure rhythm of the music of the maternal voice. The introduction of a punctuating rhythm appears as a primordial act whereby the real, "transcended," puts the *infans* in the position of being able to dance even before it can speak. The word "dance" is metaphorical: a child suffering from a motor paralysis would be no less apt than another at experiencing the lulling rhythm transmitted by the maternal voice. By virtue of this rhythm, the *infans* is preserved from the pure determinism of the real, falling instead under the ascendancy of the unary trait, which, by pulsating, bestows on the subject to come origins with three dimensions: the unheard-of, the invisible, and the immaterial. Through the void separating two notes, the *subject-to-come* learns of the existence of an "in-between" transmitting an unheard-of silence through which the absence of manifestation on the part of the Other appears as the promise of a possible return. In learning about this unheard-of interval, the *infans* also learns that what specifies the expected note, which has not yet been heard, is also that it does not let itself be seen, that it is of the order of

## Chapter Five – The Time of the Subject of the Unconscious: Speech

the invisible.[305] Finally, through dance, the actual materiality of the body ceases to be exclusively subject to the law of gravity and now attains the symbolic dimension of a body acquiring the *significance* of weightlessness and immateriality.

I am suggesting, therefore, that by virtue of this original musical rhythm a law is introduced that gives the first psychic structure onto which speech will subsequently be grafted. But it will not be possible for this graft to occur harmoniously because the discovery of the sexual trauma will be specified by the eruption of a real, which will turn out to have the power to cancel, to nullify, the efficacy of this first symbolic law, which is that of musical rhythm. The paradox posed by such a law is that the *subject-to-come* has been led to recognize the presence of a primal *y a d'l'Un*.[306] Therefore he will be able, retrospectively, to conceive of the traumatic news, namely, the discovery of maternal castration. I interpret this as the violent eruption of a new message: "*y a pas d'Un*."

That the One is what makes it possible to think the traumatic message, "There is not such a thing as One," puts us in the position to suppose that an originary foreclosure of the primordial One deprives the subject of the very possibility of gaining access to the trauma. The terror by means of which the lack is conceivable was thus made possible by the existence of a law that, moreover, proves incapable of getting the subject out of the trauma to which it had introduced him. If this is the case, it is because music has given the subject the possibility of symbolizing the rhythmic alternation between *y a d'l'Un* and it's negation *y a pas d'Un*. However, it did not allow symbolizing the new type of lack introduced by the trauma according to which the statements "there is" and "there is not" cease to be successive, becoming simultaneous. The recognition of maternal privation is recognition of the fact that the presence *of* her body and the absence *in* her body are transmitted simultaneously in a state of chaotic entanglement. Just as before the act of separating light from darkness there existed between them an indistinct state in which it can be said that the light was

---

[305] See "The Blue Note," 247–249.

[306] See Jacques Lacan, seminars of March 15, 1972, April 19, 1972, May 17, 1972, June 21, 1972, *Le Séminaire livre XIX: ...ou pire*, ed. Jacques-Alain Miller (Paris: Éditions du Seuil, 2011); seminars of May 4, 1972 and June 1, 1972, *Le savoir du psychanalyste*, unpublished seminar; *Encore, op. cit.*, 22–23, 66–67, 128–129, 143.

"shrouded in darkness," we can say that the trauma introduces a nullification of the symbolic law that, by ceasing to govern a world where presence and absence are separated, allows the reign of the abject to emerge where presence and absence are indistinguishable.[307] This ascendancy that the indistinct reign of the real acquires over the symbolic law of distinction means that the traumatized subject, ceasing to be sustained by the symbolic law, falls out of the symbolic. This is a process of expulsion, the subjective effect of which is, to use Freud's words, an experience of "mortification."[308]

The beyond of the pleasure principle will bring the subject back repeatedly to the traumatic point that has not been symbolized. The clinical experience of repetition shows, beyond particular destinies, a point of absolute monotony that allows us to see an intangible structural point at the level of which human dereliction can only express itself through monotonous determinism. It is thus fair to assume that the recapitulation of the translations that the subject will give retroactively of his traumatic repetitions allows us to reconstruct what the originary experience of traumatic mortification may have been.

This translation demonstrates the expression of an authentic ethical experience of malediction.

*a) Betrayal*

Because he is endowed with an interpretative capacity, the subject abandoned by the symbolic law cannot fail to give this abandonment a sense: that of a betrayal. While the maternal Other was for him the source and guarantee of a plenitude of meaning, the sense that he gives to the instant when the *"troumatic"* news is revealed, announcing the Other has been deprived of its consistency because it is lacking, is this: "I have been betrayed: the rhythm had given me to understand that there was meaning, but the meaning has just sunk into the hole of what is lacking."

I am assuming that it is in this time, when the Other suddenly reveals itself as being untrustworthy, that the experience of reliability

---

[307] Genesis 1: 4.
[308] Sigmund Freud, *Studies on Hysteria* (1895), *The Standard Edition of the Complete Psychological Works of Sigmund Freud II* (London: Hogarth, 1961), 8.

acquires meaning. It is because the subject has lost faith in the Other that, ultimately, the signification of a possible act of faith in the signifier will emerge. It is thus in recognizing the fact that the Other is not reliable that the subject, deeming that he has been betrayed, has his first experience of what may be called evil. What makes the subject suffer is thus linked to the fact that he cannot fail to find meaning even where, precisely, meaning is lost—that is to say, in the difference between the sexes.

## b) The Loss of the Call

Owing to this fall of the symbolic law of rhythm, the subject, ceasing to be supported, falls in turn and is expelled from the symbolic. If this expulsion has the structure of a foreclosure (*Verwerfung*), it will have the character of a definitive fall depriving the subject of any possibility of returning to the symbolic. Such an interpretation of the fall is, as we shall see later, strangely close to the Paulinian conception of original sin.

But Freud's ethic is not Christian, even if at the end of *Moses and Monotheism* he accorded some validity to this Christian doctrine of original sin.[309] Also, the term *werfen*, which he uses in negation, indicates that he prefers to replace the notion of a foreclosure without return with that of an expulsion from which the subject can return to the symbolic.

The most obvious clinical effect of the fall of the subject consists in the fact that his destitution outside of the symbolic institutes him as a pure object. The turd that the "Wolf Man" deposits at the traumatic moment of the primal scene is, for example, the manifestation of what the fallen subject is reduced to. As a pure object, he has become the cursed part that will retain, each time the symbolic law collapses, the power of falling again into the obscene stage of the real. That this collapse of the law can be obtained by an insult ("shitty," "pissy," "snotty"), which names as waste matter what has been withdrawn from significance, warns us that the malediction that is the insult derives its

---

[309] Sigmund Freud, *Moses and Monotheism* (1939), *The Standard Edition of the Complete Psychological Works of Sigmund Freud XXIII* (London: Hogarth, 1961), 135–137.

## Chapter Five – The Time of the Subject of the Unconscious: Speech

power from the fact that the subject has never emerged *once and for all* from his originary traumatic fall.

That such a collapse of the law could be put to the service of a death industry producing waste matter is the novelty of our century: Was not Auschwitz described by the Nazis as the "world's anus"?

In the experience of distress linked to the absence *of* the mother, the infant has the possibility of crying out to call for "help," whereas in the experience of trauma as conceptualized by Freud, where the *infans* encounters a hole *in* the mother, he is reduced to an absolute silence (since for him there is no longer an Other who is sufficiently reliable to be called on). It seems to me, therefore, that the mother that Ferenczi calls into question is structurally different from the maternal function conceptualized by Freud. For Ferenczi, the mother is good or bad depending on her capacity to respond to the call of the *infans*. In this respect, she embodies, rightly or wrongly, what I have called the symbolic law of rhythm insofar as she incarnates the law governing the presence or the absence *of* the mother. On the contrary, the mother portrayed by Freud in the trauma incarnates—at least provisionally, and in a way that goes beyond her good or bad quality—a situation in which the structure of language, insofar as it is determined by castration (absence *in* the mother), is exposed.

In this unveiling of maternal privation, the symbolic distinction between absence and presence is abolished and leads to the reappearance of the originary lack of distinction between the real and the signifier. If it is indeed such a blend between real and symbolic that has a traumatic effect (we have defined the terror caused by the monster as a subjective reaction to this blending), we assume that the experience of the monstrous has its roots in trauma. I am establishing a connection between the silence that takes hold of the subject fascinated by the absolute silence that inhabits the monster and the silence that shows itself through the gaping hole of the open-mouthed, traumatized *infans*. This gaping hole, unlike that of the dream navel, is visible; it teaches us that the evil revealed by the trauma is not an *evil* in which the unheard-of real can be heard, but rather a stupefying evil linked to what can be seen. The trauma does not introduce us to the badly heard but to a badly seen: to an evil eye.

*Chapter Five – The Time of the Subject of the Unconscious: Speech*

### c) *The Medusa's Gaze and the Loss of Being Incognito*

That a mere hole in the real has the power of giving birth to the dimension of the gaze is something of which language bears several traces. It speaks to us of the gaze (*regard*) of a skylight or window, of a basement window, or of a geological fault-line.[310] In his novel *Les Misérables*, Victor Hugo condenses this affinity between hole and gaze as follows: "What used to be called a furrow, is now called gallery; what used to be called hole, is now called a look out point."[311] The opening of a window is a framed hole: the frame that delimits it is the effect of a law that, by delimiting the hole, brings it to symbolization. On the contrary, the hole revealed by the "*troumatism*" is inaccessible to the symbolic, for, like the abyss, it has neither an edge nor a bottom: it incarnates absolute disorder.

The gaze that wells up from such a hole is in no way comparable with the poetic gaze of a skylight: it is a malefic gaze that Greek genius isolated as Medusa's gaze. This myth tells us that, under this gaze, the body loses its living status characterized by its mobility and is transformed into a pillar of stone. This mortal petrification is the traumatic operation that occurs each time that the cursed part of man, ceasing to be knotted with the unconscious signifier, becomes unknotted and falls into the real. In this fall, the lightness that my body received from the sustaining signifier disappeared. This body (I had forgotten, moreover, that it was a heavy body) suddenly begins to have weight as if it no longer obeyed anything but the law of the real, which is the law of gravity.

Human depression, which is the first subjective effect of the internal perception of the pressure exerted by gravity, reminds me that one of the fundamental functions of the unconscious was to bestow on me this unconsciousness of the real that enabled me, without even having to think about it, to walk, to jump, and to dance. Without the unconscious law, the body leaves the symbolic stage to appear on that other stage, an obscene stage, where it begins, like any other inanimate body, to obey the law of falling bodies. For the melancholic,

---

[310] ["*Regard*," in addition to meaning "gaze" in French, can also mean "an opening to facilitate the insertion of a conduit [i.e., skylight or window]" or "geographic orientation of the map of a fault" (Paris: Petit Larousse, 1976).]

[311] Victor Hugo, *Les Misérables*, trans. Norman Denny (New York: Penguin, 1982).

*Chapter Five – The Time of the Subject of the Unconscious: Speech*

this obedience can even go as far as to consign this body to the law of falling bodies by throwing it out of the window. By this he shows that if what the body tumbles towards is its tomb, it is because the cursed part of the body is the double, the invisible companion that is the potential corpse.[312]

That it is necessary to forget this cursed part in order to live indicates that analytic work is not only a struggle against forgetting: more fundamentally, it is the conquest of a forgetting that dispenses life. Its acquisition implies that the subject is able to forget the message of absolute knowledge, which, gazing at him with dismay, says to him: "That's all you are, a fallen object; you are not that thing which is speech and which can move from one place to another, thereby escaping from the one and only place to which my gaze assigns you."

It is because the omniscience of this gaze that signifies, "No part of you can be hidden from me," is at the same time a signifying omnipotence, "Nothing in you can contradict my omnipotence," that the Medusa has the power to kill. That certain sudden deaths, which are inexplicable for medicine, are due to a violation of a taboo against contact seems to me to be something worth considering.[313] In this respect, the writer Milan Kundera speaks of the circumstances in which his friend, the dissident Prochaska, suddenly found he was dying from a fulminating illness. His death occurred after the Czech Communist Party, having secretly recorded his most private conversations, decided to divulge on the radio the content of these recordings. Prochaska died one week later.

The fact that he died from this public revelation of his private being embodies the mode of action of the deadly vengeance of the taboo. The public's gaze, like the Medusa's gaze, killed Prochaska by touching in him not the unthinkable, the prohibited, but rather the untouchable taboo.

That a subject can thus be deprived of life when what is most private and most intimate in him is violated by contact with an eye whose power to turn the intimate secret inside out, transforming it

---

[312] [*Il démontre, par cette défenestration, que si vers quoi tombe le corps, c'est ça tombe, c'est parce que la part maudite du corps est ce double, ce compagnon invisible qu'est le cadavre en puissance.*]

[313] The following four pages are taken from my contribution to *Fin d'une analyse*, op. cit., 12–14.

## Chapter Five – The Time of the Subject of the Unconscious: Speech

for the outside world, for the public, into an open secret, leads me to ask the following question: What is the connection between the fact that Prochaska, dumbfounded, died very suddenly from cancer and the fact that this illness appears to be propagated by contact, by silent proliferation?

Fear of contact, which is not fear of something prohibited but rather of a taboo, can be observed most frequently in the phobia of cancer. If we do not observe a phobia of myocardia heart attack—despite its gravity—it is because, for the unconscious, the alteration of the heart appears as a rhythmic symbolic alteration, as a "noble" illness. On the contrary, cancer (for the unconscious) obeys the mode of transmission characteristic of the real, which strives to impose continuity on the symbolic and the imaginary relations, destroying discontinuity. This angst, linked to the setting up of a new frontier showing the blending between the continuous and the discontinuous, is the same angst that, since time immemorial, caused the emergence of the monster, of the being that loses its unity by showing the reign of confusion between the world of the human form and formlessness.

It is impossible to overlook the ethical consequences introduced by the fear of contamination. Racist attitudes are nothing other than an attempt to resolve such fears. What else, in fact, is the racist thinking if not the "final solution," which strives to foreclose, to get rid of, the contaminating agent—for example, Jewish blood, insofar as it has the power to contaminate Aryan blood. If, in racist thinking, the child born of a union between a Jew and an Aryan can only be Jewish, it is because Jewish blood obeys the law of the transmission of the real. It has the power to be incorruptible and indestructible and that of corrupting Aryan purity, which therefore would not carry a self-sustaining, self-authorizing symbolic consistency. This raises the problem of the aberration that occurs when a singular fear, linked to the fear of taboo contamination, becomes organized into a collective racist discourse concerning a corruptive agent.

What power does the symbolic give the analyst to introduce into this clinical experience of the monstrosity of the body a separation, an interdiction, at the very point where deadly contact is active? The following fragment of analysis will help me to show how one day I found an answer to this question that each analyst is faced with.

It concerns a young woman who was sent to me by a dermatologist because she was subject to increasingly frequent erythematous

## Chapter Five – The Time of the Subject of the Unconscious: Speech

eruptions on her neck, which induced in her a progressive state of claustrophobia. Not only did she no longer venture out of her home, but "she no longer uttered a word [*elle n'en sort plus Une*]," for she was reduced to silence by the appearance of the marks. She associated her silence with the fact that what these marks showed put her in the position of no longer being able to hide anything, even though she did not know what she was unable to hide. Nonetheless, she felt that there must be a secret place in her that impeded her from speaking. What she was pointing out here is that speech can only be deployed effectively if it transmits something beyond itself, an elsewhere, a place "ex," from which this speech "ex-sists." If there is no transmission of this interval, which establishes an "inter" between the moment something is said and the saying itself—an "inter" that is nothing other than the interdicted—if, in short, instead of the foundational separation of discontinuity there is confusion, a continuity established by the gaze, then, indeed, speech dies. Just as Prochaska died. It dies because the "elsewhere," the secret of being, insofar as it was showing itself "here," through these epidermic marks, dies.

This young woman discovered in her analysis that a true secret does not need to be hidden; a true secret can be revealed in broad daylight without losing anything of itself. How was this truth conveyed to her one day? Not by a striking interpretation of the analyst taking her back to some point in her history she was unaware of, but by a manifestation of the analyst's presence referring her to something ahistorical, structural, in her. It involved something that had been very moving for her, but which I myself had not been aware of at the time. She told me how, on that day, I had greeted her by saying, "Good morning," while looking at her in a completely new way. This look had moved her deeply, as it had astonished her, since it no longer referred her to the dialectics of being and appearance. Up to that point she had supposed that, behind her appearance, something consistent was hidden that is called "being." Her symptom made her feel this was accessible to the gaze of the Other insofar as she situated this "being" at the level of the marks on her neck.

Why did this new gaze have the power to astonish her so radically? Because if, under this gaze, she felt "naked," she also discovered that it was no longer the same nakedness. For the first time, she discovered that her nudity, both physical and psychical, was inaccessible to the Other's gaze: it was no longer something that was accessible to

## Chapter Five – The Time of the Subject of the Unconscious: Speech

knowledge, but rather, like a secret, impossible to approach through knowledge.

If she described this so-called novelty of my way of looking at her as having something of the "eye of a painter" about it, it was to indicate that her new nudity was no longer something hidden behind a veil, but was itself constituted as a veil. Discovering that nudity was in fact the emergence of the ultimate veil, revealing itself when all the other veils had fallen, she discovered in the process that she was the bearer of a secret, that of a sexual not-knowing, that could show itself in broad daylight without being seen by an evil eye.

Will the analyst be able to kill the evil eye that stupefies the analysand? Will he be able to kill the Medusa by resorting, as Perseus did, to a ruse that enables him to decapitate it without looking at it? In other words, will he be able to kill it simply by looking at it, head on, without being stupefied by it?

That it is possible for him not to be petrified by this gaze that petrifies the analysand resides in the fact that the analyst's desire—insofar as it exists—is only articulated in his relation to his own lack. Encountering this lack that signifies that the subject of the unconscious is "not all" visible, the omniscience and omnipotence of the Medusa's gaze will be rendered inoperative. The science and power of the evil eye can only have consistency when supported by the category of the All: for absolute knowledge, there is no science without omniscience, no power without omnipotence. The fragility of all totalitarian thought, which relies—as Orwell showed brilliantly in his novel *1984*—on the omnipresent gaze of Big Brother, stems from the fact that the superego's mode of thinking of the All is rendered perishable by the introduction of this "little nothing" that is the "not all." This "little nothing"—the "incognito" belonging to the subject that was undermined by the trauma—is the cornerstone that psychoanalytic treatment must substitute for the piece of rubble that is the traumatized subject.

In losing the dimension of that which is inaccessible in him, the traumatized subject has been dispossessed of his existence. Can we say that the way out of the trauma involves getting in contact with his inaccessibility? No, he will not rediscover the disposition of his body, his image, and his speech because he has possession of them, but rather because they will be given to him by the action of the paternal metaphor.[314] Body, image, and speech will become his own by virtue of this gift, without him having ownership of them for all that. His body will only become available to him because its immateriality will have been given to him as a gift and because immateriality cannot be possessed. It has no owner; it itself is the owner of bodily matter. By the same token, the unheard-of and the invisible are gifts that he will receive and that will give substance to his speech and his image.

How is the fact that these gifts are beyond his control manifested clinically? By the fact that *he does not know* what his speech is, what his image is, or what his body is. What will happen if he finds out? He will ask himself if this speech, image, and body are worthy of what he knows. Will he ask himself what he is going to say? He will lose his capacity to speak. Or what does he look like? His beauty will immediately seem suspect to him.

The child's charm, charm itself, is nothing other than this "*je ne sais quoi*" that I possess: I speak with the weight of truth because I do not know what I am saying; I look beautiful when I do not know that I am so; I move lightly when I do not know that my body is a potential corpse.

This "I don't know" is the path whereby the subject of the unconscious can receive the metaphorical gift of speech, of the image, and of the body. The act by means of which he will receive this triple gift will require of him an act of inner assent that will or will not take place. A gift is not received automatically: it can be received or rejected.

## B) THE WAY OUT OF THE TRAUMA

The trauma appears to us as that originary experience in which the absolute *Alter* that was the mother ceases, because it shows it has been altered, to be the fellow human being that it was. We are led to assume that the subject will be able to get beyond the trauma because, during this period of time when there is no longer a fellow being for him, he will become a new type of "fellow" that Freud describes as the

---

[314] Jacques Lacan, "The Function and Field of Speech and Language in Psychoanalysis," in *Écrits, op. cit.*, 248: "Speech is in fact a gift of language, and language is not immaterial."

## Chapter Five – The Time of the Subject of the Unconscious: Speech

*Nebenmensch.* "The formula is striking to the extent that it expresses powerfully the idea of beside yet alike, separation and identity."[315]

According to Freud, the *Nebenmensch* is separated into two parts, one of which imposes itself through the constant apparatus that Freud calls *das Ding*. *Das Ding* is not governed, like the object, by the pleasure principle. It proceeds from what is beyond the pleasure principle and presents itself as the first stranger, that absolute Other, who, if it is not foreclosed, may be approached by the subject as something in which he can put his trust. Lacan points out: "The paranoid doesn't believe in that first stranger in relation to whom the subject is obliged to take his bearings. The use of the term belief seems to me to be emphasized in a less psychological sense than first seems to be the case. The radical attitude of the paranoid, as designated by Freud, concerns the deepest level of the relationship of man to reality, namely, that which is articulated as faith.... I already referred to it when I said that the motive force of paranoia is essentially the rejection of a certain support in the symbolic order...."[316] The prehistoric Other is *das Ding* in relation to which "the subject is constituted in a kind of relationship characterized by primary affect, *prior to any repression*..."[317] and in relation to which "the first choice, the first seat of subjective orientation takes place, and that I will call... the choice of neurosis."[318]

The mechanism involved here is the effect of the capacity of the signifier to insist. Inasmuch as we had understood as musical rhythm the first manifestation of the Other to transmit itself, we understand the instance of the prehistoric Other, *das Ding*, as that in the Other which insists when the traumatized subject, because he has lost the support of the symbolic law, is subjected to this state of the urgency of life (Freud's "*die not des Lebens*") that does not want to die.

---

[315] Jacques Lacan, *The Ethics of Psychoanalysis, op. cit.*, 51.
[316] *Ibid.*, 54.
[317] My emphasis.
[318] *Ibid.*

## Chapter Five – The Time of the Subject of the Unconscious: Speech

### a) The First Time of Exit from the Trauma: Originary Bewilderment

#### 1. The "You" that Precedes the "There"

My supposition is that the subject to come will be extricated from the state of traumatic helplessness by the intervention of the prehistoric Other, whose vocation is to announce to the subject that beyond the traumatic bad news—"There is no signifier [*Il y a pas de signifiant*]"—there is good news: "There is some signifier [*Il y a du signifiant*]."[319]

The stunning novelty of this message lies in the fact that it contradicts the message "there is not" on two counts. First, by letting it be *understood* that "there is a signifier," this new message frees the subject from the Medusa's damning gaze, for it institutes him as an auditor. Second, by announcing that "there is a signifier," it denounces the exclusive reign of the traumatic "there is not" and confronts the stunned subject with a logical paradox: How can the notions of "*y a de l'un*" and "*y a pas de l'un*" both be valid at one and the same time?

That the prehistoric Other, namely, the signifier of the Name-of-the-Father, was reduced to silence in the time of traumatic terror is what defines the ascendancy that the real can have over the symbolic, insofar as it can corrupt it. But the fact that the symbolic can rise from its ashes in order to let its vocation of transmission of One be heard again is, on the other hand, what specifies the enigmatic insistence with which the signifier, even though put to death by the real, had not yet had its last word. How does the bewildered subject receive the manifestation of the Other's insistence? Lacan suggests that the subject responds to this encounter with the prehistoric Other by discovering the pronoun of interpellation, the "You." The "you of devotion," Lacan says, "whereby the prehistoric Other, the unforgettable Other... suddenly threatens to surprise us and by its appearance to cast us down from on high."[320] If such an encounter can be produced by this "you," it is because it precedes primal repression: the effect of this

---

[319] Jacques Lacan, *Encore, op. cit.*, 96: "Wasn't it charitable of Freud to have allowed the misery of speaking beings to say to itself that there is—since there is the unconscious—something transcendent, truly transcendent, which is but what the species inhabits, namely, language."

[320] Jacques Lacan, *The Ethics of Psychoanalysis, op. cit.*, 56.

repression will be to convert this "you" into a "he," into an instance that, owing to the fact that it can no longer be invoked, can henceforth only be supposed.[321] Through the reappearance of the transference on to this "you"—which existed already in the musical relation with the Other—the subject, who had fallen as damned, is extricated from this impossibility of appealing, insofar as he receives this "*y a de l'un*" with which he can now sustain himself.

Why am I saying that this signifying support is bewildering? Because, as in the experience of being bewildered by a witticism, the subject is plunged into that particular state of perplexity and incomprehension prior to the moment of illumination. The inaugural encounter with this "you" is experienced in a state of bewilderment, of stupefied *jouissance*. Unlike a musical note, the signifier of the "*y a de l'un*" does not transmit its light instantaneously. The period of latency prior to this moment of illumination is the effect of the fact that ever since the trauma, the subject has ceased to be in tune with the Other and is structurally *late* in relation to it.

In this originary moment of bewilderment by the One, the subject, established sovereignly as recipient, is torn from the field of the gaze in which he was *mis-seen (mal vu)* and assigned to the field of a listening through which the *mis-* ceases to be *seen* in order to be *heard*. This moment of *mis-hearing (mal-entendu)* is the first moment of psychic latency when the subject, hearing that there is some signifier, has for the first time the means to hear—and not to look at—that there is simultaneously absence and presence in the signifier.

## 2. The Traumatic Dilemma

### a) Existence of the Dilemma

The dilemma he is faced with by this coexistence of the "there is" and the "there is not" is, as Jean-Pierre Winter points out, a real paradox: "something is traumatic when it links the subject to an impossibility of responding logically to an event with which he is faced and which, generally, is of the order of the cruelty of the world.... Freud

---

[321] It is the absence of primal repression that, for the mystic, bestows a relation of *jouissance* upon the "you" that is opposed to the transitory "*j'ouïe-sens*" of the *dritte Person*.

says, roughly, that what is of the order of reality is that which can be articulated logically. What is disturbing for the subject is when he can no longer produce this articulation... because he has been put in the position of being confronted with an unsolvable paradox."[322]

In the clinical example given by Jean-Pierre Winter to illustrate what is a traumatizing paradox, a father lays down the following law for his son: "You must not obey." It is indeed impossible to obey such a prescription, for, if the subject agreed to this injunction, "You must not obey," he would be obeying his father and therefore contravening his commandment; on the other hand, if he rejected this commandment, he would be being obedient.

In light of this clinical example, we can ask the following question: What solution can the bewildered subject find to extricate himself from the dilemma with which he is faced by the coexistence of the "there is" and the "there is not"? Must he obey the symbolic, which says, "There is," or the real, which shows that "there is not"? The problem is that, if he obeys the symbolic, he will also obey the real, for the real has ascendancy over the symbolic; if, on the other hand, he obeys the real, he will be led to obey the symbolic, for it is impossible to think the "there is not" if the subject has not first been able to think that "there is."

My clinical experience teaches me that, to overcome this paradox, the subject has at least four possibilities.

## β) The Four Possible Responses

The first two possibilities consist in suppressing one of the two contradictory terms: whereas the foreclosure of the signifying presence of the "there is" is the psychotic solution, the disavowal of the "there is not" seems to be more characteristic of the perverse solution. The third solution will retain our attention more: Will the subject interpret these two messages as the manifestation of the existence of two distinct Others, one good, the other bad, or will he interpret them as the manifestation of a single Other who is not split but rather divided?

---

[322] Jean-Pierre Winter, "Le traumatisme entre réel et réalité," *Les Carnets de psychanalyse* 5 (1994), 220–232.

## Chapter Five – The Time of the Subject of the Unconscious: Speech

The first interpretation is, in a certain way, the gnostic solution: it supposes that the creator of a badly made world, inhabited by a traumatic "commotion," cannot be the same as that of a world humanized by the law. From this point of view, there is thus an opposition between a good God, who is the dispenser of the ethical law, and the Prince of this world, who reigns over a malefic real that escapes the efficacy of the law and against whose power the good God is powerless.

It is because the coexistence of these two divinities seems to have its roots in the original experience in which the subject is confronted with the paradox of the coexistence of the abject and the world that we may suppose that gnostic thought is perhaps a leftover from prehistoric times when the subject, owing to his encounter with *das Ding*, was destined to choose his neurosis. If he maintains a split transference whereby a radically deceptive Other and an Other who cannot deceive remain irreducibly separate, he will become, for example, an inquisitor; in this respect, he will be able to send the heretic to the stake without any anxiety: Would the god who does not deceive allow himself to commit such an error?[323]

With this gnostic solution, the notion of a good God is partially saved: if his power is in fact limited by the malevolent power that governs the created world, this limit does not prevent him from being the guarantor of the truth about truth.[324] In sum, the future inquisitor is the one who has responded in the following way to the prehistoric dilemma that the trauma has posed for him: it is impossible for the signifier to disappear and appear from one and the same place; impossible that the cause of this stupefying traumatic real through which I learn that I can no longer call the Other could be, at the same time, what talks and calls me.

Gnostic seduction is so powerful that Saint Paul managed to preserve the essential aspects of it in spite of his profession of faith in a God claiming to be the unique creator of the world and the law. His doctrine of original sin allows him to substitute for a divine dualism another dualism in which there is an irreducible opposition between

---

[323] Nicolas Eymerich and Francisco Penà, *Le Manuel des Inquisiteurs* (Paris: Mouton, 1973).

[324] On this disappearance of the attribute of power, see Catherine Chalier, "Dieu sans puissance," in *Le Concept de Dieu après Auschwitz*, ed. Hans Jonas (Paris: Rivages, 1994).

the law of sin and the letter of the law. The latter, albeit given by God the Father, proves powerless to save man from sin.

Gnostic belief is not the only possible response to the traumatic dilemma. The other possible response, the fourth, is one that is based on the recognition that "If there is nothing more than a lack, the Other is wanting, and the signifier is that of his death."[325] The signifier of the death of God, which corresponds to the message that Lacan writes S (A̸),[326] is related to the "God of the message, which has absolutely nothing to do with the God of believers,"[327] and which is a principle of the message to which "a solitary individual, like Spinoza or Freud, may feel he can devote a sentiment of love, of which only a few are capable, namely, *amor intellectualis Dei*."[328]

We must now try to account for the process of the assumption of this message S (A̸).

## b) The Second Time of Exit from the Trauma: Paternal Metaphor and Primal Repression

The subject will not emerge from the traumatic experience either by making one of the terms of the traumatic dilemma disappear (foreclosure or disavowal) or by allowing them to coexist (gnostic solution), but rather by making them copulate metaphorically with each other. Through this, the "*y a de l'un*" will fertilize the "*y a pas de l'un*" in such a way as to give rise to the appearance of that third signification which is S (A̸), the signifier of the death of God.

In order to understand how this new signification can appear, it will be helpful to consider how Lacan, in the seminar *The Formations of the Unconscious*, introduces the indication of a metaphorical signification. He takes the example of the metaphor "*atterré*" (floored) and examines the process that may have led to its appearance. A semantic analysis shows that the phoneme "ter" present in "*terreur*" (terror) has been introduced, owing to a possible ambiguity, in the place of the phoneme "ter" present in "*terre*" (earth). By substituting "*terre*" for "*terreur*," the new signifier that appears with "*atterré*" introduces

---

[325] Jacques Lacan, *The Ethics of Psychoanalysis, op. cit.*, 193.
[326] *Ibid*.
[327] *Ibid*., 180.
[328] *Ibid*.

## Chapter Five – The Time of the Subject of the Unconscious: Speech

a new signification: the terror named is to some extent tamed as well as attenuated, for, owing to its new relation to the earth (*la terre*), the terror (*terreur*) is no longer absolute.

This metaphor has a threefold power: the power to act on the signifier "*terreur*" by making it resonate more pacifically; the power to act on the signifier "*terre*," so that we no longer hear it in the word "*atterré*"; and finally the power of the appearance of a signification whose novelty is neither an addition nor a subtraction of meaning, but rather a multiplication of meaning. Just as, on account of the efficiency of the signifier "*terre*," the traumatic signification of "*terreur*" undergoes a pacification of terror insofar as it is transported into the signifier "*atterré*," the traumatic signifier of the "there is not" will be pacified by the efficacy of the "there is."[329] This pacification does not mean that the dimension of absence will be absorbed by that of the signifying presence: on the contrary, it will be exalted, but by being transported into the field of significance, for the success of the metaphor consists precisely in the fact that the lack of a signifier in the Other ($\cancel{A}$) is substituted by a signifier of the lack of the signifier S ($\cancel{A}$).

$$\text{In the same way as } \frac{\text{terre}}{\text{terreur}} \rightarrow \text{atterré}, \frac{\text{there is}}{\text{there is not}} \rightarrow S\ (\cancel{A}).$$

If the new message proceeds from a poetic structure, it is because prose does not have the power to translate it. At the very most, it makes it possible to say that this S ($\cancel{A}$) is an *Aufhebung* of "there is" and of "there is not" and to translate this passing beyond by saying that it is possible to transmit the absence within the presence. Because the process of negativization (*Ausstoßung*) is correlated with a process of affirmation (*Bejahung*), it is not equivalent to foreclosure.[330]

In this connection we can say that speech, insofar as it requires the presence and the absence of the Other, can only arise if the alternation bestowed by musical rhythm is mourned. Through this mourning, the subject, losing all contemporaneity with the Other, will be out of step with him. It is on account of this gap that he will enter into a historical time that will no longer be the time of the Other, but

---

[329] See Claude Lévi-Strauss, "L'efficacité symbolique," in *Anthropologie structurale* (Paris: Plon, 1958), 205.
[330] See 290ff.

rather *his* own time. The price to be paid for this acquisition will be expressed by the fact that the subject will only enter time by being, as Franco Baldini has so aptly put it, "structurally late." "This lateness... is the unconscious in the Freudian sense, inasmuch as it is constituted by a latency of the true subject."[331] I would add that this latency, which reveals "this being who is late in relation to the 'exigency of life' (*Not des Lebens*)," is the effect of the bewildering signifier that, by chatting with the subject, is the cause of the real of this subject.[332] It is towards this real from which he is forever separated that he will constantly run; it is a lost cause, however, for he cannot know that he is structurally late in relation to this cause.

Playing with this cause, he will play the game of *Fort-Da*. This capacity to play—which he had radically lost with the trauma—will reveal his capacity to run indefinitely after what will have become his cause, namely, the wooden reel with which "he begins the incantation."[333]

It is by making a transference onto the signifier of the division of the Other that the subject chooses not to engage in a split transference involving a dualism of the Other. Escaping the gnostic solution of a world governed by light and darkness, he enters a world governed by a third point from which light and darkness are articulated. It is not a point from which the light illuminates the darkness—which, as a result, would cease to be—but rather from which the light bestows a unary trait allowing the unnamed to be named.[334] In such a way, darkness, by becoming "night," can be extracted from the traumatic real of chaos where time has ceased to beat. With "night," the order of the temporal rhythm guaranteeing the succession of day and night can begin to beat again.

This function of nomination does not exhaust the power by means of which the signifier of the Name-of-the-Father produced the "*y a de l'un*." Insofar as it is the signifier of the Name, it possesses, in addition to the power of carrying to nomination that part of the real that can be nominated, the power of carrying to significance that part of the real that cannot be named. This distinction of the functions of the Name-of-the-Father introduces us to the equivocal nature of the

---

[331] Franco Baldini, *Les Carnets de psychanalyse* 5 (1994), 74.
[332] *Ibid.*
[333] Jacques Lacan, *The Four Fundamental Concepts, op. cit.*, 62.
[334] Genesis 1: 3.

functions of the signifier S (A̸). If, on the one hand, this signifier can be articulated as such by the subject—for example, by the *passant*—on the other, it remains a signifier that cannot be articulated.[335] It is reminiscent of that which, of the real of the lack of the Other, is radically unnameable and can only be carried to significance. The "deep" portrayed in the second verse of Genesis is there to remind us of that part of the unnameable real that, at the very most, is only signifiable.

The relationship we have established between the process of the metaphor in general and that of the so-called "paternal" metaphor was not established from the outset by Lacan. Indeed, when he raises the question of the metaphor in the seminar on *The Psychoses*—where he observes the absence of metaphor in psychotic discourse—he is not yet speaking of a paternal metaphor.[336] In this seminar he simply notes that there is a certain analogy between the psychotic discourse and the discourse of Wernicke's aphasia as Jakobson analyzes it, that is, preservation of the syntax ordering the laws of the grammatical coordination of the signifier, but disappearance of the intentionality of the subject, who is no longer able to signify himself as a speaking subject.[337] It is only in the seminar of the following year that he speaks, for the first time, of the paternal metaphor, suggesting that "the father is a metaphor by means of which the paternal signifier is substituted for the maternal signifier."[338]

That this originary metaphor, the stem of every subsequent metaphor, is foreclosed from psychotic discourse leads us to try to understand what the obstacle is that prevents the *infans* from saying "yes," from realizing the *Bejahung* of the paternal signifier that induces metaphor. If the *infans* has to produce such a "yes," it is because he is not in a purely passive position in relation to the signifying gift that is transmitted to him by his ascendants. However, this gift must itself have very specific characteristics if it is to be acceptable to the

---

[335] Jacques Lacan, "Proposition of October 9, 1967," first version, *Ornicar? Analytica* VIII, 20: "...whoever can articulate this S (A̸) need take no courses... for the reason that, like S (A̸), he has his roots in that which is most radically opposed to everything that is necessary and that suffices to be recognized to be: honorability, for example."

[336] Jacques Lacan, *The Psychoses, op. cit.*, 9.

[337] Roman Jakobson, "Deux aspects du langage et deux types d'aphasie," in *Essais de linguistique générale* (Paris: Éditions de Minuit, 1963).

[338] Jacques Lacan, seminar of January 15, 1958, in *The Seminar of Jacques Lacan, Book V: The Formations of the Unconscious*, trans. Russell Grigg (Boston: Polity, 2017).

## Chapter Five – The Time of the Subject of the Unconscious: Speech

subject to come. This gift must be capable of rendering a moral commandment transmissible to the subject, this *soll*... with which Freud announces that an "I" shall be (... *ich werden*). To the extent that this imperative is interpreted by Lacan as the Cartesian ergo—*cogito, ergo*—that presses the subject to assume his own causality, it raises the question of understanding how the *infans* hears such a commandment. And, to the extent that this bewildering commandment is a commandment about which the subject understands nothing, how can he say "yes" to it?

### 1. Passivity or Sensibility of the Subject

The very possibility of a metaphorical transportation towards an "elsewhere" that is the place where the speaking subject can come into being raises the following question. The traumatized *infans* is defined by a situation of extreme passivity, so that it is impossible for him to exit from the traumatic dilemma on his own. Should we suppose that the mortified subject, acted upon by the originary paternal metaphor, will be extricated from this mortification? Or should we suppose that in this state of absolute passivity there remains in him a possibility to participate in this extrication?

I start out from the idea that the subject enters the trauma by discovering, in general through sight, that this world, contrary to what he had believed hitherto, was badly made and that he escapes it through the intervention of the bewildering commandment that transmutes this sight into a "hearing" of the traumatic evil.

In the operation whereby the badly heard substitutes for the badly seen a radical topological reorganization occurs. First of all, what does this substitution signify? Essentially, that with the dimension of listening, the chariot of time, which had stopped rolling because the fascinated subject had ceased to be in temporality, will start rolling again. The originary bewilderment appears in this respect as the originary scansion of a new time that the subject conquers in order to constitute himself as a historical subject.

Why is it a new time? Because up until the traumatic moment the subject was not unaware of time, except that it was still not *his time*, but *the time of the Other*, the time through which the Other transmitted himself through the intermediary of the musical rhythm

## Chapter Five – The Time of the Subject of the Unconscious: Speech

to which it was possible to dance, but certainly not to speak. That music cannot take charge of the trauma, as speech is required to do, does not mean that it has no relations with it. Indeed, the presence of the originary signifier is transmitted initially to the *infans* through the intermediary of the musical Other (mother's voice). The future subject, because he has gained access to the dimension of "*y a d'l'Un*," will be able to gain access to the traumatic revelation whose function is to radically contest the affirmation "there is meaning" by announcing that meaning has been lost. Let me repeat that it is because with the trauma the statements "there is" and "there is not" are simultaneous that the support that the subject received from musical rhythm collapses, inasmuch as the latter was characterized by a successive rhythmic beat between the "there is" and the "there is not" of the signifier.

It is in this traumatic point, where the subject loses the time that was bestowed on him by the musical rhythm of the Other, that he must conquer this new type of time that will be his interior time. It will not beat, like the musical time of the Other, according to a two-time rhythm, but rather to a three-time rhythm: the first time, that of the originary scansion brought by the bewildering signifier, will call forth a second time, that of insistence, which in turn will call forth the third time, that of perseverance. It is impossible to grasp the essence of what insistence and persistence are if we have not first understood the nature of the unconscious contract established during the time of the originary bewilderment. If the bewildering commandment introduces such a contract between itself and its partner (the future subject) it must first of all be recognized that the initial time of the contract inaugurates a situation that, *par excellence*, would be rightly rejected by anyone wanting to establish a contract, for it is the situation of a misunderstanding.

This misunderstanding involves a double ambiguity: on the one hand, we can say that the subject ceases to see the symbolic hole in the real that is the traumatic evil and is now able to hear the question that is put to him by the bewildering signifier. "Where are you? By falling like waste matter, you have forgotten that you were indebted to the signifier that you have already received once. Evil is not only this '*troumatism*' that you see; it is also in forgetting the possibility of using the speech that is given to you to symbolize what has not yet been symbolized." But on the other hand, even if the subject hears this question, he does not understand it. However, to the extent that this incomprehension is radically different from the one that he felt before the traumatic scene, *the incomprehension proper to bewilderment is specific*.

In his study on witticism, Freud utilizes three words to evoke the mode of incomprehension that takes hold of the subject in the fleeting moment of bewilderment preceding the laughter that greets the illumination delivered by the witticism. He says that the bewildered subject has an experience of the incomprehensible, of the unintelligible, of the enigmatic. This situation, in which the subject is invaded by the signifier without understanding the significance of it, raises a question that we have already had a glimpse of. Does this invasion signify a subject of absolute *passivity*, comparable to the delusional state of being invaded by hallucinations or to the invasion by unbound stimuli (owing to the breach of the "stimulus barrier"), which, according to Freud, constitutes trauma?

Precisely not. When the subject is invaded by hallucination or by unbound excitation, his consent is in no way required, whereas when the bewildering signifier irrupts in subjectivity, unconscious consent is necessary. That is the reason for the radical difference between trauma and bewilderment. While the traumatized subject is plunged into an *incomprehension devoid of all hope*, of all expectation, the bewildered subject is immediately *expecting* something else—as if this experience of non-sense that he had was the vehicle of a promise of sense, with the power to induce in him the dimension of hope enabling him to *endure*, to last in time. The unintelligible and the incomprehensible of which Freud speaks are transmitted as such because they appear at the same time on the horizon of the possible.

It is because the subject has unconsciously put his trust in the bewildering signifier and unconsciously said yes to its heterogeneity, without understanding it, that this experience of bewilderment shows how the subject is not *passive* towards speech, but rather is *capable of being affected* by speech. Capable, in short, of not being, like the autist, impassive to speech. Insofar as I am capable of saying, "Yes, I am not a stranger to this stranger that is the speech that speaks to me," *a subjectivity* is affirmed in me *more originary than the one that, subsequently, will speak in order to question*. We will address the richness of Derrida's considerations on the antecedence of this "yes."

By virtue of this unconscious "yes," the subject has the capacity to endure the bewildering experience of incomprehension, for this "yes" attests to the fact that beyond this incomprehension, he is not a stranger to this stranger that is the incomprehensible bewildering signifier. Whereas the traumatic non-sense is the vehicle of a fascinating uncanniness insofar as it refers to nothing else than itself, the bewildering non-sense is not a cause for despair since it brings the hope of a sense that will emerge at a later time. Owing to the fact that there is a promise of something beyond non-sense, the bewildered subject is put in the position of being able to wait. Time thus becomes his friend and he will be able to take the time that is necessary for the spirit of the paternal metaphor to be delivered according to these two logical times identified by Freud: bewilderment and illumination. From this perspective, we can say that the production of a witticism, whatever the word that induces the wit is, always acts as a commemoration of the two times necessary for the success of the originary metaphor.

In what way must the "yes" with which the subject entered the originary contract with the bewildering signifier be renewed and strengthened so it is no longer simply an ephemeral pact that made it possible to emerge from the trauma, but establishes a definitively stabilized relationship with the traumatic real?

This definitive pact between the subject and the Other is, in my view, what is formed in the act of primal repression: it requires from the subject a *new* "yes" that will or will not result in the assumption of what psychoanalysis calls "symbolic castration."

## 2. Primal Repression as an Originary Metaphorical Pact

Insofar as the trauma is an experience of an ethical order, in which the pact with the symbolic has been broken, I understand the "yes" given by the subject to the "*y a de l'un*" bestowed by the signifier of the Name-of-the-Father as the *renewal of a pact*. A new knotting between the two contracting parties, namely, the Other and the new subject will be substituted for what had been rendered invalid.

For Lacan, this knotting is not metaphorical but rather Borromean: "Nature abhors the knot, and particularly the Borromean knot.... This knot is nothing less than the *Urverdrängt*, the primordial originary repressed."[339] My hypothesis is that, through this new pact, three

---

[339] Jacques Lacan, seminar of January 14, 1975, *RSI*, unpublished seminar.

originary metaphors will be knotted, inducing three significations: the unheard-of (R/S), the invisible (S/I), and the immaterial (I/R). The knotting of these three nominations is Borromean inasmuch as the real has ascendancy over the symbolic, which has ascendancy over the imaginary, which itself has ascendancy over the real.

The creation of these three metaphors, which, as I shall to try to show, will be the effect of the assumption by the subject of the message S (A̸), introduces us to deeper understanding of the signification of originary castration.

Inasmuch as we locate this originary castration at the heart of a certain pact, we will have to consider the consequences of the fact that primal repression is not an automatic act but an *ethical pact*, since the subject can be induced to agree to it or not, as in early autism.[340]

We are led to consider these three originary metaphors as three parameters of castration, for symbolic castration does not correspond to the reductive conception of the cutting off of the penis. Such a simplification eludes the complexity of the real involved, which requires the phallus to be articulated with the body, speech, and the image, in other words, with the real, the symbolic, and the imaginary. The castrating cut will have a triple effect: it will concern the body, speech, and the image. In each of these cuts, the negativization of the subordinate term by the ascendant term produces a symbolic effect, giving rise to each of the three originary metaphors. The symbolic will retain from its negativization by the real (R/S) of the "troumatism" a scar that Freud calls the "dream navel" and that Lacan calls the "real hole in the symbolic." But this symbolic that can be negativized by the real has the power to negativize the imaginary (S/I) in such a way that beyond the image there is an unimaginable dimension that makes a hole in the specular image.

As for this image, it has the power to negativize the real (I/R); that part of the real that is hidden by the veil in the form of the *cache sexe* is its capacity for chaotic confusion.

The pact at the heart of which these metaphorical cuts will occur will put the subject in the position to receive the usufruct of a body, of a speech, and of an image that he will be able to legitimately

---

[340] See the study by Sophie Collaudin, "L'Amour sans la lettre?," *Correspondances freudiennes* 18–19 (June 1987).

## Chapter Five – The Time of the Subject of the Unconscious: Speech

enjoy if he pays the price required by the contract. If, for one reason or another, he does not pay the price, the law to which he will henceforth be subjected will no longer be the law of the symbolic contract, but rather the pure sanctioning law of the superego, which will *contest, through the production of a symptom, the fact that the subject has been given a sexed body, speech, and an image.* Under the evil eye of his superego-bound conscience, the subject will then find that this speech is stammering, that this body is heavy, and that this image is ugly.

### α) The Originary Pact

The fundamental difference between the hole established in the symbolic by foreclosure and the hole established by primal repression consists in the fact that *in foreclosure, the act of making a hole is not the result of a pact* between the subject and the signifier, but of a breach of the pact. If in primal repression there is a pact, it is because, contrary to foreclosure, in which the "no" to the symbolic is not associated with any "yes," the "no" that is the *Ausstoßung* is indissociably linked to the affirmation of a "yes" (*Bejahung*). Through this "yes," the subject is bound by fidelity on two counts: fidelity towards the Other and fidelity towards himself. The subject recognizes that he is indebted to the materiality of the signifier transmitted by the Other (S ($\bar{A}$)), insofar as it is the assumption of this hole in the Other that permits the institution in the subject of the originary symbolic hole from which he originates.

In this respect, psychoanalysis differs from the religious view of a creation *ex nihilo*. For us the procreation of the subject of the unconscious is not procreation from a *nihilo* that precedes it, but effect of the *procreation of a* nihilo *out of the precedence of the materiality of a signifier* by means of which the subject creates the immaterial.

The second aspect of the subject's indebtedness is linked to the fact that, for this originary hole to be created in him, he must pay with his person, by expelling from himself (*Ausstoßung*) a sacrificial part whose disappearance contributes to the establishment of the real hole in the symbolic. How, indeed, will the subject be able to assume his debt of fidelity towards the signifier to which he gave his originary "yes" (*Bejahung*), given that, at the same time, by saying "no" to it, by expelling (*Ausstoßung*) it into the real, he has established a triple

## Chapter Five – The Time of the Subject of the Unconscious: Speech

hole in himself? That the artist is able to demonstrate the existence of this triple hole by restoring the unheard-of, the invisible, and the immateriality of things for us raises the following question: How can the originary forgetting prove to be unforgettable?

I shall put forward the following hypothesis in this connection: if the act whereby what is primordially expelled is forgotten forever, the act through which the subject agreed (*Bejahung*) to this loss is not. The subject, without being able to remember *what* has been lost forever, retains the capacity to commemorate the fact that he said "yes" to separating from a part of himself.

There is a distinction between the originary *forgotten* and the fact that a non-forgetting can exist, not of the forgotten but *of the act* by which it was forgotten. I link this non-forgetting of the forgetting of the originary pact to the setting up of a structural transference through which the subject not only loses, purely and simply, a part of himself, but also bestows on this lost thing the signification of a symbolic gift to the Other by means of which he strives to pay his debt towards the speech that constituted him.

We are the beneficiaries of this process of transference when, by means of what we call the amazing "gift," the artist (as if he were indebted to us insofar as he puts us in the place of the Other) gives us the gracious gift of a note of music that makes us hear the unheard-of, or of a touch of color that gives us a glimpse of the invisible. In this way I can discern at least three ways in which the forgotten originary pact is, as it were, unforgettable: the first is originary guilt, which reminds us that we do not honor the pact; the second is the bewildering commandment, which calls on us to honor it; and the third is the artist, who teaches us that someone has honored it.

### β) The Institution of the Triple Veil

— Veil over the symbolic: the unheard-of

We have seen that the subject ceased to be confronted with the gnostic universe of traumatism insofar as he was put in touch with a world whose abject character ($\bcancel{A}$) ceased to be excluded from the symbolic as a result of being brought to significance: S ($\bcancel{A}$).

In fact, the assumption of the signifier of the divided Other is the work of the "*Es*" and not of the ego, which, governed by the pleasure principle, can only establish a dualistic transference obeying the categories of the good and the bad. The subject and the ego are thus heirs of two radically different conceptions of the transference. By virtue of the mechanism of the pleasure principle, the archaic ego will respond to its gnostic conception derived from the trauma by introducing through the mechanisms of *introjizieren* and *werfen* a radical split between the good and the bad.[341] The originary ego acts by introjecting into the inside everything that is good and by rejecting into the outside everything that is bad. But due to the beyond of the pleasure principle, quite another mechanism—governed by the pair *Bejahung-Ausstoßung*—comes into play.[342] It takes into account the other conception of the world it has inherited ever since the success of the primordial paternal metaphor conveyed to it that there were not two Others—one good and one bad—but a single, divided Other. It is by means of this other psychic mechanism that the subject to be will be led to assume the division of the Other and to constitute himself as divided between absence and presence.

The fundamental difference between the act of the pair *introjizierien-werfen* and that of the pair *Bejahung-Ausstoßung* consists in the fact that the effect of the first is to create a limit between the introjected symbolic and the rejected real, whereas the effect of the second is to produce a symbolic in continuity with the real. Such Moebian continuity leads me to consider the paradox whereby the "yes" through which the *Bejahung* affirms the assumption of the S ($\bar{A}$) is not in contradiction with the "no" through which the *Ausstoßung* expresses the expulsion. This non-contradiction, which is also the means whereby the subject reproduces the act that enables the paternal metaphor to overcome the contradiction posed by the dualism of the Other, may be understood in the following way. The assumption through which the subject says "yes" to the signifier of the abyss in the Other implies that the subject pays with his person, such that within him may arise the real of an abyss that is signifiable. It is because the assumption of this abyss implies that this abyss is *created by a movement of expulsion* (*Ausstoßung*) that the "yes" and the "no" are not contradictory but go

---

[341] Sigmund Freud, "Negation," *op. cit.*
[342] *Ibid.*

## Chapter Five – The Time of the Subject of the Unconscious: Speech

in the same direction of realizing this act of primal repression, which is the most enigmatic that psychoanalysis encounters on its path.

How does the subject discover that, in order to enter the symbolic world at the dawn of his life, he must carry out this act of mourning whereby he subtracts a part of himself? How does he acquire this *savoir-faire* that no one can teach him? In the observation of the mother and the obstetrician, I was led to propose the following.[343] The absence of the *savoir-faire* of such an originary mourning is the effect of a foreclosure induced in the mother when her relationship with the child's father is such that she cannot "attribute importance" to his speech.[344] In not being able to "attribute importance" to this speech or to transmit to the child the signifier of the Name-of-the-Father, she is not the only one in question. In the speech of the necessary intercessor that is the "A-father," there may be a foreclosure that prevents him from "attributing importance" to the signifier of the Name-of-the-Father.[345] This leads me to suppose three levels in foreclosure: the foreclosure whereby the *infans* does not gain access to primal repression would be the effect of a foreclosure induced in the mother by the same foreclosure that makes a hole in the father's discourse.

The difference between the rejection linked to the *Verwerfung* and that of the *Ausstoßung* lies in the fact that the latter is a "no" associated with a "yes," whereas the *Verwerfung* is an absolute "no." Whereas, through the "no-yes" of the *Ausstoßung-Bejahung*, a part of the subject disappears with the unconscious agreement of the subject—in such a way that this disappearance is expressed by the appearance of a real hole in the symbolic—through the absolute "no" of the act of *Verwerfung*, the signifier of the Name-of-the-Father excluded from the symbolic *does not disappear, but reappears as a ghost* in a place that may be defined as a symbolic hole in the real.

There is a fundamental difference between the loss linked to the symbolic hole in the real (foreclosure) and the loss linked to the real hole in the symbolic (*Ausstoßung*). While the foreclusive loss induces an absolute deprivation of sense, the symbolic loss of the originary signifier conveys the dimension of a beyond of meaning, of a point where, in getting lost, meaning paradoxically acquires an overabun-

---

[343] See 141.
[344] Jacques Lacan, "Treatment of Psychosis," in *Écrits, op. cit.*, 482.
[345] *Ibid.*, 481.

dance. In wit, at the moment when a word loses its sense, the lexical code signals that it is conveying something unheard-of. In relation to what can be heard, what does the unheard-of convey other than the fact that it makes visible the absolute ascendancy of an unlimited *pas-de-sens*?[346] By freeing the subject from his determinism by the lexical meaning of language, it establishes him in the function of "his" freedom, as Lacan defines it: "What founds the function of freedom in the sense and the radical non-sense of the subject is strictly speaking the signifier (of the *Urverdrängung*) that kills all sense... in abolishing all of them."[347]

It is by acquiescing to the bewildering commandment: "Where something was already-known, come to what is not yet known," that the subject, through a veritable *Aufhebung*, confirms the signifying determinism *while at the same time going beyond it*. This is why Lacan adds: "The signifier constitutes the subject in his freedom in relation to all sense, but this does not mean that it is not determined in it."[348]

This unlimited sense that is apprehended in experiencing the unheard-of gives man an astonishing lesson. It is at the moment when his understanding is caught in the act of not being able to embrace such a semantic excess, at the moment when this understanding lays down its arms in the face of an amplitude that is beyond it, that the aesthetic capacity appears.[349] It is as if the joy dispensed by apprehending the beauty intrinsic to the unheard-of could only develop because man *is unable to understand* what he encounters. Does he derive enjoyment because he ceases to be encumbered by the demands of his superego for intelligibility or because the paralysis of his reason permits the opening of a third eye that could only be shut by his reason? It remains that particular conditions are necessary if the unheard-of is to be able to tear itself away from the exile in which it sojourns.

The possibility of such an experience of limitlessness raises a question that we are not the first to ask ourselves: how, as finite creatures, are we to conceive of the idea of the infinite?

---

[346] [An expression that can mean both a "step of meaning" and "no meaning."]
[347] Jacques Lacan, *The Four Fundamental Concepts, op. cit.*, 252.
[348] *Ibid*.
[349] Such an experience of limitlessness is very close to Kant's analysis of the sublime, and especially of the "mathematical sublime," which he evokes in connection with Pascal's two infinites.

The fact that Descartes focused precisely on this question in order to prove the existence of God[350] reminds us of the inescapable character of the "paradoxical knot" evoked by Levinas,[351] at the level of which one can say that thought, owing to the very fact that it can think more than itself,[352] in having the idea of the infinite, attests to the fact that the dimension of transcendence can affect immanence without deforming itself in it.[353] This philosophical term of "transcendence" can be imported into analytic discourse insofar as we refer the dimension beyond sense through which the idea of the infinite can come to us in the experience of the unheard-of to an act of "internal transcendence" by means of which primal repression establishes a hole that *ex-sists* with respect to the unconscious, and that, as "ex," transcends it.[354] The existence of such an internal transcendence implies clinically that there exists, as Freud said, a beyond the pleasure principle that, insofar as it is beyond this principle, is therefore not subject to its law.

The function of this beyond is twofold. On the one hand, it tends, in diabolically repeating the situation of traumatic distress, to remind the subject that what has not been symbolized doesn't cease to insist on being symbolized.[355] On the other hand, and this aspect was left unexplored by Freud, the beyond the pleasure principle possesses another side to it than this repetitive quest for the same; from this perspective the compulsion to repeat is not an aim in itself but a silent means by which it calls, beyond the repetition of the same, for the repetition of a recommencement of something radically new.

---

[350] René Descartes, *Méditations métaphysiques* (Paris: Garnier-Flammarion), 121: "The idea that I have of a being more perfect than mine could only have been placed in me by a being that is, in reality, more perfect."

[351] Emmanuel Levinas, "Transcendence and Intelligibility," in *Emmanuel Levinas: Basic Philosophical Writings* (Bloomington: Indiana University Press, 2008).

[352] Emmanuel Levinas, *En découvrant l'existence avec Husserl et Heidegger*, op. cit., 174.

[353] Jean-Christophe Aeschlimann, *Répondre d'autrui*, entretiens avec Emmanuel Levinas (Neufchâtel: La Baconnière, 1989).

[354] Jean-Pierre Winter, unpublished seminar on Spinoza.

[355] What I call "unsymbolized" is what Freud identifies as the effect of the "unbound" excitation.

## Chapter Five – The Time of the Subject of the Unconscious: Speech

What does recommencing involve?

It involves returning to the empty box that is the point of departure, from which a part of the subject that remains *indeterminate* gives him the possibility of recommencing his destiny by escaping from the determinism of the symptom. That it is possible to stop repeating and to begin again in another way is what Freud discovered in the analysis of the dream of the botanical monograph. By recognizing the bewildering signifier and naming it as the signifier that is the "cause of the dream," he extracts himself from the repetition that constantly led him to defer his relation to the paternal debt. By virtue of this extraction, he is able to recommence his link to speech in terms of a new rapport with this symbolic debt. This possibility of recommencing appears when, being able to renounce repressing the bewildering signifier, he agrees to hear that the unheard-of commandment of this signifier requires him to find in himself the access point where an undetermined unheard-of resides.

What the unheard-of dimension of a poetic metaphor allows me to hear is this interruption, this sideration in me of that which had hitherto been determined by the finiteness of meaning. A sideration upon which I depend, like a dancer who takes flight in escaping the determinism of the law of gravity, in order to take flight myself and to be transported to a region where the determinism of meaning no longer prevails, to a place of indeterminate a-semantism where, in a lightning flash, everything becomes possible again. For at this point where I rediscover my indetermination, I am called upon to make the choice of a signifier that will tear me away from this infinite indeterminate dimension by representing myself finitely to him.

The time of being torn away is the time of de-sideration. The most precise topological definition of sideration is that which happens to the subject when he ceases to be represented by a signifier for this other signifier that is the primarily repressed signifier. He is reduced to the fact of being nothing more than this sole signifier of primal repression. It is inasmuch as he *is* this absolute lack that he *no longer* has any relation to this lack and loses his desiring position. He will only become desiring again when, de-siderated, he ceases to be the lack, since *his lack, ceasing to be pure presence, will become re-presence*, re-presented by an object that is the cause of desire.

This process of de-sideration is one whereby the subject is called upon to divide himself into two signifiers, for he cannot remain at the level of this indeterminate signifier of infinitude.

What is the signifier of the *Urverdrängung* that Lacan writes "binary signifier S2"?[356]

Lacan, in the commentary on the case of the "Wolf Man," comments on this possibility as follows: "The subject as X can be constituted only from the *Urverdrängung*, from the necessary fall of this first signifier. He is constituted around the *Urverdrängung*, but *he cannot subsist there as such*,[357] since this would require the representation of one signifier for another, whereas here there is only one, the first."[358]

This impossibility of subsistence of which Lacan speaks refers us to the first logical time in which the bewildered subject is in an in-between, where he cannot remain if he wants to find his place in historical temporality. He finds himself between the traumatic past from which he was extricated by primal repression, and the future to which he must come by finding, through a new signifier, the finiteness of an audible meaning that will represent him before the signifier of the unheard-of infiniteness of meaning.

The means by which Lacan introduces this dimension of the infinite, of which the lost signifier of primal repression is the bearer, involves the comparison of the appearance of this loss with the appearance of the mathematical zero: "Everyone knows that if zero appears in the denominator, the value of the fraction no longer has meaning, but assumes by convention what mathematicians call an infinite value. In a way, this is one of the times in the constitution of the subject. Insofar as the primary signifier is pure non-sense, it becomes the bearer of the infinitization of the value of the subject."[359] It is at the level of taking charge of this "infinitization of the value of the subject" that the question arises of the appearance of sex and its sublimation. The artist is the ambassador of this infinite realm: by rendering the unheard-of and the invisible transmissible, his task is to remind man of the Thing

---

[356] Jacques Lacan, *The Four Fundamental Concepts, op. cit.*, 218: "this (binary) signifier constitutes the central point of the *Urverdrängung*"; "which is constituted out of the primal repression of the fall of the binary signifier."
[357] My emphasis.
[358] *Ibid.*, 218.
[359] *Ibid.*, 219.

that lives in exile in him; he does not deliver this Thing from its exile but allows it to be seen and heard as definitively exiled.

On this point, Levinas' meditation on the human face offers the psychoanalyst the possibility to consider the face as the trace that the artist, *qua* Creator, has left on the human body—a trace that permits man to see and hear the "idea of infinity" that comes to him in an unheard-of way.[360] While sublimation could thus be understood as the transmission by a signifier of the infinitization of the subject, the sexual could be understood as a taking charge of this infinite dimension by a signifier—the phallic signifier—that, having been incarnated in the body, introduces the dimension of finiteness to it.

It is striking see that, in their way of thinking about "the idea of the infinite" or "the infinitization of the values of the subject," Levinas and Lacan are both led to introduce the notion of "knot." If, for Levinas, it is a metaphorical knot, and for Lacan, a real knot, it is still the case that the institution of the hole of primal repression may be thought of as the setting up between the subject and the Other of a pact that, for us analysts, is "knotted" with the structure of a Borromean knot.

What Freud discovered by being the first to account for the fact that man "only thinks of that," of sex, was that man's thought is inexorably oriented by the point of primal repression where sense has fallen. The signifier of the loss of the signifier, the phallus, as the ambassador of the navel that makes a hole in unconscious thought, puts the subject in the position of "only thinking of that," that is, of only thinking around this point where nothing is thinkable. The phallic signifier as the effect of this contradiction whereby something significant is affirmed and, at the same time, is radically concealed, is expressed by the structural ambiguity of the *cache sexe*. The veil is both the presence of a signifier that can unveil itself and that, in so doing, reveals the absolute veil that is the phallus, as it symbolizes the real where significance is veiled forever.

---

[360] Emmanuel Levinas, *Totality and Infinity* (La Haye: Nishof, 1961); "Transcendence and Intelligibility," *op. cit.*; *En découvrant l'existence avec Husserl et Heidegger*, *op. cit.*

## Chapter Five – The Time of the Subject of the Unconscious: Speech

— Speech as pact

The speech given by the Other will only become the speech of the subject if the relation between giver and receiver is governed by an act. For the subject not to be indifferent, like the autist, to the speech given, there must be something in the speech of the Other that lends itself to a possible reception. Whereas the receivable gift will be translated by the fact that the speech given appears to be legitimately mine, the gift of speech, when it is not receivable, is translated by the fact that the *jouissance* of this speech appears to me as the usurpation of a possession that cannot be mine.

Clinically, this results in the feeling that at the very moment of speaking one does not have the sense that it is they themselves who are speaking, but rather that they are repeating someone else's words, as if they were not borne by speech, but only the speech-bearers of the Other. It is as if they could hear a voice that was saying to them, "I can definitely hear words coming out of your mouth, but is it you who is speaking? Are you not simply repeating a speech that precedes you without it being yours?" With this question, which can result in a renunciation of speaking, we are introduced to the supposition of the existence of a flaw or formal error in the originary pact between the Other and the subject.

Analysis constantly reminds us at what point parents are unable to understand why their child shows them that what is given to them is un-assumable. The mother who is fretting about her anorexic baby does not understand that her way of giving herself without reservation, when she puts the infant to her breast, arouses the reservations in the infant. She does not understand it because she does not know that what a child expects of a gift is not the object given, but the manner in which this object is given. In particular, the child does not expect the giver to be wholly within what is given, but rather beyond what is given, in such a way that there is no confusion between what is given and the giver.

A father does not understand that his son has no choice but to refuse the money that he wants to give him, for he does not see that by his manner of giving he is asking to be exonerated from the fact he did not know how to give the child the absolutely free gift that he was expecting—namely, his speech. The child in question, who was expecting to be redeemed by a gift of speech, could not be bought by money.

## Chapter Five – The Time of the Subject of the Unconscious: Speech

These two examples allow us to say what an assumable gift of speech is: such a gift is characterized by not being a giving of *oneself* whereby the giver, who offers himself wholly in a sacrificial manner, has nothing left in reserve once he has given. If, in this respect, he gives himself again, his gift, inasmuch as it is devoid of any dimension beyond it, will be identical with itself and will not transmit the essential feature of a true symbolic gift, namely, that of never giving oneself twice in the same way. This novelty consists in the fact that, through the symbolic gift, what is transmitted is fundamentally the permanent and inexhaustible reserve that exceeds what is given insofar as it attests to a beyond that no gift can exhaust. It is because the giver does not own this transcendent reserve that the symbolic gift is fundamentally a gift of love. When Lacan says that "love is giving what one does not have," he indicates implicitly that the structure of a Harpagon father is that of a father who, by confiding his possessions to the limits of a cash box, has given up the possibility of passing on to his heirs what he does not have:[361] this beyond that only "the signification of a limitless love" can make accessible.[362]

The question raised here is that of the impact of such a love in an analysis. The transference love has two fundamentally antinomical sides to it. On the one hand, it is the means, through repetition, by which the historical avatars of the analysand's misfortunes in love are recollected. On the other it is the means by which the analysand can make a symbolic transference onto this thing—*das Ding*—that, differentiating itself from every finite gift, incarnates the exception that confirms the rule according to which a gift is never free since it carries obligations.

We can now see the exceptional meaning of the debt that I am saddled with if the Other gives me what he does not have. For example, if he is an analyst, an interpretation that has the structure of a witticism. Why does the gift of wit induce such a particular debt? Because it is a gift that, as it is absolutely free, requires no recognition of debt from me; and as it requires nothing from me in return, it imposes on me, paradoxically, another test.

---

[361] [Harpagon is the main character in Moliere's play *The Miser*.]
[362] Jacques Lacan, *The Four Fundamental Concepts, op. cit.*, 276.

## Chapter Five – The Time of the Subject of the Unconscious: Speech

Indeed, it is at the moment when I receive this gracious gift that I discover in myself, with my own assent, the obligation to be grateful. Recognition, in the moral sense, which is inferred from the possibility that has been given to me of recognizing the existence of wit, introduces me to the symbolic transference that, by pulling me out of the repetitive transference, makes me encounter the procreative function of the transference. The transference onto the existence of the real (the unheard-of) is procreative when that which in the subject persists as infinitely indeterminate in its relation to the infinitude of sense, has a chance to begin speaking in another way—differently than he did before when, under the yoke of his symptom, he obeyed the determinism of the pleasure principle. In such a transference onto the unheard-of, a reversion occurs whereby the subject's debit account, insofar as he was indebted, is transmuted into a credit account. No sooner is the subject led to the act of trusting in the unheard-of, than he finds himself credited with the infinite possibility of the signifier. This credit that is thus made available to him is accorded because he has "freely" chosen—since he was not obliged to do so by the superego—to recognize his debt towards the signifier that has conferred on him the spirit of a metaphor.

It doesn't surprise us that the children of a father conducting himself with speech like Harpagon with his cash box are destined to live their relation with speech as a usurped possession. Speech is only given to the subject as his own insofar as he receives it from a giver who is able to give, in love, what he does not have: the beyond of the symbolic that is the unheard-of.

If this signifier of the unheard-of is assumed by the subject as primarily repressed, as S2, it will become the support of the "infinitization of the subject's values," the locus of the emergence of a commandment that Freud translates as "Where it was, there shall ego be," and which I prefer to translate by, "Where it was, become!" For, at this stage of primal repression, the I does not exist as yet. It is precisely that thing that has to be torn away from the intemporality of the imperfect where absolute subjectivity reigns in order to conquer time and the future of a divided subjectivity.[363] The time in which the future subject

---

[363] Jacques Lacan, "The Freudian Thing," in *Écrits, op. cit.*, 347. Lacan suggests "the production of a verb '*s'être*' that would express the mode of absolute subjectivity."

## Chapter Five – The Time of the Subject of the Unconscious: Speech

must cease to be an indeterminate signifier of infinitude in order to emerge as determined by a new signifier (whose finitude will represent it before the signifier of infinitude) is the time of desire. Here what has been created (the "*Es*") is liable to procreate in its turn by creating the act of division.

Henceforth, the subject will be positioned between two infinites: the infinitude that has acquired significance in him, and which Lacan writes as S2, has been substituted for the infinitude of meaning that appeared in the Other from the moment the signifier of a divided Other (S Ⱥ) has supplemented the duality of the Other. Sideration is *the subjective experience in which these two infinites are placed in continuity* with each other.

"That the Real surmounts the Symbolic at two points is exactly what is involved in analysis," Lacan tells us, insisting once again on the necessity for the analyst to take into account the question of the ascendancy of the real over the symbolic.[364]

This necessity is ethical. In this connection the analysand may be driven to despair if his analyst considers that the symbolic can master this impossible that is the real; he knows that "the" truth of his symptom cannot be said, but only "half-said." The analysand is not in search of a master, but of an Other who, because divided, is able to bear witness as guardian of the symbolic interdiction under the ascendancy of this master that is the impossible real. Olivier Grignon has recently given an account of this ethical requirement: "The operation that we want to produce does not lie in the field where the impossible proceeds from the interdiction .... On the contrary, if we suppose that strictly speaking it is a matter of inventing the Symbolic with the Real, it will mean making the interdiction depend on the impossible, that is to say, on the Real, and thus of having an experience of the impossible as such. Any contrary practice is a deviation from psychoanalysis, a betrayal that transforms psychoanalysis into a sort of self-righteous 'ready to wear' theory that, unfortunately, is what often happens under the cover of a pseudo-concept...."[365]

---

[364] Jacques Lacan, seminar of January 14, 1975, *RSI*, unpublished seminar.
[365] Olivier Grignon, "Les limites de la psychanalyse, c'est le psychanalyste," lecture given in Dijon, March 6, 1994.

*Chapter Five – The Time of the Subject of the Unconscious: Speech*

— The cut of the discourse

I would say that the real, by making accessible "the" truth of saying as inaccessible, tends to reveal the fact that there is no truth except as veiled. To this power of veiling has fallen the possibility of only detecting the truth because it is radically concealed. The truth that is concealed in saying, by always exceeding what detects it, puts this excess in the position of inducing an infinite insistence on unveiling through speech. If the metaphor of the unheard-of deserts the subject's speech, the articulation that this metaphor produced, by introducing into the symbolic the signification of the impossible, disappears. There then appears another articulation whereby the real, no longer being knotted with the symbolic, becomes unknotted and acts on the symbolic in a real and no longer a metaphorical way.

This is how, at the point where metaphor fails, the superego appears. In the place of a signification supported by a signifying articulation, the signification of the superego appears, sustained by an object. The eye of the conscience bears a signification that the subject always interprets as: "Don't insist!" If under this gaze, the subject desists, it is because he has lost the possibility of trusting in the unheard-of. The subject cannot invest the unheard-of transferentially, as a locus of supposed knowledge, if the knowledge that he invests is knowledge that is not supposed but that imposes itself as a guilt-inducing gaze.

— The veiled body: the immaterial

Just as the subject has at his disposal the *jouissance* of speech because the veil of the unheard-of allows him to unveil a half-hearing, he will walk and dance because the veil of the immaterial will transmit to him the *jouissance* of a body lightened by immateriality. That man *is* not a body but *has* a body that he treats "any old how... like a piece of furniture... which he puts in wagons where he lets himself be carried around..." tells us the extent to which human beings only inhabit their bodies with difficulty.[366] Can one imagine seeing a dog, or a cat, giving the impression of being uncomfortable in its body, of being cramped in it or, on the contrary, of being lost in it?

This discordance between man and his body teaches us that this bodily matter is a real that is scarcely natural. It is because speech and

---

[366] Jacques Lacan, *Scilicet* 6–7 (1976), 49.

*Chapter Five – The Time of the Subject of the Unconscious: Speech*

a specular image are grafted onto this body that it is not a pure real, but rather a mixture of real, symbolic, and imaginary. The primordial elaboration of this mixture occurs, in my view, during the enigmatic knotting process of primal repression, which, well before the mirror stage, confers on the body a pre-specular consistency that is deeper than that of secondary narcissism.

I will devote the case observation of little Lucky to the study of this consistency, which, in my view, is bestowed by the double intervention of the *cache-sexe*. By traumatically making a hole in the body, the phallic signifier introduces into it a chaotic principle of inconsistency that calls for the intervention of a consistency to come. This consistency of the body will be supplied by the asymmetrical intervention of two veils, namely, clothing and underclothing. Clothing has the double function of ensuring that the specular image is maintained and of veiling the underclothing, which is the *cache sexe*. If the *cache sexe* has to be veiled, it means that although it is a visible piece of cloth, it is not specular. In this respect, we assume that blind people living together no doubt experience the same need for their underclothing as sighted people.

— The veiled sex: the invisible

The invention of the *cache sexe* may be conceived of as the translation on the imaginary level, for the external world, of what has been radically withdrawn from the symbolic. This translation signifies that, for the unconscious psyche, the negativization bearing on the symbolic (the unheard-of) has the same signification as the negativization bearing on the body-image (the invisible): what disappears from the symbolic—as if forever unheard-of—is the same thing as what disappears from the visible.

The unconscious invention of the *cache-sexe* seems to me to be based on the same principle as the invention of the red curtain that warns the spectator that there exists a scene that it is forbidden to watch. That the non-respect of this prohibition can be life-threatening is something that a child psychoanalyst has taught us: the case in question was that of a newborn baby suffering from kidney disease for which he needed dialysis round the clock. The psychoanalyst, whom the nursing staff had contacted for a consultation, and who had pointed out that this child was clearly letting himself die, discovered a child whose body was entirely naked, with tubes everywhere. The pre-emi-

## Chapter Five – The Time of the Subject of the Unconscious: Speech

nence of the technical care given to the child was such that the nursing staff was led to restrict their care to the pure materiality of a body treated as a little machine with tubes coming out of it everywhere. The analyst's intervention was very simple: she told the child that the nursing staff had forgotten to cover his body and that she was going to ask them to rectify this.

Will anyone be surprised to learn that this child, who was letting himself die, decided he wanted to live on the very day that his right to have his genitals covered was recognized? No, for we already knew that the Medusa's eye was deadly, and so we could suspect that one of the functions of the loin-cloth was to put a humanizing veil in front of this evil eye.

The *cache sexe* thus appears as the setting up of a limit whose imaginary contour has the capacity to negativize the deadly power of the real. This negativization is necessary, for the frontier that exists—owing to the diversity of the human body—between the living human form and the formlessness of the corpse to come, is unclear. The porous nature of this frontier creates the conditions for the invasion, owing to the evil eye, of the human form by a monstrous formlessness, the ambassador of death. By negativizing the real, the veil has two essential functions: as underclothing, it prevents the real of the body from striving for monstrous formlessness by bestowing on it an invisible consistency of a pre-specular order; as clothing, it withdraws the real of the body from the pure law of falling bodies and attributes it with the possibility of lightness. In the same way as it makes something disappear from the field of the audible and from the field of the materiality of the body, primal repression makes something disappear from the field of the visible.

As a result of this primal repressed bearing on the imaginary, the specular image will be left with a hole in it: there will be something in the mirror that cannot be seen. Consequently, the imaginary will sojourn between two modalities of the invisible. On one side there will be the invisibility of the veiled phallus, and on the other side the invisibility of another structure. This latter structure, invoked by the second commandment of Moses, indicates that beyond the visible idol there exists the hidden alterity of a speech that is invisible.

The discovery of the ascendancy of the symbolic world over the imaginary world, which, moreover, is strictly in keeping with Freud's discovery that the dream image is governed by a written text, is recognition of the fact that, in order to negativize the image and to impregnate it with meaning, the signifier of the Name-of-the-Father must act through its metaphorical power. The symbolic does not make the visible disappear; it lays the imprint of the invisible on it, which transforms the visible, in allowing what exceeds it to be seen, owing to the advent of the beautiful.

By veiling the visible the symbolic creates the conditions of unveiling: this unveiling is the contrary of that type of obscene unveiling whereby a revealed secret—as in the case of blushing on account of shame—is a secret that has ceased to be one. In this respect, when the invisible shows itself, by demonstrating, as it does in a painting, that it ceases to be invisible, we can say that its mode of unveiling obeys a mode of Moebian proximity with the visible: visible and invisible are separated while remaining in continuity. If darkness is a source of anxiety, it is precisely because such proximity disappears: in the dark, the invisible, ceasing to be chained to the visible, is unleashed and tends to show itself in the form of a frightening monster.

The artist is the untiring ambassador of this triple inaccessibility to which primal repression introduces us: if he is a musician, he enables us to hear the unheard-of; if he is a painter, he enables us see the invisible; if he is a dancer, he enables us touch the immaterial.

## II. Overcoming Bewilderment and Emerging from Primal Repression

### A. THE GAME OF TENNIS AND THE ANALYTIC GAME

It is not impossible that the passion for ball games is linked, in one way or another, to the quest for that bewildering moment that one of the partners will inevitably experience when the ball has suddenly acquired temporal-spatial characteristics that are sufficiently unforeseen to bewilder him. If the spectator is unconsciously engaged by the fact of witnessing this enactment of bewilderment, it is because it reminds him of his own choice in front of the bewildering signifier—a choice between the injunction of the superego, "Don't let yourself be *verblüfft*!," and the symbolic call, "Where you were once bewildered,

## Chapter Five – The Time of the Subject of the Unconscious: Speech

become un-bewildered." Whereas bewilderment refers to the archaic experience of entering primal repression, overcoming this bewilderment is an act whereby the subject emerges from it.

But what is required of a tennis player to cease to be bewildered by the ball that passes under his nose? What must happen for this ball to cease to be inaccessible so that it can be returned? What happens to the subject who is bewildered by the tennis ball that got past him without his seeing it since, owing to its acceleration, it had become invisible for him? Has he lost his head or has he lost the ball? Does he no longer know where he is, or does he not know where the ball is? On this point, I would like to return to my commentary in the first chapter.

My contention is that, at this moment, the subject is bewildered, for he receives from the ball the following signifying message: "I am going where you can't see me, for I know where you have not yet become!" That he could have been somewhere else other than where he is reminds him that there is a "somewhere" where he could have been, but without being there.

The supposition of this "somewhere," translated by the question, "Where are you?," locates the ball in the place of a subject who is supposed to know what the subject doesn't yet know. The questioning force conveyed by the ball is thus the immediate cause of a bewildering transference comparable to the analytic transference. The effect of this transference on to another place reminds the subject of the fact that he does not know but could have known where this "elsewhere" is *from where he could have returned the ball*.

This supposition leaves him undecided and this moment of indecision is fatal for him. The ball goes more quickly than his search for the place from which he could have seen it. The fact that a subject can progress and, one day, return the ball that had hitherto bewildered him, means that he can acquire the speed that will enable him to respond without indecision, without being bewildered. The acquisition of this speed is not the effect of muscle but of that enigmatic psychic process whereby the subject overcomes his earlier state of bewilderment. How does the articulation of desire (etymologically, *desiderium*, as I have already said) occur? When the ball ceases to be an instance of questioning about the place where the subject *is* lost and instead becomes the symbol of what he *has* lost.

I would say that the subject ceases to be lost, to be bewildered, when the ball ceases to function for him as a bewildering signifier sym-

## Chapter Five – The Time of the Subject of the Unconscious: Speech

bolizing the Other. Instead, it becomes the symbol of what he has lost, namely, the *objet a* that, as cause of his desire, will allow him to play the game of *fort-da*. In this reversion whereby he ceases to *be* the lack in order to *have* a relation to the lack that is the cause of his desire, the ball no longer represents a subject who is supposed to know. It is the subject who is supposed to know how to deal with desire.

The *savoir faire* that will enable him to return the ball immediately, without indecision, is profoundly paradoxical, since it comes to him at the very moment when the subject becomes unconscious of himself, that is to say, unconscious of knowing anything at all.

How does this unconscious *savoir faire* manifest itself? First and foremost, by the fact that the subject, emerging from the state of blindness in which he was in respect of the ball, will at last see clearly. Like a witticism, the ball will deliver to him the light that it concealed in such a way that, enlightened by this light, the subject will emerge from the darkness where he was befuddled and become clear-sighted. He will know where he is and where the ball is.

This unconscious knowledge that affects space and time is expressed on the one hand by the fact that the subject will clearly see the limits of the tennis court—that is, the spatial incarnation of prohibition—within which he must return the ball. On the other hand, as he now stands in a new relation to time, he will volley the ball with an instantaneity that shows that the knowledge that enables him to react so rapidly is not in the order of a reflexive knowledge. This immediacy has two components: the subject, by making himself present and countering the ball as receiver, does not let it get past him; and then, as emitter, he returns this ball.[367]

Between the act of countering the ball and that of returning it there are two distinct logical times that, in the case of tennis, do not appear clearly because it is with one and the same stroke that the subject counters the ball and returns it to his opponent.

In this respect, fencing makes it possible to dissociate these two times very clearly, for in fencing there is not just one ball but two: the tips of each of the two foils are each comparable to a ball that must touch the opponent's body, which is thus the equivalent of the tennis

---

[367] The awakening of this instantaneity is not unrelated to the awakening of "*Satori*," the spiritual goal of Zen.

## Chapter Five – The Time of the Subject of the Unconscious: Speech

court. The art of fencing is thus based on the audible distinction of the tit for tat whereby first the parry and then the riposte can be heard.

The first "clash" corresponds to the attack of the opponent who has struck my foil; the second "clash" to the fact that I have parried it immediately.

The third moment is the one in which I will riposte by trying in turn to touch the opponent: if I touch him, he will not parry; we will not hear a third "clash."

This tit for tat response is exemplary insofar as it commemorates the two logical times in which the subject enters and emerges from primal repression.

Let us say that if the first "clash" is the time of the Other—a time when the subject receives the manifestation of the desire of the Other—the second "clash," that of the parry, is the time of the subject: a time when the subject, by signifying, "You can't get through," introduces the frontier of the separating prohibition between the Other and himself. The setting up of this frontier, where the Other is faced with the fact that the subject has become impenetrable, could be compared with the physical process that transmutes white light into color. The color green, for instance, only appears in the visible world because grass absorbs certain wavelengths and rejects, outside itself, green wavelengths. The comparison between the subject who rejects the ball and grass that rejects green wavelengths is nevertheless limited. The rejected green wavelengths are, in fact, the same as those that were already received in the white light, whereas the ball rejected by the subject is not the same as the ball received. The parrying of the ball should be conceived of as an authentic creation, for, at the very moment when the subject parries, the parried ball is no longer the same ball. It has ceased to be the ball coming from the Other, and has become the stand-in for the Other, the *objet a*. The ball that the subject parries becomes, in the same instant, an object from which he separates forever and, thereby, his lost object-cause of desire.

What characterizes the locus of this enigmatic causation is that the Other, *qua* barred, can know nothing about it, whereas the subject, for his part, knows where the cause of his desire is. If he is capable, when he ceases to be bewildered, of parrying instantly, without thinking, it is because he knows unconsciously where the ball, the cause of his desire, is. With his parry, he teaches the Other that he is no longer where the Other saw him, henceforth veiled by the master

## Chapter Five – The Time of the Subject of the Unconscious: Speech

trump card, namely, the phallic signifier that is the racket with which he has parried the ball. It is as if he was signifying to the other: "You thought you knew where I was, but I am teaching you that I am no longer where you thought I was; I am henceforth elsewhere." This "elsewhere," which is henceforth untouchable, inaccessible to the racket of the Other, is the radically incognito point from which the subject is caused in his desire.

In fact, what makes this "elsewhere" truly inaccessible is not that the Other does not know where the subject is hidden. The statement, "You do not know where I am hidden," produces a hiding place whose secret is fundamentally precarious. The vulnerability of such a hiding place lies in the fact that the very fact of hiding myself from your gaze sets up a transference whereby I suppose that a third party has the possibility of being the one from whom one cannot hide anything. If Dupin can see the purloined letter, it means that the hiding place invented by the queen, however astute it is, overlooks the structural fact that it suffices for an object to be veiled to elicit immediately the appearance of a revealing gaze. If the tennis player who has countered the bewildering ball signifies to the Other that he is in a truly invisible "elsewhere," it means that he is not in the position of the queen who knows what she is hiding. The player is in the position of the subject who, insofar as he is unconscious, is hidden, *without knowing that he is hidden*. It is precisely because, unlike the queen, *he does not know either that he is hidden or where he is hidden that he is genuinely hidden*.

The paradox of the one who is forgetful of himself is that if, by forgetting himself, he has forgotten the subject who is supposed to know, he does not forget, on the other hand, where the ball that is the cause of his desire is. We thus find Lacan's conception of the trajectory of the transference in analysis in this path from a transference of knowledge on to the bewildering Other to a transference of desire onto the *objet a*. The beginning of the analysis, when the analyst is in the position of the Other who is supposed to know, stands in stark contrast with the end of the analysis when the analyst is removed from this place and falls as *objet a* cause of the analysand's desire—who, as a result, becomes the subject who is supposed to know how to deal with his desire.

This comparison between the analytic game and the game of tennis is particularly meaningful from the angle of the similitude that can be noticed between the subjective position of the analysand concluding his analysis and the position of the player who, after the time of countering, concludes, in a third time, with a winning shot. The winning shot is characterized by the fact that, as the desire of the Other has been fended off, the desire of the subject is articulated as separated from the ball. By means of this separation, he transfers the parameters of inaccessibility that were within himself on to the object he has rejected outside of himself. Whereas, when he was bewildered by the ball of the Other, *he* was invisible, unheard-of, immaterial, it is now *the ball* that has acquired these characteristics and then becomes stunning for his partner.

In this connection, we can say that the analyst can be stunned by what happens at the end of analysis.[368] Indeed, it is the analysand who makes the separating blow, which the analyst recognizes without being aware of it. Whereas by parrying, the player had put a veil between his opponent and himself signifying: "I am not where you thought I was," by riposting, he reveals himself, signifying this time: "I am there where you were not expecting the receiver that I am to return, as emitter, his own message in a stunning form."

In this game of "I am not here, I am there" in which the subject conceals and reveals himself, he shows that he can only affirm the *da* of his presence because he has previously had the experience of the influence with which the stunning ball of the Other made him absent. Concerning this primacy of the *fort* over the *da*, there is the possibility of identifying something Heidegger does not take into account in his concept of *Dasein*, namely, the question of the precedence of the Other. Does the fundamental reason that prevents Heidegger from thinking about ethics lie in this absence of the precedence of a *Fortsein* in relation to a *Dasein*?

In the rhythm whereby the time of riposte follows the time of parrying, I identify the two modes of emerging from certain sexual symptoms. I interpret frigidity as being linked to the fact that the woman is unable to overcome her sideration in relation to the phallus, and impotency as linked to the fact that the man is unable to constitute his partner as a lost object, the cause of his desire. From this point of view,

---

[368] Lacan speaks in this connection of the analyst's "loss of being" ("*désêtre*"). One of the questions I will discuss in a forthcoming book is the following: Was Freud, the analyst, capable of being stunned by the discourse of an analysand towards the end of an analysis?

## Chapter Five – The Time of the Subject of the Unconscious: Speech

abandoning frigidity involves the possibility of being able to parry the stunning aspects of the phallus and to be able to appropriate, to make her own, the spirit of the phallus.

As for the disappearance of impotency, it seems to be linked to the possibility of finding the path of the second "clash," the path along which the subject finds his desire in constituting the object as separate. If this separation is not fully achieved, if, at the moment of hitting the ball, the player yields unconsciously to the temptation of catching it in order to enjoy it, then the ball, won over for *jouissance*, will be lost for desire.

Between the ball, object-cause of his desire, and the racket, a phallic signifier that represents this desire, there is thus an incommensurable tension: the desire signified by the erection of the phallic signifier is at once a wish to make desire last by deferring *jouissance* and a wish to abolish desire by encountering phallic *jouissance*. What makes a champion is no doubt linked to a capacity to sublimate *jouissance* in such a way that, when hitting the ball, there is no hesitation, no ambivalence between the nostalgia of *jouissance* and between the wish for desire, which implies a persevering attitude in renewing the loss of the object cause of desire.

In the same way as the player will only produce a winning shot if his racket is sufficiently *stiff* to separate him from the object, a man will only be *stiff* if, paradoxically, the companion that is the body of his partner is not too close to him. In its extreme proximity, this body must at one and the same time be endowed with the extreme remoteness that confers it with its alterity in order to be, like the tennis ball that is moving away, the cause of his desire.

Is there nothing more obvious than a tennis ball bouncing off a racket? And yet, the time in which there is a contact between the phallic signifier and the *objet a* followed by a separation is related to the most immemorial human time when the subject tore himself away from being a single signifier in order to divide himself into two parts. With one part, the phallic signifier, he signifies himself; with the other, the *objet a*, he objectizes himself.

I need to explain why these two times seem to me to be constitutive, one of the feminine position, the other of the masculine. In the time of parrying of the Other, the subject is represented by a new signifier marked by finitude—the phallic signifier that is the racket—onto which are transferred the potentially infinite properties of the

## Chapter Five – The Time of the Subject of the Unconscious: Speech

primordially repressed signifier. Insofar as it represents the infinitely impenetrable aspects of the subject, the erection of this phallic signifier veils the body, bestowing on it an impenetrability. The ego corporal surface becomes impermeable and ceases to be pierceable by the ball of the Other.

This first time of veiling is followed by the time of the unveiling of desire caused by separation from the object.

That these two times seem to me to correspond to the feminine and masculine position is something that is confirmed by the early distinction made in games according to which a little boy plays soccer whereas a little girl jumps rope. The fundamental distinction between these two games consists in the fact that, in soccer, the little boy is constantly separating himself from a ball that he shoots, whereas in jumping rope the little girl does not separate herself from herself but from the ground. Whereas in soccer, the boy has a phallus—the foot—with which he sends the object into the outside, in jumping rope, the girl does not, like the boy, throw an *objet a* outside herself, for it is her body, it is herself, that she tosses in the air.

This reminds us of Michèle Montrelay's intuition that a girl's coordinates of desire are profoundly different from those of a boy. They do not strive, as do the boy's, to separate from a divisible object in order to gain access to desire. It is because she does not play the *fort-da* game with a wooden reel but with her own body that, to the best of my knowledge, the most profound nostalgia that each woman carries within her is that of not having devoted her life to dance. If a woman knows that she was made for dancing, and that she could have bounced like the little girl I referred to earlier, it is, I think, because, unlike a man, she is not "all" in the phallic position. If she knows that when her feet touch the ground she can take off again without any muscular effort, it is because for her the ground possesses a different, elastic energy, extracting her, as if magically, from her weighty materiality. She knows this because she knows that the surface of the ground—like that of a racket—is the stage from which the signifier of the Other, as the power broker [*passeur*] of the Other, can transmit to her the elastic power of transporting her body, by constituting it as an object that is momentarily lost as far as gravity is concerned.

Lacan gave an account in his seminar *Encore* of this unconscious knowledge that places a woman in a causal relationship, not like a man with a stand-in for the Other (the *objet a*), but with the very place where the signifier of the Other transmits itself.[369] The time of parrying, the first time of un-stunning, is the stage in which the subject constitutes himself as surface associating the fact of assuring the reception of the signifier of the Other and that of being transformed by this reception. In this transformation, he recapitulates instantaneously the different subjective transmutations by means of which he emerged, first from the trauma, and then from primal repression. By emerging from the trauma, he constitutes himself as signifier of the lack in the Other (S $\bar{A}$) and, by emerging from primal repression, he separates himself into phallic signifier and object.

This originary separation in which the ball has stopped is not yet the separation in which the ball will be returned. It is a separation that is comparable with that which the little girl makes when she rebounds off the ground. She does not enact the object that the subject *has* but the object that the subject *is*.

## B) THE UNFORGETTABLE FORGETTING

### a) *The Urgent Necessity to Forget: Of the Psychotic, the Mystic, and the Psychoanalyst*

To the extent that a parallel can be drawn between the instant when I hit the ball, sending it back to the sender, and the instant when I speak in order to send the message back to the sender, who thus receives his own message in an inverted form, a question arises: Can I, as an emitter of speech, speak up if, in the same instant, I remain a recipient who hears the speech coming from the Other? No, I cannot at one and the same time hear and make myself heard. The drama of hallucinatory psychosis teaches us in this respect that the impossibility of becoming a speaking subject lies in the fact that the subject, insofar as he cannot extricate himself from his position as a recipient of the voice that hallucinates him, is in the impossibility of forgetting the Other and, consequently, of forgetting himself and of producing himself as a speaking subject.

---

[369] Jacques Lacan, *Encore, op. cit.*, 78.

No one better than the female mystic knows what this impossibility of forgetting oneself is, inasmuch as she is not, like the psychotic, abandoned to the voice of the Other, but rather abandons herself deliberately. The mystic, by virtue of this very choice, has a terrible lucidity concerning the impossibility of forgetting this Other. Marie Pesenti-Irrmann thus speaks of the abhorrence Thérèse d'Avila felt towards the dictatorship of her memory, which could never forget the will of God: "It remains engraved in my memory," she says, "in such a way that I can never forget it.... This memory tires me, I loathe it."[370]

What is it, generally, that enables a subject to forget this Other place where chatter never ceases, if not the sway of the fellow being who, by speaking to him, by looking at him, turns his attention away from the big Other?[371] In order to ensure a permanent openness towards the beyond, it is precisely at this point that the female mystic—like Marguerite Alacoque as evoked by Lacan in the seminar on *Ethics*—deploys a strategy of absolute closure here on earth. In effect, she makes herself "deaf, mute, blind, and insensitive to every earthly thing."[372]

This choice of deafness, muteness, and blindness opposed to the big Other is nothing other than the choice of primal repression. The act of speaking, of listening, and of looking at the little other are only possible for the subject if he commits the act of originary infidelity. This consists in forgetting the big Other by overcoming the state of bewilderment.

The possibility for the subject of forgetting himself, of becoming a subject who is unconscious of himself, implies the possibility of being able to forget the Other. For the subject to be able to speak, it is necessary for the Other to let a silence be heard that, like the blank sheet of paper that allows writing to be inscribed on it, will permit speech to have its specific impact.

How are we to understand the structure of such a forgetting of the Other? Is it the forgetting of secondary repression? No, the de-subjectivizing forgetting produced by secondary repression is not the subjectivizing repression produced by the appearance of a blank, of

---

[370] M. Pesenti-Irmann, "Le mysticism, une écriture de la passion," *Apertura* 10 (1994).
[371] The sway of the little other.
[372] *Ibid*.

## Chapter Five – The Time of the Subject of the Unconscious: Speech

a blank page, of a bar attesting to the fact that the Other has barred itself. What, then, is the structure of a forgetting of the Other that is not that of secondary repression?

One of Freud's remarks puts us on its tracks. What did he mean when he gave the recommendation to analysts, "In each new case, forget everything you know"? When the analyst has to intervene with his analysand, he mustn't do it based on what he already knows, but rather on what he does not know as yet. What would happen, indeed, if he only spoke with what he knew already? He would be led to introduce a body of knowledge that he owed to Freud, but he would not have paid the price for it to be truly his.

What does this "truly" mean? That the analyst has to go back to the primordial "yes" that had been forgotten ever since, as a result of primal repression, "the trace of footsteps was replaced by a no trace."[373] By going back to this bewildering "no trace," like a tennis player who is capable of avoiding the bewildering ball in order to counter-attack, a signifier of this "no trace" is produced. In this way he attests to a non-impossibility of symbolizing the impossibility of the "no trace."

If the Freudian recommendation, "Forget everything you know," is not a call to the desubjectivizing forgetting of secondary repression, but to the assumption of the subjectivizing forgetting of primal repression, a question arises: What is the meaning of the analyst's resistance to forgetting what he already knows and to letting himself be surprised by what he does not know yet?

Freud interpreted this resistance of analysts to forgetting the "already known" when he came to understand that his theory was not invested by them symbolically but in a superego-based way. After realizing with stupefaction that analysts were transforming the recommendations that he had given them into prescriptions to which they submitted, he wrote this to Ferenczi in 1928: "Docile analysts did not perceive the elasticity of the rules I had laid down and submitted to them as if they were taboos."

In this strange preference that can push analysts to substitute a superego commandment for what was a symbolic commandment we

---

[373] ["À la trace de pas a été substitué un pas de trace." There is a play here on the word "*pas*," which can mean both "footstep" and "no."]

can identify the human appetite for the law of the superego. Whereas the symbolic commandment, "Forget everything that you know," is constantly forgotten, for it is forgettable, the superego commandment imposes itself as structurally unforgettable knowledge. That its unforgettable character is precisely what prevents the subject from gaining access to unconsciousness is what is made obvious by insomnia. How can one find the path of self-forgetting if, in the darkness, the eye of consciousness is too unforgettable to allow this fall into unconsciousness that is sleep?

## b) What Unforgettable Forgetting Is

For theory to be forgettable in a manner that is subjectivizing, it must be situated, for the analyst, in a topological point combining the fact of not being forgettable according to secondary repression and, at the same time, of not being unforgettable, as is the superego. Such a paradox—simultaneously associating something forgettable that is different from secondary repression and something unforgettable that is different from the superego or from hallucination—is realizable inasmuch as it introduces us to the recognition of the existence of an *unforgettable forgetting* that is the very mark of what specifies the mode of forgetting proper to primal repression.

We are thus led to recognize that the bewildering signifier, characterized by being capable of an unforgettable forgetting, combines the properties of the signifier in the real that is the superego-related signifier and that of the signifier in the symbolic that is the signifier of secondary repression. Unforgettable like the signifier in the real, without being incapable of being forgotten, and forgettable like the signifier in the symbolic, while remaining unforgettable, it is topologically situated at the point of intersection between the real and the symbolic, partaking of both. This intersection is written by Lacan by the parenthesis associating the symbolic presence of the signifier with its real absence: S ($\bcancel{A}$).[374]

---

[374] Thus, I would say that, unlike the return of the secondary repressed—which is a return in the symbolic—the stunning signifier is a return of the signifier of the Name-of-the-Father in the real.

The topological specificity of such a return of the signifier of the Name-of-the-Father consists in the fact that it is radically different from a return in the real following its fore-

## Chapter Five – The Time of the Subject of the Unconscious: Speech

This paradox is established during what I have identified as being the two "times" of the process of overcoming the state of bewilderment. The time of the parade is the time of the feminine position in which the bewildering alterity of the ball is received in an unforgettable manner. Whereas, in the time of riposte—that of the masculine position—the subject forgets the bewildering signifier, for he has substituted a stand-in for it, namely the ball, from which he separates in order to conquer his desire. This substitution whereby the subject will cease to look for the Other in order to seek the lost object is not established as an absolute discontinuity. The transferential transmutation by virtue of which the ball returned is heterogeneous with the ball sent is not absolute. A secret continuity passes from one to the other. Such continuity is maintained owing to the fact that the lost object retains, inscribed within it, the trace of the Other, who, insofar as he has disappeared, has ceased to be visible, material, and audible. It is by virtue of the invisible, immaterial, and extraordinary character of the ball, as a lost object, that the character of the Other, which is both inaccessible insofar as it has been forgotten and accessible insofar as it is unforgettable, is transmitted to it.[375] The ball, rendered invisible, commemorates the fact that the Other, insofar as it is forgotten, has acquired an invisibility that, by virtue of the very fact of being symbolized by the ball, makes it unforgettable. This is a question of commemoration and not of remembering, because the Other, insofar as it is radically forgotten, is not memorable as such. On the other hand, what is commemorable by the subject is the path he finds again when he *discovers* that he has forgotten the Other. In finding this path again, he rediscovers not *what* he has forgotten—which is forever immemorable—but *the fact that he has forgotten*.

Returning to this originary act of forgetting, he thus raises it to the paradoxical status *of a forgetting that he cannot forget*. It is as if the subject had constituted himself structurally as someone who is forgetful of the Other and only committed himself with fidelity towards the Other after having carried out, in relation to him, an act of infidelity. The bewildering commandment, "Don't forget that you have

---

closure. The parenthesis associating S with A—S (A)—evokes this mode of return of the signifier in the real.

[375] Is it not true that woman embodies for man this absolute paradox insofar as she is for him both an unforgettable presence and a presence that is constantly forgotten?

## Chapter Five – The Time of the Subject of the Unconscious: Speech

forgotten your originary 'yes,'" reminds him of this. The unforgettable forgetting is thus an act of returning to oneself whereby the subject gains access to the possibility of not forgetting his constitutive act as someone forgetful. This non-forgetting of forgetting is the assumption of the fact that the subject has not remained a stranger to that absolute stranger that is the Other.[376] It requires the bewildered subject to return to the first "yes" that he gave to the Other before forgetting him in his riposte. In this return, the subject does not return to the Other—who is not remembered—but to the *originary time when he said "yes"* to the bewildering Other.

This is how the subject's insistence is born insofar as he confirms that his first "yes" cannot be forgotten, but is restated according to the pact of a "yes-of-yes." It is owing to the insistence of this "yes-of-yes" that fidelity to oneself is accomplished, which has nothing to do with narcissistic belief in oneself. This fidelity towards oneself does not proceed from a subjective movement turned towards the identical but rather from a movement whereby the subject, bewildered by the signifier, has said "yes" to the absolute alterity of the signifier.

What, then, is the act of the subject who derives his authorization from "himself," if not the act by means of which he tears himself away from dereliction by attaching himself, not to the Other (who has become immemorable), but to the rediscovery of the originary "yes" that he twice gave to this Other?

Thus, by authorizing himself, the subject is not referred to a "himself" signifying an identity with oneself of an ego-related order, but rather to an alterity on which he can lean as if he were leaning on an assumed "himself." The subject therefore only derives his authorization "from himself" when, having broken with his ego-related ties, he accedes to a *non-forgetting of forgetting* of the originary "yes" that is not however an accession to the remembering of the forgotten. This non-forgetting of forgetting does not lift the originary forgetting of the Other; on the contrary, it exalts it, by raising it to the dignity of a commemoration. The living persistence of this originary forgetting is rendered transmissible, insofar as unforgettable, by something un-

---

[376] Nothing transmits the idea of this non-forgetting of forgetting better than music: The affect created by music, which Freud was oblivious to, reminds the subject, does it not, that, in spite of the originary forgetting of the Other, something of the Other continues to remain unforgettable and to affect the subject?

heard-of that a musical note transmits or by the invisible revealed by painting.[377]

### c) The Contribution of Derrida

Through the artist's activity we are brought back to that absolute point of origin beyond the philosopher's questioning where the subject, well before he is able to speak in a questioning way, incarnates a locus that is not impassive to speech—a locus capable of responding with an originary "yes." This is the knot of this "question of the question" to which Derrida devotes some dazzling lines, worthy of comment.[378]

Meditating on the two sides of originary speech, Derrida, commenting on Heidegger, is led to recognize that speech "cannot not promise as soon as it speaks; it is promise, but it cannot fail to break its promise."[379]

In this dialectic where the corruption of the promise [*Verwesen*] is opposed to the promise [*Versprechen*], we are at the heart of the conflict established in the subject, owing to the fact that the *saying* that he receives is simultaneously the knotting of a *well said* [*bien dire*] and a *badly said* [*mal dire*]. If man is susceptible to not being impassive to the stunning commandment of the saying, he is at the same time susceptible to being traumatized by this broken promise,

---

[377] The function of certain religious rites seems to me to be linked to the commemoration of these two foundational moments when, after having said an originary "yes," the pre-subject betrays his oath by forgetting this "yes" (primal repression).

The prayer of the Kol Nidre, which inaugurates the eve of Yom Kippur—analyzed by Reik, Abraham, and, recently, by Muriel Djerebi (seminar on psychoanalytic anthropology of February 8, 1993)—is, in this respect, profoundly significant. This is the solemn formulation read out by the officiating Rabbi: "All vows, oaths... maledictions, anathemas... which we may have vowed or bound ourselves to from this day of Atonement to the next, we do repent. May they be deemed absolved, forgiven, annulled, and made of no effect...."

This invocation signifies that the act (primal repression) through which the subject betrayed the sworn oath (*Bejahung*) is recognized as structurally necessary for the institution of a speaking subject and, furthermore, that this act creates the conditions of a return to the originary "yes" (the *Brith*), which has the effect of lifting the inherent malediction in the perjury.

[378] Jacques Derrida, *De l'Esprit* (Paris: Galilée, 1987), 146–152.

[379] *Ibid.*, 146.

## Chapter Five – The Time of the Subject of the Unconscious: Speech

which is the profound meaning of the Freudian trauma. However, to the extent that we have acknowledged that the traumatic experience of the "*y a pas d'Un*" could only be inscribed in the aftermath of the transmission of the "*y a d'l'Un*" transmitted by musical rhythm, we recognize that music has the power to transmit a real that elicits from the subject the earliest of the "yeses," since it is such an absolute "yes" that it cannot even suspect the existence of a "no." Does not the gratitude that we feel towards the artist reside precisely in the fact that the unheard-of and invisible product that he delivers frees us, even if only fleetingly, from our intellectual aptitude for thinking "no"?

The pacifying effect of the artistic gift is linked to the enigmatic transmission of a "promise of spirit," which announces to the subject that even before he constitutes himself as questioning he is instituted as a hoping subject.[380] Derrida stresses this: "It remains to be known whether this *Versprechen* is not the promise that, opening every act of speech, makes the question possible and therefore precedes it without belonging to it: the dissymmetry of an affirmation, of a yes before all opposition of yes and no."[381]

This dissymmetry between a "yes" that does not know a "no" and a "yes" that knows the "no," refers us to the dissymmetry between the tree of life and the tree of the knowledge of good and evil. We are then obliged not to forget that, if it is with Biblical monotheism that the question of the promise is introduced, it is because this monotheism poses the following question: What is speech insofar as it lays down the law?

Although Heidegger does not refer his method of deconstructing Western metaphysics to the Hebraic heritage, it is obvious, as Marlène Zarader has shown,[382] that the conception of the *Zusage*, on the basis of which he questions the essence of speech, takes account, whether he realizes it or not, of the Hebraic heritage. The notion of "*Zusage*," which "brings together significations that we dissociate in general, that of promise, acquiescence, and consent," is of particular interest for us.[383] It alerts us to the fact that a philosopher, through his

---

[380] *Ibid.*, 146.
[381] *Ibid.*
[382] Marlène Zarader, *La Dette impensée: Heidegger et l'héritage hébraïque* (Paris: Éditions du Seuil, 1990).
[383] Jacques Derrida, *De l'Esprit, op. cit.*, 148.

## Chapter Five – The Time of the Subject of the Unconscious: Speech

singular approach, can be led to turn his thought towards this initial, absolute time when, for the psychoanalyst, the enigmatic pact established in the time of primal repression was formed.

I prefer to translate by "pact" what Derrida prefers to call "pledge."[384] The notion of pact introduces us to the fact that the subject, as a contracting party, is not exposed to the "absolute originary abandonment" evoked by Heidegger, and does not receive the promise of the spirit passively. If, instead, he receives it because of his susceptibility to it, it is because he is liable for a cost for accepting it. Indeed, he is liable to the pain of symbolic castration, which he chooses actively as an ethical choice.

Why does this ethical dimension, whereby the subject accepting the promise of the spirit is led at the same time to accept the symbolic law, escape Heidegger? Because, in his conception of ontological difference, the being is released into Being, without any cost, without any real imposition, in an exuberant and Dionysiac playfulness in which human responsibility vanishes.[385]

Heidegger remains extremely discreet in relation to this question of the responsibility of the subject, so powerfully underlined by Levinas. Nonetheless, he has the considerable merit of having placed the accent on the originary operation that, preceding the time when the subject began to speak, harks back to an earlier time. Speech, by the very fact of speaking to us, could not fail to promise to "ally" itself with us in a pact whose trustworthiness seemed sufficiently real to the subject for him to answer "yes" to it.

Derrida implicitly poses a daunting question by pointing out that this originary "yes" binds us to "... a faith that defies every narrative. No erasure is possible for such a pledge. No going back."[386] Will the subject, without realizing it, not remain unswervingly bound to the originary trustworthiness of the first pact, owing to the impossibility of "going back"? Despite the traumatic experience that the speech that has been given cannot fail to fall short of what it promises? The rage and hatred that this subject will be led to feel in his life can be inter-

---

[384] *Ibid.*: "Pre-originary pledge [*gage*] that precedes any other involvement in language or in action..., which does not mean that it is foreign to it."

[385] See the study of G. Petitdemange, "La querelle de l'ontologie: Heidegger et Levinas," *Les Cahiers de la nuit surveillée* 3 (1984), 37–49.

[386] Jacques Derrida, *De l'Esprit, op. cit.*, 149.

preted as the effect of the fact that each time he experiences a betrayal of the speech that has been given, in spite of himself he perseveres in having faith in the originary trustworthiness of speech.

With this implicit idea of an *imprescriptibility of the pact*, Derrida asks the psychoanalyst a radical question about psychosis. If the foreclosure of the Name-of-the-Father has rendered the imprescriptibility of the originary act impossible and inoperative, what is required of the subject and his ascendants in order for the originary *Bejahung*, in which Freud identifies the originary assumption of the signifier, to be produced? On this point, Derrida proposes three directions of research that, if examined more closely, could shed light on the obscure mechanism of foreclosure. He thus asks himself what founds:[387]

1) the imputability of the subject by speech;
2) the possibility of the subject's assuming the signifying promise;
3) the originary trustworthiness of speech.

These three questions distinguish different axes of research: that the subject is imputable—we could say supposable—does not imply, however, that he can assume speech. Let us say, in this respect, that he will be put in the position of being able to assume speech if he is unconsciously lived by his ascendants as being imputable to speech. However, it is not because a newborn baby is unconsciously lived by his ascendants as imputable to speech that they will necessarily transmit to this descendant a speech pregnant with trustworthiness. In this knot that exists between imputability, the possibility of assumption, and the trustworthiness of speech, we can identify as many different points of entry as there are different foreclusive procedures.

The difference between foreclosure and primal repression consists in the fact that the act of negativization characteristic of primal repression is a "no" (*Ausstoßung*) associated with a "yes" (*Bejahung*), whereas the act of negativization of foreclosure is a pure "no" (*Verwerfung*) in which the signifier of the Name-of-the-Father, withdrawn from the symbolic order, leaves a hole. As this hole is not of the order of the forgotten, it cannot have access through the medium of artistic production to the commemoration of a "non-forgetting of forgetting," for it can only be perceived through the medium of that strange product that is hallucination.

---

[387] *Ibid.*, 151–152.

# TO CONCLUDE:
## THE CONQUEST OF TIME

When I said that the subject responded to speech that, before appearing on the stage, knocked three times at his door by saying, "Enter, make yourself at home!," I was only telling a half-truth. The "yes" with which the subject agrees to the pact of subjection to speech is a saying of which a part—the cursed part—is a retraction. Ever since the day—the day of the trauma—when speech did not arrive at the right moment, did not "come well," the cursed part of the subject attests to the fact that speech, having betrayed its originary promise, is unwelcome. This broken promise is not the rupture without any possibility of return that is foreclosure. The Freudian Thing will be able to join up again with speech by replacing the originary pact that was rendered invalid by the trauma. In this second pact, it will be able to allow itself to be by confirming the originary "yes" that it had given to the signifier of the Name-of-the-Father, when it was musical rhythm, with a second "yes"—"yes-of-yes"—given to the naming speech transmitted by the Name-of-the-Father. The conquest of this insistence remains precarious, for what I have identified as the second superego (censorship) intervenes here as an injunction, "Don't insist!," thereby pushing the subject to desist.

If the subject does not retract what he has said, he exposes himself to the stunning question of the *Che vuoi?* posed by a third superego. This questions the subject about his possibility of maintaining himself in the perseverance of a "yes-of-yes-of-yes," which I define as desire realizing the ultimate assuming of his originary "yes." That speech, if it is to be conquered, has to be marked by the triple stamp of a "yes" tells us that it does not appear—like Athena emerging fully armed from her father's brain—dramatically and once and for all. Its appearance is the fruit of a process of germination during which what seeks to prevent its appearance and passage, namely, the superego, must be overcome. Thus I understand speech as a hypothesis whose presence resides in the fact that it is at once mortgaged by superego-related guilt and the effect of an eventual lifting of this mortgage.

This lifting does not happen all at once, but rather in a series of fits and starts. The superego is, in this respect, comparable to the Lernaean Hydra: when one of its heads is cut off, another grows in its place, except that the new head that grows is not the same as the one that was cut off. The censorship that succeeds the archaic superego does not proceed from the same structure and does not possess the same powers. Moreover, the superego does not possess an infinite number of heads: in my view, it has at least three, which incarnate three specifically different modalities of contesting speech.

Thus, between the symbolic law that insists in order to attest speech and the symbolic law that persists in contesting the emergence and passage of this speech, there is a dialectical tension that is at the origin of the generation of human time. It is because the chariot of time tends to be interrupted at least three times by superego-related guilt that human time acquires its signification of conquest.

What I am identifying as the conquest of human time is the movement whereby the time of the Other, which is a musical diachronic time received primordially by the subject as absolutely exterior to him, becomes, with the process of primal repression, an interiorized synchronic time.

The conquest of human time is the effect of two processes. On the one hand, it is the effect of the *primal repression of the musical* by speech. By means of this repression, speech institutes a *profane time* that, by profaning the ahistorical, sacred time of the Other, allows it to subsist as immemorial, but commemorable. On the other hand, it tends to replace superego-related power, which tends to immobilize time by fixing the subject in a perpetual present, with a historical time, which has the power to uproot the subject from the atemporal by introducing him to becoming.

### Dialectic of the Interruptions and Resumptions of Time

#### — The first interruption of time: foreclosure of the "Become"

The human Thing, in phase with the Other who was dancing a rhythm and a melody, in responding to the musical call "become," traumatically discovers himself out of phase, betrayed, abandoned by the musical power of the Other. The "become," which was borne by the musical call, is no longer of any recourse, of any help for symbolizing the traumatic real, insofar as this dumfounding real has the power to foreclose the way in which the Name-of-the-Father manifests itself in music. The rhythmic succession of the "there is" and the "there is not" cannot answer for their traumatic simultaneity.

The *foreclosure of the musical by the trauma* is structural and structuring, for it requires the passage of speech into the world. It is radically different from pathogenic foreclosure, which, in my view, is a pre-traumatic foreclosure of the music of the maternal voice.

— *First resumption of time: originary bewilderment and the commandment, "Become again"*

The first scansion that extricates the subject from the life imprisonment that the world becomes when it ceases to be inhabitable by time is that whereby the traumatized subject is withdrawn from the Medusa's gaze. The bewildering misunderstanding is substituted for the badly seen. In this time of originary bewilderment, the signifier of the Name-of-the-Father, whose commandment—"Become!"—was foreclosed by the traumatic real, returns in the form of a bewildering commandment that may be formulated as: "Become again!"

Through this second pact, which represses the first, the human real will no longer suffer from a musical note, but rather from a bewildering speech that calls upon the subject to constitute himself as pure listener bewildered by the signifier. This originary state implies a first unconscious choice. Either the subject is liable for being bewildered or—subscribing to the commandment of the censorship, "Don't let yourself be bewildered"—he renders himself, like the autist, impassive towards the signifier.

If he is open to bewilderment, the subject undergoes an experience analogous to mystical experience. He hears the Other, but without necessarily being a good listener. In this respect, he is comparable to a person with hearing difficulties who is put in the position of having to endure his condition until he becomes a good listener. This endurance corresponds to the enigmatic phase of latency between the *jouissance* of sideration and the "*j'ouïe-sens*" of wit.[388]

---

[388] [A play on *jouissance* and "I hear sense."]

— *Second interruption of time:* "*Don't let yourself be un-stunned!*"

The check that the bewildering signifier puts on the fascinating real is not a definitive check on the superego. Symbolization has merely succeeded in pushing back the power of censorship in such a way that, having given up any hope that the subject will be able to avoid being bewildered by the signifier, it will now lay down new demands. It is as if the censorship's calculation was as follows: "Since you have been bewildered by the signifier, you might as well remain in the stupor of bewilderment and forget about becoming a desiring, un-stunned subject."

This commandment concerns the second signifier ($S_1$), which the subject must discover if he is to become—as in wit—the good listener of the spirit of the bewildering signifier. It is as if the censor, recognizing that the subject was already subjected to the reign of the signifier and no longer to that of the fascinating gaze, wanted to preserve a final right of inspection for the eye of conscience: the right to contest the legitimacy of the signifying order.

In this respect, if the subject, like certain mystics, has so much difficulty in extricating himself from the Other's *jouissance* caused by the bewildering signifier, it is because he receives from the eye of conscience the following message: "There is nothing to listen to in the bewildering message that you are enjoying! Do not be taken in by the signifying call that would like to make you understand that you could, if you found the right signifying key, become the good listener of the hidden spirit of the Word." This injunction implies a second unconscious choice. Either the subject disregards the second commandment of the censorship and constitutes himself as a good listener or he obeys the censorship and, having given up the hope of finding the second signifier (the swarm of $S_1$), which would have opened the door of meaning for him, he will remain bewildered, forever fixed as a pure auditor of a voice in relation to which he will never succeed in becoming the good listener who could greet the Other. To be able to greet the ***dritte Person***, the subject must separate himself from the Other while mourning his *jouissance*. Without this mourning, he remains in the position of Saint Theresa, exhausted from not being able to forget: "It remains engraved on my memory in such a way that I can never forget it…. This memory tires me…."

*To Conclude: The Conquest of Time*

— *Second resumption of time: the time of hearing well*
Transgressing the second commandment of the censorship, the un-stunned subject has torn himself away from the Other's *jouissance* in order to greet, through his new *j'ouïe-sens*, the Spirit of the *dritte Person*, which had not liberated itself during the time of bewilderment.

The question that arises immediately is this: now that the subject has heard the speech of the Other well, will he become a subject who will assume this speech in order to *say well*?

— *Third interruption of time: "Don't insist!"*
That it is possible to hear speech without, however, daring to assume it takes us back to that mode of fear—*timere*—that so intimidates the timid subject as to make him babble. What is the timid subject doing when he babbles if not confessing that he knows very well what he wants but cannot accomplish it. In this respect, is he not in a position to say: "Wanting the good is within my reach, but accomplishing it is not. I do not do the good that I want [well saying my desire], but I babble the evil that I do not want"? This saying of St. Paul is worth our attention inasmuch as it exemplifies the position of a subject who, as an auditor, has heard the law perfectly well ("In my inner being I delight in God's law"), but who, as an agent, is unable to convert the signification heard into a signification that could be put into action by him.[389]

This co-existence of two "I's"—an "I" that hears and an "I" that cannot act—defines very exactly the fear that takes hold of man *at the moment when the possibility of a third "I" appears*. The censorship intervenes in its third and last commandment by signifying to him: "Don't insist! No third 'I' is possible."

If, for the censor, this third "I"—the subject of speech—is fundamentally the bad subject, the one through whom evil comes, it is because, for the inquisitor that he is, the speaking subject is fundamentally heretical.

— *Third resumption of time: the subject insists*
Following Lacan's teaching, I interpret this fear due to a third "I" speaking as being linked to what the assumption of the Name-of-the-Father requires in order for a *quilting point* to appear between the

---

[389] Romans 7: 22.

signifier and the signified.[390] This assumption may be defined as the capacity of the subject not to remain, like Saint Theresa, in the permanent *jouissance* of the Name-of-the-Father. Rather, it is the assumption of a de-stunning, with the result that the subject, like Abraham, through his speech, can respond to the stunning call of the Other by saying these three words, "I am here," which have founded the *quilting point* of a civilization.

If the inquisitor is perfectly right in considering that any subject who says, "Here I am," is a bad subject, it is because, through this enunciation, the "speaking being" assumes a type of real that creates a definitive disorder in the ordered world of the censor. By saying, "Here I am, determined by the signifier," he has to assume a triple task.

In the first place, he will have to accept the ascendancy of the signifier, before which he will efface himself by saying: "After you." Next, the paradox of simultaneously being absolutely determined by the signifier as well as by the locus where "the function of freedom... insofar as the primordial signifier kills all meanings" is produced.[391] This invalidation of all meanings is, in effect, liberty, since it is a possible invalidation of determinism.

Finally, if this liberty bestowed by the symbolic is unacceptable for the superego, it is because it signifies that the subject is not free not to take charge of what has fallen from the symbolic. While the inquisitor wants to expel this waste matter that, for him, represents the absolute exteriority of the impure, the bad subject radically contests the superego because *he knows that he is not a stranger* to the decline of the real. As Lacan says, this is because the subject knows himself to be culpable to the real, because he knows that the price for his maturation to symbolic existence has been paid for by a forfeiture. He knows that he must go back to that which was badly made at the beginning in order to give this cursed thing the chance, one day, of being, if not well said, at least better said.

Consequently, the fear that makes me tremble at the instant of speaking is justified, is it not? Will I be able to measure up to this triple commandment that I receive from speech, as soon as I assume it in order to let it speak?

---

[390] Jacques Lacan, *The Psychoses, op. cit.*, 267.
[391] *Ibid.*, 268.

*— Fourth interruption of time: "Will you persevere?"*
The question of my perseverance is put to me by the *Che vuoi?* from the moment when, having transgressed the censorship, I am no longer faced with the adversity of an injunction to desist as a speaking subject. It is thus, faced with the void, when my desire no longer has an adversary to justify it and has no other support than its own possibility of enduring, that a last scansion is posited, which is the test of truth itself: What is the temptation to desist in the face of the absolute choice?

The speech carried to a point of insistence by the *savoir-faire* of the analyst has reopened the gaping hole of the absolute demand that the analysand, captivated by the lure of the object of his desire, had forgotten. With this insistence, a dimension of transference that eluded Freud is affirmed. Beyond the historical transference, there is a structural, ahistorical transference that invokes the Other through the insistence of that which demands to begin again. It is because, during the time when the Other finds himself responding to this invocation by the ad-vocation that is the question *Che vuoi?*, "What do you want?," the subject is cornered. This question, in effect, takes him at his word: "Will you, who lets me hear in your demand the call that you have received from the irreducible incognito through which the *Urverdrängung* insists in you, be able to give this demand for love the expression of a desire caused by this gap itself? In that instant when you are in the void, will you be able to find the signifier that can both knot and signify, in a transmissible manner, what there is in you that is unheard-of, invisible, and immaterial?"

It is a daunting question because it has the power to put the subject in a position where he can no longer avoid responding to the absolute choice with which he is faced. Will he choose again the pact of confidence whereby he decided, one day, to be absolutely determined by the signifier? Or will he choose again the traumatic instant in which the experience of the broken promise taught him that he could no longer allow himself to be taken in by the signifier and should henceforth have nothing but mistrust towards it?

With this choice concerning his determinism, the subject of the unconscious will be unable to avoid choosing between Eros and Thanatos. The choice of diabolical hatred is the most evident: it is the choice according to which the *signifier is accused* by the figure of Satan. It is justifiably accused for, on two occasions, the subject has had the experience of being betrayed. After being betrayed by the Other in the time of the trauma, he was the one who, in the time of primal repression, betrayed the Other by forgetting him. Owing to these two moments in time in which the real turns out to have ascendancy over the symbolic on two counts, the subject remains marked forever by two types of hatred.[392] The subject's hatred for the Other, insofar as he has been betrayed, and the Other's supposed hatred for the subject, insofar as the subject's originary guilt is the effect of his having forgotten the Other in primal repression.

The choice of what Lacan calls "real love" is much more enigmatic: it is what happens when the subject loves with what he is lacking and gambles on being loved by the Other for what the Other does not have.[393] In this case, what the Other does not have is the means to tell the subject what he must do to be able to answer the question "*Che vuoi?*" From this point of view, it is at the point where the Other transmits himself through the gift of a signifying silence—a silence that he is not guaranteed to give—that the subject can receive this gift of what the Other does not have.

"Real" love for signifying determinism is fundamentally the assumption of a choice of an Other who gives what he does not have, implying that the contract between the subject and speech is not the contract whereby a transfer of *jouissance* allows a tenant to *enjoy what belongs to the owner* as long as he pays the price fixed by the contract. Since the exact price of enjoying the signifier (symbolic castration) is not known, the contract, by which the speech received will become the speech of the subject, will be transmitted as fundamentally unconscious. Since the Other does not possess—as an owner does—a written contract, the subject, receiving what the Other does not have, must learn to interpret the clauses of an unconscious contract.

To what extent will the subject be able to have access to this field of speech that reigns as far as the field of the Other extends? This will depend on how he receives the pact, since his speech will not be the same depending on whether he receives it with or without guilt. The emergence of this originary guilt stems from the fact that the subject has forgotten the originary pact with speech due to primal

---

[392] Jacques Lacan, seminar of January 14, 1975, *RSI*, unpublished seminar: "That the real surmounts the symbolic on two points is precisely what is involved in analysis."

[393] Jacques Lacan, seminar of January 16, 1963, *Anxiety, op. cit.*

repression. He finds himself faced, retrospectively, with the fact that what he has forgotten proves to be unforgettable insofar as the pact was, in fact, as Derrida has pointed out, imprescriptible. It is owing to this very imprescriptibility that the originary pact will continue to be transmitted to the subject, reminding him, as soon as he is unfaithful, that he has always been bound—whether he knows it or not, whether he likes it or not—by an originary faithfulness from which he is unable to free himself.

The strangeness of this pact consists in the fact that—even though he has forgotten the fact that he once entered into it—the subject is obliged to recognize that he is party to the contract. His originary guilt leads him to recognize that he is unfaithful to a *law that lays down obligations without stating what the obligations are*, without knowing, however, what this faithfulness consists in. It is exactly on this point that the bewildering commandment proposes to disregard originary guilt and hate. It does not strive to remind the subject—as guilt does—that he has transgressed the contractual obligation, but rather to summon him to discover the extent of the amplitude of this obligation not stated by the written law.

The strangeness of this obligation, transmitted by the bewildering speech, resides not only in the fact that the Ten Commandments do not exhaust the power of obligation. Enunciation of this speech, insofar as it takes charge of this inexhaustible excess, has absolute ascendancy over the statement of the written law. How is it that Abraham, well before the law was transmitted to Moses on Mount Sinai, had knowledge of it? Should we not understand, in this respect, that, in the assumption of the bewildering speech, "Where are you?," to which he replied, "I am here," there is an assumption of a double recognition: recognition of how the foundational *saying*, by transmitting life to speech, is transmitted, at the same time, as an interdiction that has the function of preventing this speech from being put to death by murder or incest. That Abraham was able to hear the *latent existence of the interdiction in the stunning saying* of the Other teaches us that an "I," whose existence is supposed in the originary pact ("Where are you?"), can tear itself away from the supposition in order to take up the position of "I" as enunciator ("Here I am").

There is a transmission to this "I" of an unconscious knowledge about two aspects of the law, which are the tree of life and the tree of the knowledge of good and evil. While knowledge about good and evil is knowledge about the *limits imposed* by the interdiction, knowledge about the tree of life is an unconscious knowledge about the *unlimited obligation* into which the subject is propelled from the moment when, becoming a being of speech, he succumbs to the infinite. Henceforth, speech will wait infinitely for him to become, owing to the very fact of the infinite powers that it delegates to him as the delegate of the infinite.

The extreme difficulty that exists in finding out how to draw support from the infinite consists in the fact that this discovery implies renouncing all forms of guilt. We have seen that, even in the case of a man like Freud, attachment to guilt could be such that, while he acknowledged receipt of the bewildering *Che vuoi?*, he preferred to consider that he had been unjustly accused, rather than interrogated by the pertinence of this calling into question. This gives us a good idea of the scale of the dizziness that takes hold of the subject if he renounces the support of guilt.

The renunciation that he is invited to make when the advocation of the bewildering commandment resounds is radical, since it pertains to each of the three forms of guilt, namely, superego-related guilt, symbolic guilt induced by the law, and originary guilt founded by the originary pact.

The radicality of this last unconscious choice is matched by the radicality of the subject's response. He could respond by renewing his ties with the *jouissance* of the first superego through a foreclosure of the bewildering signifier. The case of the terrorist that we studied taught us that the superego asked for nothing better than to offer its services, to stand in for the symbolic, as soon as the subject, unwilling to be taken in or duped by the signifier, chose to free himself from the "originary "yes" that bound him to speech. More ordinarily, he will respond by repressing the experience of bewilderment. This repression, which lends itself to universality, is the very essence of the discovery of St. Paul. The dogma that he promotes signifies that the bewildering question, "Where are you?," has become null and void for any possibility of redemption. For Paul, the fall of Adam implies that, in the absence of the redeeming Son, man can no longer return to the bewildering Word that, as a result, falls into disuse, into the forgetting of repression.

Foreclosure and repression do not exhaust the subject's capacity for choice, for the question of the "yes," of the *Bejahung* towards

## To Conclude: The Conquest of Time

the originary signifier, always remains open. Since his first seminar, Lacan accentuated this question as follows: "Which *Bejahung*, which assumption by the ego, which yes, is involved in analytic progress? Which *Bejahung* is it a matter of obtaining, which constitutes the unveiling that is essential to the progress of an analysis?"[394]

The assumption of a persevering "yes" leads to more radical consequences than the assumption of an insistent "yes." In the possibility of responding to the bewildering commandment, the subject shows that when he has lost everything—the support from prohibition and the superego—he is able to revisit this thing that, having become human by saying "yes" one day to speech, was lost from the moment he had forgotten this originary "yes."

It is to this transgressive visitation that he will return by affirming this return to the non-forgetting of forgetting through the insistence of a "yes-of-yes" that wants nothing more than to give birth to the perseverance of a "yes-of-yes-of-yes."

---

[394] *Ibid.*

Titles Published by the Sea Horse Imprint:

Betty Bernardo Fuks – *Freud and the Invention of Jewishness* (2008)

Gérard Haddad – *Eating the Book: Dietary Rites and Paternal Function* (2013)

Erik Porge – *Truth and Knowledge in the Clinic: Working with Freud and Lacan* (2016)

Paola Mieli – *Figures of Space: Subject, Body, Place* (2017)

Alain Didier-Weill – *The Three Times of the Law* (2017)

www.ingramcontent.com/pod-product-compliance
Lightning Source LLC
Chambersburg PA
CBHW021139080526
44588CB00008B/123